FRONTIER MISSION

Walter Brownlow Posey

FRONTIER MISSION

*A History of
Religion West of the
Southern Appalachians
to 1861*

UNIVERSITY OF KENTUCKY PRESS
LEXINGTON, 1966

TO THE MEMORY OF

WILLIAM WARREN SWEET

Splendid Teacher and Generous Friend

PREFACE

AFTER THE PUBLICATION of my study of the Baptist churches (1957), the editor of a university press urged me to combine this book with earlier works on the Methodist (1933) and Presbyterian churches (1952) into a study of "The Democratic Churches in the Old South." This suggestion was accepted and diligently followed, but later it seemed wise to include all of the important churches that spread into the Southern area beyond the colonial fringe. What promised to be an easy task was greatly changed by the addition of four churches—Roman Catholic, Protestant Episcopal, Cumberland Presbyterian, and Disciples of Christ—and by the extension of the study to the time of the Civil War. The region studied was in a great era of expansion during this period. From this territory had come by 1821 six new states for the Union—Kentucky, Tennessee, Louisiana, Mississippi, Alabama, and Missouri—and by 1845 two others, Arkansas and Texas. Although the South's religions were brought from the Atlantic and Gulf regions, in time they developed aspects more Southern and Southwestern than Western; so I have reached beyond the prescribed geographical limitations to include related events in other states, particularly in Georgia and South Carolina.

I have not hesitated to use materials and passages from my other books. The Weatherford Printing Company, the John Knox Press, and the University of Kentucky Press have graciously permitted me to use portions of the Methodist, Presbyterian, and Baptist books.

My appreciation is extended to approximately one hundred libraries scattered from Boston to Savannah, New Orleans, St. Louis, and Chicago. Several of these libraries generously lent rare books and scarce microfilm. Especially do I owe a debt of gratitude to Florence E. Smith, associate professor of history at Agnes Scott College, whose close scrutiny in reading the entire manuscript saved me from numerous awkward sentences and poorly chosen words. The portions of this book relating to the Roman Catholic Church have been read by Monsignor John Tracy Ellis of the University of San Francisco. I am grateful for his counselling, which I needed for a proper perspective. The complex calculations which were the bases for the diagrams in the Appendix were made by my colleague Henry A. Robinson, chairman of the Mathematics Department of Agnes Scott College. His skill has reduced the likelihood of error to a very low point. A grant from the Board of Christian Education of the Presbyterian Church in the United States paid part of the cost of research. Generous allowances of time by Agnes Scott College and Emory University made the writing possible.

WALTER BROWNLOW POSEY

CONTENTS

NEBRASKA TERRITORY
INDIAN TERRITORY
MISSOURI R.
ARKANSAS R.
RED R.
BRAZOS R.
SABINE R.
TEXAS
Fort Gibson
Doaksville
Anderson
Austin
San Antonio
Gonzales
Victoria
MISSOURI
ARKANSAS
LOUISIANA
Jacksonville
ILLINOIS
MISSISSIPPI R.
Vincennes
St. Louis
Ste. Genevieve
New Madrid
Fort Smith
Little Rock
Arkansas Post
Pine Bluff
Natchitoches
Opelousas
St. Martinville
Baton Rouge
New Orleans
INDIANA
OHIO
Bethany
Cincinnati
Louisville
Frankfort
Maysville
Cane Ridge
Lexington
Bardstown
Pleasant Hill
OHIO
KENTUCKY
Princeton
CUMBERLAND GAP
Abingdon
CLINCH R.
HOLSTON R.
VIRGINIA
Staunton
Manakintown
NORTH CAROLINA
SOUTH CAROLINA
REELFOOT LAKE
TENNESSEE
Nashville
Murfreesboro
Knoxville
Memphis
Sewanee
Chattanooga
Holly Springs
Huntsville
La Grange
Chatsworth
Calhoun
Florence
Columbus
YAZOO R.
PEARL R.
Tuscaloosa
Marion
Jackson
Port Gibson
Natchez
Montgomery
MISSISSIPPI
ALABAMA
GEORGIA
Columbus
Mobile
Pensacola
FLORIDA

1

INTO THE VALLEY

THE VAST REGION beyond the Appalachian Mountains served
as a beacon to restless folk who saw there the bright new
day of economic betterment. Fertile land nestling in river
bottoms like those of the Cumberland, Tennessee, and Mississippi was abundant and beckoned to the white man.
For many thousands this region was to become the home
where they would find greater social and financial equality
than in the East. Daring and self-reliant, these frontier
people hunted, explored, surveyed, cleared land, built cabins,
organized communities, and established local and state gov-
ernments. This territory contributed by 1845 eight states to
the Union. By then, in Kentucky, Tennessee, Louisiana,
Mississippi, Alabama, Missouri, Arkansas, and Texas, the
Catholic and Protestant churches were giving moral stability
to the region they had helped to develop. The Protestant
churches had had little influence in the West before the
American Revolution; the colonists were too preoccupied
with wresting a living from a new land. Representatives
of the Roman Catholic Church had come early with explorers
into the area; unhampered by domestic concerns, their
purposeful missionary endeavors carried them up the St.
Lawrence River and across the Great Lakes to secure a
tenuous foothold in the Mississippi Valley.

Near the middle of the sixteenth century Catholic priests
accompanied the De Soto expedition of nearly a thousand
men which traveled through much of the southern part of

North America. Sailing into Tampa Bay, the expedition touched land in May 1539 and claimed it for the Spanish king. For nearly a century and a half thereafter, Dominican, Capuchin, and Jesuit priests moved from post to post in the region bordering the Gulf of Mexico.[1]

After La Salle had descended the Mississippi River in 1682 and claimed the entire area as French territory, the Seminary of Quebec was permitted to send three missionaries to establish missions in the lower part of the region. The men reached the mouth of the Arkansas River in 1699 and began work among the Tensaw and Natchez Indians. In 1727 an effort to establish a mission at the mouth of the Yazoo River incited the Indians to massacre more than a third of the seven hundred settlers. The retribution taken in 1729 by a French military force was so terrible that the Natchez disappeared as a nation.[2]

In August 1727 twelve Ursuline nuns, traveling at the expense of the Western (later called the Indies) Company, arrived in New Orleans to begin a work which has continued to the present. Governor Jean Baptiste le Moyne Bienville, foreseeing the need for a school for girls, had appealed to Father Nicholas I. Beaubois, the superior of the Jesuits in Louisiana, who in turn sought aid from the Ursulines in Rouen. For forty years during the French period and for

[1] Theodore Maynard, *The Story of American Catholicism* (New York, 1941), Chap. II; [Mary T. A. Carroll], *A Catholic History of Alabama and the Floridas* (New York, 1908), Chaps. I-IV; John T. Ellis (ed.), *Documents of American Catholic History* (Milwaukee, 1956), 84-89; John G. Shea, *A History of the Catholic Church in the United States* (4 vols.; New York, 1886-1892), I, 479-80, 547; Jean Delanglez, *The French Jesuits in Lower Louisiana, 1700-1763* (Washington, 1935), passim.

[2] Richard O. Gerow, *Catholicity in Mississippi* (Natchez, 1939), 11-17; Norman W. Caldwell, "Tonty and the Beginning of Arkansas Post," *Arkansas Historical Quarterly*, VIII (1949), 189-205; John E. Rothensteiner, *History of the Archdiocese of St. Louis* (2 vols.; St. Louis, 1928), I, 25-26; Martin J. Spalding, *Sketches of the Life, Times, and Character of the Rt. Rev. Benedict Joseph Flaget* (Louisville, 1852), 151-57; *Sketch of the Catholic Church in the City of Natchez, Miss.* (n. p., 1886), 9-11.

another forty years under Spanish rule, these nuns were the "Guardian Angels" of the young girls in New Orleans. They taught the children, the Negroes, and the Indians, nursed the sick, and took care of the children who had been made orphans by the Indian massacre at Natchez.[3]

By agreement between the Bishop of Quebec and the Western Company's council the Mississippi Valley was divided in 1722 into three jurisdictions. The region to the north of the Ohio River, including the Illinois settlements and territory along the Missouri River, was given to the Jesuits. The district from the Perdido River along the coast and up the Alabama and Mobile rivers, with headquarters in Mobile, was assigned to the Discalced Carmelites. The third territory, comprising the French and Indian settlements in the area from the mouth of the Mississippi to that of the Ohio River, was Capuchin territory. Later, because of the small number of Capuchin priests, the company was forced in 1726 to place all the Indian tribes under the Jesuits also who could perform no ecclesiastical functions, however, without the consent of the Capuchins.[4]

During the whole of the French rule in Louisiana, no bishop was sent to that vast region. In 1783 Father Cirillo de Barcelona, a Spanish Capuchin, became Louisiana's first resident auxiliary bishop. Ten years later he was relieved of his office, having been charged unjustly with permitting a deplorable lack of religious and ecclesiastical discipline. In December 1793 Luis Peñalver y Cardenas, a native of Havana, was appointed bishop of the newly created diocese of Louisiana and the Floridas. During eight years of valiant

[3] M. A. C., "Education in Louisiana in French Colonial Days," *American Catholic Quarterly Review* (Philadelphia), XI (1886), 398-404; Delanglez, *French Jesuits*, 130-37; Jane F. Heaney, "A Century of Pioneering: A History of the Ursuline Nuns in New Orleans, 1727-1827" (Ph.D. dissertation, St. Louis University, 1949), passim.

[4] Ellis, *Documents*, 87; Claude L. Vogel, *The Capuchins in French Louisiana, 1722-1766* (Washington, 1928), 15-50, 92-96.

struggling against disorder, he was unable to make any apparent progress.[5]

As early as 1756 some Acadians, ruthlessly expelled from Canada by the British, made their way to Louisiana, where they were given immediate aid by French officials and the inhabitants of New Orleans and in time granted lands. Other Acadians came in the succeeding years, with the largest influx in 1763. In 1765 a commission was granted to the Acadian settlement at Attakapas which became known as New Acadia. A frame church was built at St. Martinville, the most celebrated haven for the exiles.[6]

The Mobile and the Alabama missions among the Indians had been little disturbed by controversy among the Carmelite, Capuchin, and Jesuit orders. From 1723 to 1769 there were, as a rule, two Capuchin priests who attended to the churches at Mobile and on Dauphin Island and to the Indian missions among the Apalachees and Tensaws. At various times Catholic missionaries were dispatched to Fort Jackson, near Montgomery, to the Choctaws in the southwest, and to the Chickasaws on the upper part of the Tombigbee River.[7]

Dating from about 1734, Ste. Genevieve, to which priests were sent from Cahokia in Illinois, was the first Catholic settlement in Missouri. When St. Louis was founded in 1764, the entire area had only two Catholic priests. Soon after Father Pierre Gibault reached St. Louis in 1768, he erected a small church of upright logs—the first church building in the immediate territory. A Capuchin was resident priest in St. Louis from 1772 until 1789. No existing

[5] Vogel, Capuchins, 102-18; Roger Baudier, The Catholic Church in Louisiana (New Orleans, 1939), 213-46; Ellis, Documents, 181-84; Albert H. Biever, The Jesuits in New Orleans and the Mississippi Valley (New Orleans, 1924), 55-63.

[6] For Acadians and St. Martinville see index in Baudier. Also see [Carroll], Catholic History, 161, 172-73.

[7] Michael Kenny, Catholic Culture in Alabama: Centenary Story of Spring Hill College, 1830-1930 (New York, 1931), 16-20.

records reveal a resident priest for the next several years, and by 1800 St. Louis and the territory west of the Mississippi River had been under five church jurisdictions, all of which apparently had accomplished very little.[8]

The first Roman Catholics to settle in Kentucky were members of the Coomes family who came from Charles County, Maryland, to Harrodsburg in the spring of 1775. Mrs. Coomes opened a school which was probably the first elementary school in Kentucky. The Coomes family later moved near Bardstown, secured several tracts of land, and in 1804 gave a farm of more than one hundred acres to the church. Unsatisfactory conditions in the East and news of attractive opportunities in the West led to the formation in Maryland of a Catholic colonization league which influenced a group of Catholics to leave Maryland in 1785 and to settle in the Pottinger's Creek region a few miles from Bardstown. This band had traveled to Pittsburgh and then had come down the Ohio River to Kentucky. Other Catholic groups came to Kentucky overland by the way of the Cumberland Gap.[9]

French-born priests Stephen T. Badin and Michael Barriere, selected by John Carroll, Bishop of Baltimore, to go to Kentucky, arrived there in November 1793. After a few months Barriere departed, leaving Badin alone to serve the vast area. The twenty-five-year old priest, the first to be ordained in the United States, was handicapped by a meager knowledge of the English language and.less acquainted with the customs of Kentuckians. Between 1797 and 1799 three

[8] John E. Rothensteiner, "Historical Sketch of Catholic New Madrid," *St. Louis Catholic Historical Review*, IV (1922), 115-21; James J. Conway, *Historical Sketch of the Church and Parish of St. Charles Borromeo, St. Charles, Mo.* (n.p., ca. 1892), 16-17; Gilbert J. Garraghan, *The Jesuits of the Middle United States* (3 vols.; New York, 1938), I, 6-8.

[9] Mary Ramona Mattingly, *The Catholic Church on the Kentucky Frontier, 1785-1812* (Washington, 1936), Chaps. I, II; Ben. J. Webb, *The Centenary of Catholicity in Kentucky* (Louisville, 1884), passim.

more priests arrived in Kentucky, two to find an early grave and one to withdraw because of temperament. By 1803 Badin again was alone. Within ten years the increase in the number of Catholic families made almost unbearable demands on the lone priest. The arrival of Father Charles Nerinckx in 1805 relieved Badin of some labors among his scattered flock.[10]

Catholic families did not migrate early to the region that became Tennessee. In 1790 a small party came from North Carolina, and in this group was Father Rohan who stayed only part of a year. Nearly ten years later the number of Catholics in the new state did not exceed one hundred. In 1799 Governor John Sevier of Tennessee, in an effort to increase the state's population, sought to interest Badin in the possibility of settling one hundred families there and offered to sell parcels of land as inducements. Sevier defeated his purpose, however, by setting so dear a price on the land that the Catholic families were uninterested in the offer.[11]

Only in Kentucky did the Catholics secure a foothold, and this was accomplished amidst the Protestants' overwhelming advantages—lay workers and local preachers. Into the transmontane area adjacent to the Atlantic colonies members of the Protestant denominations moved rapidly, established churches, and installed preachers of their own beliefs. The Methodist and Baptist congregations rarely had a preacher

[10] Peter Guilday, *The Life and Times of John Carroll* (Westminster, Md., 1954), Chaps. XII, XIX; Annabelle M. Melville, *John Carroll of Baltimore: Founder of the American Catholic Hierarchy* (New York, 1955), Chaps. VIII, XVI; J. Herman Schauinger, *Stephen T. Badin: Priest in the Wilderness* (Milwaukee, 1956), passim; J. Herman Schauinger, *Cathedrals in the Wilderness* (Milwaukee, 1952), 20-27; Victor F. O'Daniel, *The Light of the Church in Kentucky . . . the Very Rev. Samuel Thomas Wilson* (Washington, 1932), 83-84; Ellis, *Documents*, 184-88.

[11] George J. Flanigen, *Catholicity in Tennessee* (Nashville, 1937), 10-13; Mary de Lourdes Gohmann, *Political Nativism in Tennessee to 1860* (Washington, 1938), 34-35; Schauinger, *Badin*, 62.

who had been ordained before he came to the West, but the Presbyterian and Episcopal churches used only regularly ordained ministers, a practice which greatly limited their expansion into the new lands.

The Baptists in America had arisen as a denomination after the expulsion of Roger Williams from the Massachusetts Colony and the subsequent organization of a congregation at Providence, Rhode Island, in 1639. The Great Awakening of a century later stirred many controversies among the Congregational churches of New England and contributed a great deal to Baptist growth. The local Baptist congregations, scattered along the length of the Atlantic seaboard as far south as Georgia, were completely autonomous; no administrative office supervised the action of any congregation or dictated a program. The democratic form of Baptist church government matched the nature of its membership and appealed especially to a people of little property or culture. If a Baptist congregation needed a preacher, a man was chosen from its members and ordained. Baptists were generally regarded with disfavor by other denominations, particularly in Virginia, where they suffered severe treatment from the members of the Episcopal Church who deeply resented their inroads. Originally identified with the excesses of the Reformation and opposing themselves to long established usages, the Baptists were not always comfortable companions. Their churches frequently were a member's only opportunity for self expression, and to him his voice sounded sweet and strong.

During the American Revolution the Baptists, like the Methodists and Presbyterians, sacrificed greatly in behalf of freedom from England. Their demands for non-interference from the state and equality for all religions before the law led them to support the Constitution strongly; indeed, any objections against the new government usually arose from the fear that it would not provide sufficient religious liberty.[12]

Despite wartime loss of church buildings, Baptists had gained in membership. Hard times and persecution, however, encouraged many of them to turn westward to lands across the mountains. A Baptist preacher, Thomas Tinsley, had preached in Harrodsburg, Kentucky, as early as 1776, but it was five years later under the shade of a maple tree at Severns Valley that eighteen people organized the first Baptist church west of the mountains. John Garrard served as pastor of this church until he was captured and murdered by the Indians. The Baptist ranks increased rapidly: by 1785 in Kentucky there were eighteen churches, nineteen preachers, and the Elkhorn and Salem associations. A third association was formed in 1787, at which time Baptists, both Regular and Separate, numbered more than three thousand in a total population of about seventy thousand. So great had been the Baptist migration westward that one-fourth of the Baptists in Virginia moved to Kentucky between 1791 and 1810.[13]

The Baptist migration into Tennessee paralleled the Kentucky movement. A permanent church was formed in 1780 at Buffalo Ridge on Boone's Creek by a group which had moved in a body from a congregation at Sandy Creek in North Carolina. Within six years there were enough congregations in east Tennessee to form the Holston Association. A church was organized in 1786 in middle Tennessee, on a branch of the Red River, and within ten years the Mero

[12] See "The Status of the Baptists in America at the Close of the Revolution," Chap. I in William W. Sweet (ed.), *Religion on the American Frontier: The Baptists, 1783-1830* (New York, 1931).

[13] Charles D. Kirk, "The Progress of Baptists and Baptist Principles," *Christian Repository* (Louisville), I (1852), 160-61; John H. Spencer, *A History of Kentucky Baptists* (2 vols.; Cincinnati, 1885), I, passim; John L. Waller, *Historical Sketch of the Baptist Church* (n. p., n. d.), 108.

Association was formed from the many churches in that section.[14]

From the coastal settlements, the Baptists moved farther west and south than the pleasant places of Tennessee and Kentucky. In 1780 a band of emigrants, among them many Baptists, left South Carolina for the Natchez region. After a perilous trip down the Holston, Tennessee, Ohio, and Mississippi rivers, the group made a permanent landing at the mouth of Cole's Creek about twenty miles north of Natchez. Richard Curtis, a licensed preacher, having obtained the consent of a church in South Carolina to preach, to exercise discipline, and to baptize, gathered the Baptists often for religious meetings in the homes of interested persons. Although Spanish officials permitted only the Roman Catholic form of worship, they did not molest the Baptists for several years. As Curtis's work spread to other settlements, the Spanish authorities issued warnings which went unheeded. In April 1795 Curtis was brought before Governor Gayoso who confronted him with his persistent violations and abuses of the privilege of occasional meetings. Facing arrest, Curtis fled to South Carolina where he stayed until the Natchez country fell to the United States. Returning in midsummer of 1798, Curtis organized the Salem Church, the first of several churches erected about the same time.

A group of Scotch-Irish Presbyterians, twice expatriated, had made a settlement on the Eastern Shore of Maryland about 1649. Influenced in some degree by the attractive offer of Lord Baltimore, they had turned to America as the land of hope and had found so many of their kin already there that in a relatively short time a native organization of

[14] For the beginnings of the Baptist Church in the West see Walter B. Posey, *The Baptist Church in the Lower Mississippi Valley, 1776-1845* (Lexington, Ky., 1957), 1-7, et passim.

large scope was easy to achieve. At the opening of the eighteenth century immigrants from Scotland and Ireland flooded into Boston, Philadelphia, and Charleston, the chief ports of entry. Settling in all of the thirteen colonies, they had established by the time of the American Revolution five hundred Presbyterian communities, half of which were in the Southern colonies. They swept through the seaboard regions to take possession of frontier land in the rich valleys of Virginia and the Carolinas and in the grasslands of Kentucky and Tennessee. According to an old saying, the Presbyterians "kept the Sabbath and everything else." Whenever and wherever a group of Presbyterians found themselves living together, they gave a religious tone to the settlements by organizing a church. As a rule, the preacher was able to set religion on a firmer basis than mere emotion and to exert a strong influence in the community. His was a steady and continuing influence, for he was unlikely to move on to greener fields. But there were all too few of these sturdy Scotch-Irish ministers who sought to redeem the men of the West.[15]

In 1740 John Craig, an Irishman educated at the University of Edinburgh, began a long pastorate near Staunton in the western part of Virginia. Two years after he was graduated from Princeton, Hugh McAden came into the back country of Virginia and the Carolinas and preached there in 1755. The Ebbing Spring and Sinking Spring churches, on the Holston River in Virginia near the boundary of Tennessee, secured in 1773 the services of Charles Cummings for a stipulated salary of ninety pounds a year. For more than three decades this fearless native of Ireland preached in that section to various congregations, in which every man had his rifle at his side.

Samuel Doak, another graduate of Princeton, settled in

15 For the Presbyterians see Walter B. Posey, *The Presbyterian Church in the Old Southwest, 1778-1838* (Richmond, 1952), 11-21, et passim; Ernest T. Thompson, *Presbyterians in the South* (Richmond, 1963), Chap. VIII.

Tennessee in 1778, and by doing so became the first minister of any denomination in this region. After preaching in Sullivan County for two years, Doak moved to Washington County and there combined preaching and teaching. His school, which eventually became Washington College, earned the distinction of being the first institution offering literary courses in the Mississippi Valley. Inured to the dangers of the West, Doak never quailed from fear or danger. Once in the midst of a sermon he heard the cry of "Indians! Indians!" Immediately he grabbed his gun and led the chase. Another alarm caused him to dismiss his school and hurry to the camp of Colonel John Sevier.

Terah Templin, a licentiate from the Hanover Presbytery in Virginia, was probably the first Presbyterian minister in Kentucky, where he settled permanently in the early 1780s. David Rice from Bedford County, Virginia, visited Kentucky in 1783 in search of good land for his large family, and encouraged by a subscription paper signed by three hundred people offering him inducements to settle with them, he accepted the invitation. Rice returned to Kentucky to play the leading role in planting Presbyterianism and to win for himself the greatly deserved title of "Father of Western Presbyterianism."

Despite the dangers from Indian fighting, the land-hungry pioneer was willing to stake a claim for the virgin soil of Kentucky. Reports of bounteous yields coaxed people to the region; the population increased rapidly and so did the number of Presbyterians. By 1785 there were twelve Presbyterian congregations in central Kentucky and in the following year four ministers and five ruling elders formed the Transylvania Presbytery which covered all of Kentucky, the Cumberland region in middle Tennessee, and settlements on the Big and Little Miami rivers in Ohio.

Before the end of the century the voice of Presbyterian preachers had been heard in Cincinnati, Kaskaskia, and among the Chickasaw Indians in Mississippi. In 1800 the Synod of the Carolinas sent James Hall on a missionary reconnaissance to Mississippi. Arriving in December, he remained in the territory until April and particularly enjoyed the hospitality of Natchez, which he thought "may vie with any part of the Union."[16] During this visit he found only one Episcopal, one Methodist, and two Baptist preachers—all illiterate except the Episcopalian.

The Presbyterian Church as a whole had emerged from the American Revolution in good condition and was exceeded in size only by the Congregational Church. Members and ministers had been active and prominent in supporting the revolutionary cause of the American colonies, in securing colonial liberties, and in forming a constitution for the new government. After the war the organization of the church was intact, its people were exultant over victory, and its determination to grow and expand was strong. Perhaps no other church gained so great a benefit from the successful prosecution of the war. Of all the churches in the South, only the Presbyterian denomination maintained a vigorous life during the Revolution.

The Presbyterian Church had been the first to send missionaries across the mountains with its migrating members. Presbyterians in the back country begged the Synod of New York and Philadelphia to send ministers. When a request came in 1779 from the Hanover Presbytery in Virginia, the synod stated that "it is greatly for the interest of the church to pay particular attention to the Southern and Western parts of this continent," for unless advantage is taken of the opportunity now theirs "in a few years [they] may be utterly lost by the prevalency and preoccupying of many ignorant and irreligious sectaries."[17]

[16] James Hall, "A Brief History of the Mississippi Territory," *Publications of the Mississippi Historical Society*, IX (1906), 560.

[17] William W. Sweet (ed.), *Religion on the American Frontier: The Presbyterians, 1783-1840* (New York, 1936), 8.

Presbyterianism was not destined, however, to remain the leading religion of the frontier. The Methodists and the Baptists, far more democratic and less demanding than the Presbyterians, soon got control of the great masses of people. The basic belief in Calvinism left man alone in the presence of his God, and this was too helpless a state to suit many frontiersmen. The requirements for educated ministers limited the number available to the Presbyterians and handicapped the church in its competitive struggle with other churches that demanded little intellectual attainment from their preachers.

General worldliness and desecration of the Sabbath so disturbed the Presbyterian Church that the General Assembly of 1789 addressed a pastoral letter to the churches pointing out the "pain and fearful apprehension" which it experienced over the sad state of religion. The framers noted that "profligacy and corruption of the public morals have advanced with a progress proportioned to our declension in religion. Profaneness, pride, luxury, injustice, intemperance, lewdness, and every species of debauchery and loose indulgence greatly abound." Much of this accusation was, of course, directed to Presbyterians over the mountains.[18]

The Methodist movement, beginning in a small society of Anglican churchmen who desired a moving, personal religious experience, mushroomed in America. Its systems of leaders, classes, and circuits were peculiarly fitted to a widely scattered people. When the Bishop of London declined the request to send clergy to the American Methodists, John Wesley in 1784 ordained Thomas Coke, a presbyter of the Church of England, and sent him as superintendent to America with full power to ordain other

[18] *Minutes of the General Assembly of the Presbyterian Church [1789-1820]* (Philadelphia, ca. 1835), 153.

preachers. Coke and Francis Asbury, a Methodist missionary who had been sent to America by Wesley in 1771, assumed a bishop's title and functions, organized a compact empire, cut the Methodist societies from the Anglican Church, and started the Methodist Episcopal Church on its independent way, free to create its own bishops, ordain its clergy, and adopt a discipline that would comport with the changing needs of America.

Despite the suspicion and prejudice under which the Methodists labored during the American Revolution, the church increased in membership and ministry. The people who identified themselves with the Methodist movement were aggressive and zealous, and because of their enthusiasms they were often unpopular with other folk in the communities. It was said that the Methodist preachers had only one sermon; without manuscripts they preached about an offended God, a perishing world, and a saving Christ. There must have been some power in repetition, for at the close of the war the Methodist Church had almost fifteen thousand members and nearly one hundred preachers in the American colonies.

In 1783 the Holston Circuit was formed in Tennessee and included settlements on the Watauga, Holston, and Nolichucky rivers. Jeremiah Lambert, a traveling preacher from Delaware, served this far flung area. In 1786 Acuff's Chapel, the first Methodist church building in Tennessee, was erected near the present Blountville. The Cumberland settlements felt the power of Methodism through the preaching of Benjamin Ogden who came from Kentucky in 1787. Two or three years later a stone church was erected in the heart of the new town of Nashville, and James Robertson, a founder and a leading citizen of the town, and his wife joined the Methodist Church. Bishop Asbury crossed the mountains in 1788 to attend the first conference in the West held at Keywood's on the Holston River in Washington County, Virginia. The entire region was upset by the civil disturbances growing out of the abortive State of Franklin. The bishop did not allow the political trouble to disturb the conference which included the few preachers in the Holston region and those in Kentucky. Although Asbury's *Journal* records a few instances of hostility displayed in the course of years by members and ministers of other denominations, particularly by the Baptists, he made numerous references to the demonstrations of good will. Some of the early Methodists felt that they had been persecuted or ridiculed by the Presbyterians, but the harsh relations had been modified at the opening of the Great Revival period. At the close of the century 2,500 Methodists in Tennessee had been organized into six circuits.[19]

The spirit of Methodism spread into Kentucky at about the same time as its early preachers went to Tennessee. In 1783 a Methodist local preacher, Francis Clark, moved from Mercer County, Virginia, to Kentucky where he immediately organized a class of Methodists and appointed John Durham as the class leader. Evidently Clark worked successfully wherever he lived, for by 1785 there were enough Methodists in the state for two preachers to be sent to the Kentucky Circuit. James Haw and Benjamin Ogden were assigned by Bishop Asbury to this initial organization of Methodists in Kentucky. In the spring of 1790 Asbury again crossed the mountains, the second of thirty-one trips, in order to attend the Kentucky Conference held at Masterson's Station five miles from Lexington. On his first visit to Kentucky the bishop was disappointed in Methodist accomplishments, for he commented in his diary: "The Methodists do but little here—others lead the way."[20] And the bishop could have repeated his observation many times,

[19] For a fuller discussion of Methodism in the West see Walter B. Posey, *The Development of Methodism in the Old Southwest, 1783-1824* (Tuscaloosa, Ala., 1933), passim; William W. Sweet (ed.), *Religion on the American Frontier: The Methodist, 1783-1840* (Chicago, 1946), Chaps. I-IV.

[20] Examine Walter B. Posey, "Kentucky, 1790-1815: As Seen by Bishop Francis Asbury," *Filson Club History Quarterly*, XXXI (1957), 333-48.

for the Methodists did not increase in Kentucky as they did elsewhere. The area, however, served as a springboard for Methodist activities in other states; Methodist preachers moving from Kentucky spread the faith into Tennessee and Ohio and eventually into the Mississippi Territory. By 1796 a class had been formed in Milford, Ohio, and two years later Dayton and Cincinnati were stations included in the new Miami Circuit.

The chief impetus which sent the Methodist Church into Mississippi came from the South Carolina Conference. In January 1797 Tobias Gibson was chosen by Bishop Asbury to serve as a missionary to the Southwest. After a seven hundred-mile trip by horseback and boat, Gibson reached Natchez; five hundred miles separated him from the nearest Methodist preacher, and four years passed before he saw one.

The circuit rider system which the Methodist preacher used in covering a vast area was effective. Many communities had too few Methodists to justify the use of a stationed preacher, and, where the membership was large enough to need a full-time preacher, they frequently were too poor to support one. The church responded to the situation by marking out a circuit, putting a rider on it, and bidding him cover it at least once a month, preaching at every possible opportunity. This system secured the greatest expansion at the least expense and triumphed in competition with the Presbyterian and Baptist method of having a preacher serve only one or two churches. Primarily a middle-class religious movement, Methodism made little effort toward a literate ministry. In face of the pressing need, the Methodist Church could not wait to train preachers. Experience was the basis of all Methodist training; men learned to exhort by exhorting, to preach by preaching, to teach by teaching.

The Church of England had first come to the American colonies with the men who planted the Jamestown Colony. Chaplain Robert Hunt read prayers on June 21, 1607, and set the pattern for others to follow. But there was never a sufficient number of priests to serve the scattered parishes, and the life of the church was maintained in family prayers and in private chapels of ease. The thriftless clergy of England that sought refuge in the colonies neither benefited the church's reputation nor fostered its growth. In order to meet urgent needs, the Society for the Propagation of the Gospel in Foreign Parts was created. This new organization, approved both by the bishop and the crown, assisted the colonists in providing missionaries to the Indians and with funds which supplemented the stipend of regular ministers in South Carolina, Georgia, and New York. Even with this new life-line, however, the Church of England planned to stay well within the bounds of settled communities. Prior to its disestablishment the church had hardly glanced toward the West.[21]

In the year 1764 the Bishop of London licensed the Reverend Samuel Hart to serve at Mobile, then in West Florida. Hart found the inhabitants of Mobile to be "strangers to the paths of virtue and sunk in dissolution and dissipation," and the task which faced him seemed so hopeless that he really never tackled it.[22] Sixty years elapsed before a second Episcopal minister visited Alabama. Although Episcopalians were numerous in Kentucky, the state did not have a settled clergyman of that faith until 1794, when

[21] Most of the content of this and the four following paragraphs has been taken from my article "The Protestant Episcopal Church: An American Adaptation," *Journal of Southern History*, XXV (1959), 3-30. For standard histories of the Episcopal Church see Charles C. Tiffany, *A History of the Protestant Episcopal Church in the United States of America* (New York, 1900); James T. Addison, *The Episcopal Church in the United States, 1789-1931* (New York, 1951); Samuel D. McConnell, *History of the American Episcopal Church* (New York, 1890).

[22] Quoted in William S. Perry, *The History of the American Episcopal Church, 1587-1883* (2 vols.; Boston, 1885), II, 210.

James Moore, a Presbyterian minister who had turned Episcopalian, came from Virginia. These gestures indicate the feeble outreach of the church.

Upon the Church of England in the Colonies the ravages of the American Revolution fell heaviest. Among the laity some felt a loyalty to their Prayer Book and not to the crown, but the members of the clergy felt that in the very act of ordination they had sworn perpetual allegiance to the king; herein lay an obligation which conscience could not easily lay aside. Upon them fell the fury of a patriotic populace: the churches were wrecked, and the lands and property were confiscated by legislation. Representative churchmen met in an advisory convention in 1784, and in the next year they adopted a skeleton organization for the reviving body. Out of the ruin arose the Protestant Episcopal Church.

Over the general debilitation serious churchmen shook their heads and made woeful comments. Bishop James Madison of Virginia shared the opinion of John Marshall that the church was "too far gone ever to be revived." Bishop William White of Pennsylvania in retrospect said, "The congregations of our communion throughout the United States were approaching annihilation." The Reverend Devereux Jarratt, rector of an Episcopal parish in Virginia, having previously served between nine hundred and a thousand communicants, lamented that he could find scarcely forty communicants after the Methodists had done their work. Consequently, Bishop White and Bishop Madison, who knew the Methodists well, were genuinely interested in the plan of reunion initiated by Thomas Coke in 1791.

The weak condition of the Protestant Episcopal Church and the dull spirit of the dioceses are best indicated by the records of the General Convention which met triennially. Two bishops, twenty-four clergymen, and less than ten of the laity sat in the convention of 1811. In 1792 the convention had appointed a committee to plan for the support of ministers in the West, but no plans materialized. In fact, the needs of the West carried so little significance that the region was omitted from the reports of the state of the church prior to 1817.

The life of any preacher was hard. The ministry was no profession for a weakling, and preaching was no calling for one who loved his comforts. The roads were so treacherous and streams so difficult to ford that the means of travel were limited to horseback or foot. When caught in a rainstorm the traveling preacher had to swim swollen streams, then walk miles in search of a cabin, and start on his way in the morning with no change of clothing. Fortunately most of the clergy possessed the strength and faculties necessary to meet the demands of a hard and exacting life in a country like Kentucky, which was described as too tough for bears who couldn't stand the biting and gouging tactics of the frontiersman. Benedict J. Flaget, the Catholic bishop in Kentucky, lived for a year in a miserable log cabin sixteen feet square which contained nothing but a bed, a few chairs, two tables, and a few planks for shelves. The garret of "this strange episcopal palace" was used by Badin when he came as the missionary. Having no clerical companion in Kentucky for three years, Father Badin had suffered moments of great despondency. Often lost in the woods, sleeping on the ground, suffering from hunger, wearing rags, he pondered the prospects for himself and his church. And for all the suffering, toil, and labor the Catholic priests sometimes met only ingratitude. Bishop Flaget, resenting the treatment of a pastor under his direction, addressed a parish and expressed his feelings in a tirade against a man who had "raised his hands and violently menaced your respectable pastor, who for nearly twenty years has moistened this ungrateful field with the sweat of his brow, sacrificing his inclinations and his tastes in order not to leave you without a priest."[23]

23 Spalding, *Flaget*, 99; Schauinger, *Cathedrals*, 167.

The irregular life of the backwoodsman, the excitement of the chase, the danger from the Indians, the insatiable greed for land, and the continuous litigation over claims contributed to the lack of gentleness and piety. According to a keen native observer, "Religion but excited the smile of scorn or rude jest."[24] The culture of those who had immigrated to the West was superior to that of the first and second generations born or reared in the new region. Some of the preachers could hardly read and a few could not read at all. Generally the preacher who accomplished the most in the new regions was both strong in body and in conviction. Many a hardened sinner was not converted until he had made the grievous mistake of physically dealing with some powerful exponent of "muscular Christianity."

The toil, sacrifice, and privation which constituted the major part of the life of all preachers and priests in the early Mississippi Valley stand among the heroics of American history. Not all the clergy, by any means, deserve to be praised, for some combined their preaching activity with their greater interest of getting land and getting ahead in worldly goods. But of that ilk, the number was relatively few. On the other hand, there were hundreds who had no income save the meager pittance from a church or from their own labor. As a rule, neither source provided the necessities of life. Some preachers, tired and hungry, with worn-out clothing and gaunt horses, were forced to seek a permanent location so that they could supplement the church's meager financial support. It was not uncommon for a congregation to take a collection in order to buy a horse for the preacher. Thirty dollars was a considerable sum in those early days, and for many preachers was good pay for a year's service. The Methodist preachers and Catholic priests were more completely dependent on the church than were the Baptist

[24] Samuel H. Ford, "History of Kentucky Baptists," *Christian Repository,* V (1856), 275.

and Presbyterian clergy. The priests, it must be pointed out, often taught school, but the work was part of their regular duties, not a supplement to their stipend. Baptist preachers were usually farmers who preached on Sunday, a task for which they often received no pay. The Presbyterian minister usually regarded his duty as two-fold—that of a preacher and a teacher. By holding a subscription school he could augment the money which the congregation paid to him.

At the opening of the nineteenth century the Catholic, Presbyterian, Baptist, and Methodist churches had been established in various parts of the frontier. The challenging job of winning souls was at hand. New churches, like the Disciples of Christ and the Cumberland Presbyterian, were to spring from a frontier background; the Protestant Episcopal Church was tardily to enter the area and compete for members and for territory; and the several Protestant denominations were soon to lose themselves in the most successful evangelizing scheme the churches had yet discovered. The camp meeting was at hand.

2

THE EARLY CAMP
MEETING ERA

Following the Revolution, most of the new Americans, elated by victory, focused their attention on material affairs.[1] Few had escaped the accompaniments of war—worldliness, immorality, and infidelity. Busy with expansion and insatiable speculation, men had great difficulty in holding to a proper sense of values. Usually leaving such matters as religion and church membership to women, the males devoted themselves to agricultural and commercial pursuits. After he had been in Kentucky for a few weeks and had preached at several places, David Rice made note that he had "found scarcely one man and but few women who supported a credible profession of religion."[2] As late as 1818 the Presbyterian Church in Nashville, Tennessee, had forty-five members, forty-two of whom were women. James Smith, a preacher in the Republican Methodist Church making a trip from Virginia to Kentucky in 1795, was much disturbed about the region where pride and profaneness had led to "great decay of true and vital religion." Two years later Bishop Asbury of the Methodist Episcopal Church visited east Tennessee and, sensing the lack of interest in religion, wrote in his journal: "when I reflect that not one in a hundred came here to get religion, but rather to get plenty of good land, I think it will be well if some or many do not eventually lose their souls."

Surrounded by uncleared lands and hostile Indians, the early settlers were driven by the unrelenting demands of conquest. They found no place on the midwestern frontier for any of the niceties of refined society. Living was mainly a struggle for bare existence. If the new land supported the pioneers, it also required in return the absorption of all their energies and left little opportunity for spiritual pursuits. Settlements were far apart; frequently members of a household endured a whole winter without the sight of a new face. The deadening routine became torture and the monotony an instrument of madness. Sunday was welcomed as a day free from work and often was spent in rowdy entertainment. Tired bodies sought relaxation through the excessive use of intoxicating liquors, and starved souls cried out for nourishment.

Into this milieu came that remarkable institution—the camp meeting. The origin of this form and manner of worship is obscure, but the leader of the revival movement in Kentucky and Tennessee was James McGready, a Presbyterian minister. Prior to his coming to Kentucky, McGready had led a religious revival in North Carolina by methods which he had observed in Virginia at Hampden-Sydney College. Rumors of his success reached Kentucky, and a hurried call went to him. In 1796 he took charge of three Presbyterian churches in Logan County, Kentucky.

McGready was a spark fallen into the tinder: at a revival meeting in May 1797 a woman "was struck with deep conviction, and in a few days was filled with joy and peace in believing." The awakening had begun in Kentucky and through the years 1798 and 1799 spread rapidly. Pinched spirits found relief through the wondrous ways of the revivals. To a four-day meeting held at McGready's church

[1] Since this chapter is largely a condensation of chapters on the camp meeting in my three books (Chap. IV of the *Baptist Church;* Chap. II of the *Presbyterian Church;* Chap. II of *Methodism*), footnotes will be given only to highly significant material or to additional material.

[2] Robert H. Bishop (ed.), *An Outline of the History of the Church in the State of Kentucky, during a Period of Forty Years: Containing the Memoirs of Rev. David Rice* (Lexington, Ky., 1824), 68.

at Gasper River in July 1800, crowds came from such distances that it was necessary to provide accommodation for them. A suggestion was made that they should all camp on or near the meeting ground; thus the "camp meeting" came into existence. Two years later a description of the camp meeting appeared in the *New York Missionary Magazine;* the observer noted that it was an agency "of an extraordinary nature" which was capable of arresting "the attention of a giddy people, who were ready to conclude that Christianity was a fable and futurity a dream."[3]

McGready, significantly, preached a modified form of Calvinism. He talked repeatedly of the new birth and the absolute necessity of a specific awareness of conversion. Prior to McGready's coming to Kentucky, the stiff, formal Presbyterian theology had small appeal chiefly because "there was no vitality—no flashing of the electric sparks of human sympathy—no trumpet call to repentance." McGready's "coarse, tremulous voice" could frighten even the stoutest; they shrank from his many references to torment and turned to "a Wesleyan way of escape leading through conversion to rebirth." Hellfire and brimstone were ever-present in his impassioned sermons that were usually devoted to the topics of regeneration, faith, and repentance. The salvation of souls became the one consuming interest of this "son of thunder." To "the fierceness of his invectives" was added terror by "the hideousness of his visage and thunder of his tones."

Having witnessed the success of McGready's meeting at Gasper River, William McGee returned to his home in middle Tennessee with the determination to try a similar method. Assisted by four other Presbyterian ministers, McGee held a five-day meeting on Drake's Creek in October 1800. On the last day William McKendree, a presiding elder, Bishop Richard Whatcoat, and Bishop Francis Asbury,

---

3 *New York Missionary Magazine*, III (1802), 92.

traveling from the first Western Conference of the Methodist Episcopal Church, stopped at the encampment. When invited to participate in the services, all three preached to the large audience of over a thousand. Concerning this, Asbury on October 21, 1800, wrote in his journal: "The ministers of God, Methodists and Presbyterians, united their labours, and mingled with the childlike simplicity of primitive times. Fires blazing here and there dispelled the darkness, and the shouts of the redeemed captives, and the cries of precious souls struggling into life, broke the silence of midnight." Asbury doubtless would have been less enthusiastic had he been able to envision the ultimate involvement of the Methodists with the camp meetings and their emotional excesses, which embarrassed the Presbyterians and the Baptists.

The rapidity with which the camp meeting spread throughout Kentucky and Tennessee best indicates its spontaneity and popularity. Quickly the camp meeting grew beyond the bounds of denominational controls and became a veritable judgment at Cane Ridge, Kentucky, where in 1801 some 25,000 people convened. Witnesses later declared that more than a thousand shouted at the same time. In truth, the camp meeting's appeal was not just to the spirit of man hungering after righteousness but to his gregarious nature seeking surcease from the loneliness and hardship of the frontier.

Homes were deserted, settlements temporarily abandoned, and fields left unworked, for the whole countryside turned out to the "holy fair." The discomfort of a wagon trip of thirty miles was a small price to pay for the social and spiritual tonic of a "religious holiday." Usually the politicians arrived early in the morning, the large crowds of receptive listeners offering opportunities too rare to miss. Late in the day the preacher arrived at the appointed place, and the meeting commenced. By evening the camp had usually settled down: the wagons had been drawn up on the outer rim, and around each the busy women tended the children, prepared food and sleeping quarters. Day and night were given over to the exercises. In addition to three definite services each day, many prayer meetings were called. If the spirit ran high, the night service continued until dawn.

At first sight these meetings presented a scene of confusion. The crowd talked freely and walked from place to place during the services, and several preachers and recruits from the laity performed simultaneously. Trees, stumps, and wagon beds served as pulpits or as rostrums for the song leaders. Each new preacher had a gathering around him, and for his hearers he depicted horrible prospects unless one "got right" with God.[4] At times as many as six hymns were sung at once, with discords punctuated by hysterical shouts so that the melodies were hardly recognizable. With conversion sinners took the stand or were hoisted to the shoulders of comrades, from which vantage point they added their exhorting to the confusion of tongues. Both laity and clergy abandoned themselves completely to excesses of emotion.

Stirred by the excitement, many participants were caught up by spasmodic movements of their bodies. The "jerks" affected some of the victims so completely that they were unable "to move from one place but jerked backward and forward in quick succession, their heads nearly touching the floor behind and before." When only the head was affected, it often twisted so quickly that "the features of the face could not be distinguished." Few seemed to be able to escape the agitations. Wicked men, seized in the midst of cursing, jerked "as though they'd be torn to atoms." The long unbraided hair of strong women was reported by

---

[4] For a background to the awakening in the West see some letters from Devereux Jarratt in Francis Asbury, *Journal of Rev. Francis Asbury* (3 vols.; New York, 1852), I, 215-18, 222-24. Also see Wesley M. Gewehr, *The Great Awakening in Virginia, 1740-1790* (Durham, 1936), passim.

John W. Monette, a skilled observer, "to lash and crack like a whip, perfectly audible at a distance of twenty feet." Twenty thousand people at the Cane Ridge meeting, according to the reliable Methodist preacher James B. Finley, were "tossed to and fro, like the tumultuous waves of the sea in a storm, or swept down like the trees of the forest under the blast of the wild tornado. . . ." A portion of the ground was usually spread with clean straw for the comfort of the mourners and for those who were sure to fall.

The attitude and behavior of the preacher affected the incidence of these displays of nervous agitation. As a rule, the preacher's lamentable ignorance and zeal far exceeded his culture or prudence, and he was willing to cater to depraved religious appetites. If salvation was expected to descend in a remarkable manner, he saw that the crowd got what it wanted. He knew that the report of the success of a camp meeting was based on the number that "fell"; consequently, his chief interest lay in how many were caught in his "gospel net," not how well they were caught. Many conversions were not permanent, but backsliders provided catches for the next castings.

Within and without the bounds of the camp grounds there was much evidence of passions "not sanctified by grace." Misconduct and moral laxity necessitated the use of vigilance committees and a set of regulations. Whisky dealers carried on a lucrative business, and prostitutes were present for whatever the trade was worth. Ruffians cut bridles and reins, heckled the preachers, and amused the crowds. One old man, having equipped himself with a stick into which he had driven a nail, found great amusement in prodding the fallen converts. But at some point he found the excitement contagious, and throwing his stick aside, he joined the mourners in the straw. The story is told of a notable revivalist preacher McNamara whose ardent admirers sang a song that contained the line "Glory to God and to

McNamara." One night, seeking to impersonate the devil, McNamara crawled on his hands and knees through the crowd that had assembled around him. After creeping a few feet, he would stop and say, "I am the old serpent that tempted Eve!" The situation got out of hand when a hearer took an unexpected role saying, "And I am the Woman that crushed him," as he kicked the preacher in the face.[5]

Looking back on the mixed activities of such religious holidays, Asbury used to remind his hearers that family and closet worship should never be abandoned. Yet Asbury was aware of the importance of numbers, and, having counted the thousands who had joined the Methodist Church, gave credit where it belonged when he confessed that "camp-meetings have done this: glory to the Great I Am!"

Although admittedly the originators and sponsors of the Western revivals, Presbyterians within a few years found themselves reluctant participants. Having made the pie and knowing there were enough plums for all, the Presbyterians had welcomed any and all denominations into this revival enterprise. In 1803 the General Assembly of the Presbyterian Church was unwilling to believe that the revivals had proved to be less "than a dispensation of the grace of God." Two years later, however, the assembly feared that bodily affectations had "greatly tended to impede the progress and to tarnish the glory of what, in its first stages, was so highly promising." In 1806 the assembly, although mildly supporting revivals, asserted that the revivals had incited "the most absurd and extravagant outrages upon Christian sobriety and decorum." Later, in the face of declining membership, the Presbyterian Church regretted the sobering restraint upon her congregations. Although eighteen Presbyterian ministers were reported as being present at the Cane Ridge meeting, less than half of them continued to support the revivalist program. When it became quite evident that the

<hr />

[5] Schauinger, *Badin*, 70.

theological drift was toward Arminianism, both Presbyterian and Baptist preachers squirmed as they thought of their Calvinism.[6]

Mature clergymen of the Presbyterian Church were alarmed when they realized that they had been preaching a free and full salvation coupled with universal redemption —doctrines incongruent with the creed of their church— and many thinking Presbyterians wished to discontinue the camp meetings. But despite the moral courage of some individuals in condemning the movement, the rushing torrent of fanaticism could not be controlled, and the camp meeting continued to flourish for the next decade.

A reaction to the emotional excesses among the older and more conservative Presbyterian clergy and laity led to a denunciation of the camp meetings and even to expulsion from church membership of some who continued to favor the revival movement. Schisms were the result. The conservatives declared themselves the true and sole expounders of God's word.[7] Even though the camp meeting may have been "peculiarly adapted" to the needs of the West, it did not seem congruent to the creed and polity of a church that had no intention of radically changing its tenets or of altering its ecclesiastical structure. Some of the younger Presbyterian preachers definitely chose to stay with the revivals because they believed that the spiritual tone of the country had been enriched and that the church rolls had been increased sufficiently to justify their deviation. From such as they arose in 1810 the Cumberland Presbyterian Church, a definite product of the revival era. Some of the less rigid denominations were to make the necessary adjust-

---

[6] *Extracts from the Minutes of the General Assembly of the Presbyterian Church in the United States of America: from A.D. 1803 to A.D. 1811* (Philadelphia, 1813), II, 11, 92, 125. Also see Thompson, *Presbyterians in the South,* Chap. IX.

[7] An interesting commentary is in T. Marshall Smith, *Legends of the War of Independence and of the Earlier Settlements in the West* (Louisville, 1855), 393-94.

ments, but the Presbyterian Church stood adamant in the very face of dissension and schism.

Since early in the new century the Baptists had been aloof to any cooperation with other denominations. They opposed any concession in the matter of baptism as a requirement for communion. When it became evident that the Methodists had largely taken control of the camp meetings, the Baptists withheld whatever participation they had previously given. After all, the frontier competition for members was between Baptists and Methodists. Although the Baptists at first held almost no camp meetings of their own, they reaped a rich harvest from the awakening. Between August 1800 and March 1801 more than two thousand members were added to the Baptist churches within a twenty-mile radius of Lexington, Kentucky. Distasteful as the extravagances were to them, the Baptists had to admit that the camp meetings were "thawing frozen hearts." In 1801 and 1802 no less than ten thousand new members were added to Baptist churches in Kentucky alone.[8] No organization could afford to scorn a device that worked so successfully. By 1803 the revivals were being generally used by Baptist churches, and the denomination carried the revival methods to all parts of the West. Within the next twenty-five years the Baptists used the terms "sacrificial meetings" and "protracted meetings" to describe their revival seasons. The camp meeting technique was employed by Baptists at the time of the annual meetings of the associations—cooperative unions composed of several adjacent churches. Such services attracted large crowds, and, except for the absence of continuous camping, the protracted meetings differed little from the Methodist camp meetings. As the church buildings became more numerous and more adequate than those in the earliest settlements,

[8] John Rippon, *The Baptist Annual Register, for 1801 and 1802* (n. p., n. d.), 655; Walter M. Lee, *A History of the Elkhorn Association* (n. p., n. d.), passim.

the protracted meetings were moved indoors. Within the confines of walls the preacher could hold the attention of his congregation, and, consequently, turbulence decreased. Occasionally encampments were made by individual churches in the 1830s and 1840s, and the old patterns of the early revivals repeated themselves later in Tennessee, Alabama, Mississippi, Louisiana, and on the new frontiers.

Perhaps because of its sensational nature, writers have been prone to devote too much space to the camp meeting to the neglect of the circuit rider, the churches themselves, and the highly effective activity of Methodist laymen. At no time was the camp meeting recognized as an official agency of the Methodist Episcopal Church; only a few references to it are found in the reports of the annual conferences; the various disciplines do not contain any rules for governing the meetings.[9] But for at least three generations after its introduction the camp meeting proved an important factor in the spread of the Methodist Church. Even with their misgivings about the propriety of the revivals, when Asbury, McKendree, and others saw the results in the field and in the printed reports, their doubts vanished. Undoubtedly, some of the preachers were guilty of indiscretions, but the great bulk of the better class demanded decency and order. A group of revivalist preachers, including Peter Cartwright, James B. Finley, and Jacob Young, entertained no serious doubt of the value and the wisdom of using the camp meeting. As a rule, they were never guilty of allowing a meeting to get out of control, and, therefore, no misgivings disturbed them. However, Robert Davidson, a learned but extremely biased historian of the early Presbyterians in Kentucky, thought the ability and quality of the revival preachers in all churches were generally of poor caliber and that "with two or three shining

[9] Charles A. Johnson, *The Frontier Camp Meeting: Religion's Harvest Time* (Dallas, 1955), 81-82; Sweet, *The Methodists*, 69.

exceptions, the majority were men barely of respectable talents, and [only] a few above mediocrity. . . ."[10]

By 1812 about four hundred Methodist camp meetings were held each year, many of them on the very edges of the moving frontier. Manuals for the regulation of the camp grounds and collections of spiritual songs and hymns were published in large numbers. These books never received official recognition from any governing body of the Methodist Church, but there is no evidence of disapproval of their use.

Statistics seem to indicate that over a long period of years the revivals constituted the chief source of new members added to the church rolls. Granted that they were ill conceived and poorly conducted, the camp meetings were fitted to the frontier character. There is little evidence, however, that the camp meetings appealed to the upper brackets of frontier society. Travelers in this period reported that most well-to-do people in Kentucky were infidels. Francois André Michaux visited Kentucky in 1802 and after observing the scene noted in his journal that "the better informed people do not share the opinion of the multitude with regard to this state of ecstacy. . . ." A somewhat similar opinion of those most affected by the camp meetings was expressed by James Flint. Flint, a sympathetic but critical Scottish observer who spent a year and a half at Jeffersonville, Indiana, in 1818-1819, wrote that he had known many Methodists who were valuable members of society and people of genuine importance but that he had never "seen any one prostrated, or even visibly affected, at the camp meeting or elsewhere, whom I knew to be men of strong minds or of much intelligence."[11] With the passage of time

[10] See Chaps. V-VII in Robert Davidson, *History of the Presbyterian Church in the State of Kentucky* (New York, 1847).

[11] François André Michaux, *Travels West of the Allegheny Mountains, 1802*, in Reuben G. Thwaites, *Early Western Travels* (32 vols.; Cleveland, 1904), III, 249; James Flint, *Letters from America, 1818-1820*, in Thwaites, *Early Travels*, X, 263-64.

the attitude of the church membership began to change in favor of good buildings, more formality in worship, and better educated, stationed ministers. When these changes matured, this American socioreligious phenomenon began to decline in importance.

Amazed at what they witnessed at camp meetings, the Catholics felt that the meetings combined all the features that were repulsive to their thought and training: an untrained clergy gave private interpretations of the Bible; the laity assumed ecclesiastical duties; converts accepted membership without preparation; the service, devoid of ritual and form, was subjected to the whimsy of self-styled clergy. Catholics viewing camp meetings at close range in Kentucky condemned the revival movement. In 1801 Father Badin recorded in unequivocal language his impressions of camp meetings which took place near him: "The Baptists continue to make much noise here, the Presbyterians have thought proper also to imitate the tricks of the former by their extasies, visions, experiences, &c." Concerning the quick baptisms following conversions Badin noted that "they baptize incessantly men who know not even the intent of baptism far from knowing the discriminating doctrines of the church they are associated to." Granting that among his own parishioners were "many Scandalous & nominal Catholics," he reported that none "has forsaken the Church since the revival of the Baptists &c."[12]

In 1805 Father Badin in a detailed account of camp meeting activities described very sensitively the religious excitements. His observations about the type of preachers are cogent: "These bold oracles are for the most part persons without education, who lacking learning, boast of their ignorance, which, they say, makes them preach like the Apostles, that which the Spirit puts on their lips." Again noticing the mass baptizings, Badin wrote: "They have

12 Mattingly, *Church on the Kentucky Frontier*, 191.

lately baptized by immersion a great part of the country people; but several of their neophytes were baptized without knowing why, purely because it was the fashion of the times." One preacher told Badin that since so many had been baptized, not enough sinners were left around Elktown, Kentucky, to have a dance. Badin harshly criticized the meetings as "infamous revels and the harbor of libertinism."[13]

A later appraisal of the Protestant revivalism on the frontier was made by Martin J. Spalding, who was Vicar General of the Diocese of Louisville at the time he wrote his observations. A Kentuckian by birth, Spalding had great understanding of all aspects of frontier life. He was surprised at the general acceptance of the revival fanaticism, despite the good sense of a few who were able "to detect the imposture." Reviewing the leading features of this movement in religion, he adjudged "the whole matter furnishes one more conclusive evidence of the weakness of the human mind, when left to itself. . . ." He thought that there existed in Kentucky at the turn of the century a "contagious frenzy," a condition characterized by fanatical tricks which should teach Protestants to cease talking "about Catholic ignorance and superstition." Having no warmth from participation the Catholics looked upon a revival as an "unholy assembly" in which "no means, however disgusting and revolting to reason, are left untried for the purpose of creating an excitement in sensitive minds. . . ." Long after the first wave of the camp meeting period, a Catholic paper described the Methodist assemblies as being "heathenish." Then the paper posed the damaging question: "What is the area around the camp but a scene for the exhibition of vice, where the profane swearer, the reeling drunkard, the rowdy, the pickpocket and such like mix among the thousands who seek only amusement?"[14]

---

[13] Mattingly, *Church on the Kentucky Frontier*, 192-93. Also see Schauinger, *Badin*, 69.
[14] Ellis, *Documents*, 277-78; *Shepherd of the Valley* (St. Louis), Sept.

Within Kentucky and Tennessee the rash of revivals had dissipated religious energies by 1810, but revivalism repeated itself on each ebbing frontier, assuming new elements or characteristics wherever it took root. Regardless of place and time the revival movement was distinguished by three stages of involvement: first, lack of organization; second, the rise of regulation; and, subsequently, a decline of effectiveness. Then, when the revival spirit became dormant, strong leadership could quickly and easily renew the flames.[15]

The hard conditions of the frontier had contributed to the rise of the camp meeting at the turn of the century. A decade later, natural phenomena in the form of a comet and a series of earthquakes brought to the Mississippi Valley increased religious enthusiasm. A comet of extreme brightness and long visibility appeared over the western hemisphere from March 1811 to August 1812. For a few weeks in the autumn the comet was visible with great brilliancy to residents of mid-America. Children were aroused from sleep to be shown the long nebulous train—a hundred million miles long, so they were told. They soon forgot this awesome sight, and the vividness of it would have dimmed in the adult minds had not unnatural events occurring in December brought immediate recall.

A series of earthquakes rocked the Mississippi Valley between the thirty-sixth and thirty-seventh parallels with an intensity which ranged from violently severe shocks to generally alarming ones. Extensive land slides occurred in the Mississippi River Basin below St. Louis; most of the buildings of New Madrid, Missouri, caved in with the river banks; over in Tennessee Reelfoot Lake was formed in the Indian country; and the Mississippi, tossed by the shifting land, changed its course and laid out new channels for itself. The tremors had been felt from Canada to New Orleans

---

15, 1832; *Catholic Advocate* (Bardstown and Louisville), Aug. 26, 1848.

[15] Carefully examine the concluding chapters of Johnson, *Frontier Camp Meeting.*

and in such unrelated places as Washington and Boston. Population in the heavily damaged areas was sparse so that the loss of human life was small. People living in the river towns had time to flee to the higher ground and from there to observe the instability of the land and to muse on the transience of human life. The scared settlers somehow connected the quakes to the comet and themselves to the terrifying events. Somewhere in the irrational processes of their mind, they interposed an angry God.[16]

Intermittent quakes continuing for several weeks sustained the initial uneasiness. The land slidings were to the people poignant reminders of moral backslidings. In genuine fear of natural consequences, many men sought to right their own waywardness. Each tremor of the earth seemed mightily like a "direct agency of Jehovah," and the preachers in the affected areas pointed out the connection between "these convulsions" and "the moral guilt of the world." For the moralists the destruction of New Madrid served as an admirable example, for its inhabitants "had been noted for their profligacy and impiety." Settlers hastened to atone for their sins and willingly gave themselves over to religious revival. Many sought grace with deep religious fervor; others rushing into the church building sought only refuge within the walls.

Jacob Bower of Muhlenberg County, Kentucky, has written a frank account of his conversion. He had been wrestling with religious doubts for some time, reluctant to make any decision to join a church until the tremors struck that area. Realizing his sad plight, he exclaimed, "Eternity, oh Eternity was just at hand, and all of us unprepared. . . ." It was an awesome sight, he remembered, to see "everything touching the earth, shakeing—quivering, trembling; and mens hearts quaking for fear of the approaching judgment." Bower became a Baptist preacher and an effective missionary in

[16] See Chap. IV in Posey, *Methodism*.

many revivals. In his judgment there "were perhaps fiewer [sic] apostates" among the "earthquake Christians" than from any revivals he had ever witnessed.[17]

The experiences of Bower were duplicated in many instances. Reuben Ross of Stewart County, Tennessee, was beseeched by a "pitiable and terror-stricken crowd" to preach. At nightfall the people were unwilling to leave Ross's cabin, and so the preaching and praying continued until dawn and Ross reaped a grand harvest for his Baptist church.[18] In Arkansas one "die-hard" sinner, greatly alarmed, sent for the local preacher to come to him at once, as he was "the worse case in all the country." In Tennessee a counterfeiter, having buried some copper coins for an aging period, assumed responsibility for the quakes in his section of the country and admitted his complete guilt.

Within the devastated areas there were not enough preachers to administer to the wants of the people. News of the "great awakening among the inhabitants" fell on ready ears, and preachers from the outlying districts hastened to share in the divine manifestation. Men who had not considered themselves as opportunists were unable to withstand the timely circumstances that gave them new power. James B. Finley admitted that he was unable to resist the urge to play on the emotions of the dozen men with whom he was meeting in a cabin. When a tremor made windows rattle and cupboard doors open, Finley jumped on a table screaming, "For the great day of his wrath is come, and who shall be able to stand?"[19]

While hearts were faint and fear smote a multitude of knees, Baptist, Presbyterian, and Methodist preachers made use of the natural catastrophes. Frontier soul-savers preached

[17] "Autobiography of Jacob Bower: A Frontier Baptist Preacher and Missionary," in Sweet, The Baptists, 188-91, 200.

[18] James Ross, Life and Times of Elder Reuben Ross (Philadelphia, n. d.), 203-204.

[19] James B. Finley, Autobiography of Rev. James B. Finley, or, Pioneer Life in the West (Cincinnati, 1854), 240.

that the end of the world was at hand and that man's only
hope lay in baptism and church membership. The Western
Conference of the Methodist Church enjoyed a most fruitful
year in 1812, a phenomenal increase in membership of 50
percent. The full impact of that figure becomes evident
when it is compared to the slight increase in the rest of the
country. The Baptist churches reaped a similar harvest in
membership as reports from some associations within the
seismical region attest. In Kentucky, for example, between
1811 and 1813 the Elkhorn Association added 605 members
and Russells Creek enrolled 622. The Presbyterian Church
shared in the benefits from the periods of excitement. The
Synod of Kentucky in 1812 expressed gratitude for "provi-
dential dealings such as Earthquakes and War—that . . .
increased attention to the Scriptures and all means of Grace
—that many additions have been made to the Church the
last year—that some have returned to our Communion who
formerly went out from us—that Infidels in general have
been more silent, and in some instances reclaimed. . . ."[20]

John M. Peck, a Baptist minister and a frequent visitor
through much of the affected region, believed there was
nothing strange about people professing religion and uniting
with a church in a disordered state of society, even if their
"subsequent lives proved their hearts were unrenewed. . . ."
Peter Cartwright had misgivings concerning the permanence
of some of the conversions of this period, and he commented:
"though many were sincere, and stood firm, yet there were
hundreds that no doubt joined from mere fright."[21]

Events within a year proved that Cartwright's misgivings
were justified. With the subsidence of the earthquakes the
people lost their intense interest in religion and turned their
attention to the Indian troubles which had plagued the

[20] MS Minutes, Synod of Kentucky, 1811-1818, Oct. 21, 1812, in Louisville Presbyterian Theological Seminary—hereafter cited as Louisville.
[21] *Baptist Banner and Western Pioneer* (Louisville), Feb. 17, 1842;
Peter Cartwright, *Autobiography of Peter Cartwright: The Backwoods
Preacher* (New York, 1857), 181.

Northwest. The questionable victory over the Shawnees and their Indian allies at the Battle of Tippecanoe in Indiana in November 1811 had brought no real end to the skirmishes, and the Westerners blamed the British for the bloodshed along the borders; many thought that the only way to make their region safe was to drive the British out of Canada. Females writing from Kentucky mentioned the disturbing conditions of war. Susan L. Martin wrote to a friend in Ohio: "We have heard of earth quakes in many places and felt some of them; and now we have war in all its horrors, war with the Indians and war with the British." The demoralizing effect of the War of 1812 on a new people in a new area was great. One writer complained that the Presbyterian Church was "tormented by a virulent outbreak of unbelief and skepticism." In the Methodist Church Finley admitted that "wars and rumors of wars are peculiarly fatal to the mild and peaceful spirit of the Gospel."[22] The general story is the same with other churches. Men's passion for conflict left only the burnt-out ash of revivalism.

The war brought property damage, human suffering, loss of life, rising cost of living, loss of markets for staple crops, and troubles and anxieties of all sorts. These conditions made it extremely easy for interest in religion to lag, for churches to lose their hold on the people, for some ministers to become speculators and landgrabbers, and for a decrease in membership in all churches. A great number of the "earthquake converts" fell from grace and from membership and "returned to their evil habits." As late as 1814 Asbury in surveying the scene moaned that "there is distress everywhere; in the Church, and abroad in the United States." Great difficulty plagued those seeking to extend the church. The Presbyterian General Assembly of 1816 was deeply

[22] Susan L. Martin to Polly Dickey, Aug. 2, 1812, in Presbyterian Historical Society, Philadelphia—hereafter cited as Philadelphia. W. C. Humphrey, *Historical Sketch of the Synod of Kentucky, 1802-1902* (n. p., ca. 1902), 25; Finley, *Autobiography,* 258.

disturbed over the "secular pursuits" on the Sabbath and the failure to keep the day holy. In Frankfort, Kentucky, a town of twelve hundred people, Isaac Reed found no member of the Presbyterian Church and only one house of worship—a Roman Catholic chapel. Thirty counties in Kentucky had no Presbyterian minister. In 1814 Robert Donnell, a Cumberland Presbyterian minister, was preaching in Madison County, Alabama, but he was greatly discouraged over his prospects as the "people are carried away with the world, so that they talk of little else but corn, cotton, [and] the price of land" which was then selling for ten to fifteen dollars an acre.[23] A missionary in Tennessee reported in 1820 the section was practically destitute of ministers. The Sequatchie Valley, according to one reporter, in 1829 contained one Presbyterian—a woman.

In the overall appraisal of the value of the camp meetings and revivals, there are two schools of thought. One believes that the meetings never performed any substantial good, and that the entire movement should be characterized as "one of the errors of the past." Another group thinks, as does William W. Sweet, that they "served a very large social and religious need." Charles A. Johnson, author of a recent study of the camp meeting, likewise insists that the camp meeting arose in response to a great and impelling need and that "it was a vital socioreligious institution" which was "a wholesome weapon of the church."[24] It appears that the camp meeting did bring salvation to many—but to others only an emotional experience to be followed by reversion to the old way.

[23] Asbury, *Journal*, III, 433-34; Posey, *Presbyterian Church*, 113; Isaac Reed, *The Christian Traveller* (New York, 1828), 55-72, passim; David Lowry, *Life and Labors of the Late Rev. Robert Donnell* (Alton, Ill., 1867), 102.

[24] William W. Sweet, *The Story of Religions in America* (New York, 1930), 8; Johnson, *Frontier Camp Meeting*, 240-41, 299-300. For an interesting Catholic endorsement of a Baptist appraisal of the camp meeting see "Revivals," *Catholic Advocate*, April 29, 1848.

3

SOME DENOMINATIONAL
SPLINTERS

THE PROTESTANT CHURCHES in America have been distinguished by the dissensions that sprang up so freely in them.
Sectarianism has been regarded as a disease by some students
of church history and as healthy mutation by others. No
denomination escaped an occasional drift in its orthodoxy.
Some churches were able to curb free-thinking members:
some tolerated them; but other churches expelled the
recalcitrants. The widespread settlements in America so
stretched the lines of communication that contacts with
centers of authority were difficult to maintain and in some
instances impossible to keep. The same scattering of people
made for narrow conservatism and radical liberalism—the
turn depending on the intellectual processes that were at
work in the new environments. A community tucked in the
hills of Tennessee could well decide to think as it pleased,
and then to delight in its independence. Other remote settlements could have an awareness of their slipping from the
faith of the fathers and yet gather all together with a new
bond of orthodoxy. Occasionally a preacher, having gone to
New England or the Tidewater settlements of the South,
returned home with some ideas of the intellectuals he had
met and then stirred the complacency of his old congregation.

One notable shift on the frontier was the reaction against
Calvinism. The sense of freedom and independence engendered on the frontier doubtless worked against many of the

doctrines of strict Calvinism. The great increase in lay preachers that resulted from the revivals weakened the control exercised by church authorities and encouraged the development of religious freedom. The moderate Calvinism and the young, democratically inclined Presbyterian ministers on the frontier contributed materially to the success of the revivals and to the growth of schisms. In the west a number of dissensions troubled the Presbyterians as a consequence of frontier independence.

During the decade of 1785-1795, prior to the dissensions over the revivals, the unity of the Presbyterian Church had been torn by Adam Rankin in Kentucky and Hezekiah Balch in Tennessee. Rankin had been born in western Pennsylvania in 1755. At the age of twenty-seven he was licensed by the Hanover Presbytery in Virginia. He soon received calls from the Holston and Nolichucky neighborhoods but declined because of disputes over psalmody. A contentious and self-willed individual from youth, obstinate and opinionated, he was susceptible to dreams—one of which turned him against Watts's version of the Psalms. Accepting a call from a church in Lexington, Kentucky, in 1784, he readily collected a large and faithful congregation. Often as many as five hundred people were present on sacramental occasions before which he launched attacks against the use of Watts's psalms. Fanatically, he attacked his opponents by calling them swine, hypocrites, blasphemers, and deists. At a conference in 1785, a year before the formation of the first presbytery in Kentucky, Rankin brought up the matter of psalmody. Alone in his views, he went without commission to the General Assembly of 1789 determined to force the rejection of Watts's versification. The assembly listened at length, denied action on psalmody, and then recommended that he should not disturb the peace of the church on this matter.

Returning home more vehement than before and contending that a divine warrant in dreams supported his opinion, Rankin continued his assault on the Presbyterian clergy and barred from the communion table all who favored Watts's psalms. No longer could this go unnoticed by the Transylvania Presbytery. In April 1792 he was suspended, and in the following October his pastoral charge was declared vacant.[1]

So calculatedly and artfully did Rankin state his case in a published narrative of ninety-six pages that he was regarded by many members of his church "as a martyr in the cause of truth, persecuted for righteousness' sake."[2] While able to retain possession of his church and the loyal support of most of its members, Rankin made a connection in 1793 with the Associate Reformed Church. Later he broke away from this church and became independent. Although his following declined until it became insignificant, scarcely a Presbyterian congregation in Kentucky escaped the disputes which he had aroused.

While the Presbyterians were wasting their strength on a secondary doctrinal point, other churches were rapidly gaining. In Tennessee the Presbyterian Church had lost ground through the Hopkinsian controversy led by Hezekiah Balch, a native of Maryland, a graduate of Princeton, and in 1785 the third Presbyterian minister to reach east Tennessee. Because of his age and experience he took the lead in organizing churches. After a decade he made a trip to New England in quest of funds for his school. While there he became a devotee of Hopkinsianism, a departure from strict Calvinism. Upon his return Balch published these new

[1] Samuel J. Baird (compiler), A Collection of the Acts, Deliverances, and Testimonies of the Supreme Judiciary of the Presbyterian Church (Philadelphia, 1855), 209; Ezra H. Gillett, History of the Presbyterian Church in the United States of America (2 vols.; Philadelphia, 1864), I, 412; Sweet, The Presbyterians, 138-39.

[2] Davidson, Presbyterian Church, 93 and Chap. III, "The Rankin Schism."

opinions in the form of Articles of Faith in the Knoxville *Gazette.* At first his church reacted impassively to the new teachings. Balch was an indiscreet person with strong convictions who often acted upon a quick impulse. Many thought him "overbearing and abusive" in his views. The matter was taken to the Abingdon Presbytery and dismissed "upon some unmeaning apologies from Balch." But the excitement led five of the leading ministers in the presbytery to withdraw and form the Independent Abingdon Presbytery in 1797.[3]

Later the matter was the subject of extended discussion by the Synod of the Carolinas in 1797 and then referred to the General Assembly meeting in the following year. After Balch acknowledged that he had erred in the publication of his creed, he was admonished not to foment divisions as he had previously done. Although the assembly exonerated Balch from the accusation of heresy, it charged him with "imprudent and unwarrantable conduct" and warned him against teachings that would "tend to produce serious and lamentable evils." Despite the censure, Balch continued his unorthodox and forceful teachings along Hopkinsian lines. One observer was certain that the hurt caused "by Balch and his party is almost beyond description."[4]

Other divisions and dissensions occurred in the West. Thomas B. Craighead, a graduate of Princeton, reached Nashville in 1785, and for thirty years continued to be a perennial storm center in middle Tennessee. In the early

---

[3] Baird, *Collection,* 629-34. Hopkinsianism was advanced by Samuel Hopkins (1721-1803) who "believed that the inability of the unregenerate is owing to moral and not to natural causes, and that sinners are free agents and deserving of punishment, though all acts, sinful as well as righteous, are the result of the decrees of providence. The essence of sin, he thought, consisted in the disposition and the intention of the mind." James G. Wilson and John Fiske (eds.), *Appleton's Cyclopedia of American Biography* (6 vols.; New York, 1898-1899), III, 258.

[4] *Minutes of the General Assembly, 1789-1820,* 151-57; Edward Crawford to James Crawford, Sept. 18, 1797, Philadelphia.

1800s he embraced elements of Pelagianism, and in 1806 preached a sermon before the Synod of Kentucky for which he was arraigned and admonished to be cautious in the future. Four years later he published a blasting attack on Calvinism about which James Blythe, a Presbyterian minister, in writing to a friend said: "I have never felt so uncomfortable under any publication. . . . It had proved to [be] a kindling flame, an overwhelming deluge."[5] Suspended by the synod in 1810 and deposed in 1811, Craighead continued to preach until 1824. Numerous people believed that Craighead's influence led to an infiltration of Unitarian sentiments and to the appointment of Horace Holley to the presidency of Transylvania University.

Harmony in the General Conference of the Methodist Episcopal Church meeting in Baltimore in 1792 was broken by the dissension centering on James O'Kelly, an influential preacher in Virginia. He spoke out boldly against the authority of the bishop, particularly against the appointing power from which there was no recourse. O'Kelly introduced a resolution which provided that a preacher, dissatisfied with an assignment by the bishop, would have the right of appeal to the annual conference, and, if the conference approved the objection, the bishop must then appoint the preacher to another circuit. O'Kelly, believing that he was the spokesman for democracy, was unprepared for the defeat of his resolution. He knew that he was not alone in opposing the power of the bishop, but he had not reckoned with the influence of an absent man nor the fickleness of human nature. Asbury, disabled by a slight physical disorder, addressed the assembly by a letter, which

[5] Blythe to William Williamson, ca. 1810, Philadelphia. Also see Sweet, *The Presbyterians*, 352 et passim; Gillett, *Presbyterian Church*, II, 199. Pelagianism denied the doctrine of original sin and defended the freedom of will.

probably said far more than he would have said on the floor in opposition to the resolution.[6]

On the morning after the defeat of his resolution, O'Kelly and several other preachers framed a statement of their intention to withdraw from the conference in session. A committee immediately sought to persuade the dissidents to return, but the request was refused. Within three days O'Kelly, accompanied by the preachers under his influence, left the city. Incensed over O'Kelly's actions, Asbury accused O'Kelly of desertion because of his failure to "settle him for life in the South District of Virginia." Other people charged that O'Kelly was ambitious to become a bishop.[7]

The General Conference of 1792 rejected every effort to modify its autocratic methods in favor of a limited degree of control by the laity. Some Methodists believed that the less the laity knew about church matters the better. But this opinion was not accepted by the writers of the constitution for the Protestant Episcopal Church, adopted in the same year, which granted equal representation to clergy and laity in the House of Deputies. Indeed, the reforming element in the Methodist Church spent twenty years in an effort to secure the point at issue when O'Kelly and his group walked out of the conference.[8]

O'Kelly for several years had been a critic of Francis Asbury. He could not agree with the assumption of power

[6] John J. Tigert, A Constitutional History of American Episcopal Methodism (Nashville, 1894), 243-54; Jesse Lee, A Short History of the Methodists (Boston, 1810), 149-53, 179; Edward J. Drinkhouse, History of Methodist Reform . . . the Methodist Protestant Church (2 vols.; Baltimore, 1899), I, 407, 432-36. On numerous points in regard to O'Kelly I have relied on a Ph.D. dissertation that I assisted in directing at Emory University. See Charles F. Kilgore, The James O'Kelly Schism in the Methodist Episcopal Church (Mexico City, 1963).

[7] W. E. MacClenny, The Life of Rev. James O'Kelly (Indianapolis, 1950), 98-102 et passim; George C. Smith, Life and Labors of Francis Asbury (Nashville, 1896), 180-81.

[8] Drinkhouse, Methodist Reform, I, 425. In 1872 laymen were grudgingly admitted to the General Conference of the Methodist Episcopal Church; in 1910 they were admitted in equal number with the ministers.

by Asbury, whom John Wesley had reproved for calling himself bishop, a title Wesley never assumed.[9] He had opposed the council form of church government since its inception in 1789. The council was composed of the bishop and eleven presiding elders, which the bishop appointed and could remove at his will. As a member of the council, O'Kelly had requested the removal of various rules and restrictions and had heartily advocated a general conference of all preachers. The real issues under consideration, however, were easily lost in the personal confrontations of Asbury and O'Kelly. Each had loyal followers.

When the Virginia Conference met in 1793, the O'Kelly partisans pleaded with Asbury for a compromise in church government and requested that they be continued as members of the Methodist Church. When Asbury would not consider the subject, the O'Kelly group had no alternative to secession. On December 25, 1793, in Manakintown, Virginia, they formed the Republican Methodist Church. It was so named because republican principles were prevalent in Virginia at that time. In August of the next year the Reverend Rice Haggard stood up in a conference in Surrey County, Virginia, held up a copy of the New Testament, and said that, because the disciples were called Christians, he moved that adherents to the new movement be called Christians. This became the permanent name of the denomination, with the Scriptures as its only creed and rule of faith and practice. In doctrine the Christians differed little from the Methodists, but in the matter of government the difference was great. There would be no grades allowed in the ministry; each church would chose its own pastor; the laity

[9] See Herbert Asbury, *A Methodist Saint: The Life of Bishop Asbury* (New York, 1927), Chap. IX, for Bishop Asbury's opinion that "the trend of American Methodism was away from John Wesley" and Bishop Thomas Coke. In 1788 Wesley wrote Asbury a letter in which he severely reprimanded him. "I study to be little; you study to be great. I creep; you strut along." "How can you, how dare you, suffer yourself to be called a bishop? I shudder, I start at the very thought!" Smith, *Asbury*, 118.

would be given the balance of power; and executive authority would be left to local congregations.

Among those who strongly favored O'Kelly's position was William McKendree, who for four years had served on a circuit under O'Kelly's supervision. At the General Conference of 1792, when the resolution was under discussion, McKendree had made a forceful speech against the power of a bishop to appoint without the right of appeal. He said that the procedure was "such an arbitrary stretch of power, so tyrannical [or] despotic, that I cannot [or] will not submit to it."[10] He refused an appointment from Asbury and cast his lot with O'Kelly. Freeborn Garrettson, Richard Ivey, Hope Hull, and others of equal importance likewise joined the democratic faction.

For McKendree the glitter of the "glorious Church" without slavery soon dimmed, and within a year, having been approached by Asbury to ride with him for a while, he returned to the Methodist ranks. Asbury appointed him a presiding elder in 1795 and guided him into the office of bishop in 1808. At this point McKendree advanced extreme demands for administrative authority and resented interference from the conferences. "It would almost seem as though the type of man capable of rising to preeminence in the hard school of the frontier was bound to be the type of man who would rebel against having his hands tied by democratic paraphernalia once he was secure in high office."[11]

As could be expected the Christian Church moved in uncertain directions. Some thirty preachers had withdrawn from the Methodist Church with O'Kelly, and their number had been increased by stray preachers who sought employ-

[10] Drinkhouse, *Methodist Reform*, I, 435; Robert Paine, *Life and Times of William M'Kendree* (2 vols.; Nashville, 1869), I, 59, 65. Both M'Kendree and McKendree are used.

[11] Elizabeth K. Nottingham, *Methodism and the Frontier: Indiana Proving Ground* (New York, 1941), 102.

ment in the new pulpits. The very independence of the lot fostered jealousy and bickerings. O'Kelly was a man of considerable ability and natural charm, but his qualities did not make him an effective leader of a dissenting group. Despite these conditions, excitement about the new church was infectious. In Virginia and North Carolina, where O'Kelly had preached for sixteen years, entire congregations followed him out of the Methodist churches. In the Cumberland country of Tennessee and Kentucky the new church got a foothold. Two itinerants, James Haw and Benjamin Ogden, who had been planting seeds of Methodism in this region since 1785, forsook their charges and circuits to join the O'Kelly movement. Haw, a very persuasive man, was able to proselyte every traveling and local Methodist preacher in the Cumberland region except one. Ogden was a man of less activity than Haw; he became a stationed preacher soon after he moved to Kentucky and as a result his influence was limited. In his old age he returned to the Methodists. Between 1796 and 1801 the increase in Methodist membership in Kentucky and Tennessee was almost negligible. The total membership in both states was 2,296 for 1796 and 2,488 for 1801.[12]

In order to combat the devastating influence of Haw, the Methodists in 1795 placed William Burke on a circuit that included a large section of middle Tennessee and middle Kentucky—the identical area in which Haw had led so many from the church. To Burke, a young elder, was assigned the job of stopping Haw, the experienced and popular preacher who had been in the country for a decade. Burke accepted a challenge to debate Haw at Station Camp, a point near a large number of societies of Methodists in central Kentucky. According to his own reminiscences, Burke triumphed so completely that Haw "lost his influence

[12] For statistics on membership see Kilgore, *O'Kelly Schism;* MacClenny, *O'Kelly; Minutes of the Annual Conferences of the Methodist Episcopal Church,* I (New York, 1840), passim.

among the Methodists, and his usefulness as a preacher," and finally joined the Presbyterian Church.[13]

The loss of members by the Methodist Church is the best commentary on the seriousness of the O'Kelly defection. During the three years after the conference of 1792 membership declined by about eleven thousand, and ten years passed before it exceeded the figure for 1791. In all secession had cost the Methodist Church about one-fifth of its membership. For a short time the revolt against authority in behalf of a more democratic church had an attraction for so many people that it threatened to disrupt the parent church in many sections. By 1810 O'Kelly's Christian Church claimed that its boundaries extended from Philadelphia, down the Ohio River to the Mississippi, down that river to a point due east of the southern line of Georgia, thence along this line to the Atlantic, and then up the coast to Washington and on to Philadelphia.

Some years after the organization of the Christian Church, two other movements originating independently merged with O'Kelly's group. One movement, largely of Baptist origin, arose under the leadership of Elias Smith and Abner Jones in New England. The second was the familiar Stone defection chiefly from Presbyterians and Baptists in Kentucky. All three groups clearly rejected Calvinism and adopted the Scriptures as their rule of faith and their only creed. When each of the three learned of the other, each sought fellowship and cooperation. In May 1809 Christian ministers from Virginia, North Carolina, and South Carolina assembled in Virginia and sent a message to their brethren in New England. Three New England ministers returned the greeting. In 1811 Elias Smith visited the Southern group

13 James B. Finley, *Sketches of Western Methodism* (Cincinnati, 1857), 48. For early efforts in Kentucky and Tennessee see Albert H. Redford, *The History of Methodism in Kentucky* (3 vols.; Nashville, 1868-1870); John B. McFerrin, *History of Methodism in Tennessee* (3 vols.; Nashville, 1871-1874).

and worked out a general agreement of union. Although the churches in the three areas had much in common, denominational consciousness developed very slowly. Churches that had arisen out of opposition to a curtailment of liberties were naturally apprehensive of entering a new union. A conference of the Christian Church with official delegates first met in 1820, and after that assembled quadrennially until 1854 when the church split over slavery.[14]

What was the effect of the O'Kelly defection from the Methodist Church? Two results stand unquestioned. The Methodists lost members and a new sect came into existence. Beyond these and probably even more important, there remains the inevitable conclusion that O'Kelly's resistance against oppressive church government tempered the autocratic government of the Methodist Church and brought it more in line with prevailing civil liberties.[15]

On the frontier schisms and defections popped up at random, and among the more unstable folk talk spread of a millennial church. Whispers became prophecies, and eager expectancy reached out to the Shakers who arrived in the West early in the nineteenth century.

This peculiar and now almost extinct sect had its origin in France in 1688 when some Dauphiné peasants sought a return to the early Christian faith. Persecuted by Louis XIV, a few extremists escaped to England. In 1758 Ann Lee, an illiterate daughter of a blacksmith from Manchester, identified herself with the Shakers. Marked with ability and initiative, Ann Lee easily assumed leadership, and, finally despairing of making headway for her associates in England, "Mother Ann," as she was then called, brought

---

[14] Reunited in 1894, the church lost its identity when it combined with the Congregational Church to form the Congregational Christian Church in 1931. As will be seen later, most of Stone's following had united with Campbell in 1832 to form the Disciples of Christ.

[15] See "Centralized Control in Church Government," in Peter G. Mode, *The Frontier Spirit in American Christianity* (New York, 1923), Chap. VII.

eight of her disciples to America in 1774. The "Believers" settled on a tract of land at Watervliet, across the Hudson River from Albany, New York.[16]

In 1779 events around New Lebanon, New York, brought a windfall to the Shaker community: the failure of a series of revivals that had attracted many Baptists, some Presbyterians and Methodists, and a scattering of onlookers turned many of these people to the Shakers. Additional substance was given the Shakers when they assumed the more meaningful name of The United Society of Believers in Christ's Second Appearing.

The origin of a large measure of the Shaker theology is usually attributed to Ann Lee. Having had a vision of Christ, Ann developed the idea that in her was realized Christ's second appearance on earth. The idea was accepted by her followers and developed into a dual concept of the deity in the Father-Mother God. The Shakers claimed that they represented the true church and stated that "revelation, spiritualism, celibacy, oral confession, community, non-resistance, peace, the gift of healing, miracles, physical health, and separation from the world are foundations of the new heavens."[17] The feminist feature of Shaker theology made a tremendous appeal to women, particularly to spinsters and widows whose lot in frontier society was usually dull and unhappy. The opportunity to live in a community without the domination of men was attractive to them, and in some Shaker communities or villages women outnumbered the men two to one.

As early as 1780 Mother Ann had made a prediction that

[16] This brief sketch of the Shakers draws heavily on my article, "The Shakers Move West," *Emory University Quarterly*, XLVIII (1962), 38-46. For the beginnings of Shakerism see Thomas Brown, *An Account of the People Called Shakers: Their Faith Doctrines and Practice* (Troy, N. Y., 1812); Edward D. Andrews, *The People Called Shakers: A Search for the Perfect Society* (New York, 1953). The Shakers were originally known as "Shaking Quakers" because of their trembling during worship.

[17] H. K. Carroll, *The Religious Forces of the United States* (New York, 1912), 112.

the Shaker gospel would thrive in the Western country. For twenty years her predictions seemed vain; the eleven colonies which the Shakers had established in New York State and in New England were small, poor, and promised little for the expansion of the sect. Almost miraculously the situation changed in 1805, and a new field opened in Kentucky and Ohio. Upon hearing of the great revival movement in Kentucky, the leaders of the Shakers recognized "the manifestations of a spirit akin to their own." Recalling the advantages that had come from the New Lebanon revival in 1779, Lucy Wright, who had succeeded Ann Lee as leader of the Shakers, decided to capitalize on the opportunity that had arisen. On January 1, 1805, she dispatched John Meacham, Benjamin S. Youngs, and Issacher Bates to the West with no appointed destination except the centers of the revivals. In addition to $5,467 in missionary funds, official greetings, and some explicit instructions, the missionaries carried a letter from the central office urging people to confess their sins and to take up the Cross. On their way to the West they heard rumors of a new sect called Christians whose members in strong religious excitement fell into trances, jerked head and body, danced, shouted, sang, and uttered strange sounds. While walking all but sixty of the nearly thirteen hundred miles to Kentucky, the missionaries had time and opportunity to get a good picture of social and religious conditions of the country. Arriving in Garrard County, Kentucky, on the first Sunday in March 1805, they spoke to an assembled group of Presbyterians at Paint Lick on their first evening in the village. Matthew Houston, pastor of the congregation, gave a ready ear to the message which the travelers brought and within a month he was prepared to renounce his connection with the presbytery.[18]

[18] Marguerite F. Melcher, *The Shaker Adventure* (Princeton, 1941), Chap. IV; Julia Neal, *By Their Fruits: The Story of Shakerism in South Union, Kentucky* (Chapel Hill, 1947), 22; Davidson, *Presbyterian Church*, 207-208.

After a few days spent at Paint Lick, the evangelists went
to Cane Ridge, where, according to their testimony, Barton
Stone, at that time a Presbyterian minister, "sucked in our
light as greedily as ever an ox drank water." Recalling his
early impressions of the Shakers, Stone said, "They were
eminently qualified for their mission. Their appearance was
prepossessing—their dress was plain and neat—they were
grave and unassuming at first in their manners—very intelligent and ready in the Scriptures, and of great boldness in
their faith." For a short time Stone verged on full acceptance
of the Shaker belief, but was repulsed by their doctrine of
the resurrection and their repudiation of marriage. As he
lost his initial enthusiasm for the new faith, he became
more objective in his assessment of its offerings. Looking
at all the uneasiness which the travelers had caused, Stone
wrote, "The worm of Shakerism was busy at the root of all
the sects, and brought on them great distress; for multitudes
of them, both preachers and common people, also joined
the Shakers." Stone found hard to swallow the Shakers'
claim to the power of miracles. When he challenged this
power by asking for a demonstration which they refused,
Stone denounced the missionaries as "wolves in sheep's
clothing, [who] have smelt us from afar, and have come to
tear, rend and devour. . . ."[19]

Stone, in appraising the successes of the Shakers, admitted
that he with other defectionists had paved the way for these
conversions. Squarely on the shoulders of Robert Marshall,
John Dunlavy, John Thompson, Richard McNemar, and
himself, Stone laid the responsibility for fomenting the revolt
against the Westminster Confession. Explaining this, he
said: "Some of us were verging on fanaticism; some were so
disgusted at the spirit of opposition against us, and the

[19] Sweet, *The Presbyterians*, 98; John Rogers, *The Biography of Eld.
Barton Warren Stone, Written by Himself: with Additions and Reflections*
(Cincinnati, 1847), 62-63; Richard McNemar, *The Kentucky Revival* (New
York, 1846), 102.

evils of division, that they were almost led to doubt the truth of religion *in toto;* and some were earnestly breathing after perfection in holiness, of which attainment they were almost despairing, by reason of remaining depravity."[20]

Other voices did not speak out so violently against the Shakers. To their satisfaction the missionaries had found the soil prepared for their coming; in the people was aroused a consciousness of wickedness and they were ready to revolt against Calvinism. Stirring the religious waters wherever they went, the Shaker missionaries moved on to Lexington, then to Cincinnati, and on to Warren County, Ohio, where Malcolm Worley had large holdings on Turtle Creek. No doubt these itinerants moved purposefully. Worley, a prominent man in the community, had already defected from his Presbyterian upbringing and had identified himself with the New Light Church whose minister was Richard McNemar, a colleague of Stone in the revival movement. Worley welcomed the three Shakers to the generous hospitality of his log home. In less than a week Worley had accepted wholeheartedly the Shaker teachings and became the first believer in the West. About a month later McNemar "opened his mind and united with the Believers." Most of McNemar's congregation followed him into the new group, so that by May the Shakers had forty members at Turtle Creek. Worley's house became the nucleus for the Shaker settlement of Union Village, and this place became the center for the administration of all the communities in the West.[21]

The time was more auspicious for the Shakers than they had anticipated. Swamped by converts, the three missionaries needed helpers, and at their request nineteen more

---

[20] Rogers, *Stone,* 64.

[21] Neal, *Shakerism,* 23; McNemar, *Kentucky Revival,* 81-94, passim. Davidson (*Presbyterian Church,* 208) says that Worley "had been one of the wildest of the New Lights, and was like tinder ready for the spark" of Shaker proselyting.

workers came to the West to organize societies or colonies. Settling in the midst of strong schismatic preachers, the missionaries continued to be the center of interest and of controversy. Stone, now steadfast in his opposition to the new faith and the practices of its adherents, lost his accustomed sweetness and mildness in order to broadcast damaging reports about the Shakers. From him came accusations that the Shakers were using the rule of celibacy in order to acquire property through the separation of man and wife. In an effort to nullify this attack, the missionaries used part of their money to purchase some land in Bourbon County. There they settled several "families" and, in the midst of critical onlookers, gave proof of the commune that Believers could enjoy. Naturally it was not easy to break down opposition, and the members of the community endured many indignities: property was damaged by vandals, and buildings were set afire. Their strangeness engendered suspicion, and their prosperity fostered jealousy. The policy of self-sufficiency seemed to have created a separateness that prevented any cordiality toward the new sect.[22]

From the beginning the Shakers had been spiritualists, holding that there is "a most intricate connection and the most common communion between themselves and the inhabitants of the world of spirits." But they were not deeply concerned with spiritualism until 1838-1845. This was the period of their greatest prosperity, and it is possible to surmise that economic independence allowed time and energy for flights of fancy. Whatever the reason, the Shakers did indulge themselves to the extent that their religious services were little more than seances. Visitors to such meetings were shocked by the fanaticism displayed, and, after the word about them became common knowledge, the governing elders barred all visitors.[23]

[22] Brown, *Shakers*, 351-62; Andrews, *Shakers*, 80.
[23] Carroll, *Religious Forces*, 112. "The first victims of the spiritualist craze were the New England Shakers, the somewhat boring decorum of

The various settlements, except New Lebanon, were divided into units or families, each occupying a double house, usually three stories high, with separate entrances and stairs for men and for women. At the head of each house was an elder and eldress with limited authority subject to the approval of the family. To some were delegated responsibility for the agrarian economy which supported the community. According to his strength, each member worked at crafts indoors or in active farm duties. However, it was the duty of all to witness for the Shaker beliefs; all were preachers but none so called. To the committee of overseers was given the title "the ministry" only because of their administrative duties. Shaker communalism was expressive of the underlying belief in brotherhood. A statement of principles declares: "The bond of union which unites all Shakers is spiritual and religious, hence unselfish. All are equal before God and one another; and, as in the institutions of the primitive Christian church, all share one interest in spiritual and temporal blessings, according to individual needs; no rich, no poor. The strong bear the infirmities of the weak and all are sustained, promoting each other in Christian fellowship, as one family of brethren and sisters in Christ."[24] Such statements were far more than hollow words; they were ideals daily practiced in the fields, barns, mills, and kitchens. The Shakers excelled in all things except educational pursuits. They feared the restlessness of a cultivated mind, hence provided only elementary schools for the children in the community.

A great deal of Shaker success in the West turned on the conversion of Worley and McNemar. The latter has been described as a striking person, tall, erect, possessing "native

---

their peaceful communal life making them peculiarly susceptible to this call of the wild." Ernest S. Bates, *American Faith: Its Religious, Political, and Economic Foundations* (New York, 1940), 421.

[24] Bates, *American Faith*, 365-66. See "The Shaker Communities," Chap. VII in Alice T. Felts, *Freedom's Ferment* (New York, 1962).

endowment, toilsome acquirement, studious training. . . .
His mind was ever open for more light. He accorded to
others the same rights he reserved for himself."[25] McNemar
became the spokesman for the Western Shakers whose
activities he recorded well in *The Kentucky Revival*, an on-
the-spot report written in 1807. He promoted hymnology,
wrote many songs, and started the *Western Review*. When
McNemar died in 1839, literary efforts among the Western
Shakers virtually came to an end.

In 1806 some Believers settled on land purchased in
Mercer County near Lexington, Kentucky. The new community, named Pleasant Hill, began to take permanent form
with the erection of the first stone building in 1809. Between
1807 and 1810 another community, South Union, began to
take shape in Logan County, near the Tennessee boundary.
South Union and Pleasant Hill developed along similar
lines. Sturdy stone buildings attest to the industry and toil
of the workers and to the wisdom of their administrators.
On the large acreage attached to each center diversified
farming and crop rotation produced a greater yield than the
needs of the community required. The Shakers expanded
their labors by adding trades and crafts and sold their
finished products throughout the state and beyond. The
facilities of Pleasant Hill and South Union were filled to the
maximum accommodation of 604 residents.

Despite outside opposition to the communes, the Believers
grew in number and increased their land holdings. Their
farm endeavors produced a very satisfactory economic base,
and in time their industrious ways won the respect of people
outside the fold. The Shakers had only two real sources
for new members. Welfare agencies were non-existent, and
the communities provided a home for orphans or unwanted
children. Also, following camp meetings and revivals, the
Shakers offered continued emotional enthusiasm to people

[25] Melcher, *Shaker Adventure*, 274.

who had been temporarily aroused and had found no lasting satisfaction in their own denominations. The Shakers were active proselyters wherever they settled.

Under the direction of Lucy Wright the Shaker expansion had reached its maximum of nineteen centers with seven located in the West. No new communities were established after her death in 1821. The membership, however, reached its peak between 1840 and 1860, at which time the yearly membership was about six thousand. If one measured influence and impact by means of numerical strength alone, he would miss the full import of the Shaker communities. Among more than one hundred communal societies established in the United States, the United Society of Believers was the most successful in establishing and maintaining colonies. South Union, its last remaining settlement in the West, was closed in 1922,[26] and now the inroad which the Shakers made among the Presbyterian strongholds exists only in print.

The history of the Baptist denomination in America has been replete with a record of missionary efforts, but the Baptist alone of all the churches suffered a lengthy and disastrous fight over the missionary movement in a region where an early church often received aid from the East and, in the case of the Catholic Church, even from Europe. As early as 1755 the Charleston Association committed itself to the support of a missionary in the West and initiated Baptist mission work in that part of the United States. This decision antedated by more than half a century the formation of the Baptist General Convention in 1814. The organization, soon to be known as the Triennial Convention, sent Luther Rice as a missionary to the West in 1815. Spending several years there, he found the people, especially in Ken-

[26] See the interesting "Statistical View of Shaker Communities," Andrews, *Shakers*, 290-92.

tucky, willing to support the work with generous contributions of money. At its second meeting in 1817 the Triennial Convention increased its efforts by sending James E. Welch of Kentucky and John M. Peck of Connecticut to Missouri with instructions to preach to both whites and Indians and to establish schools. Peck spent the remainder of a long life in a region where his name became a household word. Probably no missionary in any church in the Mississippi Valley ever equalled Peck in the extent of the territory he covered or in the amount of work which he performed.

Largely because of the accomplishments of Rice and Peck, interest in Baptist missions spread rapidly through the Mississippi Valley. In 1817 a Baptist missionary society was organized in Mississippi. In the following year this society made elaborate plans for its work including an annual collection of money. The Triennial Convention accepted in 1817 the offer of James A. Ranaldson to go as a missionary to the city of New Orleans and the state of Louisiana. Living expenses were so high that he left the region,[27] but in 1823 Ranaldson took the lead in organizing the Alabama State Convention which sent fifteen missionaries to various sections of the state for six weeks of service. In Alabama and in other parts of the Lower South the missionary program was promising to spread widely when it ran headlong into an antimissionary movement with which it would battle fiercely and heroically for more than a quarter of a century.

At first glance it seems an anachronism and a contradiction that a church rooted and grounded in the spirit of missions should find itself faced with an antimissionary antagonist that threatened its destruction. This new force gained its strength from three rather remarkable Baptist preachers strategically located and from extremely favorable conditions for success—temporary though it proved to be.

---

[27] His letter is printed in John T. Christian, *A History of the Baptists of Louisiana* (Shreveport, 1923), 60-61.

On the border of Tennessee and Kentucky lived Daniel Parker, an implacable foe of missions in any form. Despite his unattractive physical features he possessed genuine leadership among the poorly educated class of frontier folk. He traveled widely, preached incessantly, and wrote a stream of pamphlets and books which literally covered his part of the country. Parker opposed ministerial education and charged that missions constituted a scheme of collecting money for an unworthy group of men. Parker's effectiveness brought many missionary societies to dissolution and many programs to an end.

John Taylor, next in importance to Parker, migrated in 1782 to Kentucky from Virginia and became for a period of several years the most influential Baptist minister in Kentucky. As a pastor of ten different churches at various times and a large landowner he wielded tremendous power among a much higher level of frontier society than did Parker. When the missionary program began in Kentucky, Taylor became a determined opponent. In a widely circulated pamphlet, *Thoughts on Missions*,[28] he made a slashing attack on missionary societies as money-grabbing devices wholly contrary to the Baptist system. Taylor hurt the missionary efforts not only in Kentucky but far beyond the borders of the state.

The third person to play a leading role in the early history of the Baptist antimissionary fight was none other than Alexander Campbell, a Presbyterian until 1812, a Baptist for the next two decades, and thereafter the successful leader of the Disciples of Christ. Few figures in American church history possessed greater qualities of leadership or commanded a more loyal following than Campbell. Through the media of the pulpit and of the press he made himself and his cause known from his home at Bethany in Western

[28] John Taylor's *A History of Ten Baptist Churches* (Frankfort, Ky., 1823) remains one of the best accounts of pioneer Baptists in Kentucky. Taylor deserves a biography.

Virginia to the extreme fringes of the frontier. In his earlier days he opposed anything and everything for which he could not find clear authority in the Scriptures. Although he denied that he opposed missions *per se,* he attacked the Baptist plan as extravagant, avaricious, and dishonest. After he formed the Disciples of Christ, he renounced his early opposition to missions, but his attacks had taken a heavy toll.

Probably much of the sympathy for this antimissionary movement in the Baptist churches arose directly from their ultrademocratic form of government. The denomination was built on a strictly voluntary basis that guaranteed each individual church to be a separate, distinct, autonomous unit. The Baptist idea of the freedom of the individual did not find agreeable the authority of a missionary board that could send a missionary wherever it pleased. Election, predestination, the nature and extent of atonement, and the final perseverance of the saints were the chief themes dwelt upon by the majority of Baptist preachers. It was easy to convince church members who needed their money for many purposes that to send missionaries to Indians and to Negroes was definite interference with God's work. Many readily believed that it was sinful for a preacher to accept money for preaching. No wonder that an association like the Buttahatchee in Mississippi firmly declared itself against missions: "Surely you must have a great thirst for money that you should beg it in the name of converting the heathen!—for if you know anything about God, you know this, that it is his prerogative to convert the heathen, or as many of them as he wants converted. And he holds the means in his own hands to do it . . . without your horse-leach system—cry, give, give!"[29]

The battle between the two forces often reached a heated point. One man in the Conecuh River Association in Ala-

[29] Jesse L. Boyd, *A Popular History of the Baptists in Mississippi* (Jackson, 1930), 50-51.

bama threatened to use his rifle on any missionary who invaded his community. The ministers in some of the pulpits delivered slashing condemnations of missions and missionaries. Parkerism and Campbellism rapidly moved into many erstwhile missionary Baptist churches causing the cessation of missionary societies, the deterioration of religion, and the division of numerous churches. The very existence of the Baptist denomination in the Mississippi Valley had been threatened.

The panic years around 1837 undoubtedly played some part in the failure of many people to support missions, but by 1840 the future of missions began to brighten. The contention with Campbell had been quieted in some sections, but Campbell was no longer a member of a Baptist church and that lessened a great tension. Parker, the most vigorous and most effective of all the foes of missions, had moved to Texas in 1833. John Taylor had reversed his former position and in this manner removed the third member of the opposing triumvirate. Prosperous years brought money, and Baptists began to demand education for their children and their preachers. The tide had turned in favor of missions. The cost had been great in effort, money, and spirit, but the Baptists had brought most of their churches in line with the expanding forces of liberalism in religious matters.

Out of this antimission fight came the Primitive and the Two-Seed-in-the-Spirit Baptists—two of the numerous groups into which the Baptists have divided. The Primitive or Hardshell Baptists are principally known for the old custom of washing the feet of the members of the church. In Alabama, where the Hardshells were especially strong, the question of washing feet was often considered by churches and by associations. Some ruled that it was not an ordinance of the gospel, while others considered it "a divine appointment." The Hardshells, claiming apostolic descent, were often accused of speculating on decrees and purposes of

God rather than directing their attention to the unchurched people.

Parker first developed the Two-Seed doctrine, a type of antinomianism which exalted predestination to an extreme point. This doctrine is a modification of ancient Manichaeism which divides all mankind into two classes. One group is endowed with a good spiritual seed implanted by God into Adam and Eve. After the fall of man, Satan implanted in Eve "the seed of the serpent." All descendants of the divine seed are assured of salvation, while those born of the evil seed are doomed to damnation. The Two-Seed and Primitive groups of Baptists became the chief protagonists of antimissionism which, according to Albert H. Newman, historian of American Baptists, "constitutes the saddest and most discreditable feature of modern Baptist history. . . ."[30]

These four religious groups, born in unusual conditions, challenged and often defied the older denominations. The Shakers and the O'Kellyites have faded from the scene. Today the Two-Seed Baptists number only two hundred members. The Primitive Baptists, the most strictly orthodox of all Baptists, still have about seventy thousand members. Two other groups, the Cumberland Presbyterians and the Disciples of Christ, became so successful that they grew into full-fledged denominations and both continue to the present day.

[30] See Justin A. Smith, A History of the Baptists in the Western States East of the Mississippi River (Philadelphia, 1896), 123-25; Albert H. Newman, A History of the Baptist Churches in the United States (New York, 1900), 433.

4

TWO NEW DENOMINATIONS

A FRONTIER that had accustomed itself to unlimited freedom
had little disposition to accept a "God of inexorable decrees."
A minister could hardly press upon his listeners the doctrine
of foreordination and unconditional election and at the same
time point out to a sinner his personal accountability for his
poor religious state. Soon the revivalist party in the Presbyterian Church realized that adherence to a rigid Calvinistic
faith would tend to scatter its forces in all directions, for
Presbyterians had definitely displayed their inability to adapt
their tradition to the conditions of the frontier. Although a
large portion of the Western people were partial to the
Presbyterian form of government, they could not accept the
whole of the Presbyterian doctrine. Furthermore, the Presbyterian Church never sought to be popular or to enroll the
masses.

Robert Davidson, an unfair critic of the revivals, insists
that only five Presbyterian ministers supported the revivals.
Others were unfriendly or opposed to the manner in which
the revivals were conducted.[1] Nevertheless, a disturbed
frontier had led James McGready to relax discipline in order
to meet the pressing need of a ministry that had become
helpless in the face of so many unconverted people.

Almost from the beginning of the revivals the Presbyterian
Church found itself divided into the revival and antirevival
factions. Although several rifts occurred in Presbyterian
ranks, the greatest blow was the defection known as the

Cumberland Schism which resulted in the formation of the Cumberland Presbyterian Church. Four important factors largely explain the situation that brought the new church into existence. First in order of time was the appearance of a revivalistic element within the frontier Presbyterian Church, largely composed of Presbyterians with traces of Arminian conviction, people having a somewhat lower economic, educational, and social status than the older Calvinistic group. The degree of difference between these two Presbyterian elements was greater than that between the revivalistic Presbyterians and the Methodists. Not bridged by some compromise, this unhappy situation led to division.

The second disrupting factor arose from the educational requirements for the Presbyterian ministry. When the revivals were at their height, the supply of ministers fell far short of the demand. In order to meet the urgent need, the Transylvania Presbytery in 1801 lowered the requirements and accepted four men as exhorters and catechists who, according to Thomas Cleland, "made no pretensions to the literary qualifications required by our Form of Government." The exhorters were directed to prepare discourses on different subjects and to read them at the next meeting of the presbytery. At the meeting in October 1802 Samuel King, Alexander Anderson, and Finis Ewing were licensed to preach despite a strong dissent signed by three ministers and two elders who complained that the examination "consisted only in one short sermon & an examination on experimental religion & divinity." The men "being destitute of classical learning" were without "such extraordinary talents" as to justify licensing.[2]

---

1 Davidson, *Presbyterian Church*, 223-24. Despite the unfairness displayed by Davidson, his book is a valuable source and a mine of information.

2 [Thomas Cleland], *A Brief History of the Rise, Progress, and Termination of the Proceedings of the Synod of Kentucky* (Lexington, Ky., 1823), 4; "Minutes of the Transylvania Presbytery, 1786-1837," Oct. 6-7, 1802, in

The advocates of lowering the educational requirements cited the success in the Methodist and Baptist denominations of the untrained preachers who had been largely recruited from the laity. It was acknowledged that an education was exceedingly difficult to come by, and one could reasonably question its value in a frontier meeting "where thousands were collected in the open air, to receive the bread of life . . . [from a preacher] with a voice of thunder, denouncing the curses of the law upon guilty and impenitent sinners. . . ." The ability which some uneducated preachers had demonstrated brought pressure on the Presbyterians to enlist men with similar capacities. Men with strong Christian experience but little formal education could be sent out as missionaries with good expectations for success. David Rice had made the suggestion that "under the circumstances" the classical course was not necessary and that laymen of ability should be selected to serve, when needed, as catechists or exhorters.[3] But the ruling element insisted on shutting the door to the Presbyterian ministry against all candidates who did not have the requisite formal education.

The need for more preachers became imperative when the Synod of Kentucky in 1802 divided the Transylvania Presbytery into the Transylvania and Cumberland presbyteries. The latter was formed out of the lower portion of the old presbytery and comprised the less recently settled area, south of a line along Big Barren River to its mouth and thence to the mouth of Salt River. The Cumberland Presbytery began with ten ministers equally divided between the revivalists and the antirevivalists. Almost imme-

---

Sweet, *The Presbyterians*, 189. B. W. McDonnold, *History of the Cumberland Presbyterian Church* (Nashville, 1899) remains the standard history of the church. Chaps. VI-XI contain much of value for the early years.

[3] James Smith, *History of the Christian Church . . . Including a History of the Cumberland Presbyterian Church* (Nashville, 1835), 583; George P. Hays, *Presbyterians* (New York, 1892), 147.

diately the bars on educational requirements were let down so far that the presbytery ordained men with no seminary training. Usually they were established farmers who had taught themselves to exhort. Davidson charged that "illiterate exhorters, with Arminian sentiments were multiplied, till they soon numbered seventeen." The success of these recruits, "burning with zeal" and traveling incessantly on their circuits, caused the conservatives great apprehension. Davidson commented fearfully that "unless this process had been speedily checked, the result would have been to establish a very undesirable ascendency in the Synod."[4]

When questioned by the Transylvania Presbytery on the propriety of licensing and ordaining for the ministry men who did not have a liberal education, the General Assembly made a reply so carefully worded that each faction readily found justification for its views on the subject. The assembly was of the opinion that a liberal education was not "absolutely essential to a man's usefulness in the ministry . . . but reason and experience both demonstrate its high importance and utility." Parrying further, the judicatory concluded, "We cannot lawfully and conscientiously depart from our present standards till they be changed in an orderly manner by the consent of a majority of the Presbyteries. . . ."[5]

The third factor leading to disruption arose over the question of doctrine, the topic on which some church historians wish to place most of the blame for the Cumberland Schism. The Cumberland Presbytery licensed candidates who not only had renounced the idea of fatality but also had objected to sections in the Confession in regard to infant damnation, limited atonement, and the perseverance of the saints. Further, the candidates differed so little from the Methodists in the matter of free will and grace that some of them desired to unite with the Methodist Church.

---

[4] Davidson, *Presbyterian Church*, 229.
[5] Baird, *Collection*, 81.

When numerous Presbyterian preachers in the revival period adopted the Confession of Faith, they made an exception to the idea of fatality, understood by a Cumberland Presbyterian minister as meaning "that God created a certain part of the human family to be saved, and a certain part to be lost; that is, he predestinated some to everlasting life, and foreordained others to everlasting death; and that this was done 'before the foundation of the world was laid'—before the persons themselves were created." To support his belief, this minister-author quoted at length from the third chapter of the Westminster Confession of Faith and from Davidson who called Calvinism "a complete and compact system," of which "every separate doctrine is a keystone, which cannot be abstracted without endangering the whole." To many the necessity for abandoning Calvinism had arrived, if relief "from the oppressive yoke of ecclesiastical bondage" was to be gained.[6] It had been inevitable that the new spirit of independence and freedom would turn the frontiersman away from Calvinism to Arminianism or cause him to accept a position midway between the two extremes.

In September 1803 the Synod of Kentucky (formed in 1802) brought against Richard McNemar and John Thompson charges of preaching erroneous Calvinistic doctrine, specifically declaring God's love for all the world and the individual ability of anyone to receive the means of salvation. Three other preachers who were under suspicion of "Arminian tenets," Robert Marshall, John Dunlavy, and Barton Stone, held a conference with McNemar and Thompson. The five decided to withdraw from the Kentucky Synod but not from the Presbyterian Church. Immediately they formed themselves into a presbytery which they named Springfield.

[6] MS Minutes of the Cumberland Presbytery, 1810-1813, 6, Philadelphia; T. C. Blake, *The Old Log House: A History and Defense of the Cumberland Presbyterian Church* (Nashville, 1897), 65, 76; Franceway R. Cossitt, *The Life and Times of Rev. Finis Ewing* (Louisville, 1853), 190.

The Kentucky Synod, with undue haste, suspended the five independents and declared their pulpits vacant.

The Springfield Presbytery in January 1804 issued an "apology" written in three parts: the first attempted to justify the withdrawal, the second attacked the doctrine in the Confession of Faith, and the third part defended the Bible against the creeds. This provocative broadside by the militant ministers, some of whom were very popular, threatened to sweep the Western country with a wave of enthusiasm. By the end of 1804 seven new societies were formed in Ohio and eight in Kentucky.[7]

The disturbance caused by the five colleagues suspected of Arminianism reached the General Assembly in May 1804 by means of a letter signed by a committee of the Presbytery of West Lexington requesting the assembly to heal the unhappy breach or to prevent its extension. Less than a month later the Springfield Presbytery, convinced that it only served as a hindrance to the plea for union, agreed to disband and begin an independent church. To this end the presbytery was dissolved by the issuance of a strange and facetious document entitled *The Last Will and Testament of the Presbytery of Springfield.* It had been written no doubt by McNemar and was signed by the original five protestors plus David Purviance. This instrument denounced all sectarianism, forsook the title of "Reverend," and declared the independence of each congregation. Various names were given to the new group—New Lights, Stoneites, Marshallites, and Reformers.[8]

For a while the new organization called itself the Christian Church, but the idea of freedom was so exaggerated that

[7] For the role of Stone and his colleagues in the revival movement examine Rogers, *Stone;* William G. West, *Barton Warren Stone: Early American Advocate of Christian Unity* (Nashville, 1954); Charles C. Ware, *Barton Warren Stone: Pathfinder of Christian Union* (St. Louis, 1932).

[8] See "The New-Light Heresy," in Baird, *Collection,* 634-40; Sweet, *The Presbyterians,* 94 ff.

any hope for union soon disappeared. Within this loosely organized sect, with no real bond of union, defections soon appeared. In 1806 the three Shaker missionaries from New York readily convinced McNemar and Dunlavy that their way of life was superior to the Reformer way. The Unitarianism of Stone and the controversy over baptism led Marshall and Thompson to issue a pamphlet confessing their errors. As penitents they appeared in 1811 before the Synod of Kentucky. After they had submitted to an examination, the synod removed from them the sentence of suspension and welcomed their return to the Presbyterian Church. Only Stone remained to fight for the freedom which the original five once so boldly demanded. In 1832 he merged his own branch of the Christian Church with the Disciples of Christ led by Alexander Campbell.[9]

A controversy over the rights and powers of the synods and presbyteries in the examination of ministers constituted the fourth and deciding issue. By all standards the Cumberland party stood in a logical position. The beginning of this dispute arose from the appointment of a committee of five by the Synod of Kentucky in 1804 to attend the next meeting of the Cumberland Presbytery and report on its educational requirements for the ministry. This step was largely taken because of a complaining letter from three members of the antirevival party in the Cumberland Presbytery. The Presbytery correctly denounced the appointment of this committee as an unwarranted assumption of power and denounced as a spy the one member of the committee who dared attend. Although the presbytery wandered from the standards of a classical education as a requirement necessary for the Presbyterian ministry, the synod erred from the very

[9] Cossitt, *Ewing*, 408; Levi Purviance, *The Biography of Elder David Purviance* (Dayton, Ohio, 1848), 114-16; Gillett, *Presbyterian Church*, II, 174-77; Catherine C. Cleveland, *The Great Revival in the West, 1797-1805* (Chicago, 1936), 136-41.

beginning in its vigorous intervention in the affairs over which it had no right of control.

A committee appointed at the 1805 meeting of the Synod of Kentucky made a report on the "extremely defective" records of the Cumberland Presbytery. It mentioned numerous irregularities and made the criticism that "the mode of transacting business frequently violates our rules of discipline." After much debate on the report and expression of disapproval of many actions of the presbytery, the synod took the unfortunate step of appointing a committee of sixteen ministers and elders to compose "a Commission vested with full Synodical powers to confer" with the presbytery and adjudicate its proceedings. The meeting was ordered to be held at the Gasper meetinghouse in Logan County on the first Tuesday in December.[10]

By moving into the stronghold of revivalism, the anti-revivalist commission found itself in a hornet's nest. Its coming was thoroughly advertised throughout the community, and its purpose was represented as threefold: to stop the licensing of non-college trained ministers, to abandon the circuit system, and to halt the progress of the revivals. John Lyle recorded in his journal that bitter opposition to the commission incited one congregation in the presbytery to collect and burn copies of the Circular Letter published by the synod. Hostility and resentment filled the air, and, when time came for the meeting, only one person in the neighborhood of the church offered hospitality to

10 "Minutes of the Synod of Kentucky, 1802-1811," Oct. 17, 18, 1805, in Sweet, *The Presbyterians*, 331-35. The historian of the Cumberland Presbyterian Church is on safe ground when he complains that the commission was composed of men "who had been the fiercest partisans against the revival." Among these was the well known Joshua L. Wilson who had been charged with antagonizing the Cumberland group "with a malignity which would have disgraced a Romish priest in the days of Martin Luther." Failure to include conservatives like Rice made the composition of the committee highly weighted against the accused. McDonnold, *Cumberland Presbyterian Church*, 81.

the commissioners. Undoubtedly, the synod compounded its mistakes in choosing Lyle to deliver the opening sermon. Being extremely hostile to the revival group, he had boldly described Finis Ewing as "one of the illiterate ministers of this presbytery." Following Lyle's three-hour explanation of the qualifications expected in a Presbyterian minister, the commission proceeded to the task before it.[11]

The chief trouble, as was expected, centered on the twenty-seven men who had been licensed and ordained by the Cumberland Presbytery. The candidates had been permitted to adopt the Confession with the reservation "so far as they deemed it agreeable to the word of God," and no reference had been made to this in the minutes of the presbytery. The majority of the presbytery, with James McGready as spokesman, admitted the fault as stated by the committee, but pleaded the exception of the fourteenth chapter of the Form of Government and numerous precedents. Meeting this rebuff, a committee of the synod resolved to examine and to judge the qualifications of each candidate; whereupon the majority of the Cumberland Presbytery refused to submit on the very proper ground that the presbytery had the exclusive right to examine and to license its own candidates. The commissioners from the synod then forbade the recusants from preaching or administering the ordinances until they submitted to examination. Five members of the presbytery were ordered to appear before the next meeting of the synod to answer charges of error or contumacy in refusing to force to examination the young men "who had been irregularly licensed and ordained."[12]

[11] A Narrative of Rev. John Lyle's Mission in the Bounds of the Cumberland Presbytery (1805), 20-21, 40, 57. MS in Kentucky Historical Society, Frankfort—hereafter cited as Frankfort.
[12] "Minutes of the Synod of Kentucky, 1802-1811," Dec. 9, 1805, Oct. 27, 28, 1806, in Sweet, The Presbyterians, 341-43, 351-54. See also Blake, Old Log House, Chap. IV; Gillett, Presbyterian Church, II, 182-86.

Immediately after the commission had delivered its verdict and declared itself dissolved on the eighth day of its meeting, the majority of the Cumberland Presbytery formed itself into a council which pledged its members to preach, to refrain from presbyterial actions, to keep the churches and the revivals alive, and to seek a reconciliation with the parent church. Of the five ministers ordered to appear before the Synod of Kentucky in October 1806 only two were present, and they went not in answer to the command but in an attempt to effect a reconciliation. The synod, in no mind for compromise, suspended from the ministry the two recalcitrants, dissolved the Cumberland Presbytery, and attached its church members to the Transylvania Presbytery.

The dissension came to the attention of the General Assembly through a "Letter of the Council of revival ministers to the General Assembly of 1807." The high judicatory expressed some sympathy for the revival party. In a letter directed to the Synod of Kentucky this General Assembly commended the synod on its zeal but suggested that much of the procedure of the commission was of "questionable regularity." Furthermore, the letter urged a review of the proceedings and the adoption of milder views. The assembly, by a letter to four remonstrants from the Cumberland Presbytery, admonished the licensing and ordaining of persons not possessing the qualifications required by the discipline as "highly irregular and unconstitutional." The presbytery was advised to return to the constitution of the church and to strive for peace. The General Assembly of 1808 received a second petition from the presbytery, but declined to consider the overture on the grounds that the Synod of Kentucky was the only constitutional body empowered to handle the dispute at the stage then reached.[13]

In 1809 John Lyle, as a commissioner from the Synod of

[13] Cossitt, *Ewing*, 479-86; *Minutes of the General Assembly, 1789-1820*, 389-93, 400-406.

Kentucky to the General Assembly, took to the assembly a letter defending the synod's action. Undoubtedly Lyle's dramatic presentation of the case influenced the unanimous support for the rulings made by the Synod of Kentucky against the Cumberland Presbytery. Awestruck by the assembly, Lyle was at first speechless; then, bursting into tears, he gave so impassioned an appeal that his hearers reversed their previous ruling against the action of the synod. The case against the revivalists was closed by a decision which is now "almost universally admitted" to be contrary to Presbyterian rule and custom. A Cumberland Presbyterian historian asks if any body of ministers ever did "commit so many intolerable blunders, and not only violate the constitution of the church to which they belonged, but actually transcend the very warrant giving them power to act, as well as prescribing and limiting their action?"[14]

Despite the generally accepted democracy of Presbyterian government, the session, the presbytery, and the synod can issue successive decrees against dissenters and troublemakers. The presbytery and synod possess the power of suspending ministers and dropping churches from the roll. This gives enormous authority to insure compliance with doctrine and discipline. One scholarly study of early Kentucky goes so far as to charge that "the story of Kentucky Presbyterianism is the story of the ruthless destruction of every vestige of independent theological thought which might arise among the clergy, and even among the laity." Years ago, Davidson had boastingly announced a similar position by saying that "our discipline does not contemplate clothing a man with ministerial authority in order to propagate his private and schismatic views. . . ." And again he proclaimed the power of the church in Kentucky by saying "there is no part of the Presbyterian body in the United

[14] Davidson, *Presbyterian Church*, 119, 250; Hays, *Presbyterians*, 465; Cossitt, *Ewing*, 145.

States . . . that furnishes more sturdy champions for rigid orthodoxy and efficient discipline, than the Synod of Kentucky. . . ."[15]

The council of recusants met again in August 1809 and made one final appeal to the Synod of Kentucky. Although willing to be examined on doctrinal points, its members would adopt the Confession only if permitted to except that portion which appeared to teach the doctrine of fatality. The synod refused to accept the terms and ordered a meeting for the purpose of restoring those members of the old Cumberland Presbytery who would submit to the requirements of the synod. This offer brought the return of William Hodge, Samuel Hodge, James McGready, and Thomas Nelson. Finis Ewing, Samuel McAdow, and Samuel King were the only ordained members who remained faithful to the stand taken by the revivalist element in the Kentucky Synod. By obstinate resistance to the commission the recusants had to all intents renounced the authority of the Presbyterian Church. T. C. Anderson, a contemporary Presbyterian minister of considerable prominence in east Tennessee, called Ewing, McAdow, and King "three ignorant boys" who "had put to sea without chart or compass," who, like mushrooms, "had sprung up, as it were, in a night, and would soon wither and die in the sunlight of Divine truth."[16]

Contrary to predictions Ewing, McAdow, and King held to their course. These three met in the home of McAdow in Dickson County, Tennessee, on February 4, 1810, and constituted the independent Cumberland Presbytery, which formed the nucleus for the Cumberland Presbyterian Church. The newly organized presbytery adopted a constitution which accepted the confession and discipline of the Presbyterian Church, but made a provision for relief from

[15] Niels H. Sonne, *Liberal Kentucky, 1780-1828* (New York, 1939), 18-20.
[16] T. C. Anderson, *Life of Rev. George Donnell* (Nashville, 1858), 188; McDonnold, *Cumberland Presbyterian Church*, 106.

fatality. The Cumberland fathers believed that they had adopted a medium position not "between fatality and freedom, but a medium between the Calvinism of that day and Arminianism." In March the members of the presbytery, still hoping for a reunion with the parent church, agreed that unless a reconciliation could be reached by October, no further effort would be made.

The Presbyterians worked diligently to warn people by circulars and pamphlets that the new church possessed no right to administer the ordinances. James McGready, whose failure to join the Cumberland group constituted a major loss to the defectionists, expressed grave concern over the extreme position of the new sect: "They have a flame of animation with them which they call the revival and this is what supports them and gives them importance, but . . . the contempt with which they treat some of the doctrines of the Confession of faith . . . [seems] to differ from the Spirit of Christ. . . ." In 1811 Gideon Blackburn, coauthor of an accusing letter to the West Tennessee Presbytery, made several severe accusations against the Cumberland Presbytery and concluded by reiterating his opinion that the new conception of fatality was "totally denied by every well informed Calvinist."[17]

Instead of hindering, these attacks spurred the rapidly growing Cumberland movement. In 1810 the new church distributed a circular letter which explained "the origin, progress, and termination of the difference between the Synod of Kentucky and the former Presbytery of Cumberland." Three years later the church held a synod composed of three presbyteries which had sixty congregations. At this time a committee was appointed to prepare a confession of faith and a discipline—the whole of which was presented to

[17] McGready to Archibald Cameron, Nov. 6, 1811, Philadelphia; MS Minutes, West Tennessee Presbytery, 1810-1836, Sept. 17, 1811, in Historical Foundation of the Presbyterian and Reformed Churches, Montreat, N. C.—hereafter cited as Montreat.

and adopted by the synod in 1816. By 1820 the church had
a thousand members in Kentucky, and the movement had
spread to Alabama, Arkansas, Illinois, Mississippi, and Missouri. The first General Assembly was held in Princeton,
Kentucky, in 1829. Six years later there were nine synods,
thirty-five presbyteries, three hundred ordained and one hundred licensed ministers, and seventy-five thousand communicants. The phenomenal early growth of the church
resulted largely from adoption of a revivalistic program, the
borrowing of the Methodist system of circuit riding, and
the modifying of the stern Calvinistic creed. Finally, the
leadership of Finis Ewing was a great force in the early
years. By no means the illiterate man pictured by Lyle,
Ewing was "a majestic pioneer preacher," admirably equipped
to meet the same problems faced by such noted Methodist
circuit riders as Cartwright and Finley.[18]

The early Cumberland Presbyterians adopted the doctrine
of sanctification which is "an evidence of a desire that a
revival of religion shall be made permanent in holy living."
Ewing in a lecture on sanctification grieved over the low
state of grace of Christians who "are not expecting daily
communion with God, daily access to the throne, a daily or
abiding witness that they are born of God." Several important Cumberland preachers spent great effort in a search
for holiness of life and earnestly advocated baptism by the
Holy Spirit. Davidson charged that these claims to new
discoveries in Christian doctrine were nothing except "a
mongrel mixture of Antinomianism and Arminianism," a
form of error which "blended high pretension to sanctification with equally high exaltations of human agency in
believing, and a studious silence upon the subject of the
Holy Spirit and his operations." David Rice tried to prevent

---

[18] McDonnold, *Cumberland Presbyterian Church*, Chaps. XI-XIV; J. Ber-
rien Lindsley, "Sources and Sketches of Cumberland Presbyterian History,"
Theological Medium (Nashville). These informative articles are scattered
through Vols. VI and VII (1875, 1876).

the Cumberland group from adopting a system that contained no mysteries. The frontier, however, was a fertile field for the growth of "holiness" ideas, and, despite Presbyterian charges of heretical doctrine, the Cumberland preachers and people for a period found in sanctification "the climax in Christian zeal and idealism."[19]

Viewing now in appraisal the events of 1810, one finds much evidence that the founders of the Cumberland Presbytery had no intention of creating a new church or even a schism in the old. Anticipating a spirit of compromise from the parent church, the dissenting group hardly expected or desired the sudden exclusion and independence that faced it. The dissenters entered the ecclesiastical skirmishes perplexed and uncertain, and, if they had found some tolerance and kindness in the synod, there is little likelihood that the new church would have arisen. Theodore L. Cuyler said: "Had Presbyterianism been as sagacious as Methodism in such matters, it might have harnessed the fiery enthusiasm of those frontiers-men into its chariot. Grant that those John Baptists in linsey-woolsey and leathern girdles were lacking in diplomas, and rather low in their Calvinism and wild in some of their methods; yet Presbyterianism needed just such a corps of skirmishers and sharp-shooters for its frontier campaign."[20]

The separation was complete and finished before the respective sides began to temper their judgments. Shortly before James McGready died, he is quoted as having said to his congregation: "Brethren, when I am dead and gone, the Cumberland Presbyterians will come among you and occupy this field; go with them [for] they are the people of

[19] Merrill E. Gaddis, "Religious Ideas and Attitudes in the Early Frontier," *Church History*, II (1933), 169; McDonnold, *Cumberland Presbyterian Church*, 27; Davidson, *Presbyterian Church*, 166; R. A. Johnstone, *Presbytery of Transylvania, Kentucky* (Louisville, 1876), 38-39.

[20] *Address Delivered at the Celebration of the Centennial of the General Assembly of the Presbyterian Church* (Philadelphia, 1888), 16.

God." Most of the membership of his church followed his advice and joined the Cumberland Presbyterians. An evidence of the cooling of passions is seen in the minutes of presbyteries such as that of the Alabama in 1824; it is recorded that the presbytery could not "hold fellowship" with the Cumberland Presbyterians, but it did not "wish to oppose or disparage their labors in the cause of Christ." In 1828 the *Western Luminary*, an interdenominational periodical, stated that it was willing to print news concerning the Cumberland Presbyterian denomination. A year later Finis Ewing, who had more cause to nourish ill will against the old church than any other member of the Cumberland Church, wrote for publication in the *Luminary* a gracious letter urging members of his church to subscribe to the paper, because it probably had the widest circulation of any religious paper in those states where Cumberland Presbyterians lived. The widely traveled and fair-minded James Gallaher, a Presbyterian minister and author, had no hesitancy in believing that "no body of Christian ministers in America, or even in the world, have *preached so much good, effective preaching,* and *received so little worldly compensation,* as the ministers of the Cumberland Presbyterian church."[21]

Three obscure Presbyterian ministers had founded in the wilds of the West a new church "simply and solely that they might have standing room" in an atmosphere free from ecclesiastical oppression.[22] They were deeply concerned for the welfare of "souls that were perishing" because of a shortage of ministers—a concomitant of a Presbyterian demand for a classical education. The new church met a pressing need by coping with a frontier religious situation

[21] Cossitt, *Ewing,* 166; MS Minutes, Alabama Presbytery, 1821-1826, April 2, 1824, Montreat. See issues of the *Luminary* for Dec. 24, 1828, and July 1, 1829; James Gallaher, *The Western Sketch Book* (Boston, 1850), 61.
[22] Lindsley, "Sources and Sketches," *Theological Medium,* VII (1876), 34.

in which the older church on numerous occasions had
failed.

The westward movement had weakened ecclesiastical ties
and lessened the church authority to the point that many
men contended that the Bible was in the East and freedom
was in the West. Distance and lack of communication gave
the necessary freedom to those people possessing some
different religious ideas who wished to form new sects, a
few eventually to become denominations and others to
disappear. The sect which became the most important major
denomination in the Mississippi Valley was the Disciples of
Christ. "Its simplicity, its warmhearted informality in worship, its suspicion of any lurking seeds of clericalism, its
vocal insistence upon congregational independence, all bear
the mark of the American frontier."[23]

In many respects the background for this movement was
first set in force in 1804 by Barton Stone, who, after the
dissolution of the Springfield Presbytery, favored the name
"Christian" and urged its acceptance by several Presbyterian
churches in central Kentucky and southern Ohio. By the
close of this year fifteen Christian churches had come into
existence. Stone was the accepted leader of the new movement which, according to statistics printed in 1827, had
about thirteen thousand members scattered from Ohio,
Indiana, and Illinois to Tennessee and Alabama. Stone's
idea of a church characterized by original Christianity, as
he described it, was a broad fellowship among members,
one essentially free from ecclesiastical councils. Early in
his life Stone had been troubled by numerous phases of
theological controversy. After a quarter of a century "of
intermittent polemics against the most cherished doctrines

[23] Ruth Rouse and Stephen C. Neill (eds.), *A History of the Ecumenical Movement, 1517-1948* (Philadelphia, 1954), 238-39. See also Leonard W. Bacon, *A History of American Christianity* (New York, 1921), 241-44.

of orthodoxy," he reached the practical conclusion that what really mattered the most in religion fell outside the realm of the disputes to which he had devoted so much of his efforts. Although he gladly accepted the advice to spend less time in "speculation," he had already done enough thinking to demand freedom from what he thought were old and outworn dogmas.[24]

The direct origin of the movement, however, was the left wing dissenting group, generally known as the Reformation Movement led by Thomas and Alexander Campbell, father and son, who were members of the Anti-Burgher branch of the Seceder Presbyterians. The joint effort of the Campbells never resulted in a splintering movement similar to that of the O'Kellyites or to that of the Cumberland Presbyterians. Although in the beginning many of the Campbellites were defectors from older churches, the later membership came largely through converts of the unchurched to their doctrine.

Thomas Campbell was born in Ireland and was graduated at the University of Glasgow. While serving as a minister in the Seceder Presbyterian Church in Ireland, he became a firm advocate of Christian union. Leaving his family in Scotland at the age of forty-five, he came to the United States in 1807 in search of a better climate and better economic conditions. Soon after reaching Philadelphia, he was appointed by the Anti-Burgher Synod to the Presbytery of Chartiers in southwestern Pennsylvania. Within three months a charge had been brought against Campbell for heretical views and violation of some of the rules of the church. In sum he had advanced the idea that Protestant sects could be reunited into a single church and could return to simple Biblical teachings. Thereby he had become an avowed enemy of sectarianism. He refused to abide by

[24] Winfred E. Garrison and Alfred T. DeGroot, *The Disciples of Christ: A History* (St. Louis, 1954), 115, 121.

the rule of close communion and invited all Christians to partake of the sacrament. When the presbytery confronted Campbell with censure, he appealed to the Associate Synod of North America saying that he would be willing to be judged by the standard found in the Bible. The synod released Campbell from the censure, but about a month later he withdrew from its jurisdiction.[25]

After spending nearly a year preaching in private homes in the region of Washington, Pennsylvania, Campbell took the lead on August 17, 1809, in the formation of the Christian Association of Washington, which accepted as its guide the declaration of Campbell: "Where the Scriptures speak, we speak; where the Scriptures are silent, we are silent." This association did not consider itself a church but rather a society organized for the sole purpose of reform.

During the summer of 1809 Campbell prepared *The Declaration and Address of the Christian Association of Washington,* the most important document in the history of the Campbell Reformation Movement. Later when printed as a pamphlet of fifty-six pages, it was divided into four sections—a Declaration (three pages) giving reasons for the organization, its purposes and ideas; an Address (eighteen pages) explaining the desire for Christian unity and proposal for securing it; an Appendix (thirty-one pages) answering criticisms and explaining points in the Address; and a Postscript (three pages) suggesting steps for promoting the program.

The Declaration boldly states four principles of the association: the right of private judgment, the sole authority of the Scriptures, the evils of sectarianism, and the road to union. Then follow nine resolutions designed to serve as a constitution for the association. Number IV explicitly states

[25] The chief source of information about the Campbells has long been Robert Richardson's *Memoirs of Alexander Campbell* (2 vols.; Philadelphia, 1868-70).

"that this Society by no means considers itself a Church
. . . [and not] at all associated for the peculiar purposes of
Church association; but merely as voluntary advocates for
Church reformation. . . ." The address expanded the
argument in behalf of unity of all Christians and described
the unhappy divisions in a new country so thinly settled.
The heart of the address is found in a series of thirteen
numbered propositions that urged Christians to follow the
New Testament in order to achieve an undivided church,
inasmuch as division is "antichristian," "antiscriptural," "anti-
natural," and "productive of confusion and of every evil
work."[26]

A great heartening came to Campbell with the arrival of
his family in December 1809. He found that his son Alexander, then twenty-one years of age and fresh from a year's
study at the University of Glasgow, had accepted a religious
philosophy closely akin to that of his own. Alexander read
the galley proof of the *Declaration and Address* and was
agreeably impressed with the content. He told his father
that he had immediately determined to give himself to
spreading its principles. Foreseeing the role that his son
would later play in the Reformation Movement, Mr. Campbell urged him to forsake all else and diligently study the
Bible for at least six months.

Despite the program so systematically arranged by Campbell, the Christian Association of Washington accomplished
nothing that it had hoped to do. No other ministers joined,
no missionaries scattered the news, no similar societies were
organized, no flood of favorable responses was received.
After a couple of years Thomas Campbell was sorely dissatisfied with the association. Gradually it was assuming
a character different from what he had originally intended.[27]

[26] Richardson, *Alexander Campbell*, I, 244, 261.

[27] The idea of restoring the New Testament Church has been called "a
monumental absurdity" and the cause of a great deal of sectarianism. Charles
C. Morrison, *The Unfinished Reformation* (New York, 1953), 157.

The problem facing Thomas Campbell was the prevention of the Christian Association from becoming a separate and independent church. By the spring of 1811 he gave up the battle, since there seemed to be no diverting the tide of events. On May 4 the Christian Association constituted itself the Brush Run Church, taking the name of a creek a few miles northeast of Washington, Pennsylvania. Thomas Campbell had officially been out of the Presbyterian Church for over a year, and Alexander had left the Seceder Church while he was in Scotland. This lack of clerical affiliation and church membership did not deter the group from selecting Thomas Campbell as an elder and from licensing Alexander as a preacher. Deacons were chosen and the congregational form of government was adopted. The Campbells had formed a church out of the Christian Association without the sanction of any ecclesiastical body or any person except the thirty members of the organizing group. This single church was in a sense "a separate denomination," the concept of which Thomas Campbell had specifically opposed in the Declaration.

Probably a satisfying explanation for this reversal lies in the "logic of events" which later forced Thomas Campbell to revise his views. He had asked men and women to join the association, yet he had failed to see "that it would be impossible to organize outside the communions and still not become a church." After erecting a frame building, eighteen by thirty-six feet in size, the congregation seems to have functioned as an entity. The adoption of plenary immersion as the proper mode of baptism further characterized the church and led to its petition for admission to the Redstone Baptist Association. Despite an objection by a minority of the association, Brush Run Church was admitted in 1813. In this affiliation the new group protected itself with a reservation that "we should be allowed to teach and preach whatever we learn from the Holy

Scriptures, regardless of any human creed or formula in Christendom."[28]

Young Campbell had devoted long hours to the study of the New Testament and had become convinced that infant baptism and sprinkling were not practiced in the early Christian church. After wrestling with the time, mode, and significance of the rite of baptism, the Campbells had reached a conviction that immersion at the age of accountability constituted the only true baptism and that the act of immersion after sprinkling was not a rebaptism. On June 12, 1812, the Campbells made a dramatic exhibit of their conviction. After preaching for seven hours on the subject of baptism, Thomas and Alexander Campbell and their wives were immersed in Buffalo Creek by a Baptist preacher.[29] This adoption of plenary immersion radically altered the Campbells' program henceforth. They had previously insisted that all churches had beliefs and practices so sufficiently uniform that a union could be achieved, but now the act of immersion set them apart from all denominations except the Baptist.

When the Redstone Baptist Association met near his home in August 1816, an attempt was made to prevent Alexander Campbell from preaching, but at the last minute he filled a vacancy caused by illness of the scheduled speaker. Campbell obviously had come prepared, as his sermon showed no trace of extemporaneous remarks. The analytical discourse which he called the "Sermon on the Law" presented Christianity as "a new institution and not an extension and modification of the Hebrew legal system." He drew a distinction between the Law and the Gospel, saying that the Law of Moses was applicable only to the Jewish nation and that Christians were guided by the Gospels.

[28] Lester G. McAllister, *Thomas Campbell: Man of the Book* (St. Louis, 1954), 110, 169; Garrison and DeGroot, *Disciples of Christ*, 153-58, 162.
[29] McAllister, *Thomas Campbell*, 155-59.

His hearers were startled by the implication that the Old Testament was now to be discarded. Some of the people fell into ready agreement, but many more were afraid of the words they had heard. Campbell had asserted that many of the Old Testament practices, such as baptizing infants, paying tithes, and observing holy and fast days were "repugnant to Christianity." In the course of the sermon some people including a few elders of the church "used every means openly to manifest their dissatisfaction." When a woman fainted, one of the elders came into the stand and created a disturbance designed to interrupt the speaker. During an intermission this same elder said to those people near him, "This is not our doctrine."[30]

After a brief period of unity the followers of the Campbells and the members of the Baptist churches fell into disagreement. Alexander Campbell ran afoul of the orthodox Baptists over the matter of regeneration and baptism. The Baptists required a public confession of a Christian experience prior to receiving baptism, and the Campbells believed that regeneration followed the act of baptism. The Baptists did not claim that baptism brought the remission of sins, but Campbell held that baptism assured complete absolution to "believing penitents."

Campbell's followers, calling themselves Reformers and being called Campbellites by others, were active agitators in the Baptist churches throughout the West. Frequently they led a group out of a particular congregation in order

---

[30] Richardson, *Alexander Campbell*, I, 471-72. Also see Errett Gates, *The Early Relation and Separation of Baptists and Disciples* (Chicago, 1904), Chaps. I-III, et passim; "The Creedless Frontier," Chap. XXII in Bates, *American Faith;* Colin B. Goodykoontz, *Home Missions on the American Frontier* (Caldwell, Idaho, 1939), 213-14. As late as 1830 Alexander Campbell had not changed his position, for he insisted that only such parts of the law as had been "promulged" anew by Christ constitute "a rule of life for Christians." *Millennial Harbinger* (Bethany, Va. [now W. Va.]), 1830, 83. Campbell had an excessive fondness for italics. In the majority of quotations from him, I have omitted the italics.

to form a new church along the tenets advocated by the Campbells. By 1830 the Reformers numbered between twenty and thirty thousand, most of whom had withdrawn from the Baptist congregations or had been excluded by them.

This tenuous union between the followers of the Campbells and the Baptists was terminated in 1830. The break relieved tensions and set each party in an agreeable state of freedom. The best study of the separation of the Baptists and the Disciples suggests that the lack of flexibility in the Baptist polity drove the reformers out of the association. This author enumerated several examples: the division of the Baptists into "Regulars" and "Separates"; the antimissionary sentiment of the Baptists; the creedal beliefs of the Baptists; and the hyper-Calvinism of Baptists and Presbyterians.[31]

Two appraisals of this venture into union are interesting. As Newman draws near the end of his history of the Baptists, he muses over their loss of the Disciples and explains the causes as he sees them. "If the Baptists of the Southwest had been in the third decade of the century what Baptists are to-day—if they had been more intelligent and had possessed an educated ministry, if they had laid as little stress on confessions of faith as Baptists do at present, if they had taught as evangelical a form of doctrine as that taught by the mass of the denomination to-day, if the missionary spirit had been as active then as now—it would have been impossible for such a movement as that led by Campbell to have arisen or to have gained such a following as it did." A historian of the Disciples of Christ thinks that the period of cooperation did little to lessen the differences between the Reformers and the Baptists or to introduce new points of mutuality. By association the two groups had developed more divergency and were more unlike at separa-

---

[31] Gates, *Baptists and Disciples,* Chap. VIII.

tion in 1830 than at their union in 1813. Neither had the will for concession or compromise.[32]

Prospects were good for the Campbells. Having separated themselves early from the Presbyterians, they were accustomed to working outside any specific denomination, and the new rift with the Baptists did not hamper their program. The West was an open field and offered more opportunity for new religious groups than ever before. With Andrew Jackson in the White House a new emphasis was felt in American life. The Campbells had few misgivings about their intent to take advantage of the situation. It is probably true that neither Thomas nor Alexander Campbell brought any new theology, but it is definitely true that they, especially the son, brought new ideas of man's personal power and his relations to God. In the congregations of the Campbellites religion was simplified. After confessing that "Jesus is the Son of God," one could receive immersion without any account of a previous religious experience.[33]

In 1824 Alexander Campbell and Barton Stone had met and at once were aware of a spiritual attraction. Although not in accord on numerous points, their ideas became increasingly akin, and in 1832 they entered into an agreement that bound their followers into a loose union. Stone, however, was reluctant to accept some of Campbell's views on free will, original sin, and total depravity. For a long time after Campbell was baptizing on a confession of faith, Stone was using a mourner's bench and teaching immediate conversion in contrast to his Presbyterian heritage. Stone

[32] Newman, *Baptist Churches*, 491-92; Alonzo W. Fortune, *Origin and Development of the Disciples* (St. Louis, 1947), 87-88.

[33] *One Hundredth Anniversary of the Disciples of Christ* (Cincinnati, ca. 1909), 344-45. "The denomination was part of the movement of the 'common man' which developed in the frontier region of the Middle West, and which showed itself in the election of Andrew Jackson to the presidency in 1828." Anson P. Stokes, *Church and State in the United States* (3 vols.; New York, 1950), I, 770. Also see "The Rise of Jacksonian Democracy," Stokes, *Church and State*, I, 696-702.

was seeking a midway position between baptism as an end in itself and as an act of no particular significance. He advocated the doctrine that Christ had died for all sinners and that the sinner had power to accept Christ at any time. Winfred E. Garrison, one of the best authorities on the Disciples, declares that "the actual union was a gradual process conditioned by the growth of acquaintance and the discovery of community of spirit and purpose on the part of individual members and local churches." Another writer succinctly explains that the arrangement between Campbell and Stone was "on the sole basis of a common faith in Christ and a common acceptance of the divine authority of the Bible." The united fellowship had great difficulty holding together; its looseness allowed extremes of independence which endangered the slight bonds and threatened the willingness to cooperate.[34]

In many respects the new combination of Disciples under Campbell and the Christians under Stone was in a highly satisfactory position. These movements sprang up among the so-called common people. The early preachers were generally from the local folk and had no theological training. Much of their preaching was effective, marked by emotional appeal and spontaneity. "Given a man dead in earnest, with a book like the Bible, viewed as it was in those days, a book read and re-read and largely committed to memory; and given a man whose mind, thoroughly awakened, was charged to the brain with Scripture, and solemnized by prayer-vigil and lonely meditation; and given the motion and fire of delivery prevalent in those days, and you have a generator of tremendous sensations and impressions."[35]

---

[34] Ware, *Stone*, 268; Bishop, *Church in the State of Kentucky*, 137; West, *Stone*, 165; Winfred E. Garrison, *Religion Follows the Frontier: A History of the Disciples of Christ* (New York, 1931), 154; Bacon, *American Christianity*, 242.

[35] Milo T. Morrill, *A History of the Christian Denomination in America* (Dayton, Ohio, 1912), 103-104.

Of the four persons generally regarded as the founders of the Disciples of Christ, the youngest was Walter Scott, born in Moffatt, Scotland, in 1796 and educated at the University of Edinburgh. At the urging of an uncle in New York, young Scott came to the United States in 1818. A year later, when infected by the spirit of the West, he walked to Pittsburgh. There he made the acquaintance of a fellow countryman named George Forrester, who aided him in securing a teaching job. Forrester was a preacher of the Haldanean school and served as a pastor of a small "primitive Christianity" church that Scott attended. After Forrester's accidental death, Scott became pastor of this congregation.[36]

In the winter of 1821-1822 Scott and Alexander Campbell met and found in each other qualities that led to a lifelong friendship. At this time Campbell was about ready to issue a monthly paper for which he was considering the name *The Christian*. Scott suggested that the *Christian Baptist* had more significance, for Campbell was then a member of the Brush Run Church connected with the Redstone Baptist Association. This name would please the Baptists, he said, and they in turn would support the paper.

After living in Pittsburgh for eight years, Scott moved to Steubenville, Ohio. At once he was appointed an evangelist for the Mahoning Baptist Association which included churches in the Western Reserve of northeastern Ohio. Preaching a simple Christian fellowship, Scott stated that all the bases for Christian union were found in the New Testament and that no church had any right to change them. He devised a scheme by which he stressed the simplicity of his doctrine; his "five finger exercise" indicated the steps to salvation—faith, repentance, baptism, remission

[36] A. S. Hayden, *Early History of the Disciples in the Western Reserve, Ohio* (Cincinnati, 1875), 61-65, et passim; Alanson Wilcox, *A History of the Disciples of Christ in Ohio* (Cincinnati, 1918), Chap. XVIII.

of sins, and the gift of the Holy Spirit. The popularity of
this device spread so rapidly that one thousand converts
had been added by the end of his first year of evangelism.
He placed so much emphasis on "the importance of the
practical restoration of the design of baptism" that he
claimed "this was in reality the restoration of the gospel."
This concept had great appeal to Scott, and he denominated
his own preaching method "The Gospel Restored." He gave
much attention to the cause of Christian union, joined forces
with those of Alexander Campbell, and contributed greatly
to their common endeavor. Although living in Ohio, Scott
had great influence in Kentucky where he often visited.
One writer has dared to say that the Disciples of Christ
might never have come into being without Scott.[37]

Thomas Campbell had witnessed the disastrous effects of
divided religious forces and had set himself to heal divisions
and to bring unity. His was the creative personality of a
new Reformation Movement. It was left to his son to
become the interpreter of his father's ideas. According to
his biographer Robert Richardson, Alexander's reaction to
the sectarianism of the day was "to increase his reverence
for the Scriptures as the only infallible guide in religion,
to weaken the force of sectarian prejudices, and to deepen
his conviction that the existence of sects and parties was
one of the greatest hindrances to the success of the gospel."[38]
Contrary to their intentions, the efforts of father and son
to bring unity eventually added to the divisions by causing
a new denomination to be formed.

During a period of some two decades Alexander Campbell
was an energetic iconoclast condemning salaried ministers,
Bible, tract and missionary societies, Sunday schools, and

[37] Richardson, *Alexander Campbell*, II, 442-43; Ware, *Stone*, 233; Garrison and DeGroot, *Disciples of Christ*, 182; Alonzo W. Fortune, *The Disciples in Kentucky* (n. p., 1932), passim.

[38] In Clarence R. Athearn, *The Religious Education of Alexander Campbell: Morning Star of the Reformation* (St. Louis, 1928), 133.

religious associations of any variety. Some of these he called "milking schemes" designed to impoverish the many for the benefit of a few. Current theological ideas he discarded, and he rejected creeds as lacking authority. He insisted on no distinction between clergy and laity and dropped titles of distinction such as "Reverend" and even "Pastor." Criticism was heaped on other churches and on those people who disagreed with him. In an effort to achieve his goal of Christian union, Campbell stressed the means so vigorously that his plan became submerged. He came close to fanaticism and narrowly missed the extreme practices, such as foot washing and the holy kiss, that had destroyed some predecessors like the Scotch Baptists. Fortunately, his learning, culture, and intellectual powers saved him. Under the influence of his colleague Walter Scott, Campbell in 1830 changed the name of the *Christian Baptist*, a paper he had published for seven years, to *Millennial Harbinger*. When his following had severed all connections with other denominations, Campbell found himself in the role of a leader, and then the second and constructive period of his life began. On many issues he completely reversed himself and assumed the lead in that which he had formerly opposed.[39]

In self-defense the Campbellites abandoned the idea of a unified Protestantism and moved rapidly toward the formation of what ultimately constituted a new denomination. By so doing Alexander Campbell faced an almost solid wall of opposition, since denominations in the West seldom extended the generosity so often attributed to them. When Campbell's newly-founded church threatened to take members from older groups, bitter and continuing attacks were

[39] The Disciples' insistence that what was not in the Bible could not be accepted led Scott to say that "the Bible is revealed, and beyond its sacred pages the true religion does not exist." The *Evangelist* (published by Scott in Cincinnati), I (1832), 259. Also see Walter W. Jennings, *A Short History of the Disciples of Christ* (St. Louis, 1929), 153-54; Colby D. Hall, *Texas Disciples* (Fort Worth, 1953), 136-37; James H. Garrison, *The Reformation of the Nineteenth Century* (St. Louis, 1901), passim.

made. Sometimes these went to extremes and even led to charges that Campbell's teachings were destructive to the principles of Christianity. These charges were substantiated by Presbyterian and Congregational missionaries reporting from the Mississippi Valley to the American Home Missionary Society. One letter accused Campbellism of being "the *great* curse of the West—more destructive & more injurious to the cause of religion than avowed Infidelity itself. There is evidence of wonderful cunning in the system, and in those who seek to carry it out. It presents something like a form of godliness, which may answer temporal purposes, and serve for those who cannot silence conscience without something in the semblance of religion." The Philadelphia *Presbyterian* of April 10, 1833, said that "few living errorists have done so much to rend and corrupt the church in that region." For many of these attacks Campbell was in a large measure to blame. As a shrewd and unsparing debater and journalist he struck hard at any and all who threatened the progress of his endeavor. John B. Purcell, Catholic Bishop of Cincinnati, who knew and admired Campbell, said that he was "regarded as a kind of religious Goliath" who delighted in accepting challenges to debate and to defend his peculiar views. "Campbell floored his opponents in a few moments. Their arguments fell to pieces as if they had no more strength than a potter's vessel. . . . The people saw all of this and it made Campbell thousands of proselytes; their children and their children's children have to this day stuck to his church like grim death, and they will stick for generations to come."[40]

What did the people actually see and hear when Campbell took the debater's rostrum? One who knew him in his late

[40] Goodykoontz, *Home Missions*, 211; *Millennial Harbinger*, 1833, 226; John T. Christian, *A History of the Baptists of the United States* (Nashville, 1926), 424. The opposition to Campbell and his subsequent victory are treated at length in Walter B. Posey, *Religious Strife on the Southern Frontier* (Baton Rouge, 1965), Chap. II.

years has described him as a tall, gaunt, slightly stooped man with a great amount of hair, a hawk nose, blue-gray eyes that peered from under heavy brows. His voice, though not strong, was clear and his words fell with great fluency. He was at ease in the pulpit with questions and statements logically arranged to secure the results he desired. The observer was aware of tremendous energy and vitality; in fact, one could say that Campbell looked like a reformer.[41]

Born in a region recently emerged from a frontier condition, the new church had no problem in appealing to converts and to those seeking salvation. Alexander Campbell's plan was simple and clear. It included belief, repentance, confession, and baptism. Fortunately, the Disciples did not pass through the early period of excessive revivalism experienced by the Methodists and the Baptists; accordingly, they escaped the intense emotional fervor. The Disciples rapidly outgrew the crudities of their frontier origin, quickly abandoning "an undiluted horror of culture and symbolism." Richard Niebuhr accurately appraises the situation of the new church: "It was somewhat more interested in the social principle of union than in the individual principle of the salvation of souls. Perhaps this was why it was less aggressive than its rivals. It was representative of a West which had passed the storm and stress period of social adolescence and was recovering from its youthful extremities of hope and fear, without having lost the characteristic features the formative years had impressed upon it."[42]

[41] *Millennial Harbinger*, 1850, 272-73. Campbell copied from *The Watchman of the Prairies* an unflattering description of himself. "Few persons have ever possessed more of the qualities of a demagogue than Alexander Campbell. Eloquent in speech, adroit in argument, witty, ambitious, unscrupulous, and fond of public notoriety," he traveled from state to state charming the masses. *Millennial Harbinger*, 1851, 83.

[42] Andrew L. Drummond, *Story of American Protestantism* (London, 1951), 246; H. Richard Niebuhr, *The Social Sources of Denominationalism* (New York, 1929), 180-81.

5

PRACTICES OF
LOCAL CHURCHES

THE USUAL METHOD of beginning a church at any given place was the same among the several denominations, with the possible exception of the Catholics who often got financial aid from some European source. Most of the early church meetings were conducted by a minister in some log cabin to which the neighbors had come from a radius of several miles. It was in these rude and homely places that sermons first fell upon the frontiersmen's ears. When the West became more populous and the church groups had increased in number, separate meetinghouses became necessary. Several factors entered into the selection of a site for a church building: a central location in the community, proximity to a spring or stream of running water, and land enough to provide a burying ground—a solemn, convincing factor. Sometimes a church was located near an influential family who gave the land. In later years churches were often located at the edge of towns in order to increase the value of the surrounding property. It has been said that some churches were erected in isolated locations through the influence of some old preacher who did not wish educated townspeople to attend.

An account of the evolution of the church structure for one congregation tells substantially the story of similar churches on the frontier. The Presbyterians built the first meetinghouse in Marion County, Kentucky, in 1789. Constructed five logs high and sixteen feet square with an earthen floor, the building contained no windows. Unchinked cracks between the logs admitted enough air but not enough light. Within six years the membership had grown so that a larger building was needed. This new church, measuring twenty by twenty-eight feet, was equipped with a floor, benches, and a small window behind the pulpit. Nine years later an even larger church was necessary, and this was a frame building with several windows.[1]

An interesting provision in the Disciplines of the Methodist Church, from its organization in 1784 until its division in 1845, stated: "Let all our churches be plain and decent; but not more expensive than is absolutely unavoidable; otherwise the necessity of raising money will make rich men necessary to us. But if so, we must be dependent upon them, yea, and governed by them. And then farewell to Methodist discipline, if not doctrine too." Certainly the admonition in behalf of "plain" churches was absolutely unnecessary in the West for many years. A Methodist church in the early 1800s in Clark County, Kentucky, was of rude log construction, with a dirt floor. The preacher "delivered the word" from a platform with a puncheon floor, at the edge of which two poles had been set in the ground with a board placed across for a speaker's stand. This and hundreds of similar churches met the simple requirement laid down in the Disciplines.[2]

Since the meetinghouses were similar to the crude cabin homes, the people had no reason to grumble over the lack of ornamentation. An early Catholic missionary spoke for many: "For precious stones and marbles, we employed only bark, but the path to heaven is as open through a roof of bark as through arched ceilings of silver and gold."[3]

[1] W. T. Knott, *History of the Presbyterian Church in What Is Now Marion County and City of Lebanon, Kentucky* (n. p., ca. 1895), 9-12.

[2] In the 1812 edition of *The Doctrines and Discipline of the Methodist Episcopal Church* (New York), 181; A. H. Redford, *Western Cavaliers: Embracing the History of the Methodist Episcopal Church in Kentucky from 1832 to 1844* (Nashville, 1876), 103.

[3] [Carroll], *Catholic History*, 240.

Stumps of trees served as seats, which were later made more comfortable by the laying of slabs from stump to stump. Some people brought initialed chairs for the personal use of the women in their family. Warmth was a comfort for which there was little provision. The aged placed their feet on heated stones which had been wrapped in bed quilts, and the hardier sat near the door in order to get heat from the fire burning outside. Fireplaces and stoves later improved the heating arrangement during the long sermons. Many years were to elapse before a mahogany melodeon, wooden spittoons, oil lamps, and other appurtenances would be a part of any of these church buildings.

In some Southern cities the Episcopalians erected substantial churches. The cornerstone of the present Christ Church in Mobile was laid in 1835. The building was solidly constructed with walls four feet thick at the base, built of brick and covered with plaster. In 1837 William Jackson left St. Stephen's Church in New York to accept the pastorate of Christ Church in Louisville. This congregation had "a large commodious church—one of the finest specimens of Gothic architecture at that time west of the mountains." It was quite proud of a furnace and gas lights.[4]

In rural sections or small towns the exceptional generosity of a well-to-do planter occasionally made possible the building of a fine church. Bishop James H. Otey in 1842 consecrated St. John's Episcopal Church, a neat brick structure set in a grove of great oak trees six miles from Columbia, Tennessee. It was a gift of Bishop Leonidas Polk and three of his brothers who had large land holdings in that vicinity.[5]

[4] Herman C. Duncan (comp.), *The Diocese of Louisiana: Some of Its History, 1838-1888* (New Orleans, 1888), 49-52; *Christ Church Parish, Mobile, Ala.: A Record of the Century, 1823-1923* (n. p., n. d.), 3-5; Margaret A. Jackson, *Memoirs of the Rev. William Jackson* (New York, 1861), 243-45.

[5] Trezevant P. Yeatman, Jr., "St. John's—A Plantation Church of the Old South," *Tennessee Historical Quarterly*, X (1951), 334-43; George W. Polk, "St. John's Church," *Tennessee Historical Magazine*, VII (1921-1922), 147-53; *Spirit of Missions* (Burlington, N. J.), July 1842, 202-203.

Except for the larger churches in the cities, most Episcopal church buildings were not distinguishable from the rude structures of the other Protestant denominations. As a rule, they were made in the form of a plain rectangle with two doors evenly spaced in the front wall. A high plastered ceiling made the acoustics very poor. Frequently there was no altar, and for the lack of a communion table the minister could not follow the rubrics. Vested choirs were shunned, for the early minister hesitated to introduce the new regalia among a people all too quick to accuse Episcopalians of being Catholics in disguise.[6]

Catholic efforts to build churches followed somewhat the same patterns as those of the Protestants, but they seem to have resulted in a proportionately larger number of permanent churches and cathedrals. In 1792 when Father Rohan built Holy Cross Chapel on Pottinger's Creek in Kentucky, the building, covered with clapboard, was without glass in the windows, and had a rough hewn slab of wood for an altar. About 1805 Father Nerinckx built St. Charles Church which had no benches until a male member constructed one for himself and one for his wife. Other men soon made the same additions for themselves and their families. The first brick Catholic church west of the mountains was that of St. Rose completed in 1809 in Kentucky. Such a structure was rare, and log churches continued to be built for a long time. One was constructed in McEwen, Tennessee, as late as 1856.[7]

The way that a congregation went about constructing a church building often varied in detail, but the basic steps were the same. The simple plans of the Elkhorn (Kentucky) Baptist Church were recorded in the minutes. In October 1816 the members "Tuck up the motion Refered from our

[6] Walter C. Whitaker, *History of the Protestant Episcopal Church in Alabama, 1763-1891* (Birmingham, 1898), 72-73.

[7] Schauinger, *Cathedrals*, 15; Victor F. O'Daniel, *The Father of the Church in Tennessee . . . Richard Pius Miles* (New York, 1926), 107, 304, 317.

last meating ReSpecting Bilding a new meating house and the Church has Concluded to bild one on the present lot of ground whare the old one Stands." A committee was appointed to draw up a subscription to "Rase funds to bild Said house and make Report" to the next meeting in February. Then the church ordered the committee to continue the subscription and to report again in April, at which time the contract would be let as soon as the sum of two thousand dollars was raised. In a legalistic business session the Trinity Episcopal Church in Natchez made detailed plans in 1822. To the trustees was entrusted the property; to a committee was given the duty of selecting a site and letting a contract; to another committee, the duty of raising subscriptions, all of which would be held by the treasurer. The trustees were then empowered to seek an act of incorporation from the Mississippi legislature.[8]

The average Protestant church had no source of income beyond contributions from members or gifts from a church agency. Some denominations and scattered congregations of other connections used various methods to alleviate their financial difficulties. The Episcopalians, having known the support from glebe lands, made a poor but profitable substitution by renting and selling pews, although some of their churches had free slips. The Catholic churches in some cases both sold and rented pews, although this was not a widespread practice. In churches using the pews as a source of income, the price varied depending on what the traffic would bear. Pew rent was exceedingly low at St. Michael's Church in Fredericktown, Missouri, where the rate was only $1.75 per year. St. Boniface in Louisville had annual rentals in 1839 ranging from four to sixteen dollars. Many of the Catholic hierarchy protested against the system,

[8] "Records of the Forks of Elkhorn Baptist Church, Kentucky, 1800-1820," Oct. 12, 1816, Feb. 8, April 12, 1817, in Sweet, *The Baptists,* 396-98; Charles Stietenrath, *One Hundred Years with 'Old Trinity' Church, Natchez, Miss.* (Natchez, 1922), 11-16.

and Bishop England enumerated ten reasons why he did not want pews sold or rented in his church. A few Presbyterian churches resorted to the sale of pews. In 1815 the Second Presbyterian Church in Lexington, Kentucky, averaging more than two hundred dollars for each pew, realized enough money from a sale to pay for the entire cost of the building. In several instances, especially in the Lower South, money for churches was raised by a lottery authorized by the state legislature. More than half of the $45,000 indebtedness of Theodore Clapp's New Orleans Presbyterian Church was cleared by a lottery.[9]

The early church records contain few references to the money received for such specific purposes as missions, benevolences, and education, but they frequently include a list of subscribers to the general support of the church and the minister. Probably the examination of a few churches in a single denomination—here the Presbyterian because the available records are better—will adequately reveal the prevailing situation. The Washington (Mississippi) Church in 1807 had a subscription list of forty-five names with pledges ranging from five to thirty dollars. Apparently these names included all the white male members of the church. As the years unfold and particularly by the 1830s, the session and presbytery records contain many references to contributions and supply much evidence that the giving was commensurate with most of the pressing needs. An examination of the minutes of the session of the New Providence (Kentucky) Church reveals much in regard to various contributions and donations. In 1829 a donation of

[9] Hodding Carter and Betty W. Carter, *So Great a Good: A History of the Episcopal Church in Louisiana* (Sewanee, Tenn., 1955), 89; John E. Rothensteiner, *Chronicles of an Old Missouri Parish* (Cape Girardeau, Mo., 1928), 36; John B. Wuest (comp.), *One Hundred Years of St. Boniface Parish, Louisville, Kentucky* (Louisville, 1937), 28; John England, *Diurnal of the Right Rev. John England . . . 1820-1823* (Philadelphia, 1895), 46-47; Jesse Herrmann, *James McChord—A Portrait* (Lexington, 1940), 58; Theodore Clapp, *Autobiographical Sketches and Recollections* (Boston, 1857), 93-94.

$260 was made to the theological seminary of Centre College and $117 to the education fund. Two years later the women of the church subscribed $42 to the American Education Society and the church gave $105 to Centre. It is hardly probable that a church no larger than New Providence would make today similar gifts to education. Missions were rather generously supported. In 1829 the Pine Ridge (Mississippi) Church appropriated $125 for the missionary to the Choctaw Nation. In the same year the Louisville (Kentucky) Church gave $1,300 to the missionary fund, and in 1839 the Tuscaloosa Presbytery promised $1,500 yearly to send Daniel Baker as a missionary to Texas. In the latter year the Plum Creek (Kentucky) Church gave $255 for foreign and domestic missions. The national missionary board of the church assisted struggling churches as in the case of the Baton Rouge Church which received $200 to aid its ministers.[10]

All churches, Catholic and Protestant, had a priest or minister as the person responsible in church affairs. Only in the matter of raising a subscription, erecting a building, and general financial affairs did the laity constitute the governing body in most of the Protestant churches. The ancient power of the Catholic priest was sometimes disturbed by a group of trustees, but this tendency soon collapsed.

In churches other than those of the Methodist and Catholic connections the system of calling and employing a minister was extremely informal and indefinite. The majority of Presbyterian and Episcopal ministers went to the West strictly on invitations from particular congregations, with the consent of the presbytery in the former denomination and the bishop in the latter. The Baptist congregations were rarely lacking a preacher. Usually some

[10] For this paragraph see notes 29-35, pp. 175-76 in Posey, *Presbyterian Church.*

member with a willingness to preach could be recruited by churches near him. When an ordained Baptist preacher moved into a community, he was not long without a charge, for upon hearing of his presence, a church would invite him to use its pulpit. A Methodist conference and a Catholic diocese arbitrarily assigned preachers or priests to particular posts. After the settlements began to grow in the West and the South, a large number of ministers served the Methodist, Baptist, and Presbyterian churches in the immediate area in which they were reared. For a long period virtually all of the Catholic priests came from Europe and those in the Episcopal Church chiefly came from the Atlantic seaboard.

Regardless of the denomination, financial support for churches and clergy was grudgingly and sparingly given by congregations. This unfortunate attitude grew out of a variety of causes: the small amount of money in circulation, the great need for legal tender in the buying of land, and the prevailing idea that religion should be dispensed without cost. The clergy and officers of all churches complained about their inadequate support, and most of them combined their preaching with another profession or employment so as to provide the necessities of life.

Indeed, preachers were rarely men of one profession. Those of the Methodist, Baptist, Disciples, and Cumberland Presbyterian denominations belonged generally to the farmer-preacher group. Ministers of the Presbyterians and Episcopalians more likely sought the teacher-preacher combination of livelihood. Numerous Episcopal ministers were farmers, a few on a large scale, but this work seemed less dignified than teaching, and whenever possible they made the shift to the schoolroom. Many of the clergy acquired great skills in various fields. One who intimately knew Father Cellini in Missouri testified that he was not only a priest, but a physician, a mailman, and a mason. A rescript from the

Pope permitted Cellini to practice medicine in the country districts and villages "where owing to the people's poverty, it were to be desired that they could get gratuitously medical advice." Since doctors were scarce and their services expensive, Catholic priests were often called "for a fainting or some other little accident." One of the best known of all early peddlers of patent medicines was the shrewd and crafty Lorenzo Dow, a Methodist preacher who by official action in 1820 of the United States Patent Office offered for sale "Dow's Family Medicine." An advertisement of this concoction certified that it served as a cathartic, a digestive stimulant, and was particularly good as an aid to "females in a debilitated or declining state." Such varied and rigorous endeavors give evidence of an energetic and practical ministry.[11]

In the matter of contracts that churches made with ministers, an amazing variety of arrangements extended from no monetary obligations, as with the Baptists and the Disciples of Christ, to written contracts by Presbyterians and Episcopalians. A detailed arrangement was made in 1794 by the Little Mountain and Springfield (Kentucky) Presbyterian churches which received from their presbyteries permission to request the services of Joseph P. Howe. Ninety-seven persons signed the invitation which promised Howe one hundred pound sterling, one-third to be paid in cash and two-thirds in "Marchantable Produce." A less specific contract was made between the First Presbyterian Church of Louisville, Kentucky, at the time of its formation in 1816 and Daniel C. Banks of Fairfield, Connecticut. In the usual manner the invitation stated that the congregation was "well satisfyed of the ministerial qualifications of you Daniel

11 "Documents from Our Archives," St. Louis Catholic Historical Review, III (1931), 107-108; Frederick J. Easterly, The Life of Rt. Rev. Joseph Rosati (Washington, 1942), 43; Charles C. Sellers, Lorenzo Dow: The Bearer of the Word (New York, 1928), 200, 202.

C. Banks & having good hopes . . . that your administrations in the gospel will be profitable to our spiritual interests do earnestly call you and desire you . . . promising you . . . all proper support, encouragement and obedience. . . ." Occasionally a Presbyterian congregation felt that whenever a minister had sufficient income from elsewhere, then the church should be relieved of its financial contributions. David Rice, successful both in business and in the Presbyterian pulpit, tersely expressed his opinion about this indifferent attitude, "The people are starving the ministers, and the ministers are starving the people for it."[12]

As a general rule, the early Baptist churches made no provision or gave only slight consideration to paying their preachers. A historian of that denomination, David Benedict, regretted to hear of the conversion to his faith of ministers of other creeds because he feared "they might become disappointed and discontented" especially because "of the parsimony of our people . . . in the support of ministers, and in their doings generally in aid of benevolent undertakings." A few old preachers spoke out against a salaried clergy. In a prideful manner, one preacher claimed that he had served churches in Virginia and Alabama for forty-two years without a regular salary. Another preacher in Alabama had to ride his plow horse ninety miles a month in order to preach to a congregation which paid him less than twenty dollars for two years of service. Support was likewise poor in Kentucky. Reports show that in 1837 not one Baptist preacher in Kentucky was fairly compensated and that three-fourths of all preachers in the state had to support their families by other forms of employment. As the demands of individual churches grew, the idea of supporting ministers changed. Congregations located in

<hr>

[12] Joseph P. Howe Papers, Philadelphia; MS Session Records, Louisville Presbyterian Church, 1819-1828, 3-5, Montreat; Bishop, *Church in the State of Kentucky*, 110.

the centers of population began to pay respectable salaries. For example, a church in Nashville paid one thousand dollars in 1835, and one in Columbus, Mississippi, paid its preacher fifteen hundred dollars in 1844. The new trend was clearly indicated in a resolution passed in 1845 by the Severns Valley (Kentucky) Church. The members of this congregation stated that "it is one of the greatest sins of the church that they do not reward the brother for his hire."[13]

In the Methodist Church the early salary for preacher and bishop alike was fixed at sixty-four dollars a year. No provision was made for a wife or family until 1792 when sixty-four dollars was given to a wife, sixteen dollars for each child under six years of age, and twenty-four for each over six and under eleven, in addition to traveling expenses for the preacher. By 1816 the salary clause called for one hundred dollars for the preacher, the same amount for his wife, and slightly increased provisions for children. However, these amounts were not always collected. James B. Finley evidently failed to receive all of his allotment, for he wrote: "I sold the boots off my feet to purchase provisions," and "I borrowed a blanket, and wore it instead of a great-coat through the winter. . . ." And such poverty was not his alone. Bishop Asbury noted that he had "found the preachers indifferently clad, with emaciated bodies and subject to hard fare. . . ."[14]

At first there was much opposition by the Disciples to a hired ministry. But time and Alexander Campbell changed this attitude. At one time he had attacked the "hireling clergy," but later he became convinced that the duties which a preacher must discharge "will engross much of his time and attention," and stated that "the idea of remuneration for his service was attached to the office from the first

[13] For this paragraph and additional illustrations of Baptist attitudes toward salaries for preachers, see Posey, *Baptist Church*, 32-34.

[14] James B. Finley, *Sketches of Western Methodism* (Cincinnati, 1857), 53, 91; Finley, *Autobiography*, 193, 194; Asbury, *Journal*, II, 79.

institution."[15] Barton Stone reasoned in a similar vein. He favored support for the ministers in order to prevent the cares and anxieties of the world from distracting their minds. In the face of expediency and common sense the early opposition to a hired ministry died out, and most of the churches acquired a minister who was recognized as the pastor of the church.

Church records indicate that the Episcopal ministers never suffered from want as did the Methodists and Baptists. This may be attributed to the economic bracket from which the Episcopal congregations drew their members and the late date of the denomination's arrival in the West. In 1831 a church in Missouri offered to pay its rector three hundred dollars a year, and this amount seems to have been the prevailing salary. Exceptions, however, are not hard to find. In Mississippi a minister serving a church on a three-year contract received only fifty dollars annually, but from his school patrons came a sufficient amount for living. Bishop Nicholas H. Cobbs of Alabama was paid in 1847 only five hundred dollars by his diocese, but within two years it increased his remuneration to seventeen hundred.[16]

Beyond question the Catholic priests and missionaries lived frugally and frequently were in dire want. In 1850 John M. Odin, the Vicar Apostolic of Texas, and three priests lived for a period on a total of four dollars a week. Odin wrote to his parents of their distressing plight: "Sometime discouragement almost seizes me, when I know not what means to adopt to procure even the most indispensible provisions; but God is a good father and always comes to our help." In 1855 a Catholic father in the same state

---

[15] *Christian Baptist* (Bethany, Va. [W. Va.]), Aug. 1828, 260; Richardson, *Alexander Campbell*, II, 128.

[16] Alexander T. Douglass to William R. Whittingham, Aug. 22, 1831, in Whittingham Papers, Duke University; *Spirit of Missions*, Dec. 1846, 415; Greenhough White, *A Saint of the Southern Church . . . Nicholas Hamner Cobbs* (New York, 1897), 115; *Journal of the Nineteenth Annual Convention* (Tuscaloosa, Ala., 1850), 36.

admitted that he could not afford sugar in his coffee, for he had received only ninety-two dollars during the entire previous year.[17]

The poverty of the clergy was evident in the poor clothes of Catholic and Protestant alike. Most of the ministers wore the common garb of their fellow citizens, and nothing set them apart unless it were lean figures and lined faces. It is pleasant to imagine the thrilling effect of Bishop Louis W. DuBourg's arrival in Ste. Genevieve late in December 1817. Accompanied by Bishop Flaget in pontifical robe, DuBourg, walking under a canopy, was led through the village by a procession of twenty-four choir children. Such pomp and ceremony was rarely seen outside towns like New Orleans, St. Louis, and Louisville. Descriptions of the ceremony were repeated and grew in magnitude with each telling.

The saddlebag could be considered an insignia of office of a Methodist preacher. In it the traveling or circuit riding preacher carried Bible, hymn book, and sometimes a change of clothing. An umbrella was probably tied to the pommel of the saddle and a greatcoat was strapped behind the saddle. The preacher's suit was very likely threadbare and stained by long and hard wear. John Brooks told of a Methodist preacher who "looked so different from any other that I had ever seen . . . he seemed to be an inhabitant of Eternity, though a man on earth. Never, never, shall I forget his looks. I felt my strength give way as he passed me, and I had like to have fallen to the ground."[18]

Frequently an itinerant preacher or missionary rode twenty or thirty miles without seeing a house. When he reached his destination or overnight stop, it probably was a single-room cabin, twelve or fourteen feet square, already running over with children. The chances are that the preacher slept

[17] P. F. Parisot, *The Reminiscences of a Texas Missionary* (San Antonio, 1899), 25-26.

[18] John Brooks, *The Life and Times of the Rev. John Brooks . . . Written by Himself* (Nashville, 1848), 9.

in front of a fire and on a rug so full of fleas that the ground would have been preferable.

Little care was used by some denominations in the method of licensing a minister. A Baptist association in Kentucky decided that any candidate for the ministry should receive a license if the sponsoring congregation thought him worthy. Sometimes Methodist and Baptist churches encouraged a good prospect to apply for a license. Although the local Methodist church had no authority to admit a person to the ministry, the district conference made the process very easy. The standards of the Cumberland Presbyterian Church were far below that of the parent church, as exemplified by the action in 1811 of the Cumberland Presbytery which recommended that Mr. Rice "Study english gramer."[19] In great haste to function, neither Stone nor Campbell churches exercised the required care in the selection of their early ministers.

The lack of education was a matter of little concern to early Baptist, Cumberland Presbyterian, and Methodist ministers. One Hardshell Baptist group in Mississippi opposed education, challenging "the learned world to show any divine authority for sending a man to school after God called him to enter the ministry. . . ." Peter Cartwright believed that as late as 1821 "there was not a single literary man" among the 280 Methodist itinerants in the West. Some of the Methodist and Baptist preachers could hardly read, and a few could not read at all. But the lack of reading skill was no great handicap in some areas. Timothy Flint, a Congregational minister who traveled extensively in the West, was convinced that the ill-trained Methodist preacher who spoke the native dialect and entered into the feelings of the people could succeed where more polished ministers would fail. A qualified Baptist observer

[19] MS Minutes, South Alabama Presbytery, 1828-1832, April 3, 1829, Montreat.

insisted that in 1828 three-fourths of the Baptist preachers in Kentucky could not distinguish between a verb and a noun. In their hurry to get established, the Disciples likewise temporarily brushed education aside in favor of preachers of flaming hearts and fiery tongues. Evidently Peter Ham had little education, for he admitted that he was "a poor home-made preacher." After the first wave of Disciples enthusiasm subsided, Alexander Campbell clearly realized the great advantage education had given his father and himself and the great need for the education of his ministers. In 1843 he declared: "The proper education of young men devoted to the ministry of the Word . . . is on all hands confessed to be of unspeakable importance."[20]

The Presbyterian and Episcopal churches adhered rigidly and faithfully to educational standards which were exceedingly difficult for ministerial candidates to attain and maintain. A college education or its equivalent from the personal tutorage of an ordained minister was the usual preparation for ordination by the Episcopal and Presbyterian churches. In 1811 the West Tennessee Presbytery opposed "heart religion" by declaring that "those who would deny the utility of Academical study to qualify men for business either in Church or state, must take leave of their senses. . . ."[21] Some of the early Presbyterian ministers in Kentucky and Tennessee were graduates of Princeton and some had received honorary doctor of divinity degrees from Eastern institutions. Of the first five Episcopal bishops chosen between 1832 and 1850 to head the dioceses of Kentucky, Tennessee, Louisiana, Georgia, Alabama, and Mississippi,

[20] Boyd, *Baptists in Mississippi*, 52; Cartwright, *Autobiography*, 197; Timothy Flint, *The History and Geography of the Mississippi Valley* (2 vols.; Cincinnati, 1832), I, 146; John H. Spencer, *The Life of Thomas Jefferson Fisher* (Louisville, 1866), 19; *Ecclesiastical Reformer* (Frankfort), 1851, 11; Harold L. Lunger, *The Political Ethics of Alexander Campbell* (St. Louis, 1954), 118.

[21] MS Minutes, West Tennessee Presbytery, 1810-1836, Sept. 11, 1811, Montreat.

all were college graduates except Cobbs of Alabama. It should be pointed out, however, that two had been born in Virginia, two in North Carolina, one in South Carolina, and one in Rhode Island, and not a single one received his education in any state west of the Appalachians.

Catholic priests and missionaries were usually graduates of European seminaries, carefully taught and prepared for religious work. Some possessed all the requisites of scholars, such as Father Francis P. Kenrick whose knowledge of Hebrew, Greek, patristic and ecclesiastical literature, and the classics was considered profound. An even better case may be that of Father Simon Brute, later Bishop of Vincennes, who graduated in medicine with such honor that he attracted the attention of Napoleon Bonaparte. Little wonder that Catholics looked with alarm at the illiterate or poorly educated Protestant preachers in the West.[22]

There was no uniformity in preparation or presentation of the sermons. The Presbyterian minister laboriously and carefully prepared his sermon, often writing in full essay form. He usually opened with a text, then compared the text with other scriptural passages and concluded with numerous parables and prophecies. Generally the Presbyterian sermon was a lengthy affair. Once Gideon Blackburn held fifteen hundred people for two hours in a graveyard while "a constant but not hard" rain fell.[23] Among Baptists and Methodists there was universal opposition to preachers who read their sermons—and some of the Presbyterians thought likewise. The Episcopal sermon was brief, but comparable to that of the Presbyterian in mode of presentation. It should be pointed out, however, that in each case the congregation was probably composed of a group of people of better-than-average education to which the "dull" sermon was not wholly unacceptable. The moderate tone

<hr>

[22] Schauinger, *Cathedrals*, 120-21, 189.
[23] Isaac Anderson to W. H. Parks, April 21, 1824, Philadelphia.

of Episcopal sermons had little appeal to people of less refined sentiments who wanted damnation or salvation spelled out. Disturbed by their lack of popular appeal, many of the Episcopal rectors tended to adopt a revivalistic form of preaching which the church earlier had so carefully shunned.

Since the Methodist and Baptist preachers considered themselves called by the Lord, they looked to the Lord for a text and its development. Personal experience and not theological reference usually dominated the sermon. With little or no preparation, the preacher usually divided his sermon into several topics which he discussed in order. Much spiritualizing and many imaginative interpretations were given to the Scriptures which were quoted to support the subject. Usually he thundered forth in "unnatural tones, accompanied by violent physical exercises and manifest emotional excitement." Often he spoke with a twang, called the "holy whine" which had great influence upon the emotions of the congregation.[24] An observer would have found little difference between Methodist and Baptist preaching with reference to style and effectiveness. Lack of education and lack of time produced a Methodist clergy which exhorted in a simple, direct, and forceful language unadorned by rhetorical flourishes and in a style unfettered by a manuscript. A frightening sermon and a stirring hymn usually brought the sinner to his knees. There is a temptation to say that, given the Methodist hymns, a church like the Presbyterian would have had a much larger membership.

Alexander Campbell injected into the religious picture a highly analytical form of preaching that succeeded in rapidly adding thousands of converts to his newly organized sect. His sermons were generally well prepared and highly effective, although he once admitted that in Murfreesboro, Tennessee, he preached "on all things in general, some

---

[24] See Newman, *Baptist Churches*, 382.

things in particular, and certain other things," but all directed toward man as he has been, is, and will be hereafter. A letter to Campbell in 1855 gave a vivid description of the manner of preaching at a meeting just closed in Kentucky. The writer declared that the sermon was plain and simple and that the speaker made "no attempts to catch the ear—no labored efforts at high sounding declamation—no beautiful flourishes of musical rhetoric, mars the faithful picture of the bloody Cross."[25]

Doctrine among the majority of the Protestant churches was suited to the area; therefore it was not elaborate. For the Methodists, the doctrine of individual responsibility had the greatest appeal: much satisfaction was found in the close relationship between God and man. Maybe the Methodist preacher did not know what he stood for, but he did know what he stood against—Calvinism. The Presbyterians, on the other hand, preached a stern and unbending doctrine concerned with the Trinity, the covenant, regeneration, the nature of faith and repentance, election, and predestination. To many the church seemed inconsistent in its emphasis on the personal responsibility of the soul and on the doctrine of foreordination and unconditional election. The effect of this stern doctrine is witnessed in the secession of members to form the Cumberland Presbyterian Church, which tended toward a midway position between Calvinism and Arminianism. The Baptists, in general, held to five principles— separation of church and state, conversion before admission to church membership, individual responsibility to God, congregational church government, and immersion as the only form of scriptural baptism. The Disciples accepted the fifth of these Baptist principles and gave to it an additional emphasis that submission to baptism brought "divine assurance of remission of sins and acceptance with God."[26]

[25] *Millennial Harbinger*, 1855, 145, 1856, 536.
[26] Smith, *Baptists in the Western States*, 134.

Passages in the New Testament which spoke of the "remission of sins" in connection with baptism were interpreted literally; thus baptism was exalted beyond the Baptist view. The Episcopal and Catholic churches made little compromise with the present in the matter of doctrine. In both the bishops were aware of the needs of the area and the ecclesiastical adjustments necessary to bring the church into agreement with Western life. To their credit it must be said that neither church was willing to compromise its fundamental beliefs in order to meet some of the demands of the rising democracy of the new sections. For this reason these churches failed to enroll many people who were ready to pour into churches not bound by tradition.

No denomination ever had too many clergymen: the cry was always for more and more ministers. The Catholic priests went to the Mississippi Valley for various reasons, but the persecution of the French Revolution caused a great many, equipped for work among various nationalities, to flee to America. The small number of priests in the West in comparison to the number in the East was probably indicative of their preference for the Eastern areas where a much larger number of Catholics resided. Since the priests were unmarried and unencumbered with home ties, they were subject to frequent transfer and free to devote all their time and energy to the work for which they had been commissioned. With the Protestant minister the situation was entirely different. Born and bred in America, encumbered with a family, needing support over and beyond his meager income from some church, he often spent his entire life in a single community.

With the passing of time the crude frontier gave way to educational and cultural forces which demanded a new type of minister. The old and uneducated preacher was replaced by one better trained, especially in the Baptist, Methodist, and Cumberland Presbyterian churches. Since the Disciples came on the scene late, this group never had a great adjustment to make. Academies, colleges, and seminaries developed in the West and South, thereby elevating people as well as ministers. Robert B. C. Howell, a wise Baptist leader, editor, and preacher, has well stated an awareness of the poor spiritual fare which had been offered in the pulpit: "Of ministers, who give six days in every week to their farms and their merchandise, who go to church on the seventh, there talk about farming, market, politics, &c. till 12 O'clock, and then preach a swinging, singsong sermon of two hours, beginning in Genesis and closing in Revelations, and then off again to their worldly business, we have our share."[27] The leaders were sensing the need for a change.

An enlightening and amusing result of this attitude was seen in the great desire of ministers, especially in the Baptist and Methodist churches, to secure an honorary degree of doctor of divinity. The maneuvers became so revolting to Alexander Campbell that in 1826 he commented on them in his *Christian Baptist*: "We are sorry to observe a hankering after titles among some baptists, every way incompatible with their profession. . . ." Well before the Civil War these degrees had been bestowed so freely that the editors of the *Christian Journal* of Harrodsburg, Kentucky, glibly declared that doctors of divinity were as plentiful as "blackberries."[28]

The growing appreciation of the need for a better trained clergy was well expressed by a Baptist who sent his son to college. "I was of the opinion," he said, "that educating young ministers was worse than useless, for I thought the Lord would qualify those whom he calls to his great work. . . . When I was young and the people were less *knowing* than now, learning seemed to be wholly unneces-

[27] *Baptist Banner*, Jan. 30, 1840.
[28] *Christian Baptist*, Feb. 1826, 219; *Christian Journal* (Harrodsburg, Ky.), Dec. 16, 1843. Also see Posey, "Ecclesiastical Hankerings," *Tennessee Historical Quarterly*, XXIII (1964), 136-44.

sary; but as the world is becoming more enlightened, especially in towns, I feel it to be the duty of preachers to keep pace with others."[29] From all churches there came an acknowledgment of the duty to support the education of the ministry so that the churches might keep step with the problems arising in the rapidly expanding area.

In addition to the usual preaching services the activities of the denominations were many and varied. Among all Protestant and Catholic churches, the one activity in common was the Sunday school, although its form varied in different churches and in different sections. The credit for the introduction of the Sunday school to America continues to be a mooted question. The first Discipline (1784) of the Methodist Church in America urged preachers to train and instruct the children in the ways of the Lord. In 1786 Francis Asbury organized a school in Hanover County, Virginia, and four years later he conducted one in Charleston, South Carolina, for both black and white children. In "Notes to the Discipline" (1796) the Methodist bishops urged the people to establish Sunday schools wherever practicable "for the benefit of the children of the poor." It is quite obvious that the schools were restricted to the teaching of poor children to read in order that they might be brought under the influence of the church—a result achieved in the parochial schools of the Catholic denomination. In the beginning the plan did not include the children of pious members of the church, but later it was extended to all children.

One of the early nondenominational Sunday schools in the West was organized at Nashville, Tennessee. In 1820 a group led by Mrs. Felix Grundy, a Presbyterian, and Samuel Ament, a Methodist, organized a Sunday school of some fifteen children. The books used were Webster's

[29] *Christian Index* (Philadelphia, Washington, Ga., and Atlanta), July 16, 1831.

Spelling Book and the New Testament. Regularly each
Sunday morning at eight o'clock the class met and followed
a program of singing, praying, and studying. No sooner had
the school been organized than the leaders were accused
of being Sabbath breakers, violators of the law, and disturbers of the peace. The churches, strange to say, were
the leaders of the opposition to the Sunday school. Permission was asked to move the meeting place from a shabby,
unsuitable building to the basement of the Methodist church.
When this request was refused, the school closed for the
winter but reopened in the spring in the basement of an old
house originally used as a cabinet shop. On a Sunday
morning people walking along Church Street saw suspended
from the door of the Methodist church a large pasteboard
on which had been written "No desecration of the holy
Sabbath, by teaching on the Sabbath in this Church." The
Reverend Thomas Maddin, pastor of the Methodist church,
and several leading citizens of the city came to the aid of
the little Sunday school, and in November 1822 the churches
opened their doors and invited this group to accept quarters.[30]

By 1827 the Methodists definitely committed themselves
to the support of Sunday schools by the creation of the
Sunday School Union. Three years later more than 2,400
schools and 158,000 scholars were reported from the whole
of American Methodism, but only 20,000 had been reported
from the West in 1828. It was not, however, until 1836 that
the General Conference instructed preachers to form Sunday
schools in their charge whenever it was practicable.[31] At
last the church had recognized the great value of the
Sunday school and incorporated it as part of its whole

[30] See McFerrin, *Methodism in Tennessee*, III, 152-55.
[31] Halford E. Luccock and Paul Hutchinson, *The Story of Methodism*
(Cincinnati, 1926), 455; Charles C. Jarrell, *Methodism on the March* (Nashville, 1924), 205.

system of ecclesiastical work. Little by little the old English
plan of instruction in reading and writing to children of
poor parents was abandoned in favor of religious schools
open to all children on a broad democratic basis.

Evidence clearly points to earlier and more extensive
efforts of the Presbyterians in behalf of Sunday schools in
the West than those of any other Protestant denomination.
As early as 1805 fourteen men in Kentucky entered into an
agreement to give Negroes and others "an opportunity of
learning to read the Holy Scriptures." Probably the first
Sunday school in the state was established in Frankfort in
the home of Mrs. John Brown who had persuaded Michael
Arthur, a Presbyterian minister and school teacher, to devote
one hour each Sunday to teaching the catechism and the
Bible to children. In 1819 Mrs. Brown and six teachers
began a Sunday school with eighteen female members.
Nearly a decade later a boys' department was added. The
Synod of Tennessee by 1819 had opened several schools
for the "instruction of the ignorant," especially the Negroes.
Some ten years later the work had increased to such an
extent that the South Alabama Presbytery sought an agent
to establish schools throughout its bounds. About the same
time a Sunday school in Greene County, Tennessee, reported
more than 150 pupils. In 1834 a Presbyterian church in
Blount County, Tennessee, had established in its neighboring territory fourteen schools that enrolled 558 children. In
addition to the Bible and the catechism, spelling books were
used and readers which contained "dull, prosy biographies
of unnaturally good children, who all died young." Memo-
rizing was the routine exercise in which bright scholars
often recited whole chapters of the Bible or entire hymns.
Most of the schools were held in homes rather than in
churches because the countryside was so sparsely settled.
Undoubtedly the Sunday school was a contributing factor to
the success of the Presbyterian church. For example, a

church in Louisiana reported that its school was the only force that had held the church together during a trying period.[32]

The slight interest of the early Baptists in Sunday school work is similar to that of the Methodists and probably for the same reason—lack of sufficient interest in education. Tormented by antimissionary movements and a general opposition to organizations within the churches, the Baptists were reluctant to organize Sunday schools. The earliest Baptist school in the West was begun by a woman in St. Francis County in southeastern Missouri in 1807. A decade later the Baptist missionaries, Peck and Welch, established in St. Louis a Sunday school for Negroes which soon had about one hundred pupils who learned to read and understand portions of the Bible. Although a school was reported in 1817 to be in operation in New Orleans, the opposition to it was so great that seventeen years passed before the Louisiana Association recommended that all churches establish Sunday schools. In 1835 an official church paper in Tennessee reported that many Baptists were discarding Sunday schools because they were deemed of no value. In the larger cities this condition was not always true. In 1839 the First Baptist Church in Louisville, for example, had a school with thirty teachers and two hundred pupils. Apparently growth was slow in Mississippi, for as late as 1839 the Columbus Association refused membership to a church which claimed the right to establish a Sunday school.[33] Until about 1840 opposition, indifference, Parkerism, Camp-

[32] The agreement is in the Shane Collection, Philadelphia. See W. H. Averill, *A History of the First Presbyterian Church, Frankfort, Kentucky* (Cincinnati, 1902), 198-209; John E. Alexander, *A Brief History of the Synod of Tennessee* (Philadelphia, 1887), 53; Posey, *Presbyterian Church,* 108.

[33] *Missouri Baptist Centennial, 1906* (Columbia, 1907), 149-50; *American Baptist Magazine* (Boston), I (1817-1818), 414; Christian, *Baptists of Louisiana,* 127; *The Baptist* (Nashville), I (1835), 75, V (1839), 45-46; *Baptist Banner,* May 23, 1839.

bellism, and, in some sense, abolitionism nullified Baptist efforts to build Sunday schools.

At first Barton Stone and Alexander Campbell were suspicious of the Sunday school movement, chiefly because they thought it was a proselytizing agency and its teachings tended to be sectarian. In the Disciples and Christian churches in the South and West the program moved slowly. But occasionally the movement received some encouragement. In 1835 one outspoken correspondent to a church paper stated that "it cannot be sectarian to teach children to read the Scriptures." The Christian church in Lexington, Kentucky, was one of the first churches in the state to have a regularly organized Sunday school. Opened in 1837 with more than fifty members and about fourteen teachers, the school sought "to induce a thorough knowledge of the sacred Scriptures untrammeled by the dogmas of the day." In 1847 the church at Nashville organized a school to teach Negroes to read and write. Two years later the church expanded the Sunday school to include 65 males and 100 female scholars in addition to two Sunday schools for Negroes with about 125 members.[34]

Among the many changes Campbell made in his positions toward various issues, none was more radical than his attitude on the Sunday schools. In 1847 he encouraged the Disciples to cooperate with the Sunday School Union and went so far as to declare that "I hold it to be rather cowardice than faith to keep away from Sunday school co-operation." By this period Stone and numerous leaders were in line with Campbell's advocacy of the new and highly successful agency. At a state meeting held in Lexington, Kentucky, in 1850 a resolution was passed which

---

[34] Winfred E. Garrison, *Christian Unity and Disciples of Christ* (St. Louis, 1955), 108, 113; William C. Bower and Ray G. Ross (eds.), *The Disciples and Religious Education* (St. Louis, 1936), 24-26, 33, 35; Morrill, *Christian Denomination*, 168; Fortune, *Disciples in Kentucky*, 322-23.

recommended "the establishment of Sunday schools in all the churches, to be under the strict supervision of the officers of said churches."[35] It was an indication that the school was henceforth to be considered an integral part of the church rather than a separate organization. The *Millennial Harbinger* of May 1857 contained an announcement of a "Sunday School and Family Library" to be issued in five series of ten volumes each and "free from all sectarian tendencies." This publication was the response to a demand for books which would consist of "original and selected works, written on various topics supposed to interest children, teachers, and parents." Henceforth, there was no doubt that Sunday schools had come to stay in Disciples churches.

In 1826 the General Protestant Episcopal Sunday School Union began its work of encouraging and stimulating Sunday schools largely through the formation of Sunday school societies in various parishes and church governing areas. Almost at once the Sunday school in the Episcopal Church began to change its form from the old-fashioned charity school to schools for everybody. In Monumental Church in Richmond, Virginia, the Sunday school was "no longer confined to the poorer classes of society; the principle is no longer acted upon, that they who can afford to provide instruction for their children on week-days are under no obligation to give them systematic religious education on the Lord's day."[36] This worthy example led to a movement which rapidly spread to the democratic small towns and to the rural areas in the West. In 1830 the Episcopal church in Nashville formed two Sunday schools attended by fifty male and female scholars. Eight years later Christ Church in Mobile had a flourishing school which followed a procedure of instruction and examination from the minister or

---

[35] Garrison, *Christian Unity*, 108; Fortune, *Disciples in Kentucky*, 323-24.
[36] Clifton H. Brewer, *A History of Religious Education in the Episcopal Church to 1835* (New Haven, 1924), 210, 215.

superintendent. On the first Sunday of each month a review covered the work of the previous month. The school of about one hundred scholars had a library of 150 volumes which were read with great interest.[37] Different arrangements prevailed in different churches but all sought to avoid a conflict with the time of the preaching services. Some of the schools had two sessions, one in the morning and the other in the afternoon. St. Paul's Church in Franklin, Tennessee, held school from eight o'clock until time for morning prayers.

Peculiarly enough, the American found small place for music in his religious life. The human voice raised in solemn hymns could be used for pious praise, but wind and string instruments were coldly received or not tolerated in a worship service. The organ was acceptable in those denominations having European origins, but it was considered as an object of sinful pleasures among most of the churches which sprang into being in the Western country. From Holland the Plymouth colonists had brought a psalm book which they continued to use for about seventy years. Much better known was the Bay Psalm Book which was printed in 1640 in the American colonies. In 1719 Isaac Watts issued his famous *Psalms of David*, which has been described as "a glow of sunlight breaking in upon a gray and cloudy day." About two decades later John Wesley published in Charleston a collection of songs. John and Charles Wesley were prolific song writers; they produced some six thousand hymns, the impact of which was so great that a biographer of John Wesley said that the Wesleys "have opened lofty gates yielding a view of glory to more souls than anybody short of Gabriel had best try counting. . . ." James Martineau, the well known Unitarian minister and writer, declared that "after the scriptures, the Wesley hymn-book appears

[37] *Journal of a Convention of the Protestant Episcopal Church in the State of Alabama* (Tuscaloosa, 1831), 11-13.

to me the grandest instrument of popular culture that Christendom has ever produced."[38] Until the compositions of Watts and the Wesleys appeared, efforts were largely directed toward versifying psalms and other portions of the Scriptures adaptable for singing. After about 1800 the various Protestant denominations began to collect hymns or to alter Watts's *Psalms*.

The revivals and camp meetings provided the source for a great variety of songs best classified as "spirituals" or "revival spirituals." Many songs took form spontaneously on the camp ground; rhyme and rhythm touched the emotions in a manner seldom accomplished by the spoken word and served as a powerful complement to the preacher and his sermon. Great emphasis was laid on an inevitable death and on a restless search for peace for the "sin-sick soul." Often the verses contained crude and hastily arranged wording, liberally interspersed with hallelujahs and refrains, and largely directed toward terms of salvation. Many songs in present-day use are reminiscent of the old sweeping appeals: "Come, Thou Fount of Every Blessing," "On Jordan's Stormy Banks I Stand," and "Come to Jesus" can easily stir a lukewarm congregation. Although the camp meeting hymn books were never officially adopted by any denomination, some of the hymns are today found in Methodist, Episcopal, and Presbyterian hymnals. The Wesleyan and the camp meeting hymns found their way into the backwoods cabin. People sang them as they plowed or rode together to church. Many carried out John Wesley's admonition for congregational singing: "Sing lustily, and with a good courage. Beware of singing as if you were half dead, or half asleep; but lift up your voices with strength."[39]

On the early frontier song books were so rare that the

---

[38] Bacon, *American Christianity*, 182-83; John D. Wade, *John Wesley* (New York, 1930), 170; Luther A. Weigle, *American Idealism* (New Haven, 1928), 149.

[39] Johnson, *Frontier Camp Meeting*, 207.

song leader would read a couple of lines, then the audience would sing them, thus they would continue through the entire song. Some people copied words on slips of paper and passed them through the crowd. After 1805 "little songsters," or booklets without tunes, began to appear. A *Methodist Pocket Hymn-Book* printed in 1813 contained 350 hymns although its pages were only three by four inches. Gradually the quality of the hymn changed until the so-called "literary hymn" came from the pens of Oliver Wendell Holmes, Samuel Longfellow, John Greenleaf Whittier, and others. By the end of the Civil War people on the fringes of the Western frontier were singing "Nearer, My God, to Thee," "Onward, Christian Soldiers," and "Stand Up for Jesus." These and other songs of a similar type became the musical basis for all the revivals from then to the present.[40]

Since money was scarce and the cost of a small organ almost prohibitive—about $250 was the lowest price in 1825—instrumental music in churches caused little disturbance. By the midcentury some Episcopal churches were using organs to the decided improvement of the music, congregational singing, and the choirs. The Methodists had not departed far enough from their Episcopal background to become unduly excited about the introduction of instrumental music. Scattered opposition to the use of instrumental accompaniment to the hymns prevailed among the Methodists, but the battle was soon lost. An unusual attitude was expressed by the Mississippi Conference when in 1838 it adopted a resolution "that the introduction of instrumental music into public worship in our churches and the conducting of the music in our churches by choirs . . . is inconsistent with the directions of our Discipline." Alfred Brunson, a frontier Methodist revivalist, sternly reproved churches that were "in the habit of praising God by proxy

---

[40] See Chap. IX in Grover C. Loud, *Evangelized America* (New York, 1928).

. . . [with] a thundering organ and a select choir to do their singing. As might be expected in such cases the services were cold and formal, nothing of the life and spirituality of religion being visible."[41]

The introduction of instrumental music into a church like the Disciples, desiring to maintain simplicity in church order and worship, naturally led to disputes. Alexander Campbell, thoroughly dissatisfied with the psalms and hymns in use, published in 1828 a hymnal containing 125 selections. Although he remained steadfastly opposed to the use of musical instruments in the church, he did not write anything against them until 1851. Irritated by their popular usage, Campbell declared in the *Harbinger* that "to all spiritually-minded Christians such aids would be as a cow-bell in a concert." In the New Testament not a syllable could be found, he insisted, about instrumental music. Easily aroused, he became increasingly indignant about the worship of "that God who delights in a splendid house, in the ornaments of crimson and scarlet, in gold and silver, in the melodies of organs and the sound of unbelieving and unsanctified choristers. . . ."[42]

In 1851 a correspondent to the *Ecclesiastical Reformer*, a paper of the Stone-Campbell cooperative movement, urged the use of music in the churches. One of the editors took him sharply to task by replying that music acted on a man's blood. An organ, he declared, was "a wooden devotion quickener" and converted a church into a place of entertainment. Among the Disciples the issue came to a head in 1859 when a melodeon was placed in the Midway (Ken-

[41] William W. Manross, *The Episcopal Church in the United States, 1800-1840* (New York, 1938), 166-68; John G. Jones, *A Complete History of Methodism as Connected with the Mississippi Conference* (2 vols.; Nashville, 1908), II, 408; Alfred Brunson, *A Western Pioneer* (2 vols.; Cincinnati, 1880), II, 281.

[42] Richardson, *Alexander Campbell*, II, 366; Benjamin L. Smith, *Alexander Campbell* (St. Louis, 1930), 194.

tucky) Church. Opponents to the innovation claimed that it "ministered to pride and worldliness, was without sanction of the New Testament precept and example and was consequently unscriptural and sinful." The most extreme case seems to have occurred in the First Christian Church of St. Louis which had bought under foreclosure an Episcopal church that contained a three thousand-dollar organ. A fight ensued over the organ which resulted in its being taken out and sold. Most of this quarreling over musical instruments came after 1860 when Campbell was too old and uninterested to become involved. Earlier his strong hand might have prevented much of the acrimony that arose from the arguments against church organs, which, added to an antimissionary fight, led in 1906 to a separation of one group which identified itself as the Churches of Christ. After William K. Pendleton, Campbell's son-in-law, in 1865 replaced Campbell as editor of the *Harbinger,* he refused to take the side of the anti-organ group saying that he had "a fondness for good music of all kinds," and enjoyed "the grand and majestic swell of the organ rolling forth, laden with the strains of our sacred music."[43]

As would be expected the Baptists encountered trouble in the use of the organ, causing serious dissension in many churches. As late as 1843 the Baptist church at Bloomfield, Kentucky, passed a resolution forbidding instrumental music on every occasion. In 1859 David Benedict feared the day when the organ "shall assume an overwhelming influence, and only a few artistic performers be retained in the singers' seats, to be directed by men who take but little interest in any of the services of the sanctuary, except what pertains to their professional duty, then a machine, harmless in itself, will be looked upon with disfavor if not with disgust

[43] Issue of March 15, 1851; Jennings, *Disciples of Christ,* 195; Garrison and DeGroot, *Disciples of Christ,* 345.

by the more pious portion of our assemblies."[44] After the Civil War, with the exception of small groups in the Disciples and Baptist churches, the opposition to instrumental music soon became an issue buried in the past. The leaders had discovered the great value inherent in song and instrumental musical arrangements.

Although the churches were not so highly organized as today with societies of all types designed for the youngest to the oldest members, even the early churches offered numerous services that played an important role in individual and community life. Most of this activity revolved about such functions as baptizing, the Lord's Supper, weddings, and funerals. In some denominations the importance of one of these seemed far more significant than another. For example, the Baptists and Disciples laid great emphasis on the mode of baptizing, which was plenary immersion rather than the simple sprinkling performed by most churches. Since baptizing by immersion was a requisite for membership in the Baptist and Disciples churches, the records of these denominations abound with interesting accounts of baptizing events. A plunge into cold water seemed no hazard to health nor a deterrent to baptism; winter posed no problem other than breaking the ice on a frozen stream. Some preachers, unwilling to delay the baptism for fear that the newly converted would change his mind, performed the service at night under very impressive conditions. Singing songs and offering praises, people stood on the banks and in the glow of the firelight, watched the convert as he was "buried with Christ in baptism." In 1788 the Maysville (Kentucky) Baptist Church administered baptism in the Ohio River while a large number of Indians on the opposite bank watched its progress with much interest. Fearing the

[44] David Benedict, *Fifty Years among the Baptists* (New York, 1860), 285.

proximity of the Indians, some churches provided an armed guard at these functions.[45]

Staid churches like the Presbyterian, Episcopal, and Catholic would have frowned upon the activity of Peter Cartwright, who once baptized a family of children on a moving train. Sure that he had proceeded wisely, Cartwright said that he "would gladly have baptized the whole car load." Such a scene, he insisted, "could not but excite some emotion among the passengers, and will make a lasting impression upon the minds of the family of children." And yet, the Methodists, having adopted the Episcopal method of sprinkling, heaped all manner of ridicule upon the Baptists and Disciples for their belief in the regenerating power of water. None saw the confusion between the spirit and the symbol clearer than Episcopal Bishop Cobbs of Alabama. Although having a great dislike for baptism by immersion, Cobbs agreed to baptize two women on two conditions—that dawn should be the time and only the immediate family could be present. Of course the women withdrew their request, for the bishop had shrewdly taken "the glory" out of the ceremony.[46]

Some churches willingly accepted baptism which had been administered by churches of a different faith. The Presbyterian Church seemed to have been the most generous in this respect. This church in Tuscaloosa accepted children baptized in other churches by entering their names in a section of the record book entitled "Baptized children of the Church." The church in Nashville admitted to membership Horace Berry upon the simple statement that he had already been baptized. Years later, when he revealed that he had transferred from a Unitarian church, he was required

[45] Martin H. Smith, *History of the Maysville Baptist Church* (Maysville, Ky., 1875), 4.

[46] Peter Cartwright, *Fifty Years as a Presiding Elder* (New York, n. d.), 280; White, *Cobbs*, 119.

to receive baptism from the Nashville church for the reason that the Unitarian Church could not be regarded as a "Christian Church."[47] Not often did Presbyterians hew so closely to this line.

For the Presbyterians the sacrament of the Lord's Supper in the early days involved "fencing" the tables and collecting tokens distributed to those deemed worthy of partaking of the bread and wine. After a lengthy sermon the communicants seated themselves around the table covered with a white cloth and laden with vessels containing the elements. The services, usually "tedious and fatiguing," often lasted until after sunset. Held less frequently than today the sacrament of holy communion invariably followed a series of meetings or a protracted meeting which usually began on Thursday and continued through Sunday. These communion services gave John Lyle the pleasing privilege to record in his diary on June 14, 1801: "I preached tenderly & wept much toward the close." At a service in the Mount Zion (Kentucky) Presbyterian Church in 1857 the clerk recorded in the session book the strange note that the sacrament had been administered "to a few professing godlings."

Contrary to the occasional communion service of the Presbyterians, the Baptists followed the custom of observing the sacrament once each month. Much confusion prevailed about procedure. One church questioned the type of bread and finally decided that thereafter only unleavened bread should be used. Another church made a regular charge of 6¼ cents per member to defray the expenses of the table. Close communion seemed to concern Baptists more than any other church question. Generally the churches followed a practice of closing the sacramental services to non-Baptists and also of excluding their own members who insisted on

[47] MS Sessional Records of the First Presbyterian Church, Nashville, Tennessee, 1833-1853, 104, in church vault, Nashville.

participating in the sacrament with congregations of other denominations.

At the time of the union of the Christians and the Disciples, Stone occupied a more liberal position than Campbell on open communion. In 1829 Campbell objected to receiving "unimmersed persons" but not "unbaptized persons." This keen distinction led to a more liberal position which permitted all persons to come to the table—generally considered by Disciples to be the chief act of weekly worship.[48]

The normal method of conducting the sacrament of Holy Communion in the Episcopal and Catholic churches varied little with the location—save the limitation brought about by the absence of buildings, plate, and elements. In Methodist churches the procedure of serving the Lord's Supper was as lax as that of its other ordinances. The Methodist preacher's schedule was so irregular he rarely observed any dates in the church calendar, preferring to do what he could when he could.

The service of the several denominations in funerals and weddings varied so little that none except the most unusual occurrence seems to have been recorded. Only the Baptists had a variety of conflicting ideas about funeral sermons. A rather widely accepted belief held that no Scriptures authorized preaching at a funeral. One association did not think a funeral sermon "necessary to the decent burial of the Dead." Another thought that funeral processions were anti-Christian and ought not to be held. In Murfreesboro, Tennessee, the Presbyterian church was willing to discontinue tolling a bell at funerals, since two bells had already been cracked in this service.[49]

With the exception of the Episcopal and Catholic churches

[48] Fortune, *Disciples in Kentucky*, 369.

[49] Spencer, *Kentucky Baptists*, I, 344, II, 53; "Minutes of the Elkhorn Baptists Association, Kentucky, 1785-1805," Aug. 14, 1797, in Sweet, *The Baptists*, 476; MS Session Records, Murfreesboro, Tennessee, 1812-1860, Oct. 21, 1832, Montreat.

there was a prevailing sameness about the services and the activities of most of the churches. By the middle of the nineteenth century churches particularly in the larger cities had Sunday schools, missionary societies, choirs, and various other agencies similar to a later period. Only in rural sections and especially among antimissionary groups would one have found a church the total activity of which was limited to the preaching of sermons. As everyday life became more complex, so did the activities of the churches.

6

GOVERNMENT OF
THE CHURCHES

THE ROMAN CATHOLIC CHURCH in America passed from an early state of proscription to one of restricted civil liberty acquired, to a large degree, through the general principles which underlay the American Revolution. At the outbreak of the fighting there may have been as many as twenty-five thousand Catholics within the area east of the Mississippi River. Most of these were living in Maryland where they were planters and in Pennsylvania where they were farmers and also merchants and shopkeepers in towns like Philadelphia. The priests numbered only twenty-four; almost all were former members of the Society of Jesus which had been dissolved by a papal decree in 1773. Against their will they had been forced to become secular priests under the jurisdiction of the Vicar Apostolic of London. Naturally after the Revolution, this relation with the English hierarchy became highly impracticable. The Maryland clergy, aware of the danger of arousing the latent prejudices in the colonies, made no effort to restore relations with England but took immediate steps to retain church property and to renew worship and discipline.[1] At the moment peace and liberty promised much to the Catholics in America, but rugged days lay immediately ahead. Since the Catholics constituted such a small religious body they quite naturally favored religious toleration and supported the separation of church and state.[2]

After his consecration in 1790 Bishop John Carroll assumed

supervision of an immense territory of nearly 900,000 square miles and about thirty thousand Catholics in a population of almost four million, all administered until 1808 by the single diocese of Baltimore. In that year Carroll became archbishop of the new ecclesiastic Province of Baltimore under whose care were the four new suffragan bishoprics of New York, Philadelphia, Boston, and Bardstown, the last of which was to comprise Kentucky, Tennessee, and the Northwest Territory. All of the United States not included in the four dioceses was left in the control of the archbishop of Baltimore. In 1805 the territory of the Louisiana Purchase had been placed under the temporal jurisdiction of Bishop Carroll. At the time of the cession the diocese had twenty-one parishes and twenty-six priests, only a few of whom remained to serve under the new government. Earlier the Catholic Church had been the beneficiary of the anti-Catholic policies of the French Revolution which, between 1791 and 1799, drove to the shores of the United States twenty-three French priests. With their aid Carroll was able to furnish several educational institutions with teachers and to extend missions in several directions. No section of the country was more indebted to the French than Kentucky which received Flaget, David, and Badin—worthy priests whose names are associated with the rise and progress of Catholicism in the first trans-Allegheny state.[3]

[1] J. A. Baisnée, "The Catholic Church in the United States, 1784-1828," *Records of the American Catholic Historical Society of Philadelphia* (Philadelphia), LVI (1945), 134-35; Bacon, *American Christianity*, 214; Thomas O'Gorman, *A History of the Roman Catholic Church in the United States* (New York, 1900), 259-60.

[2] Theodore Maynard, *The Catholic Church and the American Idea* (New York, 1953), 31-32.

[3] Louis J. Putz (ed.), *The Catholic Church, U. S. A.* (Chicago, 1956), 65; O'Gorman, *Roman Catholic Church*, 291-94. After having spent twenty years in Europe, Carroll returned to the United States in 1774. At this time Maryland did not have a single Roman Catholic church open for public worship. Daniel Dorchester, *Christianity in the United States* (New York, 1888), 328-29.

So different from that of most of the denominations in the country, the government of the Catholic Church was fixed and determined. It would make few changes through the years and few concessions to the West. Let other churches alter their procedure and their beliefs; the Catholics neither could nor would change. The church had through the centuries held to its creed and to its loyalty to the Pope. Thomas C. Hall, a Protestant theologian, says: "The Roman Catholic Church is not 'democratic,' but patriarchial, and that on principle; it is founded not on the authority of the people, but on the authority of the past, and that authority is incarnated in ordained persons with a head who, from the Catholic point of view, is endowed with infallible authority when speaking from his official seat on doctrine, and with plenary administrative authority, given him as God's representative on earth."[4]

In the Roman Catholic Church cardinals, archbishops, and bishops comprised the hierarchy. The College of Cardinals served as the counsellor of the Pope, in a sense acting as the senate of the church. An archbishop might be assigned several dioceses and serve as the principal ecclesiastical official over them. Bishops were the supreme administrators of their dioceses. They were chosen in various ways, but the final decision rested with the Holy See. The parish priest, chosen by the bishop of the diocese, was the real link between the people and the church. On the way to being inducted into the priesthood, the student passed through four minor orders before reaching the orders of subdeacon, deacon, and priest. At this point he was ordained by a bishop, from whom he received the faculties to offer the Mass and administer the sacraments, to do the work of an evangelist, and to bring people into the church. Upon the priests of the Latin rite the Holy See imposed a law of

[4] Thomas C. Hall, *The Religious Background of American Culture* (Boston, 1930), 266.

celibacy that they might more nearly serve their church with an undivided heart, released from earthly ties and encumbrances.

From the earliest days of the new republic there had been a tendency, caused by factors previously mentioned, to take a liberal point of view of theology. Bishop Carroll's strong and practical desire to adjust Catholicism to the democratic beliefs in civil and religious liberty and his generous and friendly attitude toward Protestants all prevented him from being popularly accepted by Rome. With reason the first American bishop often had difficulty with both hierarchy and priests who held to the past and to a less tolerant attempt to adjust the church to American conditions. This conflict between the American desire for liberty and Rome's absolute spiritual rule was not infrequently the subject of concern to Carroll and his successors. Out of conflicts grew a movement in the church usually called trusteeism, which began as early as 1785 when the trustees of Saint Peter's Church in New York City claimed the right to appoint and dismiss the pastors and to control the church property. In St. Louis, New Orleans, Charleston, and elsewhere the fight continued and schisms often lasted for years. The chief trouble arose from the assumption by trustees, many of whom were not practicing Catholics, of the episcopal power to select the pastors. It was inevitable that the hierarchial powers would prevail, but often it was at a cost of great irritation between priests and people and at a great loss to the church. Further it seemed perfectly clear to many Americans that this trusteeism struggle could be interpreted "as a conflict between an autocratic clergy and a democratic people."[5]

When Spain was engaged in establishing colonies in North America, the Catholic Church received money from

[5] Bacon, *American Christianity*, 215-16; Baudier, *Catholic Church in Louisiana*, 335-48; Maynard, *Catholic Church and American Idea*, 57.

the Crown. In the French colonies the church not only suffered extremely, but also received a cruel blow when the Council of Louisiana in 1763 seized and sold the property of the Jesuits. In the English colony of Maryland the priests were supported by voluntary offerings and by the income of estates—including a tract of land donated by an Indian chief. At a somewhat later period, according to Bishop Carroll, it seems that the support of the clergy depended almost wholly on contributions. In 1791 the first diocesan Synod of Baltimore declared that offerings should be divided into three parts—one for the priests, another for the poor, and a third for church supplies. The increasing number of priests, the great extent of the westward movement, the poverty of the Catholic immigrant, and the small income from revenue-producing estates made the financing of the Catholic Church in America a matter of great difficulty. In the West the poverty of some of the outposts such as Bardstown and St. Louis is evident in the story of the toil, anguish, and sacrifice of priests like Badin, Flaget, Nerinckx, and others.[6]

Despite poverty, trusteeism, and a host of other problems the church continued to grow. Archbishop Carroll died in 1815 in his eighty-first year after a quarter of a century of devoted and successful work, and his death marked the end of an era in American Catholic history. In faraway Bardstown Bishop Flaget, upon hearing of Carroll's death, wrote into his journal: "This holy man has run a glorious career; he was gifted with a wisdom and prudence which made everyone esteem and love him. . . ."[7]

After 1830 Roman Catholicism grew rapidly, in the main because of heavy Irish and German immigration. The large numbers coming to America encouraged the organization

[6] Putz, *Catholic Church, U. S. A.,* 96-97.
[7] Schauinger, *Cathedrals,* 135. Unfortunately the first four of Carroll's successors were rather inferior archbishops.

in Europe of missionary societies the chief purpose of which
was to aid their co-religionists. In 1828 the Lyons (France)
Propaganda, organized in 1822, sent to the church in the
United States more than a hundred thousand francs. The
Leopold Society in Austria, formed in 1829, was another
generous contributor to the pressing need of the struggling
church. The coming to this country of large numbers of
well-educated priests from France, Germany, and Ireland
greatly aided the recruiting of a priesthood. Eventually the
Irish predominated in the church's leadership, largely because of their advantage in the knowledge of the English
language, and because of their vigorous leadership. From
England the Protestant colonists had brought a fanatical
opposition to the Roman Catholics which was allayed only
by having a common foe during the American Revolution.
When evidence appeared that the church was rapidly
growing, Protestants made organized attempts to check
Catholic growth.[8]

The presence of the Irish, the Germans, and the French
in the role of priests and missionaries had both advantages
and disadvantages. Many priests had been sent to America
on a mission of indefinite terms and subject to recall. Lacking the normal ties which many emigrés developed, the
priests rarely adopted the new land as their home. Their
neighbors had abundant reason to question their loyalty to
American institutions, democracy, and ideals. Nevertheless,
the church continued to expand in territory and increase in
numbers. The thirty thousand members at the time Carroll
became bishop had increased twenty times by 1830. Of the
ten bishops then in the United States six were either French-
born or French in sympathy, while two were Irish-born,
and two of American birth with Irish ancestry. The division
of the bishops at the time into a French party and an Irish
party began to cause trouble within the church. When

[8] Sweet, *Religions in America*, 390-91; *Hall, Religious Background*, 260-62.

Bishop Edward D. Fenwick of Cincinnati died in 1832, Archbishop James Whitfield of Baltimore wrote to his good friend Joseph Rosati, Bishop of St. Louis, that an American should be elected in Fenwick's place, and that the church should guard particularly against adding Irish bishops.[9] The church had established a pattern to secure effective organization and possessed the will to go forward in the face of great opposition.

The major Protestant denominations that stemmed from European organizations, like the Catholics, made no radical changes in their national structures. The first to form a national body out of its old self was the Protestant Episcopal Church. Conceived in the same formative years and born out of the same set of circumstances, the government of the United States and the organization of the Protestant Episcopal Church were both molded according to the Federalists' notion of a strong central government made up of component parts. Representative churchmen had met in an advisory convention in 1784, and in the next year they adopted a constitution which would provide a skeleton for the reviving church body. It was indeed bold business to form a constitution before the accession of the episcopate, but practical necessity justified this brief, but complete, reversal of the theory on which the church had been based. "It is our unanimous opinion," a contemporary acknowledged, "that it is beginning at the wrong end to attempt to organize our church before we have obtained a head. . . ."[10] Obviously, American Episcopalians needed to act quickly on three major problems: the preservation of church worship, the conservation of church property, and the inauguration of an American episcopacy.

After securing a constitution, the resolutions of the other problems were uncertain. Representatives from Connecticut

---

[9] Goodykoontz, *Home Missions*, 223-24; John T. Ellis, *American Catholicism* (Chicago, 1956), 47-48.

[10] Tiffany, *Protestant Episcopal Church*, 333.

had taken steps in 1783 to obtain an American episcopate. They secretly sent Samuel Seabury to England for consecration, but the Church of England would not consecrate him. Seabury then went to the Episcopal Church of Scotland which consecrated him at Aberdeen in November 1784. He thus became the first bishop in the United States, but his position remained precarious until it was strengthened in 1787 by the English consecrations in Lambeth Palace of William White of Pennsylvania and Samuel Provoost of New York. The General Convention meeting in 1789 had the House of Bishops regularly constituted three months after the inauguration of President Washington. Successful union in the political field gave strength to the cause of union in the ecclesiastical field.

The governing body of the Protestant Episcopal Church consisted of a General Convention, meeting triennially, and of diocesan conventions which assembled yearly. The General Convention was made up of two houses, the lower composed of an equal number of clerical and lay delegates from each diocese and the upper formed by all the bishops. This body had the power to make rules and to amend the constitution. To the bishop who had been chosen by a diocese as its administrator was given the duty to preside over the annual diocesan convention composed of the clergy and one or more delegates from each parish. As in the General Convention the concurrence of both clerical and lay delegates was necessary for a proposed act to have the force of law. Between annual sessions of the diocesan conventions, the diocese was represented by a standing committee selected from lay and clerical members. The temporal affairs of each church were in the hands of the churchwardens and the vestry; the spiritual control remained exclusively with the rector.

The founders of the Protestant Episcopal Church readily saw that the church must not be fettered by foreign control. To exist and grow, the new church had to be adapted to American life and American ideas. "Hence it could not be simply a clerical autocracy; it must draw its strength from the source which supplied strength to the state, namely, the people."[11] As a result the laity received a large share in the management of the church from the parish level to the General Convention. Although acknowledging the English church as its mother, the new American church cut itself completely away from any connection with the state and sought to adjust itself to the new conditions that began with the American Revolution and immediately thereafter. In this evolution the powers of representative bodies, diocesan and parochial, were increased so greatly that the bishop was reduced to the role of a performer of certain assigned functions. In truth the church had lost the strict form of episcopacy and had become more nearly a church with a synodical type of government.

As if to remedy a weakness recognizable after twelve years, the Protestant Episcopal Church adopted the Thirty-Nine Articles of the Church of England, a detailed statement of theology so capable of varying interpretations that it had been acceptable to High, Low, and Broad churches. True to the Roman Catholic background, the Church of England was characterized by zeal for forms of worship rather than for theological uniformity or reformation of society. Like the English church, the Protestant Episcopal Church concerned itself with the religious life of its parishioners by rite and ritual, but did not officially regard as its province their morals or institutions of public life.[12]

For Episcopalians the parish was the center of church life,

---

[11] Tiffany, *Protestant Episcopal Church*, 295.

[12] For the reconstitution of the church in America carefully examine Clara O. Loveland, *The Critical Years: The Reconstitution of the Anglican Church . . . 1780-1789* (Greenwich, Conn., 1956); *Journals of the General Conventions of the Protestant Episcopal Church . . . from the Year 1784, to the Year 1814* (Philadelphia, 1817).

the point at which the member came into everyday contact with the activity of clergy and laymen. It could arise in a variety of ways. A missionary, a bishop, or a nearby rector could organize it. In some communities a number of Episcopalians formed a church and then sought a rector to take charge of it. Churches were even begun by a single individual who acted as a lay reader until he had enough of a congregation to ask for the services of a missionary. On occasions a wealthy Episcopalian paid a minister's salary until the charge became self-sustaining.

In forming a parish, the first step was usually the election of a vestry and wardens who formed the lay government and, with the rector, managed the temporal affairs of the parish. The vestries were either elected for a term or were self-perpetuating; the wardens were often simply senior members of the vestries. In most states, the vestry, rector, and wardens acted as a board of trustees in whom title to property was vested. After the trustees were chosen they proceeded to secure from the state legislature a charter of incorporation. Then admission to the diocesan convention was sought and usually received upon presentation of evidence of organization and acceptance of the rules and teachings of the Episcopal Church.

The parish had full and complete right to select as a minister any clergyman that it might desire. Often the parish asked advice of the bishop or some other minister, but this was not required. The new minister, as a general rule, had completed his theological education in a college or seminary, at which time he had been ordained to the diaconate, unless he was not twenty-one years old. At age twenty-four he was probably ordained in the priesthood upon presentation of testimonials of good character from twelve people in his neighborhood. The rector's salary was fixed by his agreement with the parish. Most of the income for the rector's salary and for the financing of the parish came from the sale of the pews and an annual rental payment. In addition special assessments were often made to meet some emergency as the reroofing of the church. Great difficulty often faced the efforts of dioceses to raise enough money to sustain a bishop.[13]

Members and ministers of the Presbyterian Church actively and enthusiastically supported the American colonies in securing liberty and in forming a new government. Despite losses by death of hundreds of members and the burning of some fifty meetinghouses, the Presbyterian Church emerged from the war in the best position of any church in America. In the Southern colonies only the Presbyterians had managed to maintain a vigorous and continuing existence, while some churches had almost ceased to function. On the same day, May 25, 1787, that the Constitutional Convention had secured a quorum in Philadelphia, the Presbyterian Synod of New York and Philadelphia, meeting only a few blocks away, considered the form of church government which could function best in the new nation. Keeping its basis in earlier European and colonial usage, the church adopted a constitution at the next meeting of the synod in 1788. Observers called it a "compact, comprehensive and liberal system" and saw "a certain vague resemblance" between the constitution of the church and that proposed for the federal government.[14]

The Presbyterian Church continued its characteristic feature of being governed by presbyters or elders. As the church developed, two classes of elders came to be accepted —the preaching elders and the non-preaching or ruling elders. The ruling elders (later called elders) were chosen largely to assist the minister in all matters pertaining to the

13 For the situation in Alabama in the 1840s see Whitaker, *Church in Alabama*, 85-86. The fourteen assessable congregations had great difficulty raising the bishop's salary.

14 *Centennial of the General Assembly*, 104; Robert E. Thompson, *A History of the Presbyterian Churches in the United States* (New York, 1895), 66.

life of the congregation. Usually competent individuals, the elders were of great assistance in passing judgment on any and all matters of the local session, the presbytery, or the synod. The individual church issued the call to a minister, but the presbytery had the power of ratifying the choice or calling for a new election.

The session, composed of the pastor and the elders, constituted the governing body of the individual church. The session possessed legislative, executive, and judicial power to make all necessary rules and regulations, to appoint delegates, to receive new members, and to reprimand or exclude erring members. The session kept a register which revealed the activity of the church and its members, and often contained a valuable commentary on the state of society in the community. In addition to elders, the church elected deacons whose work, essentially different from that of the elders, was largely confined to protecting the temporalities of the church and to distributing its charities. So slight was the distinction between the powers of elder and deacon that the Tuscaloosa (Alabama) Presbytery ruled that in case of doubt the deacons should yield to the elders in the church session.[15]

The most important governing body in Presbyterianism was the presbytery, composed of one elder from each congregation and all the ministers in the district. A typical presbytery met in the fall and again in the spring, beginning on Thursday and concluding on Sunday. This body examined, licensed, and ordained candidates for the ministry, installed ministers over congregations, and provided for the supervision of all the churches under its jurisdiction. The membership of the presbyteries varied greatly in size because of the difference in the extent of the territory; sometimes they were as much as two hundred miles across. At

---

[15] MS Minutes, Tuscaloosa Presbytery, 1835-1843, April 6, 1842, Montreat.

least three ministers were necessary to form a presbytery, and on occasions when three were not present at a session it would be necessary to adjourn to a later time. The life of numerous presbyteries was maintained in some areas with great difficulty.

Above the presbytery stood the synod formed from several presbyteries in an area. Composed of all the ministers in the district and an elder from each session, the synod heard and settled appeals from the presbyteries, reviewed records, erected new presbyteries, suggested proposed changes to the General Assembly, and forced members, sessions, and presbyteries to conform to church rules. Before the organization of the General Assembly the role of the single Synod of New York and Philadelphia was highly significant, for it was the only point at which "the collective wisdom and discretion of the whole body was brought to bear continuously upon the affairs of an American church."[16] Unless called into a special session, the synod met once a year for about a week.

The highest court in the Presbyterian Church was the General Assembly, formed in 1789 and required to meet once a year. It was composed of delegates, called commissioners, from the presbyteries originally in the ratio of one minister and one elder for every six ministers in each presbytery, a ratio which continued to be reduced as the church membership increased. The General Assembly had the power to review the records of the synods, to create new synods, and to exercise general discipline over the entire church.

The form of government of the Presbyterian Church was that of a republic governed not by prelates but by clerical and lay elders who had been selected by the people. The absence of authority made the local church a strong unit with an individuality which appealed to a democratic folk.

[16] Thompson, *Presbyterian Churches*, 67.

Philip Lindsley, a distinguished Presbyterian minister in Tennessee, declared that Presbyterianism was "a pure democracy," which assured "a perfect parity among the clergy." The church had "no tendency to aristocracy, much less to monarchy or despotism."[17]

The government of the Cumberland Presbyterian Church was a reasonable facsimile of the parent church. But the procedures and requirements of the Cumberland Presbyterians in regard to the training for the ministry fell far below those of the older Presbyterian church. On occasions, it should be pointed out, even the Presbyterians had to give ground as in the case of the South Alabama Presbytery which in April 1829 was forced to pass a resolution that "in consideration of the desolate conditions of our Country, it is expedient to ordain at this time the [two] Brethren" for whom the educational requirements had been relaxed. Some of the Cumberland Presbyterian preachers departed so far from the rigid doctrines of Calvinism that Peter Cartwright claims they proposed to join the Methodist Church but the offer was declined.[18]

Within the Baptist congregations the offices and duties appertaining to them were not unlike those of other denominations. Although all ordained ministers in Baptist churches were called elders, there was a tendency to consider the office of elder as distinct from the ministry. Baptists preferred the term elder to that of pastor, and some churches even used the title of bishop instead of elder. The duties of a deacon often varied in different churches, but he was largely thought of as a keeper of the money of the church. He was expected to circulate the subscription paper for the support of the minister, and some churches delegated to him the duties of assisting the poor and providing bread and

---

[17] Le Roy J. Halsey (ed.), *The Works of Philip Lindsley* (3 vols.; Nashville, 1859-1866), II, 59.

[18] MS Minutes, South Alabama Presbytery, 1828-1832, April 3, 1829, Montreat; Cartwright, *Autobiography*, 47.

wine for the communion. Most churches regularly held
monthly business meetings at which the preacher usually
served as the moderator. Some churches had a regular
pastor who held one or more services each Sunday; others
had part-time preachers who came only once or twice a
month. Where there was no Baptist preacher to call a service, the members met for prayer meetings in homes. At
protracted meetings the prevailing custom was to hold
morning inquiry meetings at which the preacher instructed
the unregenerate how to find religion.

Despite the contention of Baptist historians and theo-
logians that there is no Baptist Church in the sense employed
by most Protestant denominations, the point seems hardly
warranted in the face of a trend toward an organization with
agencies endowed with considerable authority over the congregational form of individual church government. Through
the years the denomination has been gradually surrendering
some of the earlier freedoms once enjoyed, chiefly in order
to meet, so some church historians contend, the competition
of the Methodist Church with its highly effective type of
centralized administration.

The Philadelphia Baptist Association, the first in America,
was organized as early as 1707. Since then the association
has been one of the agencies that has materially infringed
upon the autonomy of the individual church.[19] The association has no binding power over a church which may withdraw at will and organize a new association. Most associations at the time of organization have adopted constitutions.
Some adopted confessions of faith while other associations
preferred to leave this matter to the churches. One association pledged itself to accept "the incontrovertible principle
that each church is sovereign and independent." Yet other
associations have not hesitated to pass resolutions, express
objections, and take various actions that made them highly

---

[19] See Chap. IX in Posey, *Baptist Church.*

effective governing agencies. The associations usually met once a year for a period of three days beginning on Saturday morning. The churches sent representatives called messengers rather than delegates, since the latter seemed to imply the idea of transfer of power. The messenger, often the preacher, was expected to carry a letter from his church stating its progress and condition. Generally a meeting was opened by a sermon from a well known preacher. This was followed by the election of a moderator and a clerk, and then the business session got under way. Various committees were appointed, reports were made, and requests were heard. Messengers from churches not members of the association might come asking for admission—a request rarely ever denied.

The meeting of an association was a great event in the rather barren lives of the people and was prepared for months in advance. Since few church buildings would hold the large crowds, most of the sermons were preached in the open. People came from great distances with the full expectation of being entertained, housed, and fed at a gathering which had many of the features of a Methodist camp meeting. Often the meeting of a large association was attended by an enormous number of people. Good order generally prevailed, although many indiscretions have been recorded. Sunday was wholly devoted to preaching and prayer meetings, with Saturday and Monday given over to the conduct of business.

Sometimes sessions were very harmonious but they could become bitter squabbles. In 1808 when the moderator of a Kentucky association refused to read two letters from a certain church, the association proceeded to impeach him. Although the association had no authority to force churches to accept its action, it expected compliance. Despite its limited powers the association rendered valuable services, especially in an advisory capacity. Quarreling congregations were often restrained, and many perplexing problems such as those caused by the antimissionary dissension were solved by the work of the associations.

As a means of communication among the member churches, the early associations in the West and South appointed one of the most intelligent members, usually a preacher, to write a Circular Letter on some particular subject or some subject of his own choice. Such familiar topics as church discipline, the Lord's Supper, and election or matters of more general interest such as the War of 1812 were often chosen. Carefully prepared, often debated, and finally corrected and edited, the letter served as an excellent voice of the association. At first these letters were handwritten and copies were sent to neighboring or corresponding associations. In 1824 the manuscript of the Circular Letter of the Elkhorn (Kentucky) Association covered twenty-two pages devoted to the question of free communion.[20] Later, when the writing consumed too much time, the letters were printed as part of the minutes of the association and distributed in that form.

Early Baptists became convinced that it was better to seek preachers who were "raised up" by the conviction of a call to the ministry. The need of ministers in the West was so great that it was easy to believe that an uneducated minister was better than no minister at all. Therefore, entrance to the Baptist ministry was exceedingly easy and simple. When an applicant was able to convince a given congregation that God had called him, he was then permitted to preach a trial sermon, which, if acceptable, secured for him a license to preach in a particular church. If on a second trial sermon he received another approval, he was then permitted to preach anywhere in the association. Ordination usually came after the new preacher received a

---

[20] MS Minutes, Elkhorn Baptist Association, 1785-1835, 257-78, Louisville.

formal call to some church. Sometimes a congregation urged a good prospect to apply for a license to preach. Of the important denominations, the Baptists had the least formal requirements for admission to the ministry.

Rivalry with the Methodists brought considerable pressure on the Baptists to limit the complete autonomy of the individual churches and to give more authority to the association. Eventually the trend resulted in a highly successful cooperative endeavor that converted the Baptists into an organized body that surpassed the Presbyterians in numbers. Only the Methodists and later the Disciples of Christ prevented the Baptists from sweeping the West. Near the close of the eighteenth century the *Baptist Annual Register* stated the case clearly for an effective association by declaring that "when men of various capacity, acquirements, habits and experiences unite in promoting one common cause, there is scarce any difficulty which they cannot surmount, or any design they cannot by perseverance accomplish."[21]

Early in the nineteenth century the need for a connecting link among associations became so evident to the officers that an organization usually called a State Convention was tried at random. By the 1830s several conventions were formed throughout the South and West. The desire to expand missionary activity was probably the most important factor encouraging the promotion of the convention. As a rule the convention was formed and planned to operate in a manner much like the association but over a far greater territory. Most of the printed minutes of the conventions contained a Circular Letter similar to that of the association. Many of the conventions survived but with great difficulty, for the association was as much a trespass on the sovereignty of the individual church as many Baptists were willing to

[21] John Rippon, *The Baptist Annual Register for 1790, 1791, 1792, and Part of 1793* (n. p., n. d.), 549.

grant. The convention was another step that threatened to
curtail autonomy and democracy. To forestall this criticism
the convention in Mississippi placed in its constitution a
limiting provision that "the Convention shall never possess
a single attribute of power or authority over any church or
association."[22] Nevertheless, the convention on both state
and national levels came to play more and more an important part in the Baptist Church.

Although English Methodism had begun in 1739, thirty
years passed before John Wesley sent any preachers to
America to take care of the scattered flocks of the newly
organized Methodist societies. In 1773 the Methodist itinerants were called to meet in Philadelphia at the first
American Methodist conference. Despite the suspicion and
prejudice directed at Methodism during the Revolution, its
membership grew until by 1784 it had nearly fifteen thousand members and more than eighty preachers.

At the Christmas conference held in 1784 in Lovely Lane
Chapel, Baltimore, the Methodist Episcopal Church in the
United States was formed. Francis Asbury refused to
accept Wesley's appointment as superintendent and ordination as deacon and elder until the American preachers
concurred. Democracy had made too much headway in
America for Asbury to submit to an arbitrary appointment
from John Wesley, so the conference unanimously chose
Asbury, the son of a gardener, as the first bishop of the
Methodist Church in America. By action of the conference
and through the leadership of Asbury, the church in America
severed its British connections and became free to create its
own bishops, to ordain its clergymen, and to adopt rules
and regulations suited to the needs of a new democratic
country, progressing rapidly along a receding frontier line.

From John Wesley American Methodists inherited a
well organized church government which was adaptable to

---

[22] *Convention of the Baptist Denomination of Mississippi* (1837), 23.

various localities and flexible to individual needs. Autocracy and democracy were, however, strongly fused in the polity and doctrine of the church. Wesley's autocratic control readily fell into the hands of Asbury, who for nearly half a century ruled as strictly as Wesley might have done under similar circumstances. James O'Kelly had objected strenuously to the absolute appointing power of the bishops. The result of the clash in 1792 brought defeat to O'Kelly without the slightest loss of authority of the bishops.

In 1792 a General Conference assembled in Baltimore and decided to meet quadrennially. Four years later a delegated conference met in New York City for a session lasting twenty-one days. This began an unbroken line of quadrennial conferences to which delegates are elected by a fixed ratio and to which even bishops are accountable.[23]

At first the traveling preachers met in what were known as district or annual conferences which had been scheduled by the bishops. Here at sessions moderated by a bishop or a president *pro tem,* reports were heard from each presiding elder and each preacher of his year's work; candidates were admitted to the ministry; all manner of questions were examined and usually decided; and preaching appointments were made for the following year.

The quarterly conference had jurisdiction over the circuit composed of the traveling and local preachers, exhorters, leaders, trustees, and stewards. The presiding elder, an appointee of the bishop, opened the usual two-day meeting on a Saturday with a sermon followed by a business meeting. In the evening another sermon was concluded with an exhortation. Sunday was devoted to a love feast, sermons, prayers, baptisms, and the communion. Often hundreds answered the call for converts. Early Monday found people on their way home.

[23] Examine an early volume of the *Journals of the General Conference of the Methodist Episcopal Church* and a volume of the *Minutes of the Annual Conferences of the Methodist Episcopal Church.*

The class meeting was a successful method of supplementing the itinerant system which made little provision for pastoral work. Here in a small unit was an opportunity for the expression of personal testimonials and experiences. Often the class leader graduated to the ranks of the ministry. The earlier plan for a leader to visit each member once a week proved impossible and gave way to a scheme of holding meetings once a week. Strict rules which governed membership forbade indulgences and excesses of any kind. The membership served as watchers over each other; demoralizing influences were guarded against; and the necessary spiritual protection was supplied. Beyond the class meeting was an even smaller organization of three or four members of either sex meeting together for a candid discussion of their worldly temptations and spiritual joys. As the years passed and church organizations shifted, the class meetings, love feasts, and bands lost their place in the church.

The three orders in the ministry were bishops, elders, and deacons. The bishops were elected for life by the General Conference. A roll call of Western and Southern bishops will readily reveal the wisdom of the conferences in their selections. Few proved inadequate to the job entrusted to them. Most of them carried the banner of the church to areas untouched before by Methodism. The local church, through the quarterly conferences, was the only avenue into the ministry. After an apprenticeship under the direction of the senior preacher on a circuit, the junior preacher, usually called a deacon, served a second probationary period under the care of the presiding elder. He then became eligible for examination by the annual conference. If accepted he received ordination and became a traveling preacher endowed with all the powers of the Methodist ministry.

Acting as an assistant to the preachers was the local preacher who, feeling unable to enter the regular ministry, retained his secular vocation. In the absence of the itinerant, the local preacher often had complete charge of marriages, funerals, and baptisms. Below the local preacher was the exhorter who was licensed merely to exhort and evangelize rather than serve as a minister. Frequently the exhorter became a local preacher and from there he moved into the regular ministry. In this manner the Methodist system effectively supplied the far-flung frontier with alert representatives of the church.

When, from the discord that arose after the Great Revival, the Christians and the Disciples of Christ sprang up as a protest against denominationalism, synods, presbyteries, and creeds, both were suspicious of clericalism, for they believed the clergy was largely to blame for the theological quibbles that had pushed aside primitive Christianity. Many years passed before these groups saw fit to participate in any interchurch effort of union or cooperation. After separation from the Baptists, Alexander Campbell found himself the leader of a group totally without any form of organization or any kind of ties beyond those of periodical meetings. Campbell early accepted the idea that a church needed only deacons and elders to administer its affairs and preachers to spread the truth. Each individual church, he contended, was independent and had complete authority to select those officials whom it chose to ordain. And even ordination conferred no authority—it merely gave recognition of authority. Campbell repudiated apostolic succession, priestly supremacy, and the authority of governing bodies such as the presbytery. However, while Campbell was still a Baptist, Stone's Christians in Kentucky were moving carefully and methodically in the direction of establishing cooperative agencies. In 1829 a general meeting was held in Clark County and in the next year a three-day meeting convened at Mays Lick.[24]

As Campbell and his followers were either pushed out

[24] Richardson, *Alexander Campbell*, I, 386-87; Garrison and DeGroot, *Disciples of Christ*, 235; Fortune, *Disciples in Kentucky*, 111.

of or seceded from the Baptist churches, his earlier opposition to cooperation began to give way rapidly. A year before the union with the Christians in 1832, Campbell declared that "a church can do what an individual disciple cannot, and so can a district of churches do what a single congregation cannot." Four years later he so firmly favored intercongregation cooperation that he wrote: "The Church is . . . not one congregation or assembly, but *the congregation of Christ,* composed of all individual congregations on earth. In this work of conversion, the whole church . . . must cooperate." In 1838 he added: "We go for the co-operation of all the members of that one church in whatever communities they may happen to be dispersed, and for their co-operation in heart and soul . . . for the salvation of their fellow-men at home and abroad." Soon his suggestions caught fire, and issue after issue of the *Millennial Harbinger* contained notices of meetings on some level—county, district, and state. The radical congregationalism of his Baptist days gave way to a middle position between that of the Baptists and that of the Presbyterians. No longer did he remain disturbed over authority for cooperative action, for he had satisfied himself that "the New Testament teaches itself, both by precept and example, the necessity of connected and concentrated action in the advancement of the kingdom."[25]

At first the cooperative meetings, especially the annual ones, resembled camp meetings or any large scale evangelistic efforts. The most effective preachers were usually present and many members were regularly enrolled. Soon the meetings became the focal points for planning on a county, district, or state level. For example, the Green River Christian Cooperation was organized at Hopkinsville, Kentucky, in December 1849 and proposed to extend the gospel

[25] Lunger, *Alexander Campbell,* 116; *Millennial Harbinger,* 1831, 237, 1835, 235, 1838, 269; Richardson, *Alexander Campbell,* II, 496-97.

through cooperation of churches. Although the area changed from time to time, the union in the main consisted of churches in four counties. Probably the greatest achievement of the union was the furnishing of one or more evangelists to work among the young churches. In the same year the first Georgia cooperation was organized at Griffin in a private home. A year later messengers from four congregations drew up a set of rules which explained both its purpose and method of operation. Many similar efforts came into existence throughout the area served by the Disciples and Christian churches.[26]

Between the 1840s and 1850s numerous Disciples churches pushed their efforts in behalf of the cooperative movement. Eventually the result was the calling of the first national convention of Disciples, held in Cincinnati from October 24 to 28, 1849. One hundred churches in eleven states sent 156 messengers to the meeting. Some messengers brought credentials and some did not. Preachers and laymen within easy reach of Cincinnati accounted for a large number of those present. In a denomination so opposed to regulation, the convention accepted all present as messengers. The convention had become a mass meeting and thus set the example for similar conventions. This convention at Cincinnati organized the American Christian Missionary Society for work in both domestic and foreign fields. Alexander Campbell was elected president of the convention and of the society—the necessary organization that gave unity to the denomination and implemented plans for the future. The impulse to evangelize had overruled the hesitancy to unite and cooperate among churches.[27]

[26] Brooks Major, *An Account of the Green River Christian Cooperation, 1849-1859* (Elkton, Ky., 1957), 1-5; J. Edward Moseley, *Disciples of Christ in Georgia* (St. Louis, 1954), 156-57.

[27] Winfred E. Garrison, *The March of Faith: The Story of Religion in America since 1865* (New York, 1933), 194; Garrison and DeGroot, *Disciples of Christ*, 245-48.

Despite the progress made, the organization continued to be very simple. The model church had to have elders, deacons, and evangelists. The elders acted as judicial or executive officers and presided over and ruled the church, administered the ordinances, and attended to public worship. Some elders were preachers and some were not. The deacons were in charge of the temporalities of the church; they cared for the poor, supervised the buildings, and served as the treasurers of the congregations. The congregation must, in whole or in part, support the evangelists who labored in the mission fields. Notwithstanding the movement in the direction of qualified authority, there is today no central body with power to bind the churches or even to adopt an official name for the denomination.

Thus, early in the history of the several churches in the West and South, administrative machinery was created to extend the churches' work and to meet the challenge offered by the prospect of adding thousands of new members, including Negroes and Indians.

7

THE INDIANS

THE INTRODUCTION of Christianity to the American Indian had been among the chief duties assigned to the Dominican missionaries in the ill-fated De Soto expedition. They found that the field was vast and workers were too few to touch many of the scattered Indian villages. Even when a priest chose to leave the expedition in order to tarry longer among particular tribes, he was rarely aware of any impact which his religious life made. With reason he could expect little, but with emotion he always hoped for more than he achieved. Persistence has long been a characteristic of the Catholic missionaries, and they continued their infrequent contacts for a hundred or more years before realizing any measure of influence. In 1700 Father Paul Du Ru visited the Houma Indians who were then living on the east side of the Mississippi River some twenty miles above the mouth of the Red River. He encouraged them to build a church fifty feet in length and to place in front of it a cross about forty feet high. Later in the year Father Jacques Gravier chanted the first high mass ever heard in the Houma village and was surprised that it aroused so little curiosity among the Indians. Concerning this indifference, the priest wrote to his brother Jesuits at the Kaskaskia mission: "Nothing is more difficult than the conversion of these savages. . . . We must first make men of them and afterwards work to make them Christians."[1]

New Orleans, founded in 1718, became the seat of gov-

ernment of the French colony of Louisiana in 1722. Four
years later the Company of the Indies and Father Ignatius
de Beaubois, acting for the Society of Jesus, entered into a
contract by which the Jesuits received full guardianship of
all Indians in Louisiana. The French government sent the
Jesuits to Louisiana for the primary purpose of evangelizing
the Indians so that they might be made more tractable.
These missionaries could also counteract the English influences already present in that area, and it was hoped that
the effectiveness of one Jesuit might be equal to that of a
garrison of soldiers—an idea that supposedly originated with
the Jesuit Father Pierre F. X. Charlevoix. In 1721 a regulation issued for the Council of Louisiana had stated that
"the Council must exhort the missionaries to labor for the
conversion of the Savages, because, independently of it
being their duty, nothing is more advantageous than to
attach these nations to France by means of religion." The
followers of Loyola were markedly successful in achieving
the ulterior purpose for which they were sent. However,
one Jesuit scholar cautions that those who find in this action
of the French government "an occasion for obloquy should
prove that such motives actuated the missionaries themselves."[2] Within the vast interior lands neither heroism nor
devotion to duty was sufficient alone to sustain a Jesuit
missionary. Obligated to learn the language of the tribe in
which he lived, the Jesuit practiced a living religion and
was able to serve both physical and spiritual needs of the
Indian.

In 1729, after the Natchez Indians revolted against the
French and destroyed Fort Rosalie on the site of the present

[1] Biever, *Jesuits in . . . the Mississippi Valley,* 43 et passim.

[2] Delanglez, *French Jesuits,* 410, 412-13, 417-19. Also see Baudier, *Catholic Church in Louisiana,* 77, 111. In 1725 Father Raphael de Luxembourg
founded a school in New Orleans and planned a separate division for the
education of Indians who would serve as aides to missionaries. Since necessary money was not forthcoming, the project collapsed.

Natchez, the Jesuits had to abandon the missions among the Choctaws, Yazoos, Chickasaws, and Arkansas Indians. At various times most of these missions were reestablished. There are no extant records of Jesuit efforts among the Alibamons, Arkansas, Yazoos, and Chickasaws, but other evidence clearly points to very limited success for the revived missions.

The Jesuits maintained a continuing complaint against the sale of intoxicating liquor, especially brandy, to the Indians. In 1750 Father Louis Vivier described for a fellow Jesuit the terrible effects of liquor on the aborigines in the Mississippi Valley. "The brandy," he wrote, "sold by the French, especially by the soldiers in spite of the King's repeated prohibitions, and that which is sometimes distributed to them under the pretext of maintaining them in our interest, has ruined this mission, and has caused the majority of them to abandon our holy religion." For some twenty years after the French established Louisiana as a colonial possession, its governors did not support the whisky traffic, but under pressure from many in authority they were forced to permit its sale. Although the trade had been forbidden among the Alibamons and the Choctaws, the commandants at the military posts ignored the order and became the first to sell liquor to Indians, Negroes, and soldiers. Father Philbert F. Watrin, who spent thirty years among the Indians, correctly complained that "brandy trade has always rendered useless the work of the missionaries, or at least has greatly impeded its fruitfulness."[3]

The Jesuit missionaries might have accomplished more had there been no language barrier and had their requirements of converts been less rigorous. The Indian already had a religion of his own which must have seemed reasonably adequate for his primitive needs. The missionary either

[3] Biever, *Jesuits in . . . the Mississippi Valley*, 50; Delanglez, *French Jesuits*, 403, 404-410.

failed to realize or refused to see that he was asking the Indian to surrender an ancient religion for the religion of the newcomer. When the white men, who were supposedly Christians, began to take Indian lands by force and by treachery, the religion of the missionary became suspect. Conversions, whatever their value to the savages, might have been more numerous had not the missionaries required of the Indians the same severe religious standard normally expected of the European. The trickery and cunning by which the Indian lived best in the forests were, when interpreted as deceit and falsehood, matters of great concern to the missionary. To one the skills were virtues; to the other, vices. To one the acceptance of nature's abundance was gratitude; to the other, laziness. So on and on, the standards of morals and the lack of congruity proved to be the greatest difficulty to success as measured by missionaries. Whatever the result, few critics question the consecration and courage of the Jesuit missionaries. A naval officer in the middle of the eighteenth century paid a graphic tribute to the Jesuit fathers in Louisiana. "Picture to yourself," he wrote, "a Jesuit four hundred leagues away in the woods, with no conveniences, no provisions, and most frequently with no resource but the liberality of people who know not God, compelled to live with them, to pass whole years without receiving any tidings, with savages who have only the countenance of human beings, among whom, instead of finding society or relief in sickness, he is daily exposed to perish and be massacred."[4]

After the Jesuits were ordered out of Louisiana in 1763, missionary activity among the Indians virtually collapsed. In the same year Spain ceded East and West Florida to England, and the new colonial government closed all the Catholic missions and converted into barracks the monastery

[4] John G. Shea, *A History of the Catholic Church* (New York, 1886), 575.

of St. Helena at St. Augustine. The Catholic Church claimed that the English made wholesale seizures of the property of the converted natives and forced many of them into the wilderness of barbarism from which they had earlier been claimed.[5]

Evidence seems to support the Catholic contention that the hands of their missionaries were cleaner in dealings with the Indians than those of the Protestant missionaries. A Catholic critic of the Protestant missionaries who worked in the Carolinas and Georgia has spared no criticism. The Indians, he wrote, "are expected to embrace Christianity at the persuasion of a speculating preacher, with a Bible in one hand and a Government grant for their land in the other. Fire-water, the rifle, and legalized robbery are the weapons of *his* spiritual warfare, varied by a barrel of bad meat, a sack of musty flour, and a shoddy blanket, as specimens of evangelical perfections, in mock fulfillment of a violated treaty." Another Catholic writer holds that frontiersmen believed that "the Indian had to be crushed before he could be civilized, and even then it was caging rather than civilizing that was attempted. The Catholic missionaries were almost the only friends the Indians had." Herbert E. Bolton, an exacting student of Catholic missions, believed that the Spanish missions in Florida and other sections constituted a force that made for the preservation of the Indians in contrast to their destruction on the Anglo-American frontier. Since they had been sent to America and were supported from Europe, the Catholic missionaries were able to stay aloof in moral rectitude from the people around them who were by any means seizing the Indian country. On the other hand, despite their own willingness

[5] J. J. O'Connell, *Catholicity in the Carolinas and Georgia* (New York, 1879), 586. Also see Philbert F. Watrin, "Memoir on the Louisiana Missions," *American Catholic Historical Researches* (Pittsburgh and Philadelphia), XVII (1917), 89-93.

to countenance injustice, the Protestant missionaries were supported by congregations near them; they could be more easily smothered in the shifts of population than their Catholic counterparts.[6]

After an absence of sixty years, the Jesuits returned in 1823 to the banks of the Mississippi to begin again the work from which they had been so unfairly snatched. They returned to find that the white man living in the Indian country had little desire to civilize the Indians. This condition and the poverty of the Catholic Church in America restricted its interest in Indian missions, for that undertaking promised little success in the face of the fierce rush to frontier land.[7]

The work of the church may well be read as it was personified in the activities of Father Stephen Badin. Having spent the best years of his life in Kentucky, Badin urged Propaganda to increase the church's mission to the Indians in the Southwest. Pressing his plea, in 1828 he sought aid from the Pope, received an audience but small encouragement because the bishops had reported practically no conversions among the Indians. Badin insisted that the Protestants were spending both men and money with some success, but even that argument availed him nothing. Then he requested and received an assignment to the Indians in the Old Northwest. There the old priest spent five disappointing years as he watched the land-hungry people push the Indians westward.[8]

The first missionary work by Protestants in the territory south of the Ohio River was performed by the Moravians, who played only a minor role in the total religious life of the area. Early pushing westward in Pennsylvania and North

  [6] O'Connell, Catholicity, 586; Maynard, Catholic Church and American Idea, 76; Bolton, "The Mission as a Frontier Institution in the Spanish American Colonies," American Historical Review, XXIII (1917-1918), 42-61.
  [7] Goodykoontz, Home Missions, 232.
  [8] Schauinger, Badin, Chaps. XVI-XIX.

Carolina, the Moravians accepted the evangelization of the Cherokee Indians as their major missionary project. After several exploratory trips by various officials of the church, Abraham Steiner in 1799 talked with leading Cherokees in council and a year later gained their consent to establish a mission among them. Obtaining a plantation, adjoining the land of the Vann family, near the present Chatsworth in northwest Georgia, the Moravians commenced religious instruction at Spring Place in the summer of 1801. More interested in education than in religion, the Cherokees demanded a school, which was opened in 1804. Among those who received schooling were John Ridge, James Vann, and Buck Oowatie, later renamed Elias Boudinot after the prominent supporter of Indian missions.

After the arrival of the Reverend John Gambold and his wife in 1805, the mission and particularly the school expanded their labors. The Gambolds, like most missionaries, counted their successes in terms of actual conversions to Christianity and additions to church membership. As they complained of their ineffectual outreach, based on the fact that nine years had elapsed before one adult accepted the white man's religion, the Gambolds failed to mention that their presence had been tolerated for sixteen years and that Indian children had been entrusted to their care. In 1821, after the death of his wife, Gambold established the Oothcalgoa Mission about fifteen miles south of Spring Place and a few miles east of Calhoun, Georgia. Both missions flourished under the active and devoted guidance of Gambold until his death in 1827. In 1830 Spring Place had thirty-one pupils and Oothcalgoa had fifteen. They continued as centers of Cherokee education until 1838—a singularly long existence.[9]

The personal interest of Gideon Blackburn, a Presbyterian

[9] Henry T. Malone, *Cherokees of the Old South* (Athens, Ga., 1956), 91-96.

minister in Maryville, Tennessee, in the Cherokees of east
Tennessee initiated the plans for a mission there. Black-
burn's enthusiasm for the work was whetted by the report
of Joseph Bullen, a Presbyterian missionary returning to
New York in 1800 from a short tour, financed by the New
York Missionary Society, to the Chickasaws in Mississippi.
Although Blackburn makes no acknowledgment of his awareness of the Moravian mission in the Cherokee Nation, it is
very likely that news of it had reached him. In 1803
Blackburn presented a request for a mission to the General
Assembly of the Presbyterian Church. The assembly appropriated two hundred dollars to educate Cherokee children
and appointed Blackburn as part-time missionary to the
Cherokees. Blackburn's friends in east Tennessee raised an
additional $430 for the undertaking. Carrying letters of
recommendation from the president of the United States and
the secretary of war, Blackburn in October 1803, at the
time of the distribution of the annuity, presented his
program to two thousand Indians assembled. From them he
received approval for the mission and a promise to send
children to a school to be established at Hiwassee. By the
spring of 1804 some twenty Cherokee children were receiving in the English language instruction that led visitors to
say the progress "exceeded all belief." Although the children's interest in learning was not great, the granting of
prizes secured happy results. Upon requests Blackburn in
1806 established a second school on South Sale Creek near
its confluence with the Tennessee River. Since the Presbyterian General Assembly would support only one school,
Blackburn found it necessary to travel a great deal in
order to solicit money from private sources. In one seven-
month tour in 1807 he obtained more than five thousand
dollars in addition to books and clothing. Within four years
from the initial effort over three hundred children had

received instruction in the two schools. No mission had a more auspicious beginning than this.[10]

Encouraged by the fine cooperation from the Indians, the General Assembly increased its financial support to five hundred dollars annually from 1806 to 1809. Having ample students and a satisfactory financial support, the missions had reasons to expect continued prosperity. Blackburn had initiated a program of agricultural improvement and had introduced a form of civil government. His concept of mission work was excellent. Taking inventory of the Indians' progress, he made a bold pronouncement: "The Cherokee nation has at length determined to become men and citizens." Then musing on his own role, he depicted himself well as a dreamer and an idealist: "If a Cherokee passing my grave may justly point his finger to the green turf, and say, there lies my deliverer, I shall think the eulogy more honorable than the bust of marble. . . ."[11]

The turn of events was soon to prove that the life of these two missions depended on the leadership of Blackburn. With a magnetic personality and "a great deal of vanity," Blackburn was able to transfer his enthusiasm and idealism to others, and by the same token to obscure his weakness. Blackburn was essentially a promoter, leaving sound management to others. For the missions he had made no solid basis for operation nor any long-range program. Pressed by financial strain and impaired health, Blackburn in 1810 decided to leave the missions. The immediate debts he met

[10] References for this paragraph can be found in Posey, *Presbyterian Church*, notes 8-17, pp. 160-61. For a recent study of Protestant missions to American Indians see Robert F. Berkhofer, Jr., *Salvation and the Savage* (Lexington, Ky., 1965).

[11] Joseph Tracy, *History of the American Board of Commissioners for Foreign Missions* (New York, 1842), 68; *Evangelical Intelligencer* (Philadelphia), II (1808), 41. Also see "An Account of the Origin and Progress of the Mission to the Cherokee Indians; in a Series of Letters from the Rev. Gideon Blackburn," *Panoplist* (Boston), III (1807-1808), 39-40, 84-86, 322-23, 416-18, 475-76, 567-68.

by the sale of his farm, but he was unable to transfer to others his power of inspiration. Despite large enrollments and adequate teaching, the two schools closed within a year.[12]

Seven years elapsed before another mission was established in the Cherokee Nation. This was sponsored by the American Board of Commissioners for Foreign Missions, whose chief concern was the advancement of missionary work among the Indians. This board had been formed in 1810 by the Congregational Church, which had invited closely related churches to participate in the program. Until 1837 this board was the common agent of the Congregational, Presbyterian, Dutch, and German Reformed churches. For a period this arrangement functioned so smoothly that it is often difficult to distinguish between the contributions of the Presbyterian and Congregational churches to the work among Southern Indians. By 1830 three-fourths of all members belonging to churches under the care of the board were North American Indians.[13]

The earliest efforts of the board in the South resulted in the establishment in 1817 of the Chickamauga Mission, renamed Brainerd a year later, on a tract of land within the city limits of present-day Chattanooga, Tennessee. When President Monroe visited the mission in 1819, he was so pleased with the plan that he ordered the Indian agent to pay an accumulated debt of the mission and to provide additional money for a much needed building. Beginning in this year Congress appropriated ten thousand dollars yearly to aid missions to the Indians. By 1821 the federal government was allotting from this sum one thousand dollars annually toward the support of Brainerd.[14]

12 Messrs. John F. Schermerhorn and Samuel J. Mills to Rev. Dr. Holmes (1813), Andover Newton Theological Seminary; Alexander, *Synod of Tennessee*, 44; J. Orin Oliphant (ed.), *Travels through the South and West with Jeremiah Evarts in 1826* (Lewisburg, Pa., 1956), 136-38.

13 John M. Linn, "The Relation of the Church to the Indian Question," *Presbyterian Review* (New York), I (1880), 682.

Emphasizing the manual labor school, the American Board erected houses and barns on the small farms on which the missions were located. Provided with tools, livestock, and time for labor, the students learned good farming methods and contributed to the support of the schools. Wise leaders like Cyrus Kingsbury and Samuel A. Worcester encouraged the participation of Indians in the active work of the church. Between 1818 and 1824 nine Indians joined the Presbyterian Church. In the next four-year period there were 219 members of this church in the Cherokee Nation. It is reasonable to attribute much of this extended outreach of the mission to the assistance from Indians who without "a systematic course of study" had been licensed to serve as catechists, to conduct sacramental meetings, and to preach. Among such distinguished Cherokees were John Huss, John Wayne, and James Holmes. The board gave encouragement to Sequoyah, a remarkable Cherokee, who developed a written language from eighty-two symbols. In 1828 he set up at New Echota a printing press which published a newspaper, the *Cherokee Phoenix*. Financed by the American Board one thousand copies of the Gospel of Matthew and eight hundred copies of hymns were printed in the Cherokee language. Working here in the several missions were men whose vision was leading to the improvement of social life for the Indian congruent with his native way and not remolding it according to the white man's pattern.[15]

The Baptist churches were slow in sending missionaries to the Indians in the West. The Triennial Convention meeting in Philadelphia in 1817 took cognizance of the need and selected Isaac McCoy to go to Indiana and Humphrey Posey to work among the Cherokees in North Carolina and

---

[14] See Robert S. Walker, *Torchlights to the Cherokees: The Brainerd Mission* (New York, 1931), passim.

[15] Tracy, *American Board*, 150, 166-67, 236; Malone, *Cherokees*, 157-70.

Tennessee. By 1820 Posey had established a mission, modeled on the pattern of the American Board, at Valley Towns on the Hiwassee River along the southern boundary of North Carolina. Adequate buildings were constructed on an eighty-acre farm, well supplied with stock and tools. Although none had joined the church until 1823, the Cherokees were cordial to the mission and within ten years about two hundred had identified themselves with it in some way. The superintendent spoke of them as "communicants," an elusive term. Among them was Jesse Bushyhead, who became an ordained preacher and an effective worker among his people. The Indians wanted workers among them who could speak their language, and since few missionaries were able or willing to learn the tribe's language, the most effective workers were recruited from the Indians. The Indians were eager to read, but a shortage of books and reading matter in the Cherokee language greatly impeded the progress of the school. From the outside the white settlers were antagonistic to the mission and opposed the work of the missionaries. In 1821 the Baptists established a second station among the Cherokees. Duncan O'Briant supervised the work at Tinsawattie in Georgia. After working seven years with no marked success, O'Briant decided that the situation was poor and that the school and mission should be moved to Hickory Log, ten miles down the Etowah River. There the mission flourished with eighty families living under O'Briant's direction.[16] When the tribe emigrated to Arkansas in 1831, O'Briant accompanied them and continued his labors until his death in 1834.

In its earlier years the Methodist Church did not distinguish itself in organized missionary activities with the

---

[16] William Gammell, *A History of American Baptist Missions* (Boston, 1849), 314-28 passim; Isaac McCoy, *History of Baptist Indian Missions* (Washington, 1840), 390-94, 572-73; *General Convention of the Baptist Denomination* (1833), 27.

Indians. Following the examples set by Wesley, Bishops
Coke and Asbury, later Methodist preachers declared all
their work to be missionary in purpose and busied themselves with the hasty extension of the church. There was
much talk about administering to the needs of the Indians,
but no one initiated a hard-core missionary program. In
July 1789 Asbury wrote a letter to Cornplanter, chief of the
Seneca Nation, and then recorded in his journal: "I hope
God will shortly visit these outcasts of men, and send
messengers to publish the glad tidings of salvation amongst
them." The attitude which his remark revealed was that
assumed by later missionaries in their relations with the
Indians. Lacking appreciation of Indian life and culture,
the missionary approached his task as a reformer. Generally
the contact of the Methodist preacher with the Indians was
brief. If the circuit took him into some Indian country, the
preacher willingly described with English words the attri-
butes of the Great White Father to any Indians he could
assemble, then rode on, leaving behind a grim picture
reflected in the actions of the land-hungry whites.[17]

Spurred by the work of James Stewart, a mulatto who had
labored independently for two years among the tribes in
the Northwest, the Ohio Conference in 1819 established the
Methodist Wyandot Mission under the care of Stewart and
James Montgomery.[18] The missionary spirit manifested itself
elsewhere about the same time. In 1819 the Missionary
Society of the Methodist Church in New York was organized, and, as the parent society, provided the impetus for
the General Conference of 1820 to encourage the formation
of auxiliaries and to support missionaries.

In the same year the Tennessee Conference of the
Methodist Church appropriated twenty-seven dollars to be

[17] Asbury, *Journal*, II, 57.
[18] See Chap. IV in William W. Sweet, *Circuit-Rider Days along the Ohio*
(New York, 1923).

divided between two preachers to be appointed to the mission in Jackson's Purchase, the western portion of Kentucky and Tennessee only recently acquired from the Chickasaw Indians. The mission was divided into two parts: the North Mission included all the land north of the South Fork of the Obion River in the general area of Reelfoot Lake, and the South Mission extended from there to the Mississippi line. By 1822 four preachers served the two missions from which they received $162.17 plus $98.62½ from the Deficiency Fund. No wonder Lewis Garrett, one of the four preachers, felt compelled in 1823 to write these pathetic but uncomplaining words: "Under these circumstances we have the opportunity of administering to our necessities, as long as our private funds will enable us to do so; then we must desist; but our reward is with our Master." This project seems to have had no specific connection with the Indians except its location. Four itinerant preachers worked in the area, but they established no mission posts nor schools as an Indian center. In 1822 the conference report shows 576 white and 6 Negro church members in the South and North missions. However, since the *Minutes* list Indians among the whites, the procedure defeats a numerical test of the effectiveness of the mission among the Indians. One may be sure, nevertheless, that the whites were numerous in this area which had so recently been opened for settlement.[19]

In January 1821 the Methodists set in motion a genuine missionary campaign when Bishop McKendree appointed William Capers as "Missionary in South Carolina Conference and to the Indians." Few men came to a job better equipped than Capers. Thirty years old, disciplined by college training, naturally amiable and intelligent, he possessed the

---

[19] "An Account of the Mission in Jackson's Purchase," *Methodist Magazine* (New York), VI (1823), 234, 236. See *Minutes of the Annual Conferences*, I, 364, 368, 382, 387.

necessary qualifications and ability for the arduous and exacting assignment. Capers first turned his attention to the Creek Nation which the Presbyterians had neglected in favor of more promising fields. Within eighteen months he had raised $2,200—the result of traveling hundreds of miles and preaching almost that many sermons in behalf of the Indians. He immediately planned two manual labor schools for Indian children. The principal one was to be called Asbury and located near Fort Mitchell, one mile west of the Chattahoochee River; and the second school to be also in Alabama near the Indian town of Tuckabatchee on the Tallapoosa River. The plans for Asbury reached reality. Capers had an interview with the Creek chief, William McIntosh, who agreed to submit the project to a general council. In November 1821 the council consented to grant all land necessary for the mission.[20]

Asbury School was established in 1822 on a small farm. Four years later the school had only twenty-five acres in cultivation and about thirty head of cattle. Some of the Creek chiefs had opposed the admission of the missionaries to the nation, and those chiefs who had consented to the establishment of the school paid not the slightest attention to the preaching. Without cooperation from the Creeks, the school as a mission center functioned poorly. From the annual appropriation for aid to Indian schools the federal government made grants in 1824 to twenty-four schools, mostly those of the Presbyterian and Baptist origin. Asbury did not receive one dollar from the government during its existence, probably because of the inferior quality of teaching and opposition to the mission from the Indians. The Indian agent, Colonel John Crowell, was hostile to the mission and did much to hinder its work. In addition to the specific

[20] For Capers' excellent background and training see William M. Wightman, *Life of William Capers . . . Including an Autobiography* (Nashville, 1859), passim.

oppositions, there were minor feuds, migrations, and general uncertainties that militated against mission and school. Under these poor circumstances the school managed to teach some reading, writing, grammar, and arithmetic, and competent judges expressed high regard for the quality of the instruction. Although fifty "scholars" attended the school in 1829, conditions were too unstable for Asbury to remain open more than a year longer. The Creek territory proved to be the most difficult of all the fields attempted by any of the churches.[21]

The Methodist circuit rider was as warmly received by the Cherokees as had been his earlier competitor in this missionary race. The continuing cordiality speaks well for the conduct and judgment of the representatives of the Moravians, Presbyterians, American Board, and Baptists who were already established in the nation. In the spring of 1822 Richard Neely, assistant on the Paint Rock Circuit of the Huntsville District in Alabama, accepted the invitation to preach at the home of Richard Riley, a prominent Cherokee half-breed living twelve miles south of Fort Deposit. Within a short time Neely formed a society of thirty-three members and designated Riley as the teacher. The success of this beginning prompted the annual conference in October 1822 to establish a mission in the Cherokee Nation. A committee chose Andrew J. Crawford as missionary. Crawford, whose experiences at the mission in west Tennessee were profitable, selected for the mission a site near Riley's home. Following the advice of Riley, Crawford opened a school in December with twelve children who soon increased

---

[21] Wightman, *William Capers*, 241-45; Paine, *M'Kendree*, II, 447-52; Anson West, *A History of Methodism in Alabama* (Nashville, 1893), 367-80. "The proximity of the dissipated whites, and their unhallowed example, together with the confirmed habits of savageism, rendered it necessary for the missionaries, in 1830, to abandon the field in despair." William P. Strickland, *History of the Missions of the Methodist Episcopal Church* (Cincinnati, 1854), 76.

to twenty. Some mild opposition to preaching soon subsided, and the Cherokees welcomed both the teacher and the preacher.

At a two-day camp meeting, beginning on July 13, 1823, the Indians furnished comfortable accommodations and abundant food for all who attended. Many of the Indians had traveled from considerable distances to attend the white man's religious festival. Although few of the natives could understand or speak English, twenty-five adults and twenty children were baptized and admitted to the church. After the meeting closed many remained seeking "favor with the Great Spirit," or, having enjoyed the spectacle, they were reluctant to leave. One of the wealthiest Indians proposed that the meeting should continue as long as the food lasted.

In 1823 the Tennessee Conference divided the Cherokee Indian mission into the northern section lying wholly in Tennessee and the southern largely in Alabama. In the latter, free from competition with other churches, the Methodists achieved their greatest success. Here Richard Neely rode a large circuit, preaching anywhere he could get a congregation. Within five years Neely, broken in health from repeated exposures on his circuit, fell a victim to consumption and died in 1828. At this time the Cherokee Mission contained 675 members and 7 preachers in as many stations. After 1830 the membership steadily declined because of Indian migrations, inroads of whites, and competition with other churches. Work continued in the Holston region until 1838 when the last preacher to the Indians transferred to Arkansas.[22]

The Creeks had presented a resistant front to the overtures made by any denomination to send missionaries to their

[22] For Methodist missions among the Cherokees see West, *Methodism in Alabama*, 383-403; McFerrin, *Methodism in Tennessee*, III, 206-209, 269-70; "Report of the Tennessee Conference Missionary Society," *Methodist Magazine*, VII (1824), 192-95; "Cherokee Mission," *Methodist Magazine*, IX (1826), 35-36.

nation. In fact, the Creeks wanted no part of the white man's civilization, for they had long been plagued by the knavery of traders and depredations of the whites. Vulnerably located along the rivers draining into the Gulf of Mexico, the Creek territory had been invaded many times by strangers and their vices. Whisky had been brought into the country in great quantities, and the Indians consumed it excessively. In 1817 the Mississippi Baptist Association requested that two missionaries should visit the Creeks, but those sent made no tangible inroads. In 1822 in the same year which the Methodists had opened Asbury School in Alabama, the Baptists tried a similar mission among the Creeks at Withington on the Tallapoosa River near the Alabama boundary. Under the guidance of Lee Compere, the school struggled along for four years, and when the situation worsened the Charleston Association abandoned its costly effort in 1829. Its most obvious achievement was the teaching of twenty youths to read portions of the New Testament.[23]

Surprisingly the Baptists succeeded even less among the Choctaws and Chickasaws than among the Creeks. Here and there a reference is found to the appointment of a missionary to travel through the Chickasaw Nation, but no school or mission seems to have materialized. The Baptists were so short of preachers in the Mississippi region that they were unable to accept any call from the Indians. For some unjustifiable reason the Presbyterians feared the Baptists would compete with them for the opportunity of converting the Choctaw Indians.

Settlers moving into the Mississippi Territory brought news of the mission schools they had seen or heard about as they came through the Cherokee country. Rumors of such reached the Mississippi Choctaws, who numbered about

[23] Gammell, *American Baptist Missions*, 328; *American Baptist Magazine*, VII (1827), 168-69.

two thousand living in three groups. Needing help to increase their independence in the face of white infiltration, the Choctaws petitioned the American Board to establish a mission in their country. In 1818 Cyrus Kingsbury was sent from Brainerd to open a mission at Eliot, on the Yalobusha River near the site of present-day Grenada. Following the community pattern which earlier he had used successfully, Kingsbury within a year had directed the building of log cabins, a mill, carpenter and blacksmith shops, and a school house. By the winter of 1819-1820 fifty pupils were enrolled in the school. Entries in the manuscript Journal of the Brethren at Eliot for the year 1819 alternate in sentiment between gloom and hope—the recounting of needs, problems, sickness, short rations, liquor, and witchcraft interspersed with the success of teaching youngsters, generosity of whites and Indians, and the good prospects for the future. A recorder noted that on May 18, 1820, Adam Hodgson, an English traveler, had visited the school and had left a little money for the library. A second mission was established at Mayhew, near the Alabama line, in present Oktibbeha County. Both missions flourished, maintaining large schools on the locations and smaller schools at the houses of some of the Indians. The missions were so efficiently managed that a surplus existed in the operation fund, and Kingsbury in 1823 offered to return one thousand dollars to the American Board.[24]

A congenial reciprocity was maintained by the Indians and the missionaries, and by 1828 the American Board had five representatives in the Choctaw Nation. Needless to say, the missionaries were not pleased by the Indians' noncommittal attitude to religious conversions. Within the first ten years of this missionary endeavor, many Negro slaves and

[24] William B. Morrison, *The Red Man's Trail* (Richmond, 1932), 45-50. The journal is among the papers of the American Board of Commissioners for Foreign Missions, Harvard University—hereafter cited as Harvard. Also see Tracy, *American Board*, 132-33, 193.

"white vagrants" had joined the church, but only four Indians. Despite their obvious indifference, the Indians in great numbers attended the religious gatherings, and their presence quickened the perseverance of the preachers. Finally the Indians developed a slight interest in Christianity and made some inquires about its benefits. To missionaries accustomed to indifference or passive rejection, this overt interest was like a "religious wave" and some even ventured to speak of it as such. The board continued its program among the Choctaws, which reached its greatest extent in eight stations served by four missionaries with twenty-seven assistants, and slightly more than three hundred church members. Its twelve years of missionary efforts among the Choctaws alone cost a total in excess of $100,000.[25]

The successes of the American Board were at no time approximated by that of a single denomination working among the Indians. The board received considerable support from various Presbyterian organizations such as the Synod of Mississippi and Alabama. Meeting at Mayhew in November 1829 in the Choctaw Nation, the synod passed a resolution against any attempt to remove the Indians. Already the Gospel was having a salutary effect and had "begun to dispel the darkness of heathen ignorance, degradation and sin." A year later the narrative of the synod's action charged intemperance and even murder on the part of unprincipled men seeking "to produce apostacy among the native converts."[26]

A very fair comparison with the American Board is apparent in the alternations of prosperity and adversity which harassed Choctaw Academy established near George-

[25] View of the Missions (n. p., 1828), 10-11; Morrison, Red Man's Trail, 48, 51; Tracy, American Board, 208-209, 223; Mary E. Young, Redskins, Ruffleshirts, and Rednecks: Indian Allotments in Alabama and Mississippi, 1830-1860 (Norman, Okla., 1961), 18.

[26] Extracts from the Records of the Synod of Mississippi and South Alabama, from 1829 to 1835 (Princeton, N. J., 1835), 5-6, 11.

town, Kentucky, by the Kentucky Baptist Society for Propagating the Gospel. The sponsoring organization, having solicited "the assistance and patronage of the religious public" in the behalf of the "aborigines of our beloved country," established a school for boys in 1818. Opening in the spring of 1819 with eight Indian boys from Missouri, the school was largely supported by federal grants. When contributions from the Baptist churches dropped in 1820 and 1821, the board of managers deemed it wise to close the school and to open another at a new site among the Indians, but no undertaking was made for several years. About 1825 some Choctaw chiefs requested Richard M. Johnson personally to educate their children. Johnson, long sensitive to the pressing need for the evangelization of the Indians, agreed to open a school if the Baptist Mission Society would act as an overseer. In the fall of 1825 Johnson, on his estate at Blue Spring, opened his school with twenty-five pupils. Supported largely by a treaty payment from the federal government of six thousand dollars annually, the school reached its maximum enrollment of ninety-eight within three years. It continued as a private project with only a nominal Baptist control until 1845.[27]

The Cumberland Presbyterian Church, distinctly evangelical in origin, early in its existence acknowledged some responsibility for the Indians. In 1819 Samuel King and Robert Bell went as evangelists to the Chickasaws and Choctaws in Mississippi. Meeting with an assemblage of chiefs at the house of Levi Colbert, an influential Chickasaw, the missionaries arranged in 1820 to open a school at Cotton Gin Port on the Tombigbee River. Following the accepted model of a school on a farm, King and Bell arranged to buy thirty acres. The school had an average

[27] *Proceedings of the Board of Managers for the Auxiliary Baptist Mission Society* (Georgetown, Ky., ca. 1819), 2; Leland W. Meyer, *The Life and Times of Colonel Richard M. Johnson* (New York, 1932), 347-78 passim.

enrollment of thirty-five pupils, one-third of whom paid their own expenses. For the support of the school the federal government gave about three hundred dollars a year and the church contributed twice as much. Subscription lists pledging aid ranged from twenty-five cents to ten dollars and from a pair of socks to a coat. Located in the path of migration, the school shared the fluctuating fortune of the Indians when the white settlers pushed into the territory. When financial assistance from the church and the government ceased in 1830, Bell sought to continue the school as a personal project. The final chapter was closed in 1832 by the Treaty of Pontotoc Creek in which the Choctaws ceded all their lands east of the Mississippi River. This small and struggling young church could proudly claim one thousand Choctaw members by the time of the Civil War.[28]

Excited by the activity of the American Board, the Presbyterian Synod of South Carolina and Georgia sent in 1820 T. C. Stuart and Daniel Humphreys to determine the prospects for missions among the Creeks and Chickasaws in Alabama and Mississippi. Furnished with several documents from the War Department and a letter from John C. Calhoun, Secretary of War, the missionaries entered the Chickasaw Nation whose principal villages were located in the present Mississippi counties of Pontotoc, Lee, and Chickasaw. After spending a short time at the hospitable home of Levi Colbert, the missionaries met a group of chiefs at the home of James Colbert, where they outlined plans for schools to which the Indians readily agreed. A site was selected and named Monroe, not far from the present town of Pontotoc. The first building used for a church was about sixteen feet square, built of poles, with a single batten

---

[28] McDonnold, *Cumberland Presbyterian Church*, 129-41; Thomas H. Campbell, *Studies in Cumberland Presbyterian History* (Nashville, 1944), 193-95.

window held on by hinges. It was heated by a large, open fireplace built into a chimney of dirt and sticks. Within two years a farm of one hundred acres had been cleared, buildings erected, and fifty children enrolled in a school largely made up of boarders. The whole endeavor continued very satisfactorily until the Chickasaws ceded their lands in 1834. Eventually in different parts of the nation four schools were established in which over one hundred pupils annually learned to read and write, or, in the case of a few, to find an opportunity to run away. After the first two schools had been established the chiefs appropriated five thousand dollars to build two more schools and promised half the amount yearly for support. By 1831, ten years after its establishment, the mission had three stations, two missionaries, one licensed preacher, and seven assistants.[29]

Holding fast to their own missionary techniques, the Methodists relied on the itinerant preacher and the camp meeting as effective ways to reach the Indians. At a time when most missions were suffering from unstable conditions between the Indians and the settlers, the Mississippi Conference sent in 1827 Alexander Talley, a doctor turned preacher, to work without station among the Choctaws in northern Mississippi. He made a firm friendship with Greenwood Leflore, chief of the Western District, whose influence and assistance explain much of Talley's success. Complying with the request of Leflore and other leading Choctaws, Talley arranged a camp meeting, which was held in August 1828, and recruited the aid of several Methodist preachers. Proceeding after the manner of earlier camp meetings in Tennessee and Kentucky, Talley brought many Indians under the spell of his preaching; among them was Leflore and several members of his family. At this and other camp

[29] George Howe, *History of the Presbyterian Church in South Carolina* (2 vols.; Columbia, 1870-1883), II, 405-406, 429-32; E. T. Winston, *"Father" Stuart and the Monroe Mission* (Meridian, Miss., n. d.), 22. Also see Thompson, *Presbyterians in the South*, Chap. XIII.

meetings the "falling exercise" was just as common among the Indians as it had been in the earlier revivals in Kentucky and Tennessee. The general effect must have been much the same, for one writer has commented that "souls were renewed, and sins forgiven." When the next annual conference met in Tuscaloosa, Alabama, in December 1828, Talley was present, accompanied by several Indian converts. Bishop Joshua Soule and the entire conference were impressed by the report made by one of the Indians.[30]

The Methodist Church lay claim in a three-year period to four thousand Choctaws "in communion." This accession to the Methodist Church is quite large in comparison to the small number of Choctaws which identified themselves with other denominations. The churches connected with the American Board had had altogether only three hundred additions in a thirteen-year period. It is only reasonable to attribute this wide variance either to the attractive gospel preached by the Methodists or to the laxity with which the Methodists accepted converts or to both.

As the whites found the soil of Georgia, Alabama, Mississippi, and Louisiana especially fine for the growth of cotton, they made persistent demands for the Indians' lands, arguing that cultivation of such good land would benefit the national economy. The federal government was highly sympathetic, as a rule, with the demands of the frontiersmen and negotiated a series of treaties by which the Indians ceded their lands. Such treaties followed each other in rapid succession. By the treaty of Dancing Rabbit Creek, September 27, 1830, the Choctaws surrendered their title to all lands in Mississippi. Missionaries of the American Board had strenuously opposed the treaty and gave such overt expression to their opposition that they were barred from the signing ceremony. In 1830, despite much resistance

---

[30] Jones, *Methodism . . . Mississippi Conference*, II, 165-81; Strickland, *Missions of the Methodist Church*, 84.

from groups of humanitarians, Congress passed a general Indian removal bill, a measure by which the Indians were to exchange their land holdings in the East for the public domain in the West. Although the law provided no means for the removal of the Indians, President Jackson gave teeth to the bite. Within a decade the entire region containing the nations in this study had been cleared of all Indians except those who had secured allotments or had stealthily eluded the agents. All the chiefs who had worked for the treaty were given large grants of land. The Christian motives were brought into question in regard to the activities of Greenwood Leflore who was given fifteen thousand acres of land in the Mississippi delta, on which he remained until his death.[31] Having no choice and no adequate champion, the less fortunate Indian made his exodus.

Neither time nor circumstance has been able to erase or dim the heartless avarice which Georgians displayed in their relations with the Indians. In 1830 the state legislature, in order to control Indian sympathizers, passed a law requiring all white men living in Indian territory to secure a permit to reside there and to take an oath of allegiance to the state. When Samuel A. Worcester and Elizur Butler, American Board missionaries to the Indians, ignored the regulations, they were arrested and sentenced to four years in the penitentiary. Concerning the action of these men, the *Jesuit*, a paper published in Boston, made a peculiar editorial comment on April 30, 1831: "The pious missionaries found this situation, in the Cherokee country, an eligible one; their passion, for idleness, luxury, and gain, was gratified." It then commended Georgia for its stand toward the mis-

---

[31] David Folsom to Elias Cornelius, July 9, 1819, Harvard; H. S. Halbert, "The Story of the Treaty of Dancing Rabbit Creek," *Publications of the Mississippi Historical Society*, VI (1903), 373-90; Young, *Redskins, Ruffle-shirts, and Rednecks*, 47-50. Examine with care Miss Young's scholarly investigation of removal, speculation, and fraud in lands once possessed by the Indians in Mississippi and Alabama.

sionaries in their fight against Indian dispossession. This was a position perhaps not taken by any other Catholic Church paper and was completely contrary to the spirit of the Apostolic Letter of December 3, 1839, which reprimanded those who would deprive the Indian of his liberty, or buy, sell, or exchange him in slavery. This connivance or consent of the national government to Georgia's actions prompted Leonard Bacon to comment, "Never in American history has the issue been more squarely drawn between the kingdom of Satan and the kingdom of Christ." The Cherokees determinedly refused to deal with the United States commissioners who sought a treaty and successfully held their land longer than any other tribe. When pressed beyond the point of resistance, the chiefs finally ceded all their lands by treaty at New Echota in 1835. An army of seven thousand troops was required to overawe and quell the majority of the Indians who had opposed the treaty. By the winter of 1838-1839 the Cherokees were actually driven to the West in a shameful and disgraceful manner. About one-fourth of the sixteen thousand died from exposure and inadequate food.[32]

Missionaries who were on duty at the time of the actual removal of a tribe usually accompanied the Indians to their new lands in Arkansas and the Indian Territory. They were bonds with the past and the nuclei of activity as the Indians resettled themselves in new places. In many instances the removal of the Indians had been a stimulus for increased activity among the churches in the new locations. By 1833 the Methodists had organized six schools, provided nine missionaries in the Cherokee Nation, and enrolled 936 church members. Within a decade the membership had

---

[32] Malone, *Cherokees*, 175-78; Walker, *Torchlights to the Cherokees*, Chaps. XIX, XX; *Catholic Telegraph* (Cincinnati), March 14, 1840; Bacon, *American Christianity*, 267. For the removal see Grant Foreman, *Indian Removal: The Emigration of the Five Civilized Tribes* (Norman, Okla., 1932).

risen to thirteen hundred. Dr. Talley had accompanied the Choctaws from northern Mississippi and set up a school in which Choctaw was spoken. He had had portions of the Scriptures translated into the Indians' native tongue, and two hundred Indians were learning to read their language. His mission served 739 members in 1833; a year later he reported twelve schools with fifteen teachers and 362 pupils.[33]

In 1844 the Methodists formed an Indian Mission Conference bounded by the Missouri River on the north, the western state lines of Missouri and Arkansas on the east, the Red River on the south, and the Rocky Mountains on the west. Of an Indian membership totaling 4,339, the Indian Mission Conference held 3,557. In 1846 this enormous area fell within the jurisdictional limits of the newly formed Methodist Episcopal Church, South. Bishop Capers in 1847 attended the Indian conference in the Choctaw Indian Territory at Doaksville, about 140 miles southwest of Fort Smith. While there he preached at a camp meeting attended by eight hundred Indians, about half of whom could understand English to some degree. In 1854 the Methodist Church had 7,372 Indian members, while all other Protestant churches combined had only 4,945—proof of the great adaptability of the Methodists.[34]

The American Board and the Presbyterian Church followed the Indians to their new trans-Mississippi homes and increased the work already begun there. In 1820 the United Foreign Missionary Society had established a mission among the Osage Indians in western Arkansas, and in the following year had formed a second mission in Bates County, Missouri. By 1836 both missions had been abandoned. The American

[33] Wade C. Barclay, *Early American Methodism* (2 vols.; New York, 1950), II, 192-93.

[34] Barclay, *Early American Methodism*, 171; Strickland, *Missions of the Methodist Episcopal Church*, 83; Wightman, *William Capers*, 430; Paul N. Garber, *The Romance of American Methodism* (Greensboro, N. C., 1931), 315.

Board in 1820 had established Dwight Mission on Arkansas Creek and three years later had a school of sixty children. In 1831 a revival of religion occurred among the Cherokees in Arkansas. Many conversions to Christianity resulted from a three-day union meeting conducted by Presbyterians, Cumberland Presbyterians, and Methodists. Despite these apparent successes, the work lagged to the point that in 1836 the Presbyterian Church abandoned its mission in Arkansas for a field farther west with greater prospects. Although Presbyterians and the American Board scored some success, they could have done more had their missionaries held themselves less aloof from the Indians and had used "peculiar exertions to raise them from their benighted condition." D. S. Butrick, an American Board missionary at Brainerd, observed that the standards of the missionaries would not allow them to drop to the level of the Indians. Obviously he included himself in the offense when he wrote this indictment of his colleagues: "They will not come down far enough to take hold even of their blankets to lift them out of this horrible pit." He feared that the Indians would go to Baptist or Methodist meetings, "where they can find some one who does not feel above them, or they will excite such opposition as we cannot withstand."[35]

The antimissionary struggle within the various types of Baptist churches and the rise of Campbellism came at a difficult moment for the Baptists in their missionary work among the Indians. After the Indian removals the Missionary Baptist groups seem to have suddenly come to life. Concern over the fate of the Indians and activity in their behalf are evident in numerous places. In 1832 David Lewis, an ordained Baptist preacher, came to the assistance

[35] E. E. Stringfield, *Presbyterianism in the Ozarks* (n. p., 1909), 16-17; Tracy, *American Board*, 85, 94-95, 133; *Christian Intelligencer* (New York), Oct. 15, Dec. 24, 1831, Jan. 28, 1832; Butrick to American Board, Oct. 26, 1824, Harvard.

of John Davis, a Creek educated in Mississippi, who had conducted for two years a school for his people. Lewis organized a church fifteen miles west of Fort Gibson in the Indian Territory. In the same year Duncan O'Briant, who had emigrated with the Cherokees, built a church and opened a school seventy miles north of Fort Smith. The Baptists in Kentucky registered considerable concern over the fate of the Indians. The year 1842 brought concrete results to months of planning: The Long Run Association set forth a program for the "promotion of missions among the aborigines of America"; the Indian Mission Association was organized for the purpose of expanding the Indian cause throughout the Mississippi Valley, and a monthly journal *The Indian Advocate* was published in Louisville. The paper died with its editor Isaac McCoy in 1846; and the association dissolved in 1850. In 1843 the Baptist Convention of the Western District of Tennessee endorsed the work of the American Indian Mission Association. Scattered notations in the records of various associations indicate that small amounts of money were collected for its use. For example, in 1852 the Concord (Tennessee) Association raised $13.50 for the cause.[36]

The Baptists, in comparison with Methodists and Presbyterians, played a poor third role in the cause of Indian missions in the Great Valley. The individual congregations were rarely activated by support of an extensive missionary program. When financial contributions were inadequate locally, no central organization could force any compliance with the plans which had been received halfheartedly by a congregation feeling abhorrence of the Indians. The Baptist churches as such had neither the will nor the strength to defend, educate, or evangelize them.

Notwithstanding its genuine solicitude for the Indians,

[36] References for this paragraph can be found in Posey, *Baptist Church*, 86-87.

the Anglican Church in the American Colonies was of the
opinion that the Indian had "no capacity for English ways,
to say nothing for English religion." This attitude immediately defeated any chance for effective work among the
Indians, who never should have been remade according to
English fashions. Nevertheless, the English enrolled some
Indians at William and Mary College where they learned
to read and write English words which they promptly
forgot, having no need for them among their own people.
The Indian department at the college "never did the good
that its promoters had thought and hoped. The disposition
of the roving Indian who had been hemmed in only by the
gilded horizon and blue canopy of the heavens was not
adapted to academic walls. Many became dissatisfied in
school and pined away and died." The early enthusiasm for
this work came from England, but those at a distance little
understood the futility of their unwarranted optimism. After
the American Revolution the newly organized Protestant
Episcopal Church had a long struggle to remain alive. By
the decade of the thirties, when the church was getting a
tenuous hold in the West and South, the Indians had already
been removed.[37]

A church expanding across the Mississippi into Arkansas
and Texas could no longer afford to close its eyes to the
pressing need for some missionary work among the Indians.
In 1843 the Domestic Committee pleaded for a bishop to be
sent to the Indian Territory and for the raising of a twenty
thousand dollar endowment to support him. An agent was
sent to visit the area, arouse interest, and seek contributions.
In the General Convention of 1844 Bishop Stephen Elliott
pledged that two Savannah churches would pay five hundred
dollars yearly for three years in behalf of the Creeks and
Cherokees, former residents of Georgia. The domestic secretary urged support for aid to the Indian who should be

[37] Brewer, *Religious Education in the Episcopal Church*, 52.

considered as a ward of the church. The Reverend George
W. Freeman was chosen Missionary Bishop to Arkansas and
the Indian Territory. Evidently the necessary missionary
urge and church support were not adequate to the task
envisioned. As late as 1846 a correspondent to the *Western
Episcopalian,* visiting the Indian missions of the West, wrote
of "a people crushed, wronged, and peeled, who made
noble struggles for finding the true light, and rising into
importance, in spite of the devices of the enemy; and yet
what has the church done to aid these aspirations?" By
the time of the Civil War no missionary work of any consequence had been accomplished by the church among the
Indians who had been removed to the West.[38]

The followers of neither Stone nor Campbell seem to have
evinced any positive interest or activity in behalf of Indian
missions. Campbell was a late-comer on the Western religious scene, and problems germane to the building of his
new denomination pressed him daily more than those of the
Indians. The almost complete absence of references to
Indians in his two church journals, covering nearly half a
century, and in his own twelve hundred page *Memoirs* is
indicative of his unconcern for the Indians. As late as 1856
J. J. Trott, a Tennessee Disciples minister conscious of his
church's failure to serve the Indians, commented that if its
missionary society intended to do anything, there was a
promising field in the Indian Territory. Evidence of failure
is seen in Garrison and De Groot's excellent history of the
Disciples of Christ, whose ample index does not carry a
single reference to Indians. Although he kept his church from
involvement with the Indian missions, Alexander Campbell
had a deep and abiding sympathy for the Indians in their
struggles against injustices. Aroused by Georgia's treatment

[38] Julia C. Emery, *A Century of Endeavor, 1821-1921* (New York, 1921),
83-85; John N. Norton, *Life of Bishop Freeman of Arkansas* (New York,
1867), Chaps. XI, XII; *Spirit of Missions,* Oct. 1846, 353.

of the Cherokees, Campbell wrote an editorial on the greed
of capitalism. He made an appeal for justice, republicanism,
and integrity that would not allow the American people or
the Congress "to give up an innocent and harmless nation
to the cupidity of a few capitalists in Georgia or any where
else."[39]

It is doubtful that any church as an institution was pleased
with its Indian missions. A sense of competition motivated
the mission program in all denominations. Elias Cornelius,
who had toured the Southern states in 1816 for the Connecticut Missionary Society, wrote Cyrus Kingsbury at Eliot
in 1820: "I have long been satisfyed that in converting the
Heathen World—different denominations must occupy different portions of the great field & not blend their exertions
& thus interfere with each other & distract the attention of
the Heathen." He would let the Baptists have the Creeks,
the Methodists have the Chickasaws, and the American
Board keep those tribes with whom it then worked.[40]
Removed from the mission scene, a church counted success
or failure in terms of dollars spent and individuals converted
to Christianity. In that respect the books did not balance.
As a rule, however, the missions were operated on a low
cost basis. The initial outlay of money was frequently lost
because the mission was first located poorly and then moved
to a new site which had to be purchased and equipped.
After the federal government began paying annual grants to
assist in the support of the missions, the financial burden
on the churches was lessened.

All denominations tried the manual labor type mission,
using the school as the community center. The undertaking
that produced the most tangible results was the one which
had a stationed missionary who could supervise a farm

[39] *North-Western Christian Magazine* (Cincinnati), March 6, 1856, 332-
33; *Millennial Harbinger*, 1830, 46.
[40] Letter of March 8, 1820, Harvard.

program, teach techniques in food preparation to the women, and instruct the men in agricultural reforms. The missionary who had some knowledge of the languages of the Indians could work effectively as soon as he entered the mission field. While he was acquiring some language skill, he enlisted the aid of Indians who served as interpreters or actually worked independently as assistants. Huss, Bushyhead, Riley, and the Colberts were outstanding examples of Indians who served well in the missions.

The work of all missions was hampered by the lack of reading material. The missionary was forced into his own resources for teaching methods. Book learning was well received by only one tribe, and discipline was regarded as only a punitive device. As a teacher the missionary conducted himself only moderately well. As a representative of the white man's religion the missionary, with the exception of the early Catholic priest, was in a difficult position. Close contacts with mendacious settlers determined to dispossess the Indian of his fertile land did not support the spirit of love which, so the Indians had been told, was the key to Christianity. When theory and practice conflicted, the missionary lost face and his program collapsed.

Unfortunately for the missionary movement many of the accepted spokesmen for religion and for the West were definitely anti-Indian or wary of any hope of civilizing and Christianizing him. Timothy Flint believed that little success had characterized missionary efforts among the Indians and that changes could only come "among the children, whose inclinations and habits are yet to form." William H. Milburn, widely known and extensively traveled Methodist preacher, believed that "the Indian must perish," since all that had been done for him still left him as "an utter hopeless prospect." John M. Peck thought that Christianity should be carried to the Indian because he was "ferociously wicked," and a lover of fighting and plundering. Peck entertained no sympathy with "sickly sentimentality" which blamed the government or the pioneer for the frontier woes. On the other hand, a completely different picture can be found by sampling the thousands of letters written by missionaries of the American Board revealing true and abiding sympathy with the Indians surrounded by the greedy settlers. Others who worked with the red men, like Blackburn, Capers, McCoy, and Talley, would have testified, as did the Methodist Bishop Soule, that Christianity was suited for "every condition of the human race" and "whether man may be savage or civilized it is the gospel of his salvation."[41] There is much evidence to sustain the conviction of many that the missionary spent his years and efforts among the wrong people. The white settlers were really the ones who had needed a conversion to Christian ideals.

[41] Timothy Flint, *Recollections of the Last Ten Years* (Boston, 1826), 144-46; William H. Milburn, *The Pioneers, Preachers, and People of the Mississippi Valley* (New York, 1860), 457-58; John M. Peck, "The Last of the Pioneers," *Baptist Memorial* (New York), VII (1848), 190; "Extract of a Letter from the Rev. Bishop Soule," *Methodist Magazine*, XI (1828), 79.

8

THE NEGROES

SLAVERY HAD BEEN ADOPTED as a labor system in the New World early in the sixteenth century, but no general concern for the religious life of the Negroes was evident for at least two centuries. In 1724 Governor Bienville of Louisiana instituted the Black Code for the purpose of regulating and protecting the rapidly increasing slave population. Although the code imposed strict rules on the slaves, it also protected them from undue oppression from their masters, who were required to make it possible for them to enjoy the church privileges of baptism, marriage, and burial. Many of the slaveholders were Catholics often in name only; many were positively prejudiced against any work of evangelization and even opposed religious instruction on the plantations.[1]

In 1724 a Catholic missionary wrote to one of the directors of the Western Company complaining of some men who "live in a scandalous condition with their slaves." All manner of problems arose, especially with the military who were guilty of living openly and publicly with colored concubines. Evidence indicates little interest in the moral welfare of the Negroes. Not until 1729 did the Natchitoches parish record the baptism of a slave, "Piere, negrillon, son of Anera, Negro, and Fanchon, Negress."[2]

With the transfer of the Louisiana Territory to Spain in 1763 and then to the United States in 1803, the public concern for the spiritual welfare of the slaves changed little.

Bishop Cirillo de Barcelona traveled about the vast diocese and learned from the priests that there was little interest in protecting the morals of the Negroes. The bishop induced the King of Spain to issue on May 31, 1789, a Spanish Black Code which provided for chaplains on plantations, regulated work and amusement on Sunday and holy days, and insisted on marriage among slaves. The code was received with mixed emotion—favorably by some owners and guardedly by others. Neither the overseers nor the slaves had much regard for the marriage provision, and terms requiring the observance of Sunday as a day of rest were but idle words. Some Catholic writers insist that the American purchase of Louisiana brought a change for the worse, particularly since the American's philosophy of slave-holding assumed the inferior position of the Negro and classed him as mere chattel. Actually a comparatively liberal code assured to the slave a status above that of chattel, and to the freedman a position superior to that under Anglo-Saxon law or practice.[3]

However, in 1823 Father John M. Odin became so disturbed over the prevailing situation that he wrote: "American masters permit them [slaves] to marry in church and to practice their religion, but in Lower Louisiana, the French, for the most part, do not wish you to speak of instructing their slaves or of giving them the sacraments of matrimony; they are not even permitted to go to church."[4] In part this

[1] John T. Gillard, *Colored Catholics in the United States* (Baltimore, 1941), 68; John T. Gillard, *The Catholic Church and the American Negro* (Baltimore, 1929), 16-18.

[2] Baudier, *Catholic Church in Louisiana*, 33, 98, 127. See Madeleine H. Rice, *American Catholic Opinion in the Slavery Controversy* (New York, 1944), Chaps. I, II. In 1717 the French Crown granted to the Western Company, formed by the Scottish financier John Law, a charter which guaranteed a monopoly of trade in Louisiana. In return the company promised to transport three thousand slaves to the territory.

[3] Baudier, *Catholic Church in Louisiana*, 206; Rice, *Catholic Opinion*, 35-37.

[4] V. Alton Moody, "Slavery on Louisiana Sugar Plantations," *Louisiana Historical Quarterly*, VII (1924), 280.

is correct, but the Catholic Church had been so active in behalf of the slaves that it had alienated many planters by requiring that they support a chaplain to teach the Negroes. This demand caused such an economic hardship on many planters it had to be rescinded. The reaction against the regulation led to precautionary measures against meetings that might lead to insurrection. The area gained the reputation for excessive harshness toward the Negro. When some planters refused to kneel at the altar with their slaves, they were charged with driving them from the church. Isolated cases hardly warrant the charge. In fact, the records seem to support the contention that slaves received more humane treatment in the later years of Spanish control than in the English colonies in a similar period of development. Furthermore, there is evidence that some owners encouraged the Negroes to imitate them in religious customs in matters of marriage, funerals, and worship in general.

In Louisiana definite efforts were made to instruct the slaves in the Christian religion. The Ursuline nuns organized classes and taught Negro girls and women. In 1818 Bishop Louis W. DuBourg's inspiration led to the founding of the Christian Doctrine of New Orleans, an organization whose work was largely devoted to the spiritual care of the Negro. In 1842 Bishop Antoine Blanc and his vicar general, Father Etienne Rousselon, organized a community of colored sisters into the Congregation of the Sisters of the Holy Family, which was dedicated to the care of aged Negroes and orphans of Negroes. Here and there priests defied the will of the community or of the government authorities in order to instruct Negroes.[5]

Many of the Catholic settlers in early Kentucky either brought slaves or bought them later. Priests like Badin and Flaget owned and traded slaves for personal use or for

[5] Annie L. W. Stahl, "The Free Negro in Ante-Bellum Louisiana," *Louisiana Historical Quarterly*, XXV (1942), 363, 365; Baudier, *Catholic Church in Louisiana*, 104-105.

service on the church property and lands. Catholic clergymen and nuns often held slaves as gifts from members of
the church. Sometimes nuns received slaves as part of their
dowry. Badin was deeply disturbed by the Kentucky slaveowner's cruel treatment of his Negroes. Bishop Carroll
advised Badin to show the masters the error of their way
and to use his power to prevent the hiring and selling of
slaves. Badin trained a few women and children in the
fundamentals of religion so that they, in turn, could teach
the children and older Negroes. Especially did he hope
that the owners would accept their duty to teach the
catechism to the slaves and admit the Negroes to all the
sacraments, particularly that of marriage. In 1844 Bishop
Flaget, on a visit to Ste. Genevieve, Missouri, became so
incensed over the lack of respect for the sacrament of
marriage that he threatened to excommunicate masters who
deprived slaves of this rite.[6]

Father Nerinckx in his missionary trips in Kentucky
assembled slave children so that he might instruct them.
He planned an order of Negro women, the Little Society
of Friends of Mary at the Foot of the Cross, who would
serve in uplifting the slaves. Several women were accepted
as postulants, but the community failed of completion
because Nerinckx's successor thought the time inopportune.
The Sisters of Loretto, founded by Nerinckx, accepted as
one of their tasks the duty of aiding "aged, decrepit and
useless slaves."[7]

The Catholics in St. Louis assisted the Negroes in a
variety of ways. In February 1845 a school for the education of Negro girls opened in a three-story building. Their
instruction was placed in the hands of the Sisters of St.

[6] Schauinger, Badin, 17, 25, 74; Schauinger, Cathedrals, 117.
[7] John G. Shea, "A Pioneer of the West, Rev. Charles Nerinckx,"
American Catholic Quarterly Review, V (1880), 486-508 passim; Helene
Magaret, Giant in the Wilderness: A Biography of Father Charles Nerinckx
(Milwaukee, 1952), 117-19.

Joseph of Carondelet who taught the catechism and such subjects as plain needlework. Success accompanied this effort, but, when the enrollment reached one hundred, voices of opposition arose and warnings were issued to cease teaching the girls. After a threatening group gathered outside the convent, the mayor, fearful of the safety of the nuns, appealed to them to close the school. The sisters acquiesced but continued to teach the children on Sundays. In 1847 the state of Missouri passed a bill prohibiting instruction of slaves and providing both a jail term and a money fine as penalties for infraction of the law. Disregarding the legislative ban, the Sisters of Mercy opened, perhaps secretly, in St. Louis in 1856 a night school for colored children. Two years later a Jesuit, Father Peter Koning, was placed in charge of the work for Negroes in the city. Galleries in St. Xavier's (College) Church were converted into a chapel and there services for Negroes were held. Father Koning succeeded in organizing a Marian sodality for Negro girls.[8]

Father Arnold Damen, who was intensely interested in the welfare of Negroes, visited Natchez, Mississippi, in 1855 and found disturbing and distressing conditions prevalent in the religious life of the slaves. He asked the General of the Jesuits to permit him to work in the Natchez field. The church was so poor in Mississippi it was often impossible to supply the area with the barest of facilities, and this sad condition continued for many years. William H. Elder, who had become Bishop of Mississippi in 1857, made a very realistic appraisal of the difficulties facing the new apostolate. It was a picture that clearly and forcefully described conditions in several Southern dioceses on the eve of the Civil War.[9]

[8] Daniel M. Hogan, "The Catholic Church and the Negroes of Saint Louis" (M.A. thesis, St. Louis University, 1955), 17-18; Garraghan, Jesuits, III, 561.

[9] Gerow, Catholicity in Mississippi, 55; Garraghan, Jesuits, III, 560-61.

Although the Negroes often had a fear of Catholic priests, they soon came to be kindly disposed to the church, fascinated by the order of worship, and willing to accept its ministrations. "Having few comforts," Bishop Elder wrote, "& no expectations in this world, their thoughts & desires are the more easily drawn to the good things of the world to come. I say often because often again they are so entirely animal in their inclinations, so engrossed with the senses, that they have no regard for any thing above the gratifications of the body. But even among such as these, the missionary often finds a good soil. . . ." Priests should come, the bishop pleaded, in large numbers "ready to put the sickle into this abundant field." Naturally there was no place in the ministry of the Catholic Church for the untrained and illiterate Negro preacher. The editor of the *United States Catholic Miscellany* believed that "the system of negro preaching is a mischievous burlesque upon christianity" and ought to be abolished. He was of the opinion that planters managed to keep Negroes at home and satisfied by selecting a Negro preacher especially "for his cunning, his art, his impudence, his presumption and his volubility, than for his honesty or virtue. . . ."[10]

The bishop's call for workers brought poor response, and the harvest lay ungathered. Except in Maryland, the lower part of Louisiana, and widely scattered places in Kentucky, Tennessee, Florida, Alabama, and Mississippi, the Catholics seldom came into contact with Negroes in the antebellum period. As a consequence, the Catholic Church never gained a strong hold on the Negroes who, according to one authority, "were Catholic in little more than name. Whatever they have been quantitatively, qualitatively their religion had few of the deeply rooted principles which alone can influence the entire life of man." The church had sought

---

[10] Ellis, *Documents*, 336, 337; *United States Catholic Miscellany* (Charleston, S. C.), Sept. 10, 1831.

to protect and defend the right of the slave in the practice of religion and to teach the master the proper respect for the slave. Having done this, the church did not attempt to reform the prevailing society as imperfect as it was.[11]

Early Catholic provisions for the education of the Negro and his admission to the church put to shame the Anglican Church which long had adhered to an ancient English law that a Christian could not be held in bondage. A demand from slaveowners led the Virginia Assembly to rule that baptizing did not change the condition of a person's bondage or freedom. The Anglican Church early recognized slavery as an institution, and through its Society for the Propagation of the Gospel in Foreign Parts, organized in London in 1701, the church had committed itself to a missionary program for Negroes and Indians in America. In 1727 Bishop Gibson of London delivered an address which attempted to encourage and to aid the society in "carrying on the work of instructing Negroes in our Plantations abroad." Fifteen years later in South Carolina the society supplied money to purchase two intelligent Negro boys to teach other Negroes to "read the scriptures and to understand the nature of Redemption."[12] In its flourishing colonial days, the church had performed extensive work with the Negroes in the low country of the Southern colonies. Later in the new lands the church often supplied a missionary for slaves belonging to communicants of the church.

In Virginia in 1819 the Episcopal convention became deeply exercised over the moral standards of its communicants and expressed great concern for its Negro slaves. The convention approved an address and ordered it sent to the

[11] Gillard, *Colored Catholics*, 43-44; Rice, *Catholic Opinion*, 60.

[12] Carter G. Woodson, *The History of the Negro Church* (Washington, 1921), 5-8; Clifton E. Olmstead, *History of Religion in the United States* (Englewood Cliffs, N. J., 1960), 50; Emery, *Century of Endeavor*, 7; Albert S. Thomas, *Protestant Episcopal Church in South Carolina, 1820-1957* (Columbia, 1957), 780.

president of the American Colonization Society commending
the aims of the society and hoping that it would be possible
"to rescue this unhappy class of our fellow-creatures from
the ignorance, vice and degradation to which the habits
and sentiments if not the necessities of the present social
state will forever doom them while they remain in this
country. . . ."[13] This sentiment was expressed in Virginia
during an aroused interest in the colonization movement
and does not stand as representative of the Episcopal com-
mitments on slavery.

Of the Episcopal bishops in the South, probably none had
a greater interest in the welfare of the Negro slave than
Bishop Stephen Elliott of Georgia. Consecrated in 1841,
Elliott at his first convention made an earnest and compelling plea for the proper religious instruction of Negroes.
He realized that most of the Negroes in Georgia were
receiving a token religious training, but he was sure that
"for the most, [it was] a religion of excitement, occupied
entirely with the feelings. . . ." He spoke further of the
responsibility of the diocese to the Negroes: "The religious
instruction of our domestics, and of the negroes upon the
plantations, is a subject that should never be passed over
in the address of a Southern Bishop." The next year he
outlined the church's obligation to have "well-instructed
colored communicants in every Episcopal church" and to
provide "pastors to live among them." He urged. that, to
supply these pastors, the church adopt a system of diaconates
that would not require a high literary standard. "To others
it may be a matter of choice or caprice; to us of the slaveholding States it involves the whole question of the kind
of teaching these persons shall receive." Through the years
Elliott continued to study and plan the proper method of
training and preaching to the Negroes. He was convinced

---

13 White, *Cobbs*, 28-29.

that the masters were failing in their duty since they stubbornly believed that the Episcopal method was not so successful as that adopted by other churches. This he denied with great vigor. "It is manifest before our eyes," he said, "how little avail is declamatory teaching, accompanied by temporary excitement, unless there shall have been a long previous course of instruction in the doctrine of the gospel. We must first teach men what the truth is, before we can effectually urge them to embrace it. Exhortation is to succeed, or, at the utmost, accompany instruction; otherwise, it excites the feelings, without changing either the will, or the life."[14]

Bishop Thomas Atkinson of North Carolina advanced suggestions for the training of the Negroes quite similar to those of Bishop Elliott. Bishop Cobbs of Alabama likewise had a deep and abiding interest in the Negro's welfare. On a Sunday in 1846 in the chapel of St. Michael's Church in Marion, Perry County, Alabama, he preached to a large congregation of colored people. He thought that the services of the church were "eminently suited to the wants and circumstances of the colored people,"[15] because their elementary instruction and constant repetition easily fastened truth on the memory. Throughout most of the South, Episcopal churches were built with gallery seats for the slaves so that they could worship in the regular services, for they, like the children of the white family, were expected to attend all services. Upon the master was placed the duty of furnishing his slaves with religious instruction

---

[14] *Journal of the Nineteenth Annual Convention . . . in the Diocese of Georgia* (Columbus, Ga., 1841), 7; Emery, *Century of Endeavor,* 80-81; *Journal of the Thirty-Fourth Annual Convention* (Savannah, 1856), 14. See also Edgar L. Pennington, "Stephen Elliott, First Bishop of Georgia," *Historical Magazine of the Protestant Episcopal Church,* VII (1938), 203-63 passim.

[15] *Primary Charge of the Rt. Rev. Thomas Atkinson . . . to the Clergy* (Fayetteville, N. C., 1855), 8; *Journal of the Fifteenth Annual Convention* (Mobile, 1846), 14.

which, it was hoped, would lead to baptism and confirmation. Often a master successfully spent money and effort to secure a missionary to work among the Negroes on a plantation. In 1838 George Weller, a missionary stationed at Memphis, Tennessee, baptized at a nearby plantation some fifty Negroes in a very impressive service. The Episcopal church in Natchez was remodeled at a cost of nearly twenty thousand dollars in 1838, and a year later a basement was included so that it could be used for the instruction of the slaves in a Sunday school. Dr. William N. Mercer, a wealthy planter and owner of several hundred slaves, built on his plantation near Natchez a chapel and a rectory costing nearly thirty thousand dollars. To a rector he paid a yearly salary of $1,200. On a Sunday in 1842 the rector with the assistance of Bishop Otey baptized 110 Negro children.[16]

At the dedication service of St. John's Church near Columbia, Tennessee, in 1842 Bishop Otey preached to both whites and blacks who had filled the church to capacity. Some communicants had prayer books, but the lack of hymnals prompted the leader to line-off the songs. After the whites received the sacrament of holy communion, the bishop invited a number of the colored people to come forward so that he could explain to them what was expected of those who took the sacrament. It became the custom in this church for the half-hour before morning services to be devoted to teaching the prayers, and a large number were generally in attendance at these training periods.[17]

In various sections of the South numerous efforts were made by Episcopal churches or by individual Episcopalians

---

[16] *Spirit of Missions*, Dec. 1838, 388, July 1842, 202-203; Stietenrath, *One Hundred Years*, 19. Richard Niebuhr contends that "the association of white and black Christians in various churches prior to the Civil War is scarcely to be regarded as a demonstration of the Christian principle of brotherhood and equality." *Sources of Denominationalism*, 252.

[17] Yeatman, "St. John's," *Tennessee Historical Quarterly*, X, 335-38.

to give religious instruction to the Negroes. When Jackson
Kemper, Missionary Bishop of Indiana and Missouri, visited
the Southwest in 1838, he found some preachers of other
denominations were being paid by Episcopalians to preach
to the slaves when there was no Episcopal minister available. In Mobile, as early as 1840, the Reverend S. S.
Lewis preached to congregations of more than one hundred
Negroes. Six years later almost half of all the baptisms in
the Diocese of Alabama were of Negroes. Unfortunately the
confirmations were far less because many who had been
baptized proved themselves unworthy of full membership
in the church. In 1854 at a rural parish of St. John's in Lake
Washington, Mississippi, more than twelve hundred Negroes
were receiving some form of religious teaching. A year later
the Diocese of Louisiana reported thirty-six hundred colored
members on thirty-one plantations. To the north in Kentucky the diocese in 1860 heard a report on instruction of
colored people. The services and instruction of the church
were "admirably adapted," but missionaries were badly
needed to be used exclusively for the Negroes.[18]

Some instances of opposition in the early years to the
teaching or preaching by Episcopalians to the slave population have been found on the fringes of the Cotton Kingdom. Soon after the Episcopal Theological Seminary was
organized in 1834 at Lexington, Kentucky, the Reverend
Henry Caswall, a member of the faculty, and some of his
students collected about seventy-five slaves into a Sunday
school. When it was generally learned that the Negroes
were being taught to read, the mayor of Lexington requested
the teachers "to desist from such a dangerous proceeding"

[18] Manross, *Episcopal Church . . . 1800-1840*, 110-11; Whitaker, *Church in Alabama*, 81-82; Nash K. Burger, "The Rt. Rev. William Mercer Green, First Bishop of Mississippi," *Journal of Mississippi History*, XII (1950), 15; Carter and Carter, *Episcopal Church in Louisiana*, 113; *Journal of the Thirty-Second Annual Convention* (Frankfort, Ky., 1860), 23.

for fear that a mob "might level our Seminary to dust."
About the same time Christ Church on St. Simon's Island,
Georgia, reported that a sermon for the Negroes had been
preached every Sunday evening between 1830 and 1836.
Unfortunately all effort in their behalf had been obstructed
by the interference of abolitionary "busy bodies in other
men's matters."[19]

In Mississippi a society which had been organized twenty
years previously changed its name in 1849 to the Society
of the Protestant Episcopal Church for Diffusing Christian
Knowledge in the Diocese of Mississippi. According to its
constitution its duty was to aid plantation owners to give
religious instruction to slaves. By the opening of the Civil
War the members of that society had contributed over
fifteen thousand dollars to provide missionaries for the
plantations. In its annual report in 1861 this diocese called
attention to its obligation "to supply our colored population
with proper facilities for their spiritual welfare."[20] The
bishops, the clergy, and many of the communicants of the
Episcopal Church made a sincere effort to provide religious
instruction for the great number of Negroes living on many
of the substantial plantations in the cotton area.

John Wesley's preachers sought to bring an interracial
character to Methodism by insisting that all men were
children of God. When Joseph Pilmoor and Richard Board-
man, two Wesleyan preachers, arrived in New York in 1770,
they happily found Negro members of the John Street
Society. This did not mean that brotherhood was practiced,
for Pilmoor wrote into his journal in 1771 that he had "met
the negroes apart." It was not until 1787, however, that

[19] Henry Caswall, *America, and the American Church* (London, 1851),
209; *Journal of the Fourteenth Annual Convention* (Macon, Ga., 1836), 10.
[20] Nash K. Burger, "The Society for the Advancement of Christianity in
Mississippi," *Historical Magazine of the Protestant Episcopal Church*, XIV
(1945), 264-69; Burger, "William Mercer Green," *Journal of Mississippi
History*, XII, 16.

Negroes were listed separately in the records of church membership.[21]

Despite many statements made against slavery by John Wesley and Francis Asbury, early Methodist legislation regarding the Negro seems to have been directed toward the saving of souls rather than bodies. The Christmas Conference of 1784 ordered the preachers to provide religious training for Negroes. Three years later the annual conferences cautioned the delegates that nothing should be left "undone for the spiritual benefit and salvation" of the colored people. Meet them in classes, the conferences urged, and exercise "the whole Methodist discipline" over them. In 1790 the conferences encouraged the establishment of Sunday schools so that the Negro might be taught "learning and piety." A long step was taken in 1824 when the General Conference ordered that preachers "prudently" force members to teach slaves to read the Bible and allow adequate time for them to attend church.[22]

This same General Conference permitted the annual conferences to "employ colored preachers to travel and preach where their services are judged necessary," provided the men had been properly recommended. Several Negroes became preachers of considerable fame. One of the best known and most successful was "Black Harry" Hosier, a servant of Bishop Asbury. Unable to read or write, Harry preached to black and white with such great effectiveness that Asbury declared that, when a preaching engagement was announced, "Black Harry" always drew more people than he did. In 1810 when William Capers went to his appointment in Fayetteville, North Carolina, he found a Negro preacher, Henry Evan, to be "the most

[21] Barclay, *Early American Methodism*, II, 52-53.
[22] Charles B. Swaney, *Episcopal Methodism and Slavery* (Boston, 1926), 28; *Minutes of the Annual Conferences*, I, 28; W. P. Harrison, *The Gospel among the Slaves* (Nashville, 1893), 54-55; *Journals of the General Conference of the Methodist Episcopal Church*, I (New York, 1855), 294.

remarkable man" in the town. Often in Evan's audiences were white men who had become convinced that "the preaching which had proved so beneficial to their servants might be good for them also. . . ."[23]

In 1808 Capers as a youth of eighteen had been assigned to the Wateree Circuit in South Carolina which contained more than a hundred Negro members. At once he became deeply interested in the spiritual welfare of the slaves in a period of almost total neglect, caused to a degree by an address of the General Conference of 1800 and signed by Bishops Thomas Coke, Francis Asbury, and Richard Whatcoat. This address directed annual conferences "to draw up addresses for the gradual emancipation of the slaves to the legislatures of the states in which no general laws have been passed for that purpose. . . ." This action of the three bishops confirmed thousands "in the belief that all itinerant Methodist preachers were abolition emissaries and, as a consequence, promoters of insurrection and rebellion among the negroes." The extreme action by the three bishops threatened to destroy the church in the South and only repudiation of the address by Methodist preachers saved it. Through the years Capers continued his deep and undying interest in the Negro, and eventually in 1829 the South Carolina Conference established three missions. Capers was appointed superintendent of the missions, and his name became synonymous with Negro missions. Thus began Methodist domestic mission work that would spread over the entire South.

In 1830 the Georgia Conference was formed by dividing the South Carolina Conference. The new conference established the next year a mission to the slaves in the state. Following the Methodist mission examples of the South

[23] *Journals of the General Conference*, I, 337; Harrison, *Gospel among the Slaves*, 126-28, 138-40. For the next two paragraphs see 136-37, 145-48, 161, 164, 195, 325.

Carolina and Georgia conferences, the Tennessee Conference in 1831 established two missions, both located in Alabama. At the close of the next year the missions had about twenty-five hundred Negro members out of a total of twenty-six thousand in the three conferences reporting missions to slaves. By 1844 the Methodist Episcopal Church had located sixty-eight missions and eighty missionaries in ten states. Following the division of the church, the Methodist Episcopal Church, South intensified its program of work among the slaves, and, when the Civil War came, this organization had 329 missions, 327 missionaries, and had appropriated $86,358 for plantation missions among the Southern slaves.

In the new cotton sections, however, the quick-rich failed to accept the *noblesse oblige* of the older planters and older communities. As cotton and slavery fastened themselves upon Southern society, the church leaders began to adopt new doctrines, new discipline, and new polity designed to meet the demands of the members. Methodism's greatest success in evangelizing the Negroes had been prior to 1830 and in the older slaveholding states where the preachers had had the approval of the planters. The clergy ceased its denunciations against slavery and became slaveowning itself, for Methodist success largely depended on a common and mutual interest of preacher and congregation. Alfred Brunson believed that all Southern "Bishops, including Bascom, who formerly thundered so eloquently against the 'sum of all villainies' were, or became slaveholders, and contended that the system had divine authority." Peter Cartwright noticed the contrast in the free salvation preached by Methodism to "listening thousands, while their poor degraded slaves are deprived . . . of civil and religious liberty!" Preaching was made to conform to the tastes of the particular section, the churches thereby becoming "allies of the existing economic and social order." The "clergy formulated a strong Biblical and patriarchial defense of the South. Slavery, from being an institution to be lamented as an evil, became a blessing sustained by the Holy Scriptures, according to the ablest ministers of God." The course pursued appears to have been little short of "an exhibition of subserviency to the demands of the 'infernal spirit of slavery,' which for a time seem to stupefy the people."

Restrictions were placed on preaching to the Negroes, and they required that the sermons be carefully prepared from such texts as: "Servants, be obedient to your masters"; "In the sweat of thy face shalt thou eat bread, till thou return unto the ground"; "Render unto Caesar, the things that are Caesar's"; "Well done, thou good and faithful servant." A preacher would endanger his life if he chose for a text the narrative of the liberation of the Hebrews from Egyptian bondage or developed a passage like "The truth shall make you free." The clergy not only was careful with texts but also was afraid to work ardently for conversion of slaves because religious opportunities might lead to demands for social, political, and religious equality. The Great Revival which swept the Western world and turned men's hearts to studying the Bible scarcely touched the Negro's spiritual and moral status. Consequently a general pressure was not brought to bear upon the planter and many men continued to neglect the religious instruction of the slaves except where material profit was to be gained. The persuasiveness of such leaders as William Capers did make possible some religious work among the slaves which resulted in a Negro Methodist membership of almost fifty thousand by 1825. Yet this action of Capers was an individual expression rather than one typical of the clergy of the South.[24]

[24] References for this and the preceding paragraph may be found in Posey, "Influence of Slavery upon the Methodist Church in the Early South and Southwest," *Mississippi Valley Historical Review*, XVII (1930-1931), 539-40.

A citizen of Georgia bequeathed two hundred dollars for the religious training of his slaves since he thought that the Negro who had some religious obligations might also feel a duty of obedience. The idea that religious training for the Negro brought in good return affords the humorous case of the infidel master who provided religious advantages for his slaves and the more paradoxical instance of a prayer service being held after a dance. Some planters, deeply impressed with the mission work and the preaching, built chapels or churches on the plantations and often attended services with the slaves. At prayer meetings in private homes and on the plantations the blacks came under the influence of religion. A love feast offered a great opportunity to testify to God's goodness and in this act the Negro was happy. At the camp meetings the impulsive and demonstrative Negro was often in his greatest moment of religious excitement, for, according to an early commentator, the camp meeting was welcomed by no group "with more unmixed delight than by the poor slaves. It comes at a season of the year when they most need rest. It gives them all the advantages of the ordinary holiday, without its accompaniments of drunkenness and profanity . . . they can jump to their hearts' content."[25]

Despite the favorable attitude toward the church and the efforts of many planters, the work was hedged by many restrictions. Some states prohibited the assembling of Negroes. In 1833 Alabama passed a law prohibiting slaves or free Negroes from preaching except in the presence of at least five slaveowners and when authorized by some religious body. A year later Georgia's legislature ruled that neither slave nor free Negro could preach before more than seven people unless licensed by justices on the certification of three ordained ministers. Other Southern states passed

[25] Edward Ingle, *Southern Sidelights* (New York, 1896), 274; Johnson, *Frontier Camp Meeting*, 114.

similar or more drastic legislation in order to reduce the
probability of trouble that might come from unregulated
crowds. Teaching the ignorant black was often a task that
seemed impossible. James A. Ranaldson, writing from Louisiana in 1818, agreed that the poor African should not be
neglected, but "it truly requires the wisdom of the serpent
blended with the harmlessness of the dove, to teach this
wretched race of human beings."[26] Slaves were often prohibited from attending a religious service on any day except
Sunday. These and other restrictions greatly hampered the
work of preacher and missionary, but even these restrictions
did not prevent a common ground of understanding.

From the time of the American Revolution the Baptists
were active in behalf of the Negro. Struggling for civil and
religious liberty, the Baptists became greatly agitated over
slavery. At first they strongly opposed the institution and
pledged themselves to take advantage of all legal means to
bring its extirpation. By 1790 the Baptist denomination had
churches in all the Middle and South Atlantic states. A large
number of Negroes had become members, especially during
the revival seasons, but the Negro was never comfortable
in the white man's church. Where the Negroes were numerous, particularly in the towns and cities, special services were
held at which they could listen to their own brethren exhort.
These were encouraged to exercise spiritual oversight and
help the church care for others. The segregated groups led
to the rise of separate Negro churches with Negro preachers.
In the major cities of the South some of these churches
acquired a large membership and became highly effective
agencies for good among the Negro population. In 1841 the
African Baptist Church of New Orleans with 230 members
worshipped in its own building, and often as many as 800
Negroes attended the Sunday services. The Negro church
in St. Louis, arising from a Sunday school class formed in

---

[26] Woodson, *Negro Church*, 132; *American Baptist Magazine*, I (1817-
1818), 374.

1818, had a membership of 300 in 1842. The Louisville
Colored Baptist Church added 214 members by baptism in
the year 1843 and two years later had 644 members. In
1854 the First African Baptist Church in Lexington, the
largest church in Kentucky, had 1,820 members. Some
Baptist churches were almost completely black in membership. In 1846 the church at Tuscumbia, Alabama, had only
42 white members out of a total of 213; the Natchez church
had 62 of 442; and the Columbus, Mississippi, church had
about 80 of 400.[27]

In numerous sections of the South—in small towns, on
plantations, and in large cities—Negro preachers of importance toiled and succeeded among their people and sometimes among the whites. Although the latter usually supplied
the preacher, they were on the lookout for a Negro with the
gift of exhorting. Some white persons were converted by
Negro preachers who served as pastors of churches for
whites. In the early 1790s Sampson, a Negro preacher in
Savannah, frequently exhorted when the white preacher was
away at another place of worship. In 1804 Joseph Willis, a
mulatto, preached the first Protestant sermon west of the
Mississippi River at a point southwest of Baton Rouge. He
was the first moderator of Louisiana's first Baptist association. Job was an African slave who was taken to South
Carolina in 1806. Soon learning to read, he taught a Sunday
school and later became an ordained Baptist preacher spending the last part of his life in Alabama. Caesar, a Negro
slave in Alabama, was converted and ordained to preach.
When his master died, Caesar's freedom was purchased for
$625—a sum contributed by several Baptist churches.[28] Some

[27] *Baptist Banner*, July 14, 1841, Feb. 9, 1843; *Alabama Baptist* (Marion,
Ala.), Dec. 16, 1843; Spencer, *Kentucky Baptists*, II, 656; *Baptist Home
Missions in North America* (New York, 1883), 390.
[28] Rippon, *Annual Register for . . . 1793*, 342; Christian, *Baptists of
Louisiana*, 50-53; William E. Paxton, *A History of the Baptists of Louisiana*
(St. Louis, 1888), 139-41; Benjamin F. Riley, *History of the Baptists of
Alabama* (Birmingham, 1895), 79-80.

Negro preachers refused to be purchased from their masters
and set free, since this often tended to cause loss of face
among their Negro brethren.

One of the best known of all Negro preachers in any part
of the South was Andrew Bryan, pastor of the First Colored
Church of Savannah, who suffered great persecution by the
whites before he was accepted as a force for good rather
than one whose work hinted of insurrection. Henry Holcombe, a Baptist minister who knew Bryan well, wrote
about him in 1812, the year he died: "His fleecy and well-
sett [sic] locks have been bleached by eighty winters; and
dressed like a bishop of London, he rides, moderately corpu-
lent, in his chair, and with manly features, of a jetty hue,
fills every person to whom he gracefully bows, with pleasure
and veneration by displaying, in smiles, even rows of natural
teeth, white as ivory, and a pair of fine black eyes sparkling
with intelligence, benevolence, and joy."[29]

In a somewhat later period the outstanding Negro Baptist
preacher was London Ferrill, pastor of the First African
Baptist Church in Lexington, Kentucky. Descended from
an African chieftain's family, he was born a slave in Virginia.
Upon the death of his master he was freed from slavery and
moved to Lexington, where he served his church for thirty-
two years. Respected by all who knew him, Ferrill enjoyed
social prestige; some citizens thought "his influence was
more potent to keep order among the blacks than the police
force of the city." When he died in 1854, the funeral
procession through the streets of Lexington had been exceeded in length only by that which followed the corpse of
Henry Clay.[30]

In spite of interest of Christians in the spiritual life of
their slaves, there was a definite temptation, especially

---

[29] Henry Holcombe, *The First Fruits, in a Series of Letters* (Philadelphia,
1812), 116.
[30] Spencer, *Kentucky Baptists*, II, 656-57.

among Baptists and Methodists, to use religion as an instrument of further enslavement. Some wanted to use the threat of expulsion from membership for those who ran away. In Missouri an avowed infidel slaveholder noticed the great improvement in the conduct of his slave Dick. Upon investigation his daughters confirmed that they had witnessed Dick's baptism by a Baptist preacher. Thereupon the owner remarked: "I wish to God he would baptize all my negroes, if it would make them as good as Dick."[31]

As the church and the planter began to see eye to eye on the slavery issue, most of the earlier problems lessened or even disappeared. For example, the Alabama Baptist State Convention in 1844 recognized "the duty of using all practicable and legal methods for communicating religious instruction, as far as may be in their power." In the following year this same association believed that the Negro was most likely to profit from meetings free from whites and that masters, even when not "pious," were favorable to oral instruction of servants in religious truths.[32] Deeply concerned over the lax morals of the Negro, the Baptists through their system of watch-care found much to condemn among the colored members, whose misdemeanors were as varied as human relationships. Before congregational meetings the Negroes were arraigned for lying, stealing, conjuring, drinking, and adultery. The church usually found the Negro guilty of the charges, placed him on probation, and in cases of continued violation of the moral code deprived him of membership.

As a whole Baptists were eager and determined to improve the lot of the Negro slave. A few typical examples must suffice. In 1847 the Union Baptist Association of Alabama,

[31] R. S. Duncan, A History of the Baptists in Missouri (St. Louis, 1882), 62-63.
[32] Thomas M. Owen, History of Alabama (4 vols.; Chicago, 1921), I, 108; Proceedings of the Alabama Baptist State Convention (Tuscaloosa, Ala., 1846), 4.

disturbed by the failure of slaveowners "to reflect seriously" on their duty to their slaves, urged that masters "teach servants more fully the precepts of religion." Six years later the Gilgal Church in Alabama proposed to employ a minister to the slaves and appealed to the planters for financial support. In 1858 the Columbus, Mississippi, Association urged that slaves be instructed in the doctrines of faith, for they "toil in the field to make our bread and meat," but the church body warned against "that great enthusiasm to which they are so liable."[33]

Undoubtedly the Baptists contributed heavily to the evangelization of the Southern Negroes. They began an early program and continued it unceasingly. At first, as people of limited means and opposed to slavery, they had a great bond of sympathy with the Negro. Willing to worship with him, pray alongside the altar rail, commune with him, and be baptized in the same water by the same preacher, the white Baptists easily established a worshiping relation.

The stable position enjoyed by the Presbyterian Church at the close of the American Revolution permitted and encouraged it to adopt policies that seem on the surface to be wiser and better planned than those adopted by the Baptists and Methodists. Hardly had the Revolution closed before the Synod of New York and Philadelphia in 1787 urged Presbyterians to give Negroes the advantage of education. Seven years later the Transylvania Presbytery in Kentucky instructed its members to teach slaves under fifteen years to read the Bible. In 1809 the Synod of Kentucky ordered the presbyteries under its jurisdiction to supply religious instruction so that the slaves might have "a human and Christian treatment." In other Southern states

---

[33] T. C. Schilling, *Abstract History of the Mississippi Baptist Association* (New Orleans, 1908), 22; Henry B. Foster, *History of the Tuscaloosa County Baptist Association* (Tuscaloosa, Ala., 1934), 64; *Minutes of the Columbus Baptist Association* (Jackson, Miss., 1858), 11.

the procedure of the church followed a pattern quite similar to that which had developed in Kentucky. Although efforts were made by the General Assembly to encourage and to provide religious instruction for slaves, little was accomplished for several years. About 1830, when interest in the Negro on the part of the assembly seemed to fade, activity on the local scene arose. Various presbyteries and synods in Alabama, Mississippi, Kentucky, Tennessee, Louisiana, and Georgia began to take action in behalf of the Negro. For example, in 1839 the Synod of Mississippi commissioned two of its ministers to write a catechism for slaves.[34]

The Presbyterian minister whose work among the Negroes exceeds that of any minister of any denomination was Charles C. Jones, born on his father's Georgia plantation near Midway Church in 1804. After studying at Andover and Princeton, he served for two years as pastor of the First Presbyterian Church of Savannah. Then he returned to his own plantation, located in an area with a heavy slave population, and entered upon a life chiefly devoted to the evangelization of the slaves. Until his death in 1863 he preached, implored, wrote a catechism, organized associations, taught in a theological seminary, corresponded far and wide with results that affected not only the Presbyterian Church but all churches interested in the welfare of the Negro. Jones firmly believed that the advantages of contact with the master in religious services far outweighed the claims made for separate churches. He feared that an independent Negro church of any denomination would accomplish far less of value than one attended by both races. Jones, however, believed that most of the slaveowners

---

[34] *Records of the Presbyterian Church* (Philadelphia, 1841), 540; "Minutes of the Transylvania Presbytery, 1786-1837," Oct. 13, 1794, in Sweet, *The Presbyterians*, 147; "Minutes of the Synod of Kentucky, 1802-1811," Oct. 18, 1809, in Sweet, *The Presbyterians*, 382; John Robinson, *The Testimony and Practice of the Presbyterian Church in Reference to American Slavery* (Cincinnati, 1852), 154.

hindered the efforts of the church by taking advantage of religion as a controlling and disciplining device.[35]

In his preaching to the Negroes the Presbyterian minister talked a great deal about various sinful behavior—quarreling, drinking, stealing, and loose living. Some writers estimate that three-fourths of all cases of church discipline of Negroes concerned sexual relations. Whisky was the cause of much trouble and a continuing matter for discipline. "Living in open rebellion against God" was a general charge often found in the records, for which the Negro usually received expulsion from the church rolls. Evidence points an accusing finger toward the Presbyterian Church courts in cases that involved redress for wrongs by whites against slaves. A surprisingly small number of entries concern inhumane, barbarous, or unfair treatment of slaves. Of course there were many persons who objected to slavery and tried to adjust their position in accord. A Presbyterian in Tennessee asked that his children be baptized but made it clear that he had no intention of participating in the sacrament of the Lord's Supper until the church ceased "to wink at the practice of slavery." The West Tennessee Presbytery refused this request for "partial standing."[36]

The late 1840s began to bring some progress in behalf of the Negro. In 1846 a minister of the American Home Missionary Society, organized by the Congregationalists in 1826, wrote from Spring Hill, Tennessee, that "we can now preach and teach among them [the slaves] without molestation." A year later the Presbytery of South Alabama reported that "perhaps without a solitary exception our ministers are devoting a considerable part of their labors to the benefit of the colored population." In 1851 from Kentucky came a

[35] Henry A. White, *Southern Presbyterian Leaders* (New York, 1911), 293-97; Charles C. Jones, *The Religious Instruction of the Negroes in the United States* (Savannah, 1842), passim; Woodson, *Negro Church*, 153-55.
[36] MS Minutes, West Tennessee Presbytery, Sept. 6, 1814, 81-82, Montreat.

letter to the American Society saying that three counties were issuing marriage licenses to Negroes and the preachers were marrying them. From middle Tennessee a correspondent wrote that his aunts wanted to give two Negro boys to the Presbyterian Church for use as missionaries in Liberia. The significance of this offer may best be read in the writer's comment that Negroes and corn could hardly be bought and that land was selling at thirty dollars an acre.[37]

Existing statistics on the Negro and his denominational affiliations are variable and inconsistent. One writer has estimated that in the 1840s there were 260,000 Negroes formally connected with churches in the South, of whom only 7,000 belonged to the Presbyterian Church. Another authority thinks 20,000 was the largest number of Negroes who were members of the Presbyterian Church at any time before the Civil War, and that nearly 500,000 Negroes were members of the several denominations in the South.[38] It is clearly evident that the Presbyterian Church held only a small percentage of the Negroes, but failure to attract the Negro to membership did not lessen the church's interest in his physical and spiritual welfare. This great social interest of the church was significant. In states free from restrictions much was accomplished in the elementary education of the Negro. When due consideration is given to the problems that inevitably arose from the very nature of slavery, the position of the Presbyterian Church in its relations with the Negro was one of generosity and studied attempts to raise the general welfare of the enslaved people.

The Cumberland Presbyterian Church, unlike other Protestant denominations, did not have a single separate church

[37] George H. Blair, Oct. 15, 1846, in American Home Missionary Society papers, Chicago Theological Seminary—hereafter cited as AHMS and CTS. Benjamin Mills, Frankfort, Ky., Oct. 25, 1851, CTS; N. L. Murphy to William R. Whittingham, June 16, 1851, Duke.

[38] Woodson, *Negro Church*, 97; White, *Southern Presbyterian Leaders*, 306.

for slaves. The Negroes went to the white churches and were taught the same salvation by the same preacher. A young Presbyterian, a graduate of Auburn Theological Seminary, began his ministerial career in 1824 in Henderson, Kentucky, which was a town of six hundred people, only fifty of whom were church members. The situation seemed so unpromising that the young minister thought the blacks the more hopeful part of his charge and through them he expected to reach the whites. In a few cases a Cumberland Presbyterian minister had a colored assistant who, in his presence, preached to the Negroes in the afternoon. This denomination continued the use of the camp meeting long after it had been abandoned by the Presbyterian and Baptist churches. Often the Negroes present were permitted to continue the services after the whites had retired. "When a thousand negroes, keeping time with foot and head, with arms and bodies, poured out all their souls upon the night air in a camp-meeting chorus suited to their voices and their culture, the weird and solemn grandeur and grotesqueness were indescribable."[39]

The intellectual appeal of the Presbyterian preacher, however, had only slight effect on the Negro. Preaching man's depravity, the minister had no fresh attraction to a slave who already had suffered ignominy and shame. A rational accounting for slavery made the yoke no lighter on the slave. The Negro with his limited training was better equipped to feel than to think; the earnest and intense, though poorly trained, Baptist and Methodist preachers asked far less intellectually of the Negro. The evangelical preaching and spontaneous exercises of the Methodists and Baptists "had a sort of hypnotizing effect upon the Negroes, causing them to be seized with certain emotional jerks and outward expressions of an inward movement of the spirit

[39] *Home Missionary and American Pastor's Journal* (New York), VII (1835), 188-89; McDonnold, *Cumberland Presbyterian Church*, 433-34.

which made them lose control of themselves." Probably the
Methodist advantage is best explained by Bishop Benjamin
T. Tanner of the African Methodist Episcopal Church, who
said the Presbyterian Church "strove to lift up without
coming down and while the good Presbyterian parson was
writing his discourses, rounding off the sentences, the
Methodist itinerant had traveled forty miles with his horse
and saddle bags; while the parson was adjusting his specta-
cles to read his manuscript, the itinerant had given hell and
damnation to his unrepentant hearers; while the disciple of
Calvin was waiting to have his church completed, the disciple of Wesley took to the woods, and made them reëcho
with the voice of free grace. . . ."[40]

Negroes were members of Stone's early church at Cane
Ridge, Kentucky, and of Campbell's church at Brush Run,
Pennsylvania, and of numerous other congregations of Disciples. Although not attracted in large numbers to this
sect, Negroes probably accepted their masters' choice in the
same proportion in the Disciples as in other churches.
According to Robert L. Jordan, historian of Negro Disciples,
"some of the slaves being deeply impressed, sought spiritual
guidance. They were already in Hades and to hear a man
of God tell them how they might secure peace and sit down
at the welcome table pleased them very much. They did
not choose to go to a torment greater than the one already
experienced." In the usual church relations with the Negro
there seems to have been little difference between the
Disciples and the Baptists in the matter of teaching, preaching, and seating. As a rule, the Disciples segregated the
Negroes by allotting them a part of the church. A very
different arrangement, however, was made by the Bethesda
Church in Washington, Georgia. Segregation there was
maintained by the erection of a partition between whites
and Negroes. When the whites built a new church, the

---

[40] Woodson, *Negro Church*, 97-98, 143.

old building was given to the Negroes, who organized a second Bethesda which is still in existence.[41]

A few remarkable Negroes contributed a great deal to the advancement of their race in the Disciples churches. Such was the slave who by some manipulation, either of his master or of a mission board, secured his freedom, took the name "Alexander Campbell," and sought employment in Lexington, Kentucky. While working as a porter, he attended Transylvania University long enough to become a preacher. Then he took the lead in forming at Midway, Kentucky, a church that soon had three hundred members. After three years of preaching he was able to buy the freedom of his wife. Two sons followed him into the Disciples ministry. In a few instances Disciples churches, following the plan of other religious bodies, bought the freedom of a Negro preacher. In 1853 the church in Hopkinsville, Kentucky, assisted by neighboring churches, raised $530 to purchase Alexander Cross, who was sent to Liberia as a missionary. Unfortunately his service was short, for Cross died within a few months after reaching Africa.[42]

The attitude of the Disciples of Christ was similar to that of Alexander Campbell whose neutral position on the slavery issue was largely due to his tremendous job of organizing a new denomination in which the more pressing problems had to be settled first. Nevertheless, he was keenly aware of and alert to the charges of mistreatment of the Negroes. On various occasions he urged that the discipline be used against masters who violated their duties as laid down in the injunctions of the New Testament. In his extensive travels over the South Campbell found Negroes in numerous churches and often baptized them with his own hands. In 1856 at Cheneyville, Louisiana, he visited the Disciples

[41] Garrison and DeGroot, *Disciples of Christ,* 470; Moseley, *Disciples of Christ,* 187.

[42] Garrison and DeGroot, *Disciples of Christ,* 472; Major, *Green River Christian Cooperation,* 10-11.

church which had about a hundred members, black and white. Both sat in similarly cushioned seats, but it was quite evident to Campbell that the Negroes possessed "the more fervent devotion."[43] The Disciples records about the Negroes are slight, the references are relatively few, and the supposition seems warranted that the church expended the least effort in behalf of the Negro of all the major churches of the Mississippi Valley.

An attempt to assess precisely the total contribution of the several religious groups to the civilizing and Christianizing of the Negro seems impossible. But the toil of preachers and missionaries, the support of thousands of lay workers, the sympathy and compassion of churches—all indicate a concerted and continuing effort to mitigate the harshness of slavery, and, eventually, to prepare the Negro for a position of decency and respectability in a new land. The existence of nearly half a million Negro members of the several denominations of the South on the eve of the Civil War reveals positive evidence of the Negro's acceptance of the church of the white man.

[43] Lunger, *Alexander Campbell*, 40-41; *Millennial Harbinger*, 1857, 312-13.

9

CATHOLIC EXPANSION

THE PRINCELY Don Andreas Almonaster y Roxas, according
to contemporary reports, spent the equivalent of four million
dollars embellishing New Orleans, the city of his adoption.
Chief among his munificent gifts was the stately parish
church which became St. Louis Cathedral. Construction of
the building began in 1789 and, despite many obstacles and
interruptions, was finally completed in December 1794.
Some seven months later Bishop Luis Peñalver y Cardenas,
a native of Havana, arrived to take charge of the recently
organized Diocese of Louisiana, the second diocese to be
established by the Roman Catholic Church in the present
United States. Because moral conditions in New Orleans
had reached such a deplorable state, the new bishop was
moved to say that Catholics there lived in disreputable
corruption. Although the population of the city was predominantly Catholic, no more than one-fourth of the professing Catholics attended mass regularly. The European
concept of family life provided marked freedom for men
and constraint for the women. To a large segment of the
male population of New Orleans extramarital license was no
more than a natural right, but to the outsider such conduct
appeared scandalous. The military officers and a large number of other males lived with colored concubines by whom
they had children whose names were entered in the registries
of the parishes as natural born.[1]

Bishop Peñalver, in company with his secretary and with

Father Antonio de Sedella, pastor of the cathedral at New Orleans, traveled in 1796 over much of the diocese. They went as far west and north as Natchitoches, to the interior post of Opelousas, and later east to the Floridas. All the while they were preaching, organizing, and collecting valuable information for the church. Although he had the support of Manuel de Lemos Gayoso who was appointed governor of Louisiana in 1797, Peñalver was never in a favorable position to meet the forces of opposition, the spirit of indifference, and the low regard for religion. When Gayoso died of fever in 1799, Juan Manuel Salcedo, "an infirm old man, who was in his dotage," succeeded him as governor. Salcedo felt little responsibility for the affairs of the church and offered no support to the bishop. In a lengthy report in 1799 Bishop Peñalver, faced with rebellion, wrote that resistance to religion had always prevailed in Louisiana, but never before to such a degree. This appraisal resembles closely a similar estimate of the people around Ste. Genevieve, Missouri, made by Bishop Peñalver in the same year. After four years of careful attention and observation, he wrote: "The emigrants from the western part of the United States and the toleration of our government have introduced into this colony a gang of adventurers who have no religion and acknowledge no God, and they have made the morals of our people much worse by intercourse with them in trade. . . ." Harassed by too many opposing forces, Peñalver in 1801 gladly exchanged his post at New Orleans for that of Archbishop of Guatemala. In his comprehensive book *Catholic Church in Louisiana*, Robert Baudier declares that

[1] [Carroll], *Catholic History*, 210, 219-20; Baudier, *Catholic Church in Louisiana*, 223-27; Michael J. Curley, *Church and State in the Spanish Floridas, 1783-1822* (Washington, 1940), 259. The predominance of the Protestants in the West and South before the Civil War tends to blur and even obliterate the picture of the Catholics. Since there was a minimum of official cooperation between the two groups, it appears easier and wiser to treat the expansion of Catholicism in this separate chapter rather than to fuse it into the several earlier chapters.

Peñalver's removal was "one of the most disastrous blows ever suffered by the Church in Louisiana."[2] Once again the region was without a spiritual head; nineteen years passed before the coming of another bishop to Louisiana.

The administration of the acephalous diocese devolved upon Fathers Thomas Hassett and Patrick Walsh, two Irishmen who had been appointed vicars-general for the interim. At this time the Diocese of Louisiana had twenty-one parishes of which four were without a church building and eight without a priest. However, money for the support of the bishop and other officers seemed generous. One report states that the Bishop of Louisiana received from the government treasury a remuneration equal to four thousand dollars, and the chaplains as much as seven hundred. Revenue for the cathedral came from money paid by the king, from rent of houses and hire of pews. The parish churches were not so well endowed and frequently had an income from pew rent only. Hassett died in 1804, and Walsh was left to fight a losing battle in a schism growing out of the despotic actions of the trustees or wardens of St. Louis Cathedral.[3]

The inhabitants of Louisiana were hardly aware of the shift made from Spanish to French government in 1803, but when the United States assumed control after the Louisiana Purchase, the Catholics in the area had doubts and misgivings about the future of their church in the territory. The affairs of St. Louis Cathedral had not been administered with unity for several years. Every Catholic in New Orleans was affected by the actions of the trustees of the church who disputed the authority of the bishop and held that of the vicar-general almost in contempt. The trustees had the

<hr>

[2] Baudier, *Catholic Church in Louisiana*, 233-44, 245; John E. Rothensteiner, "Father James Maxwell of Ste. Genevieve," *St. Louis Catholic Historical Review*, IV (1922), 143.

[3] Louis J. Lowenstein, *History of the St. Louis Cathedral of New Orleans* (New Orleans, 1882), 35-49; Baudier, *Catholic Church in Louisiana*, 254-59.

support of their sinister and troublesome Capuchin pastor, Antonio de Sedella, better known in New Orleans as Père Antoine. In 1781 Sedella, accompanied by five Capuchin friars, had arrived in New Orleans. Offices were literally heaped upon him until he had become an assistant vicar-general, pastor of the cathedral, superior of the Capuchins, and assistant ecclesiastical judge. Friends and supporters were soon numbered by the hundreds. The Capuchin father began to handle matters as he willed and to defy his superiors. In 1787 Sedella had been appointed commissary of the Holy Inquisition in Louisiana. Fearing the possibility of a revolution if heretics were apprehended, Bishop Barcelona and Governor Miro ordered Sedella to return to Spain. Having been deported from Louisiana in 1790, Sedella spent the next four years in Spain. In 1794 he dared to return to New Orleans and remained there until his death in 1828. John G. Shea, an eminent Catholic historian, accuses William C. C. Claiborne, territorial governor, of supporting Sedella. Since Claiborne was glad to see the church involved in trouble, according to Shea, the governor "lent the whole influence of his position to break down the discipline of the Catholic Church and maintain in the Cathedral of New Orleans a man whose immoral character and neglect of duty were notorious, and who would in any New England village have been consigned to jail."[4] Much evidence seems to contradict this harsh charge against Claiborne.

Governor Claiborne, addressing a letter to the Secretary of War, said: "We have a Spanish priest here who is a very dangerous man. He rebelled against the Superiors of his own Church and would even rebel, I am persuaded, against this government whenever a fit occasion may serve." Claiborne, requesting Sedella to come to the Government

[4] John G. Shea, *Life and Times of the Most Rev. John Carroll* (New York, 1888), 590. Also see Kenny, *Catholic Culture in Alabama*, 34. This long and involved story of Père Antoine is scattered through many pages of Baudier's history.

House, informed the priest in the presence of city officials of the reports circulating against him. The latter denied the charges, declared his complete innocence, and pledged support of the government by taking an oath of allegiance administered by Governor Claiborne.[5]

A year after Hassett's death the president of the board of trustees wrote Bishop John Carroll of Baltimore, in charge of the vacant Diocese of Louisiana, that he and his colleagues refused to accept Walsh's authority. About the same time Walsh wrote a long letter to Rome in regard to the insubordination of Sedella. While waiting for a slow mail and further instructions, Walsh proceeded to withdraw the priest's faculties and to place his church under a limited interdict. The trustees supported Sedella in a schism which threatened to break down any discipline exercised by the Catholic Church. A letter, dated September 1805, from the Congregation de Propaganda Fide at Rome, under whose jurisdiction the church in the United States came as missionary territory, placed Louisiana under the jurisdiction of Bishop Carroll, thereby relieving Walsh of a difficult situation. About a year later Bishop Carroll explained to James Madison, Secretary of State, the disturbed conditions in Louisiana and referred to Sedella as "an artful Spanish friar." Madison, in a private letter to Carroll under date of November 20, 1806, replied that "the accounts received here [of Sedella] agree with the character you have formed of him."[6]

In 1812, after years of inaction and indecision on the part of the various church authorities, Carroll (archbishop in 1808) persuaded the Reverend Louis W. DuBourg to accept an appointment as administrator apostolic of the Diocese of Louisiana. Born in Santo Domingo in 1766, DuBourg had completed his theological studies at Paris before emi-

[5] Lowenstein, St. Louis Cathedral, 37-38.
[6] Guilday, John Carroll, 707-709. Also see Annabelle M. Melville, John Carroll of Baltimore: Founder of the American Catholic Hierarchy (New York, 1955), 238-39.

grating to America in 1794. He had served as president of Georgetown College from 1796 to 1799, and in 1800 had founded St. Mary's College at Baltimore. When he reached New Orleans, he found existing difficulties almost overwhelming—few priests, no seminary, no college, no institution for the advancement of education except that of the Ursulines with a house and a school built by Almonaster. For three years DuBourg sought to bring order out of the chaotic religious situation in Lower Louisiana which contained some fifty thousand Catholics. He was in New Orleans when the British tried to take the city and made an arousing address in support of the American forces. General Andrew Jackson publicly commended DuBourg for his patriotic efforts. Almost at the same time, DuBourg wrote Bishop Flaget in Kentucky a detailed account giving a dreary picture of the conditions and the prospects for the church in Louisiana. DuBourg revealed that he intended to go to Europe in the spring in order to seek release from a burden that had become well-nigh unbearable. It was his plan to suggest a division of the territory and the creation of a diocese in Upper Louisiana with the bishopric located in St. Louis.[7]

DuBourg's trip to Rome did not bring the results for which he had hoped. In his interview with the Pope, DuBourg so well defined the difficulties under which he had functioned in Louisiana that he appeared the logical person to overcome them. Again reluctantly DuBourg accepted the responsibilities assigned to him, and on September 28, 1815, he was duly consecrated as a bishop. His advisers in Rome were not agreeable to DuBourg's recommendation for a division of the large diocese. In view of the complaints made to Propaganda against DuBourg while he was in Europe, the decision of the Pope to return DuBourg to

[7] Guilday, *John Carroll*, 710-11; *Shepherd of the Valley*, June 6, 13, 1834; John W. Ward, *Andrew Jackson: Symbol for an Age* (New York, 1962), 101-105.

Louisiana might well indicate that no better man was available. A second bishop could not be drawn from the church's resources in America. From New Orleans came letters to the Pope expressing violent opposition to Du-Bourg's return there. The same faction sent messengers to St. Louis to arouse the people in that city against DuBourg. Wisely he chose to absent himself from his diocese while the opposition cooled in New Orleans, described a bit later by a priest as the "sewer of all vice and refuge of all that is worst on earth."[8] For two years Bishop DuBourg remained in Europe raising funds and recruiting missionaries for his extensive diocese. In October 1816 he sent ten Ursuline nuns from Bordeaux to New Orleans. By the next fall DuBourg was ready to return to America.

No easy task confronted the bishop. Prior to his arrival St. Louis had been a city without a settled priest, being served by one who came every three weeks. Since no one of authority was there to make the necessary plans for receiving the bishop, Flaget had dispatched in the early fall a group of men from St. Thomas. Placing the responsibility on Father Felix de Andreis, Flaget had admonished this Italian-born Vincentian priest to do almost the impossible in three months. Concerning this experience, Andreis has left some interesting comments. He found St. Louis in no way physically or spiritually ready for a bishop. The greater part of the population was Creole "without any religious culture, on account of the long period during which the place had been destitute of clergymen and of every means of instruction. . . ." A church was sorely needed since there was nothing to use except "a miserable log-cabin, open to every wind, and falling to pieces." He believed that there "a noble destiny" awaited to be employed among this "desolate portion of the flock of Christ in an unfaithful land."

Small hardships endured by the priests often appeared almost unbearable. It may well have been the morning after Andreis had killed as many as one hundred large ticks that he despairingly wrote: "I know that were it not for the glory of God and the salvation of souls, I would not stay where I am for all the gold in the world."[9]

Disembarking at Annapolis on September 4, 1817, Bishop DuBourg was accompanied by a suite of five priests and twenty-six young men, some of whom were to become candidates for the ministry and others to become lay brothers. Before setting out for the West, he and his retinue visited Catholic centers in Pennsylvania. On December 2 DuBourg reached St. Thomas in Kentucky, where his old friend Bishop Flaget welcomed him. Ten days later the two bishops accompanied by Father Badin started for St. Louis. Ice floes and other problems delayed the movement of the boat on the Ohio so greatly that they did not reach Ste. Genevieve until December 30. On the next day the bishops donned pontifical vestments and accompanied by communicants of all faiths proceeded to the church under a canopy carried by four citizens. On New Year's Day 1818 the new bishop celebrated mass in the little town and then continued his journey to St. Louis. Formally installed in the bishop's chair on January 5, 1818, DuBourg was deeply pleased with the generous reception given him. On the following day, Epiphany, DuBourg "preached with such admirable eloquence that he penetrated the hardest hearts and produced the most marvelous effects." He established his episcopal residence in St. Louis, and for a five-year period concentrated the greater part of his energies in the upper portion of his diocese.[10]

[9] Joseph Rosati, *Life of Very Rev. Felix De Andreis* (St. Louis, 1900), 178-97 passim.

[10] Spalding, *Flaget*, 172-75; Charles L. Souvay, "A Centennial of the Church in St. Louis," *Catholic Historical Review*, IV (1918-1919), 71-75; Schauinger, *Cathedrals*, 159.

After DuBourg's arrival in St. Louis, he moved immediately to the building of a cathedral. A cornerstone was laid on March 28, 1818, and by Christmas Day services were held in a building which was used until 1834. St. Louis College was built about the same time as the cathedral. In the library of the college DuBourg housed his fine collection of eight thousand volumes which was described as "the most complete scientific and literary repertory of the western country, if not of the western world."[11]

DuBourg was a busy, energetic bishop, going hither and yon, begging money and writing letters, alternating between hope and gloom. He visited New Madrid and found there a sad situation. The earthquakes of 1811 and 1812 had taken their great toll of real property. The old town of New Madrid had caved into the river carrying with it the St. Isidore Church, an impressive structure. Built of cherry lumber in 1799 this church had measured twenty-eight by sixty feet, and had been ornamented with ten windows, an altar of cherrywood, a large picture of the Virgin Mary, and a belfry with a bell. In addition to the church, the parish had had a comfortable residence and a garden. The expense of building and furnishing the church had been paid by the Spanish government. New Madrid had been considered spiritually dead since the transfer of Louisiana to the United States, but the presence of the church and residence had served as a token of the Catholic faith. Without the physical structures as a symbol of a once thriving religious community, its last vestiges faded with the years. In November 1820 DuBourg wrote to Father Joseph Rosati that years had passed without a priest in New Madrid; there had been no marriages, no baptisms, and no sacraments. The town desired a priest but believed that it could not support one. A year later Rosati wrote to an official in Rome that in the area "ignorance cannot go any farther. It is morally a forest

---

[11] Rothensteiner, *Archdiocese of St. Louis*, I, 271-73, 276.

to frighten the stoutest heart." A decade later the situation had changed but little, for a priest in New Madrid wrote Bishop Rosati in 1832 that at preaching "the people assembled merely to see one another for amusement and passtime. . . ."[12]

As DuBourg became acquainted with the area around St. Louis, he reversed his previous suggestion of dividing the Louisiana Territory into two bishoprics. In a letter to Propaganda in 1822 he gave five reasons for opposing the division: Lower Louisiana supported the whole see; if divided, support from the upper section must come from another source; church property in Missouri would soon yield some income; two bishops were not needed; a coadjutor could serve instead of an additional bishop. In addition to his factual appraisal, personal objection to residing in New Orleans undoubtedly bore heavily on his decision. DuBourg clearly stated his determination to resign if the territory should be divided.[13] His wishes were respected, and ultimately he saw great achievements which were especially significant when judged against the tremendous difficulties that he had overcome.

In 1823 Rosati was appointed coadjutor bishop, and DuBourg transferred his episcopal residence to New Orleans. Rosati, born and educated in Italy, early in life became a member of the Vincentian Congregation. He became a distinguished Latinist, having acquired a beautiful style, comparable to that of the early church fathers. At DuBourg's invitation he had come to Baltimore in 1816 and a year later moved to St.Louis, with the idea of founding a Lazarist college. After a change in initial plans, St. Mary's College was built at the Barrens in Perry County, Missouri, and Rosati became not only its first superior but also professor

---

[12] Rothensteiner, "Catholic New Madrid," *St. Louis Catholic Historical Review*, IV, 120, 128-29, 206-207, 211.

[13] "Documents from Our Archives," *St. Louis Catholic Historical Review*, III (1921), 117-18.

of theology, philosophy, and sacred scripture. Among his students in the seminary were Leo de Neckere, John M. Odin, and John Timon, all of whom in later years were bishops of great stature.[14]

For the purpose of his consecration, Rosati left Ste. Genevieve on February 21, 1824, on board a steamer bound for Donaldsonville, Louisiana, where by agreement he would meet Bishop DuBourg. Low water made navigation difficult, and the boat stuck on sandbars five times in 140 miles. Arriving at Donaldsonville on March 11, Rosati visited in the neighborhood for two weeks before returning for the consecration which had been arranged for March 25, on the Feast of the Annunciation. There in this country parish a cleric and thirteen priests, preceded by a bishop and a bishop-elect, took part in a stately ceremony. Bishop Rosati set out at once on a visitation through much of the diocese in Louisiana and preached in St. Louis Cathedral in New Orleans on Easter Sunday.[15]

Rosati's early years were filled with disappointments and trials little different from those of any of the early bishops in the West. He and DuBourg were soon clashing over DuBourg's change of views and his draining priests from Upper into Lower Louisiana where now lay his chief interest. Some people accused Rosati of preparing for the day when the huge diocese would be divided. In August 1823 Father Odin complained in a letter to Propaganda that in the whole of the upper half of the diocese there were only ten priests and that many congregations had been neglected. Rosati, having so little money to use and being pushed by debt, in a letter written in 1826 advised a priest to "sell the clock: I must make money by all possible means to pay my debts."[16]

[14] Easterly, *Rosati*, passim.

[15] Baudier, *Catholic Church in Louisiana*, 300.

[16] Easterly, *Rosati*, 80-82; "Diary of Bishop Rosati," *St. Louis Catholic Historical Review*, IV (1922), 248.

Without confiding his plan in anyone DuBourg in 1826 asked the Prefect of Propaganda to accept his resignation as bishop. Worry over financial problems, his disagreements with Rosati, the criticism of him in New Orleans, and especially the attacks by the newspapers contributed to the decision that he had considered for some time. Shea explains DuBourg's resignation by saying: "Discouraged at the difficulties which arose to thwart him, and confronted by bitter malevolence, he at last lost all heart and energy." Friend and foe alike rejoiced at the news. His foes believed his resignation would result in a "good riddance," while his friends thought the ecclesiastical situation had come to such an impasse only a change in bishops could solve it. Despite his romantic nature, his oversensitiveness, his lack of business acumen, and his tendency to plan on an extended scale, DuBourg deserves to be regarded as the first successful Bishop of Louisiana. He had found Catholicism at a low level in Louisiana. When he left, the region had twenty parishes with priests, churches, and schools.[17]

In November 1826 Rosati received from Propaganda a letter notifying him of his appointment as Administrator of the Diocese of New Orleans and of the proposed Diocese of St. Louis. In another letter, dated July 16, 1826, Rosati's faculties were declared to be those held by Bishop DuBourg. The resignation of DuBourg had left a volatile situation in New Orleans that demanded Rosati's presence there. In March 1827 he arrived in the city and immediately formed an episcopal council. Among the rights that he reserved to himself was the all important power of appointing pastors which the trustees had previously questioned. After three months in the South he returned to St. Louis, but he was so uneasy about conditions in New Orleans he made another visit there in November. By a Papal Brief, dated May 27,

[17] Charles L. Souvay, "Rosati's Elevation to the See of St. Louis," *Catholic Historical Review*, III (1917-1918), 173-74, 180-81; O'Gorman, *Roman Catholic Church*, 331-32; Garraghan, *Jesuits*, I, 36-37.

1827, Rosati was appointed Bishop of St. Louis, with the provision that he should continue as Administrator of the Diocese of New Orleans.

In compliance with Rosati's urgent request, Pope Leo XII issued a Brief on August 16, 1828, wherein he scathingly censured the trustees of the New Orleans parish for trying to secure a legislative act which would permit them to reject pastors appointed by the bishop. Fortunately the efforts of the trustees failed to secure the act. Sedella's death on January 19, 1829, had struck a blow to the obnoxious system, but the evil continued for years.[18]

Rosati's burden was eased a great deal and the ecclesiastical administration was improved significantly by the consecration, on June 24, 1830, of Leo de Neckere as Bishop of New Orleans. The new bishop had come from France to America on a ship with DuBourg in 1817, had studied at the seminary under Rosati, and later became its superior. This learned priest who became widely known for his masterful sermons, unfortunately, lacked a constitution equal to the physical requirements of his life as Bishop of New Orleans. De Neckere served the people of New Orleans bravely during the terrible epidemic of yellow fever and Asiatic cholera in the fall of 1832 and the summer of 1833. Sparing himself not at all, he died on September 6, 1833, from the fever which took four thousand lives between October 3 and November 13. De Neckere had won several of the ecclesiastical controversies in Louisiana and was in a good position to advance the church when death removed him.

The New Orleans diocese was without a bishop until the appointment of the Reverend Antoine Blanc, who served in this capacity from 1835 to 1850. Blanc had come to America with de Neckere and DuBourg, and, having been ordained before leaving France, he went almost immediately to

---

[18] For this and the preceding paragraph see Easterly, *Rosati*, 93-122.

Vincennes. Later at the direction of Bishop DuBourg, Blanc undertook the organization of Catholics at Natchez and Point Coupée. He was a wise and natural choice for vicar-general of the New Orleans diocese when Bishop de Neckere sought him in 1830. Taking up residence in New Orleans, Blanc served for three years with the bishop and experienced a rich apprenticeship for the duties he would assume after the death of de Neckere. Serving as one of the two administrators who conducted for two years the affairs of the vacant diocese, Blanc had an invaluable training. He came to the office of bishop, despite misgivings of his own ability, with background unequalled by his predecessors. The fifteen years which he had spent in the West and the South had well prepared Blanc for the bishopric of New Orleans.

Under Bishop Blanc's skillful and wise administration many of the disturbing factors peculiar to the New Orleans diocese diminished. He successfully curbed the usurpation by the laity of the powers of the church. His great zeal and effort in behalf of expansion of the activities of the church resulted in a greatly increased membership. Magnificent church buildings attested the growing faith in the church and in his administration. *Le Propagateur Catholique,* the first Catholic newspaper established in New Orleans, was founded largely through Bishop Blanc's desire to have an organ through which to counteract the malevolent influence of the trustees of St. Louis Cathedral and to spread Catholic news and doctrines. Parochial schools, St. Charles College at Grand Coteau, and a diocesan seminary at Plattenville attest to the growth in the realm of education. When Blanc became bishop in 1835 New Orleans had only two churches; twelve parishes in the city had been added by the time he became archbishop in 1850.[19]

[19] Baudier, *Catholic Church in Louisiana,* 315-402, contains most of the facts in this and the two preceding paragraphs.

After the large Diocese of Louisiana had been divided
and Bishop de Neckere had been installed in 1830, Rosati
became bishop of the upper portion of the Louisiana Purchase area with his see at St. Louis. Rosati was then able
to give more attention to St. Louis and especially to the
church in the Arkansas Territory. Of the more than five
thousand people in St. Louis in 1830, about three thousand
were Catholics. On October 26, 1834, the new cathedral
costing in excess of $63,000 was dedicated in sermons
preached by Bishop John B. Purcell of Cincinnati and by
Father Robert A. Abell, the Catholic orator from Kentucky.
The building of this cathedral, standing as a symbol of great
strength and stability, vastly improved the Catholic position
in St. Louis and the surrounding country, influenced as the
country was by a rising tide of anti-Catholic feeling through
the 1830s. Rosati was a wise choice as the administrator of
the St. Louis area. His deep and abiding interests in schools
had convinced many that he should not be removed from
the work he was doing for education. As bishop he increased
rather than relaxed this interest.[20]

In 1703 the Bishop of Quebec erected the first canonical
parish in Mobile which was a part of his diocese. Notwithstanding the church's early planting in Mobile, it had surprisingly small success largely because there was no permanency of priests. In some twenty-five years prior to the
seizure of Mobile in 1813 by Americans, the Catholic church
in the little town had had thirteen pastors. In 1825 Michael
Portier was made Vicar-Apostolic of Florida which included
Alabama. At this time there were but two churches in Florida,
one at St. Augustine and one at Pensacola, and three priests
served this enormous territory. Born at Lyons, France,
Portier had been ordained as a priest by Bishop DuBourg
in St. Louis in 1818. During the next year Portier was made

[20] Easterly, *Rosati*, 127-33; Paul C. Shulte (comp.), *The Catholic Heritage
of Saint Louis* (St. Louis, 1934), 191-200.

Vicar-General of the Diocese of New Orleans and established his residence in New Orleans. On November 5, 1826, this thirty-one-year old priest was consecrated a titular bishop and placed in charge of the Vicariate Apostolic of Alabama.[21] At that time he was the only priest in his vicariate. "I need two or three priests," he wrote, "but dare not ask for them, as I am afraid I cannot now support them. I have neither pectoral cross nor chapel, neither crozier, nor mitre." When finally he secured a priest for West Florida, he begged his superiors to send another priest to St. Augustine. From a trip to Europe in 1829 he returned with two priests and four ecclesiastics. During his absence Mobile was made, on May 15, 1829, into an episcopal see embracing West Florida and Alabama. Establishing his residence in Mobile, Portier was installed as bishop in a small church twenty by thirty feet in size. A two-room frame residence for the bishop stood nearby.[22]

Portier began to travel over his diocese, organizing congregations and erecting churches at Montgomery, Huntsville, Tuscaloosa, and several other large towns. In 1830 Bishop Portier secured a splendid tract of land about five miles west of Mobile and built thereon Spring Hill College which is generally accepted as the base of his enduring fame. Bishop John England of Charleston on observing Portier's successes regretted that Portier had not been appointed to the more important bishopric of New Orleans. Activities at Tuscaloosa may be observed as a typical effort made by Portier. When he first visited Tuscaloosa in 1835, he found the Catholics there had been served on infrequent visits by a priest from Mobile. Gathering a congregation Portier arranged for the use of a Masonic hall as a meeting place. Encouraged by occasional visits from the bishop, the

[21] Peter J. Hamilton, *Colonial Mobile* (Mobile, 1952), 364-65; O'Connell, *Catholicity*, 587-89; Kenny, *Catholic Culture in Alabama*, 31-38.
[22] [Carroll], *Catholic History*, 214-15.

congregation increased sufficiently to maintain a church
building which was erected in 1845. The people of the town
seemed to have had great pride in the new edifice, measuring
thirty-one by fifty-five feet, erected at a cost of twenty-eight
hundred dollars. Many Protestants contributed to the building fund, and, when one Baptist and two Methodist preachers signed the subscription list, community spirit soared. In
1850 Catholics at Mobile dedicated a splendid cathedral,
inside measurements of which were 145 by 80 feet, and the
nave ceiling towered 64 feet. The steps and upper part of
the altar were of Italian and Alabama marble. The unfinished
structure had cost eighty thousand dollars and needed
twenty thousand more to be completed.[23]

Toward the close of the eighteenth century the Natchez
district was the fastest growing center in the Spanish
Floridas. Most of the inhabitants were Anglo-American and
Irish Protestants, living in peace with the French, Spanish,
Indians, and Negroes. John F. H. Claiborne, historian of
Mississippi, declared that there was "more religious freedom
and toleration for Protestants in the Natchez district, than
Catholics, and dissenters from the ruling denomination,
enjoyed in either Old or New England." Governor Miro
had planned the erection of two parishes in the Natchez
district—one in the north and one at Cole's Creek. A church
in Natchez was completed in 1791 and another at Cole's
Creek in the following year. Apparently both were later
abandoned; a group of Irish missionaries sent to the area
remained only a short time. By 1801 the number of Catholics at Natchez had decreased until only ten families were
left and only two of these were in easy circumstances. Since
no Catholic priest was obtainable, Colonel William Vausdan
wrote to Bishop Carroll proposing that a Protestant minister

---

[23] Kenny, *Catholic Culture in Alabama*, 48-56; *Souvenir of the Centennial
of St. John's Church, Tuscaloosa, Alabama* (n. p., 1944), passim; *Catholic
Telegraph*, April 16, 1846, Dec. 28, 1850.

officiate in the church. Back came a stern letter of disapproval from the bishop. "Would not those holy places," he asked, "be profaned and the character of their consecration be effaced by their becoming the seminaries of error and false doctrines?"[24]

Some twenty-five years rolled by and the Roman Catholics in Natchez remained without a priest. In 1816 Daniel McGraw of Natchez, unaware of the death of Archbishop Carroll in December 1815 or uncertain of the name of his successor, addressed to Carroll a complaint that about a year previously the Catholics in Natchez had petitioned New Orleans to send them a priest, but the plea had been refused. A second request was sent, and generous support assured to a priest, especially if he could teach. He clearly pointed out that the priest must be one "sufficiently acquainted with the English language," so that he "can deliver an edifying and interesting discourse in that language. . . ."[25] In 1820 Father Antoine Blanc spent four months in Natchez and while there he installed a pastor who remained four years.

In 1839 the Natchez *Free Trader* pleaded that it would be an act of justice to the Catholics for all citizens to aid in the erection of a church on the site of the old building near the ancient burying ground. Waxing eloquent, the editor of the paper hoped "for the erection of a dome that shall resound with the solemn chants for the dead, and thrill with the *Misieri* [sic] and reverberate with the ancient and time honored celebration of the Mass."[26] Although the Diocese of Natchez had been formed in 1837, John Chanche, its first bishop, did not reach the city until 1841. The diocese comprised more than 46,000 square miles and about 400,000

[24] John F. H. Claiborne, *Mississippi as a Province, Territory and State* (Jackson, Miss., 1880), 136-37; Shea, *Carroll*, 505. For the early beginnings of the Catholic Church in Mississippi see Gerow, *Catholicity in Mississippi*.
[25] In *Catholic Historical Researches*, XIX (1902), 64.
[26] Reprinted in *Catholic Telegraph*, July 4, 1839.

people without a single church building and with only two priests. The efficient Chanche set out at once to build a cathedral, and in February 1842 laid the cornerstone of St. Mary's Cathedral. Bishop Blanc of New Orleans had rushed to the aid of the Mississippi diocese with about eight thousand dollars. Chanche, filling the role of a missionary bishop, continually traveled about his diocese and within ten years knew by name half of the ten thousand Catholics under his jurisdiction. Bishop Chanche died of cholera in 1852.[27]

While some problems arose in all areas served by the Catholic Church, Kentucky seems to have had the fewest. About the time the territory entered the Union in 1792, the Catholics numbered some three hundred families. The movement to the West was in full tide and hundreds of Catholics, leaving their native Maryland, moved over the mountains and down the Ohio River to settle on the good land of central Kentucky. The quality of priests in Kentucky as a whole was excellent. No Western region could boast of a group equal to Stephen T. Badin, Benedict J. Flaget, Charles Nerinckx, and John B. M. David. They lived long, devoted lives among a rural, stable, largely American-born population.

In the fall of 1805 a group of Trappists came to the state, first settling at Pottinger's Creek, then at Casey's Creek in 1807. From Kentucky they moved to Missouri in 1809, and on to Illinois in 1810 before returning to Europe in 1814. Thirty-four years later another Trappist colony arrived to settle permanently at Gethsemane on some sixteen hundred acres of land, about fourteen miles from Bardstown. In 1850 Gethsemane was elevated to the rank of an abbey.[28]

[27] James J. Pillar, *The Catholic Church in Mississippi, 1837-1865* (New Orleans, 1964), 43-50; Gerow, *Catholicity in Mississippi*, 37-41; *Catholic Church in . . . Natchez*, passim.

[28] For the early years in Kentucky see Webb, *Catholicity in Kentucky;* Schauinger, *Badin;* Schauinger, *Cathedrals;* Mattingly, *Church on the Kentucky Frontier;* Spalding, *Flaget*.

During the winter of 1804-1805 Edward D. Fenwick, a descendant of an old Maryland family and the future Bishop of Cincinnati, came to Kentucky to view the prospects for establishing the Dominican order. In May 1805 Badin addressed to Bishop Carroll a letter that outlined his deep interest and faith in Fenwick's plans to establish a Dominican monastery and college. Badin sought permission to transfer some property vested in him to the new community and to become associated with the Dominicans. Soon after this letter was written, Father Nerinckx arrived in Kentucky from Belgium and through the years became Badin's co-worker and closest friend. In October 1805 Badin wrote Bishop Carroll emphatically retracting the offer he had made to Fenwick. Beyond question the change in Badin's attitude toward the Dominican community was due to the influence of Nerinckx. Bombarding Carroll with letters denouncing the Dominicans, Badin and Nerinckx showed little charity and much jealousy. They quite obviously resented the advent of this new monastery. However, the generosity and kindness of the Dominicans nullified the hostile reception which awaited them. With his own money Fenwick had bought a farm of five hundred acres about two miles from Springfield, and there he established St. Rose's Priory. In 1808 Fenwick opened a small college which later became St. Thomas Aquinas College. St. Rose's Church, the mother house of Dominicans in America, was completed in 1809.[29]

In the period of 1800-1812 the Catholic Church in Kentucky had definite success in one field of endeavor. Three religious orders, the Dominican, the Sisters of Loretto, and the Sisters of Charity, had been established permanently and a colony of Trappists had located in the state for four

[29] In addition to material covered by the preceding note see William J. Howlett, *Life of Rev. Charles Nerinckx: Pioneer Missionary of Kentucky* (Techny, Ill., 1915); C. P. Maes, *The Life of Reverend Charles Nerinckx* (Cincinnati, 1880).

years. The signal recognition of the growth of the church
in Kentucky was made in the formation of the Bardstown
diocese. In 1808 the Baltimore diocese was erected into an
archbishopric and new dioceses of Boston, New York, Philadelphia, and Bardstown were created. To the Diocese of
Bardstown was given jurisdiction over all territory north of
the southern boundary of Tennessee and east of the Mississippi. Bardstown, incorporated by the Virginia legislature
in 1788, had become the most important town in western
Kentucky. At the time of the erection of the cathedral, the
location appeared to be ideal.[30] Unfortunately Catholic
authorities had made a poor choice, for Bardstown proved
to have little future in competition with Louisville, so
admirably situated on the Ohio River.

Having been suggested to the Holy See by Archbishop
Carroll, the Reverend Benedict J. Flaget was named the
first Bishop of Bardstown. Flaget was not happy with his
new elevation; he liked his work in Baltimore and for two
years withheld his acceptance of the bishopric, finally yielding to the persuasion of the Superior General of the Sulpi-
cians. Flaget, born and educated in France, had been
obliged to flee the country during the French Revolution.
Arriving in Baltimore in 1792, Flaget at the instruction of
Bishop Carroll had gone immediately to Vincennes, then a
military post. Recalled in 1795 to Baltimore, he had served
in various educational posts before he was assigned to
Bardstown. After he had reluctantly accepted the appointment, Flaget wrote to Badin: "God seems to require of me
to bow my head and to suffer this burden to be placed on it,
though it is likely to crush me. Alas! if I stop long to
consider my weakness, I shall become so far depressed in
spirits, as not to be able to take one step on the long path

[30] William J. Howlett, "St. Joseph's, the Cathedral Church of the Diocese
of Bardstown, Kentucky," *Illinois Catholic Historical Review*, IV (1921),
275-85, 372-80; Webb, *Catholicity in Kentucky*, 269-73.

which . . . I must now traverse."[31] Accompanied by Father David, two priests, and three seminarians, Flaget reached Bardstown on June 8, 1811.

Administration of the diocese was not easy for Flaget. He was hampered in all he did by the lack of financial support by the parishes. Money was scarce in the West, but not so scarce as the paucity of the contributions to the program of the church would indicate. The separation of church and state had placed the church on the same basis as any private enterprise, and it suffered for lack of funds. The role of patron was not part of the Western man's repertory and was one that he did not easily assume. Only in the twentieth century has the American become a generous giver. To priests accustomed to the European tradition of patronage and royal subsidy supporters of the church in the West seemed unnecessarily parsimonious. Father Anthony Salmon, writing from Kentucky in the winter of 1798-1799, had spoken of the people's attitude to Bishop Carroll: "Our people have no idea of generosity and are quite strangers with the disposition of making any sacrifice. They are mean, narrow-minded." In 1801 Badin in a letter to Carroll had complained about the stinginess of the church members. He cited the case of one Jared Boorman who had not paid a single penny to the church during the three or four years he had been in Kentucky.[32]

No aura of luxury distinguished Flaget as a hierarch of the church. His small log episcopal residence provided no comforts, and his scant trappings could little enhance the stature of the man. Once when recapitulating the material resources of the diocese, Badin rightly described Flaget as "the poorest bishop in the Christian world."[33]

[31] Schauinger, *Badin,* 161.
[32] In *Catholic Historical Researches,* XXVIII (1911), 107; *Records, American Catholic Historical Society,* XXIII (1912), 142.
[33] Mattingly, *Church on the Kentucky Frontier,* 209.

When Flaget had reached Kentucky, he found there only three secular priests and the four Dominican fathers in their priory at St. Rose. This small ministry had the care of thirty-six congregations consisting of about one thousand families or some six thousand people. The material holdings comprised ten churches, all but one built of logs, a few pastoral residences, and six plantations. In a tour made through his province soon after his arrival, Flaget detected a slackness in the religious life of the people and judged that religion played no stronger part in their lives than Badin had estimated in 1805. Badin was of the opinion that no more than half of the people in the state had any religious affiliation. The lack of priests had caused some people to slip away from the church. In the Limestone community, now Maysville, Flaget located only one Catholic. In that section of his diocese conditions were not promising: the Negroes were ignorant of religion and the whites were indifferent to it. All was not grim, however; some prospects encouraged Flaget: Catholic-Protestant relations were generally cordial and an excellent basis had been laid for future cooperation. Badin, Flaget, David, and other church leaders had numerous Protestant friends to whom they could turn for financial and other aid. In the immediate future many Protestants would entrust the education of their sons and daughters to the superior Catholic schools. The soil in Kentucky was good, crops abundant, climate gentle, and life not too harsh for the growth and prosperity of the monasteries.[34]

One unfortunate incident damaged the favorable Catholic position in Kentucky. Before the Diocese of Bardstown was created, the title to church property had been vested in Badin as vicar-general. When Bishop Flaget reached the state and asked Badin to transfer the property to him, Badin

[34] Mattingly, *Church on the Kentucky Frontier*, Chaps. IV, VIII; Spalding, *Flaget*, 97-114 passim.

refused upon various grounds. After much argument, many letters, and threats of censure by Flaget, Badin drew up a deed conveying the property of St. Thomas to the bishop. Later Flaget learned that the deed was drawn in such a manner that only part of the property had been transferred, and that Badin even boasted of his chicanery. When Badin left Kentucky in 1819 to spend nine years traveling in Europe, the disturbing problem solved itself. In most respects the diocesan authorities worked in great harmony toward a concerted good.[35]

By 1815 Flaget reported to the Pope that Kentucky had nineteen churches, ten priests, and about ten thousand Catholics. He mentioned that the area across the Ohio under his jurisdiction needed several priests. Some Indian tribes still retained lingering traces of the religion which had been preached to them by the early Jesuit fathers, and beyond the Mississippi other tribes were pleading for Catholic missionaries.

In 1816 Flaget's untiring efforts and those of his colleagues made it possible to lay the cornerstone of the cathedral at Bardstown. The building was designed to be 120 feet long, 65 feet wide, Corinthian in style, and to cost between fifteen and twenty thousand dollars. To this cathedral, the first west of the Allegheny Mountains, Protestants subscribed some ten thousand dollars and constituted half of the six directors in charge of the building program. Times were hard and money scarce, but faith and enthusiasm continued through the three years devoted to the construction. The honor of delivering the consecration sermon on August 8, 1819, fell to Robert A. Abell. On Christmas Eve, five years later, a correspondent to the *Catholic Miscellany* attended services at the cathedral, which was filled to capacity. The singing and the brilliance of the lighting of the building, the music from the organ, and the discourse of a college

[35] Guilday, *John Carroll*, 696; Schauinger, *Badin*, Chap. XIII.

president assured him that nothing in Europe could have excited such feelings as "the ceremonies of Christmas morning, in this *back-wood* Cathedral."[36] Everyone with whom the visitor had a conversation praised Flaget's accomplishment in an area with limited financial resources. The graceful cathedral has withstood the years and today stands apparently as firm as it was on that dedication day nearly a century and a half ago.

Holy Mass had been celebrated in Louisville as early as 1792. French and Irish Catholics were numerous enough in the vicinity to warrant Badin's faith in the erection of a small church in Louisville in 1811. When the building became too small for the communicants, a larger one was erected in 1830. Seven years later some German Catholics, about two thousand of whom were in Louisville, built a brick church, forty-five by seventy-five feet, costing fourteen thousand dollars. Although he objected to the taste used in ornamentation, a visitor described it as having "a truly beautiful ecclesiastical appearance." Among the benefactors was a Protestant family who lent the church their costliest plate.[37]

With the exception of Louisville Catholic church members in Kentucky were for the most part native-born Americans. A striking contrast lay in those churches organized on the north side of the Ohio River, a region where recent immigrants literally overwhelmed the earlier settlers. In 1817 Father John David became coadjutor of the diocese and in 1832 succeeded to the bishopric from which Flaget had resigned. Only a year later David, unhappy in his promotion and faced with general dissatisfaction over the loss of Flaget, resigned his office. Flaget became bishop once again to continue until his death in 1850. In 1841 the

[36] Columba Fox, *The Life of the Right Reverend John Baptist Mary David* (New York, 1925), 83-86; Webb, *Catholicity in Kentucky*, 269-75; *Catholic Miscellany*, Dec. 29, 1824.

[37] Wuest, *St. Boniface Parish*, 9-25.

seat of the diocese was transferred from Bardstown to Louisville. Because Bardstown had not enjoyed the growth which
it had expected, the church see needed to be located in a
more thriving area.

The early and continuing growth of the church in Kentucky was not shared by its installations in Tennessee. This
situation was largely the result of the lines of transportation
which brought few European immigrants and few Catholics
from the adjoining state of North Carolina. Although in
1799 a report spread that about a hundred Catholic families
were residing in the Knoxville area, little evidence supports
the hearsay. No church was built nor priest permanently
settled in the state before 1820. The presence of some
communicants is indicated by the invitation which Father
Badin received in the fall of 1807 from Patrick Campbell
of Knoxville to visit the Catholics there. A year later Badin
spent eight days in the town, where he met with six or
seven Catholic families, heard four confessions, baptized
twenty persons, and preached four times in the state house.
He returned to Knoxville in October 1809 and again in May
1810. By then some twelve Catholic families had formed a
congregation named St. Andrews, but they built no church
for years. Apparently no priest reached east Tennessee
between the time of Badin's last visit in 1810 and 1837,
when the Reverend Richard P. Miles was made Bishop of
Nashville. According to the biographer of Miles, this period
constitutes "one of the saddest silences in the annals of our
American Church."[38]

In a report to Rome in 1815 Flaget stated that about
twenty-five Catholic families in Nashville were "deprived
of all the aids of the Church." On May 10, 1821, Bishop
Flaget and Father Abell reached the town, where they
assembled about sixty Catholics. On the day after their
arrival the first mass offered by a bishop on Tennessee soil

[38] Schauinger, *Badin*, 62; O'Daniel, *Miles*, 291.

was celebrated in the home of a Frenchman named Mont Brun. Catholics in Nashville were few and poor, but the bishop was not disheartened. A subscription, circulated for a church building, received signatures from both Protestants and Catholics, and the offer of a building lot was made by the Grand Master of the Masonic Lodge. A story persists that a number of Irish Catholics, temporarily living in the city while a bridge was being erected across the Cumberland River, had become quite vocal over the lack of a priest and a church and had threatened to quit the job. Be this as it may, many civic-minded people contributed to the proposed church building.

To a hastily built frame structure located on Campbell Hill was given the distinction of being the first Catholic church in Tennessee. Frequent visits from Father Abell held the congregation together and inspired the building of a brick structure completed in 1830—long after the Irish workmen had finished the bridge in 1825. Abell continued his visits for four or five years, but with the single exception of the temporary assignment of the Reverend James Cosgrove in 1828, no priest was stationed in the entire state until 1836 or 1837, about the time it became a diocese. Bishop Flaget was accused by some of his brethren of such selfishness for the Kentucky portion of his diocese that he rarely ever assigned a priest beyond its borders. In face of his failure to station a priest permanently in Nashville, Bishop Flaget in a letter to Propaganda in 1826 stated that a missionary would visit the state twice a year. Two years later some Catholics in Tennessee begged a Charleston priest to pay them a visit. Eventually about 1836 Father Elisha J. Durbin was appointed pastor at Nashville, and a new day for the church began.[39]

On July 28, 1837, Nashville was elevated to an episcopal

[39] O'Daniel, *Miles*, 292, 306.

see and the able Richard P. Miles, who had been born in Maryland but had lived in Kentucky since he was five years old, became its first bishop. At last the church in the state of Tennessee had gained a permanent foothold from which the work spread in several directions. Forty-five years of age and in splendid health, the new bishop, astride a horse given to him by his Dominican brethren at St. Rose, reached Nashville in time to celebrate the mass and then to address the congregation on Sunday, October 14, 1838. All that his entire diocese possessed in worldly goods was an unconsecrated brick church, neglected for years. Before the bishop arrived, Father Durbin had made some repairs to the church and installed "four rows of genteel, plain seats" that would accommodate about sixty of the seventy-five to a hundred communicants in the city. Within a week after his arrival at Nashville, Bishop Miles and Durbin started a visitation of the diocese which would require four or five weeks. Since Durbin's labors in Tennessee terminated in his journey with the bishop, Miles returned alone to Nashville. Within his diocese he had not one priest and was a bishop "without scrip or staff, or even whereon to lay his head!"[40] After having ridden five hundred miles and having counted every Catholic in sight, Miles found a total of three hundred scattered from Knoxville to Memphis. In a state with an area of some 42,000 square miles, the bishop weighed his problems and soon hastened to Kentucky to make urgent pleas for a priest and for financial help. The church had made a wise choice in the energetic Bishop Miles, who quickly began to gather Catholics, secure necessary aid, build churches, and move rapidly about his large diocese.

When the capitol of Tennessee was located in Nashville in 1843, city planners, seeking a prominence on which to locate the new state house, cast their eyes at Campbell

[40] O'Daniel, *Miles*, 138.

Hill on which the Catholic church was located. The Catholic congregation was agreeable to the move, bought a lot on the corner of Cedar and Sumner streets, and on June 6, 1844, the cornerstone of Seven Dolors Cathedral was laid. The bishop's heart was warmed by the knowledge that non-Catholics had given evidence of their great admiration for him and for the accomplishments of his church. They had subscribed much more to the subscription list than had the Catholics. Sixteen years of life were left to the tall, straight, and handsome prelate. During these years Catholic progress in the state was slow but steady.[41]

As the state developed, the church shared in its growth. A correspondent from Memphis wrote in November 1845 to the editors of the *Catholic Advocate* a vivid description of the busy river town. The streets of the city of some eight to nine thousand inhabitants were filled with cotton and its people were engaged in the "all absorbing subject of money-making." The Methodists were most numerous and most noisy. The Episcopalians were increasing and had a fine church building. The Catholics, numbering about five hundred, had almost finished a brick church forty by seventy feet with a spire and a cross. Unfortunately the building of the navy yard had brought to the city numerous Irish laborers who "do not evince that spirit of religious zeal which is necessary to adorn the Church of their native land." About 1850 Father John M. Jacquet managed to have built on Pine Street in Chattanooga a little frame chapel, measuring fifteen by thirty feet. This was the first Catholic church building in the largest settlement in that area of the state. Seven years later the Catholics erected a second church, more than double in size, with a basement used for a school. By 1860 the whole of east Tennessee could claim only one

[41] The content of the preceding four paragraphs was largely derived from O'Daniel, *Miles*, passim; Gohmann, *Nativism in Tennessee*, Chaps. II, III; Flanigen (ed.), *Catholicity in Tennessee*, 10-76.

priest whose territory extended over an area of about three hundred miles.[42]

The church in Arkansas had long been a matter of deep concern to Rosati. When he became coadjutor to Bishop DuBourg in 1824, Arkansas fell to his care. From the end of the Spanish regime until the spring of 1820 only one priest had gone to Arkansas, and he had remained a single year. In 1825 Rosati received a letter from John Muletti in Arkansas telling him of a thousand Creole Catholics in the neighborhood of Little Rock who had not seen a priest for twenty-five years. In answer to this urgent appeal Rosati sent Fathers John M. Odin and John Timon to Arkansas on a missionary trip. So successful were they that Rosati reported to Propaganda that the missionaries had baptized two hundred people and performed numerous marriages. "If no time is lost," he wrote in 1825, "religion will have much to gain because the Protestant ministers have not yet done much. But certainly they will not fail to establish themselves here."[43] Some five years later Rosati reported, probably in error, that there were two thousand Roman Catholics in Arkansas without a single priest to serve them.

In 1831 Rosati selected Fathers Edmund Saulnier and Peter F. Beauprez to go to Arkansas Post. The reception accorded them was such that it probably accounts for Beauprez's description of Arkansas as "this suburb of hell." Neither Saulnier nor Beauprez had a church or chapel.

---

[42] *Catholic Advocate*, Dec. 20, 1845. Also see George J. Flanigen (comp.), *The Centenary of Sts. Peter and Paul's Parish, Chattanooga, Tennessee* (Chattanooga, 1952), 9-10; Gohmann, *Nativism in Tennessee*, 160.

[43] Charles W. Sloane, "Arkansas," *Catholic Encyclopedia*, I, 726; Easterly, *Rosati*, 79. In 1858, the Reverend James W. Moore, known as "The Father of Presbyterianism in Arkansas," related that in 1828 he found only a few Catholics on the lower Arkansas River and around Arkansas Post. "But," he exultantly declared, "God, in remembrance of his covenant promise, broke these bands asunder and delivered over this territory to his Son." Moore, "Presbyterianism in Arkansas," *Journal of the Presbyterian Historical Society*, III (1905-1906), 58.

Saulnier became disgusted with Beauprez's laziness and in February sent him to Pine Bluff to get rid of him. Then Saulnier went to New Orleans where he collected enough money to pay for the building of a chapel. In July 1832, however, he announced his intention of leaving Arkansas. At once Rosati sent Father Annemond Dupuy to Arkansas Post. When he arrived on a Sunday a crowd gathered, and from it a sneering heckler cried: "This one won't stay long," but he was wrong, for Dupuy remained five years. In November 1832 he wrote Rosati that everybody looked at him with an evil eye. "I have never seen," he said, "people more attached to the things of this world." Discouraged after two years of labor, he reported no spiritual improvement could be expected soon.[44]

In letters to Rosati in December 1833 and April 1834 Dupuy urged the establishment of a church in Little Rock, where no priest served the two hundred German Catholics. He urged the bishop to act in haste "otherwise the [Protestant] preachers will take possession of it." After a trip to Little Rock in the summer of 1834, Dupuy again wrote to Rosati of the distressing situation. He had found twenty Catholic families getting their religion from "a false minister." Most of these families had subscribed to the support of two Presbyterian churches. The Protestants, he said, were mostly Deists and the Catholics not much different.[45]

By 1837 the situation in Arkansas began to improve. A new priest named P. R. Donnelly replaced Dupuy who had so well laid the groundwork in the new state. Soon Donnelly got a subscription of nine hundred dollars for a school below Pine Bluff and also built a church at Saint Mary's costing

---

[44] Frederick G. Holweck, "The Beginnings of the Church in Little Rock," *Catholic Historical Review,* VI (1920-1921), 159; Frederick G. Holweck, "The Arkansas Mission under Rosati," *St. Louis Catholic Historical Review,* I (1918), 259-61; *Catholic Telegraph,* Aug. 11, 1832.

[45] Holweck, "Church in Little Rock," *Catholic Historical Review,* VI, 160-61, 168-70.

about a thousand dollars. Donnelly's enthusiasm overreached practicality, and he laid plans that could never be realized. In October 1839 his successor, Joseph Richard-Bole, wrote Rosati a letter complaining that Donnelly had ruined everything with wild promises about building a church in Little Rock, a predominantly Protestant town. Richard-Bole had stepped into an embarrassing situation in which he had found that Donnelly's conduct "shows duplicity, [and] absolutely no delicacy." The Protestants were willing to assist the new priest to straighten out the deception, but the task was not easy. Evidently some taint lingered over the Catholics and Richard-Bole was sick of the sorry mess, for he wrote that he had the aid of some Catholics, "but in the case of a great number of them, I would wish they were Protestants." Despite tentative plans to erect a church in Little Rock, no beginning had been made when Bishop Andrew Byrne arrived in 1844.[46]

Byrne had been born in Ireland and had accompanied Bishop John England to the United States in 1820. Ordained in 1827, Byrne served stations in North and South Carolina. After a great variety of services for the church, he was assigned in 1844 to the newly created Diocese of Little Rock which included the area of the state and the Cherokee and Choctaw nations. When the new bishop reached his diocese, he could not find therein more than seven hundred Catholics and these were scattered through every county in the state. He had one priest and two churches burdened with debt in an area where, according to Shea, "the prevailing ignorance and vice were deplorable and almost insurmountable." After three and a half years Byrne had collected only thirty-one dollars from communicants in his diocese.[47]

[46] Holweck, "The Arkansas Mission," *St. Louis Catholic Historical Review,* I, 263-67; Holweck, "Church in Little Rock," *Catholic Historical Review,* VI, 169.
[47] Sloane, "Arkansas," *Catholic Encyclopedia,* I, 724-26.

Bishop Byrne quickly became convinced that the only hope for success in Arkansas was through schools. He made a trip to Ireland in 1844 and returned with a number of priests, nuns, and catechists for work in his diocese. In Ireland Byrne had stirred up considerable interest in the cheap land in Arkansas. As a result, Thomas Hore, a native of Ireland who had served a few years as a missionary in Virginia, emigrated with about seventy-five families in 1849. After a hard ocean voyage, many fell victims of cholera soon after their arrival in Arkansas. The group became disheartened, abandoned their projected new home, and apparently most of them moved to St. Louis.[48]

In 1850, on a second trip to his native Ireland, Byrne procured a colony of four sisters and eight postulants of the Sisters of Mercy, which reached Little Rock in February 1851. This community of nuns established St. Mary's Academy at Little Rock. Bishop Byrne later founded four other convents of the order. Arkansas was a difficult region for any church, but Byrne remained and refused to give up. By 1852 his diocese had ten priests, eight churches, and two chapels in a Catholic population of not more than one thousand.[49]

The cost of numerous missions in Texas constituted a heavy drain on Spain's resources. Her poor position in the closing years of the eighteenth century had forced her to curtail many activities. In January 1792 a decree ordered the secularization of the mission at San Antonio de Valero. In 1813, the year of the first proclamation of Mexican independence, the Spanish Cortes ordered secularization of all missions in Texas. Despite the order seven active missions

[48] Catholic Advocate, June 14, 1845; Mary Gilbert Kelly, Catholic Immigrant Colonization Projects in the United States, 1815-1860 (New York, 1939), 177-79.

[49] Mary Eulalia Herron, "Work of the Sisters of Mercy in the United States," Records, American Catholic Historical Society, XXXIII (1922), 317-19; O'Gorman, Roman Catholic Church, 404.

remained until their suppression in 1823. Not until 1827 was the last of the mission lands distributed.[50]

When Zebulon M. Pike reached Texas in his 1805-1806 expedition, he was impressed with the rectitude of Catholic priests and the happiness and morality of the people. After settlements were made by newcomers from the United States, most of whom were Protestants, the number of priests declined until only a few remained at the time of the Texas Revolution. Stephen F. Austin's first colony was completed about 1824 at the time of the adoption of the first liberal constitution. He urged colonists to recognize and remember that Catholicism was the religion of Mexico, but the settlers were more concerned over Mexican hostility to slavery than hostility to Protestant religion. In fact, Austin himself seemed to have had little concern for Catholic religion. The cause for separation from Mexico grew out of a contest of nationalities rather than a struggle over religion. "Religion, while it may have been outstanding in the minds of individuals, on the whole played a small part, regardless of its emphasis in the colonization law." Probably nine-tenths of the colonists neither observed nor believed in the Roman Catholic religion, and it is also likely that few were members of any church.[51]

Austin tried in vain to have Catholic priests sent to Texas, especially to officiate at weddings and funerals. During the colonial period between 1822 and 1836 only a few priests made trips through Texas. More Protestant ministers might have been found than Catholic priests, for at the time of Texas independence there were only two settled priests in the new republic. Both were in San Antonio and both had led scandalous lives. Under the terms of the republic's

[50] Mary Angela Fitzmorris, *Four Decades of Catholicism in Texas, 1820-1860* (Washington, 1926), 3-9; *United States Catholic Magazine* (Baltimore), III (1844), 724-25.

[51] John F. O'Shea, "Texas," *Catholic Encyclopedia*, XIV, 548; Fitzmorris, *Catholicism in Texas*, 17-18, 35.

constitution religious toleration was guaranteed. The flood-
gates were down and immediately ministers of the Baptist,
Methodist, Presbyterian, and other denominations rushed in
and organized churches.[52]

The *Catholic Telegraph* of November 15, 1838, warned
Catholics going to Texas of the disturbed political conditions, abandonment of Indian missions, and absence of authority to hold a council or diocesan synod. A few old
Mexican priests who spoke English held services, but there
was little else to claim for the church. The situation had
deteriorated to such a degree that a group in the latter part
of 1837 drew up a petition and presented it to Catholic
officials at Baltimore asking for one or more priests for
Texas. Several names were suggested including that of John
Timon. Bishop Blanc of New Orleans recommended the
appointment of Timon then serving under the jurisdiction
of Bishop Rosati of St. Louis. In December 1838 Timon
reached Texas. After a trip through the Catholic centers
he went to New Orleans to give an account of the total
situation. Disturbing indeed was Timon's report that towns
were taking over pre-Revolution Catholic property, restoration of which became one of Timon's determined goals. In
April 1840 he received notice of his appointment as prefect-
apostolic of Texas. He was able to secure the appointment
of his friend and traveling companion, John M. Odin, as
vice-prefect. Accompanied by three Spanish students sent
to be trained for missionary work, Odin went immediately
to San Antonio. There they removed the two priests who
had brought the church to a miserable state. After three
months in San Antonio Odin visited Seguin, Gonzales,
Victoria, Labaca, and Austin. Encountering great difficulty
in traveling, Odin was forced to ask hospitality of both

[52] Jesse G. Smith, *Heroes of the Saddle Bags* (San Antonio, 1951), 137-
40; John O. Murray, *A Popular History of the Catholic Church in the
United States* (New York, 1876), 255.

Catholics and Protestants. He thought he had earlier experienced hard life as a missionary, but Texas was worse than any situation he had previously known. Little wonder that he advised priests not to come to Texas unless they had "zeal, pure, disinterested zeal."[53]

After having gone to Rome to report in person the needs of the church, Timon returned to Texas in December 1840. He was disappointed to find buildings unfinished that were started when he had left for Europe. Affairs of the church reflected the generally poor economic condition of Texas. The currency of the republic had been inflated until it had no value, and all businesses suffered from the inflation. Timon bore a letter from the Vatican to President Mirabeau B. Lamar imploring the return of property which had belonged to the church. On January 13, 1841, a law was enacted restoring the property and recognizing the prefect and his successors as the lawful trustees. The repossession of former property improved the position of the church in Texas.[54]

In 1845 Odin returned to France to seek missionaries for Texas. Among those who came was Abbé Emmanuel Domenech, a twenty-year old priest who spent seven rugged and exhausting years in San Antonio and Castroville, Texas. After he returned to France he wrote a highly interesting book, *Journal d'un Missionaire au Texas et au Mexique* (Paris, 1856) which relates harrowing experiences, danger from Indians, searing heat, poverty, poor housing, terrible food, and often no food at all. Such men as Domenech made it possible for Odin and Timon to advance the cause of the

[53] Smith, *Heroes*, 143-45; "Bishop Timon's Account of His Visitation in 1840-41," *Catholic Historical Researches*, XIV (1897), 187-89; *Catholic Magazine*, III (1844), 726-30; Mary Benignus Sheridan, "Bishop Odin and the New Era of the Catholic Church in Texas, 1840-1860" (Ph.D. dissertation, St. Louis University, 1938), 135.

[54] *Catholic Historical Researches*, IX (1892), 88-89; Ralph Bayard, *Lone-Star Vanguard: The Catholic Reoccupation of Texas* (San Antonio, 1945), passim.

church in Texas. When Odin became Archbishop of New Orleans in 1861, the Catholics in Texas could proudly claim forty-two priests, fifty churches and chapels, four academies for girls, and five schools for boys and girls.[55]

As early as 1834 an ardent Catholic paper, the *Shepherd of the Valley* of St. Louis, waxed eloquent about the progress of religion in the West. "Savage rudeness," it declared, "has given place to refinement, ignorance and superstition to learning and almost universal knowledge."[56] Beyond any question the Catholic Church had had a significant part in bringing about this improved condition of society in the first half of the nineteenth century.

[55] Francis J. Tschan, "The Catholic Church in the United States, 1852-1868: A Survey," *Records, American Catholic Historical Society*, LVIII (1947), 187.
[56] Issue of Dec. 13.

10

MEDIA OF EDUCATION

THE CONGREGATIONAL UNION of England and Wales in
1835 sent two ministers on a fraternal visit to the Presbyterian and Congregational bodies in the United States. Their
narrative report is here mentioned because it so well illus-
trates the errors in quick, surface observations. Finding
education in many places dominated by the Catholics, the
visitors interpreted the situation as a monopoly planned by
the Pope. In the report they said: "Every thing is done to
captivate, and to liberalize, in appearance, a system essentially despotic. The sagacity of the effort is discovered, in
avoiding to attack and shock the prejudices of the adult,
that they may direct the education of the young. They look
to the future; and they really have great advantages in
doing so. They send out teachers excellently qualified;
superior, certainly, to the run of native teachers. Some value
the European modes of education, as the more excellent;
others value them as the mark of fashion: the demand for
instruction, too, is always beyond the supply, so that they
find little difficulty in obtaining the charge of Protestant
children."[1] Unfamiliar as they were with the American
scene, the ministers had not looked at the conditions which
had created this situation. It is not to be denied that the
church which provided a school for the community did
enjoy an enviable position, a place which some Protestant
denominations were incapable of assuming. The Roman
Catholic priests were usually better equipped to teach, by

virtue of their excellent education and training, than most of the Protestant preachers. Wherever and whenever a settlement or two supported or even received a resident priest, he initiated a school program if he could find the material resources to do so.

Scarcely had a settlement been made at New Orleans before the Capuchin order established a school there. In 1725 Father Raphael de Luxembourg began for boys "a little college" whose sole teacher was the choirmaster of the St. Louis parish. A few months later a lay brother who knew mathematics, drawing, and singing was employed as an instructor. Unfortunately Father Raphael was unable to impress the Western Company with the obligation of providing necessary support, and so the school closed about 1731. More than two decades elapsed before the French government made any genuine effort in behalf of education.[2]

In 1743 Governor Bienville and Edme G. Salmon, the intendant, addressed a letter to the comte de Maurepas, Minister of the Navy and Colonies, urging that a college be founded in New Orleans.[3] It was too expensive to send children to France, the letter declared, and, when they came back to Louisiana, they were unwilling to remain. Maurepas replied that since the colony had not made the requisite progress, he could not send financial aid. Conditions in Louisiana during the closing days of French control had an unfortunate effect upon the educational efforts of the Catholic Church. When the Jesuit schools were closed in 1764, the Ursulines lost their directors and loyal supporters but managed to sustain themselves. About thirty years later Bishop Peñalver reported that the convent was doing excellent work and that girls continued to be educated there.[4]

[1] Andrew Reed and James Matheson, *A Narrative of the Visit to the American Churches* (2 vols.; New York, 1835), II, 78.

[2] Delanglez, *French Jesuits*, 287; Vogel, *Capuchins*, 69-70.

[3] For the early Catholic schools in Louisiana see Baudier, *Catholic Church in Louisiana*, 100-107.

Late in the fall of 1805 the Reverend Samuel T. Wilson, one of four Dominican priests sent to Kentucky by Bishop Carroll, stopped at the home of Henry Boone, a Catholic living in the Cartwright settlement near Springfield, Kentucky. When persuaded to stay, Wilson gathered a few boys who had expressed interest in preparing for the priesthood and opened a school in Boone's house. "This little makeshift of a school" was the beginning of the College of Saint Thomas Aquinas, the first attempt at a Catholic institution of higher learning west of the Alleghenies. Father Edward D. Fenwick, the leader of the Dominican group, used his patrimony to purchase the Waller plantation near Springfield and in May 1807 opened a secondary school with twenty-six boys. He added a college department the next year, although its building, some ninety by fifty feet in size, was not completed until 1812. The curriculum included literature, history, Latin, French, German, Italian, and music. St. Thomas had about as many non-Catholic as Catholic students; parents shelved their religious prejudices in the desire to secure an education for their children. Enrollment soon reached one hundred and continued to grow until two hundred boys were in the school. In 1816 Jefferson Davis as a boy of eight, was brought from Wilkinson County, Mississippi, to attend the preparatory school for two years. The distinguished Southern statesman always retained a strong affection for Father Wilson and for the school of St. Thomas.[5]

Early in the westward movement of the Catholics the hierarchy of the church sensed the great need for a clergy educated on American soil to serve a population composed largely of English stock. Priests who spoke the English language with difficulty worked under a great handicap.

---

[4] Delanglez, *French Jesuits*, 289-90; M. A. C., "Education in New Orleans," *American Catholic Quarterly Review*, XII (1887), 259.

[5] O'Daniel, *Wilson*, 105 et passim; O'Daniel, *Miles*, 71, 147-53.

Foreseeing the requirements from heavy immigrations of the next decades, the church sought to increase its supply of teachers and priests by establishing seminaries in the West and by widening the curricula of schools already organized.

In 1819 a seminary was begun in connection with St. Joseph's Cathedral at Bardstown, Kentucky. An incompleted building, intended to serve as the bishop's residence, housed the seminary which opened with twelve students. Immediately the people of Bardstown urged the bishop to establish a school for boys. The request was answered in the same fall by opening in the basement of the seminary a school called St. Joseph's College. Protestant and Catholic boys from Bardstown and the neighboring communities came in such numbers that the quarters were immediately inadequate. By 1820 a separate building had been erected and occupied, and three years later the presence of sixteen boarders made necessary the addition of a wing. In 1824 a Catholic school in New Orleans under the direction of Father Bertrand Martial faced the necessity of closing. With the consent of his patronage, Martial transferred himself and seventy-four students to St. Joseph's during 1824 and 1825. As a result of this merger, the college had nearly two hundred students—one-half of whom were boarders. This early Kentucky college could count among its alumni two congressmen from Mississippi, two governors of Louisiana, a cabinet officer in Lincoln's administration, and a large group of Kentuckians of prominence including Cassius M. Clay and Governor Lazarus M. Powell.[6]

Near Lebanon in Marion County, Kentucky, the Reverend William Byrne began St. Mary's College in 1821, housing the school in a former distillery. At first he was not only the president but also the sole teacher, relying on the assistance of the better students. In this group of assistants was a

---

[6] Spalding, *Flaget*, 298-300; Schauinger, *Cathedrals*, 181, 224-26.

fourteen-year old boy named Martin John Spalding, who became Bishop of Louisville and finally Archbishop of Baltimore. An advertisement of the college appeared in some Kentucky newspapers in 1833 listing the subjects taught and expenses at the college. For a session of five and one-half months, the cost for tuition, room, board, and washing was twenty-two dollars; for day students the tuition ranged between six and twelve dollars. All students gave one day per week to manual labor on the three hundred acre farm which was the school's chief source of support. The school became the property of the Jesuits in 1832, and under their direction it prospered for several years. Advertisements were placed in newspapers as far away as New Orleans, Mexico City, and Havana. The largest enrollment was reached in 1840 with 125 boarders and 18 day students, and after that date the school gradually declined. In 1846 the Jesuits surrendered control of the school to Bishop Guy Chabrat, blaming their failure on the panic of 1837, the competition of new schools and colleges, the rise of nativist agitation in Kentucky, and the attacks of the Presbyterians.[7]

Another educational activity grew up around Mary Rhodes, a young woman educated in a Catholic convent in Maryland, who taught her young cousins while visiting in Kentucky. She taught the Dant children in their home and then began to worry about the education of the neighbor's children. Early in 1812 Miss Rhodes consulted with Father Charles Nerinckx, and together they decided to open a school in an abandoned cabin on Hardin's Creek in Marion County. Children for miles around the school crowded the converted cabin so that Miss Rhodes soon had more children than she could teach. When joined by a second and then a third young assistant, she proposed to them some type of religious community. On April 25, 1812, in a special ceremony the three women pledged themselves to a life of religious

[7] Francis X. Curran, "The Jesuits in Kentucky, 1831-1846," *Mid-America,* XXXV (1953), 223-46.

devotion. Neighbors helped to improve the cabins, and the physical aspect of the project appeared more solid than formerly. The little community grew; additional postulants requested admission; and the number of students increased. Bishop Flaget directed Father Nerinckx to take charge of the movement now composed of six girls. Nerinckx wrote the rules for the group to be known as the Sisters of Loretto at the Foot of the Cross. Generally the group is referred to as Loretto or the Lorettines. Approved by the Holy See in 1816, "the first religious Congregation founded in America without any affiliation or connection with any other" had come into existence. In 1824 the convent moved to St. Stephen's farm, the former home of Father Badin. Twelve years after Loretto had been organized, the number of sisters had increased to more than one hundred. Within half a century the twenty-nine foundations of the Loretto Society had spread south to Louisiana and west as far as New Mexico.[8]

John David, the French-born priest who had arrived in Kentucky in 1811, easily adapted himself to the frontier and quickly sensed the need for education and the partial solution of the problem. Early in 1812 Father David, while teaching at St. Thomas' Seminary near Bardstown, discussed with Bishop Flaget the pressing need for a community of religious women to supplement the church work then under way. Others were likewise aware of the need and in November Teresa Carrico and Elizabeth Wells asked the bishop to direct them in some educational project. Presenting their case clearly, these "two pious ladies of mature age" convinced both Flaget and David of the feasibility of founding an order.[9]

---

[8] Webb, *Catholicity in Kentucky*, 234-43; Anna C. Minogue, *Loretto, Annals of the Century* (New York, 1912), Chaps. III-V; Magaret, *Nerinckx*, Chaps. XV-XX.

[9] For this and the next three paragraphs the material has been taken largely from Anna B. McGill, *The Sisters of Charity of Nazareth, Kentucky* (New York, 1917).

The bishop assigned them a small house consisting of two rooms, one above the other, located on part of the same farm on which the seminary had been established. In January 1813 Miss Wells and Miss Carrico were joined by Catherine Spalding, a very mature young woman of nineteen years. The day after Miss Spalding arrived Father David gave provisional rules to the three and explained their duties. As the community took form, the vitality and enterprise of Miss Spalding made her the natural choice for the superior of the newly organized Sisters of Charity of Nazareth. The residence of the sisters was moved about a mile from St. Thomas' farm to a new log cabin built by the seminarians, who gave further aid in the clearing of the land hewing logs, and erecting an additional house with a room for a chapel. In August 1814 Nazareth's first school opened with nine little girls. A year later the number had increased to thirty-four.

Near the close of 1818 Bishop Flaget and his students moved to nearby Bardstown. The bishop asked the Sisters of Charity to organize a school in Bardstown which became the first branch house the order had established. In 1820 the sisters opened a school in Breckinridge County and an academy in Union County. The academy flourished and attracted students from Ohio, Indiana, and Illinois. In 1822 the order bought a tract of land about three miles north of Bardstown to which the thirty-four sisters, including novices and postulants, moved and established their permanent home.

In less than a decade this second order of nuns in Kentucky had been firmly established. Additional foundations were organized in answer to requests from churches in several states and territories. The long lives of Bishop David and Bishop Flaget and the Mother Superior Spalding lent great strength to the continued growth and prosperity of Nazareth. Many girls, Protestant as well as Catholic, graced a Southern home because they had been carefully and lovingly directed by the nuns at Nazareth.

In 1818, the first year Bishop DuBourg resided in St. Louis, a Latin school for boys began at St. Louis Academy. Taught by four priests of the diocesan clergy attached to the cathedral, the academy prospered so well that within two years it was formed into a college with a similar name which points "to an organic continuity of descent" from the old to the new St. Louis College, later St. Louis University. Pressed by lack of time for teaching and money to hire assistants, the diocesan clergy closed the school during the 1826-1827 session. Benefiting by this interim, the college reopened in 1828, and, after securing three thousand dollars, entered into a period of prosperity. Four years later the Missouri legislature granted a university charter to the college. In 1842 the university added a medical school; the following year, a law department.[10]

In February 1830 Bishop Michael Portier and Father Mathias Loras began a school for six seminarians in a residence three miles west of Mobile. The bishop, having decided to make Mobile the head of the diocese which covered Alabama and Florida, wished to build there a college on a healthy spot, possessing good water and free from mosquitoes. By midsummer a few frame houses had been completed, and the transfer of the land had been made to the college. In July Spring Hill College officially opened and earned for itself the distinction of being the first permanent college in Alabama and the first permanent Catholic college in the Lower South. In the entire country only Georgetown and Mount Saint Mary's at Emmitsburg, Maryland, antedate Spring Hill as Catholic boarding colleges. Bishop Portier's dream had become a reality; enrollment was good and more buildings were needed. On October 29, 1830, the "First Prospectus of Spring Hill College" gave the educational plans and the disciplinary rules of the "essentially classic" college. Sixty students registered in November

[10] Garraghan, *Jesuits*, I, 269-308; III, 203.

1831 and 132 in January 1832. In November 1835 the legislature of Alabama granted a charter. After entrusting the administration of the college to the Fathers of Mercy between 1840 and 1842 and to the Eudist fathers in 1844 and 1845, Bishop Portier finally committed the institution to the safe hands of the Jesuits in 1847 and in their care it continues today.[11]

By 1840 of the some two hundred Catholic parochial schools in the United States, at least half of them were west of the Alleghenies.[12] Space permits the selection from the Catholic as well as from other denominations of only a few representative educational institutions in this effort to explain the contribution of each church and eventually the sum total of educational endeavor in the area under examination.

The excellence of Catholic schools was already evidenced by the number of Protestant children enrolled and in the alarm of Protestants at the number and the quality of these schools. Catholic and Protestant schools offered the standard curriculum to which the teachers added instruction in their respective religions. The attention given to the education of women was interpreted by some Protestants as an attempt to give "Romish" mothers to future Americans. Leonard Bacon concluded that the best defense which serious Protestants could offer was a school program equal to that of the Catholics.[13]

Presbyterians from their first arrival in America gave attention to the education of their members and their ministry. The early requirement that all candidates for the ministry should possess a minimum of a bachelor of arts degree or its equivalent set a high level that was difficult to maintain. At first the pressing need was for schools to train

---

[11] See Kenny, *Catholic Culture in Alabama*, passim.
[12] Ellis, *American Catholicism*, 55.
[13] Goodykoontz, *Home Missions*, 364.

the clergy. Unable to enlist the ministers necessary for the Western country, the Presbyterian Church as well as all other churches realized the stark necessity of educating young ministers. Numerous "lay colleges" soon dotted the fringes of the frontier. One of these later became Hampden-Sydney College in western Virginia.

Three of the early Presbyterian ministers in Tennessee were graduates of the seminary at Princeton. A worthy representative of this group was Samuel Doak, whose name is inseparably tied to education in the state. Having taught at Hampden-Sydney for one year, Doak came to Washington County, Tennessee, in 1777 and established Martin Academy, the first school in Tennessee. After six years, Martin Academy received a charter in 1783 from the assembly of North Carolina. Twelve years later, by a charter from the Territory South of the Ohio River, the academy was reorganized as Washington College. After forty years of devoted service to the academy and college, Doak resigned in 1818 relinquishing his duties to his son John. In the same year with the aid of his son Samuel, Doak opened Tusculum Academy in Greene County, and there he taught until his death in 1830. About 1783 Hezekiah Balch, a graduate of Princeton, moved to Greene County, purchased a plantation, and in 1794 received a charter from the territorial legislature to establish Greeneville College. Wisely Balch spent several years collecting funds and books and laying preparatory plans for the school. When he opened the college in 1802, he had a good working organization, and within a year the college had a hundred students. Reports of the fine school increased the enrollment and within ten years students were registered from nine states. Thomas B. Craighead, the first Presbyterian minister to locate in the Nashville area, felt the same compulsion as other Princeton graduates and opened in 1786 Davidson Academy, which later became Davidson College. It was consolidated briefly with Cumberland College and that union took new form as the University of Nashville, of which the first president was the distinguished Philip Lindsley. Eventually from these several mergers came the present George Peabody College for Teachers.[14]

Other preachers without the Princeton tradition served the cause of education well in Tennessee. In 1793 Samuel Carrick began in his home in Knoxville a seminary which a year later received a charter as Blount College. Instruction was offered in a wide variety of courses—Greek, Latin, English, rhetoric, logic, natural and moral philosophy, geography, and astronomy. While rich in curriculum, the school was always short of funds. Carrick did not attend well to financial matters; after years of struggling to meet his obligations, he agreed to merge his school with East Tennessee College—an institution that eventually became the University of Tennessee. Isaac Anderson, personally concerned over the lack of young ministers in the West, made a trip in 1819 to Princeton where he hoped to recruit some seminarians. Discouraged over the failure of his appeal, Anderson returned to Maryville determined to open a private school of theology. Beginning with a little class in 1819, the school flourished and enrolled ninety students a decade later. Such responses provided the best evidence of the need for a seminary. When control passed in 1825 to the Presbyterian Synod of Tennessee, the school was properly called Southern and Western Theological Seminary and so functioned for another ten years. By this time more than sixty ministers had been educated and sent forth to regions destitute of Presbyterian preaching. In 1836 the seminary

[14] James Phelan, *History of Tennessee* (Boston, 1889), Chap. XXIV; Alexander, *Synod of Tennessee*, 18-19, 65-69; Allen E. Ragan, *A History of Tusculum College* (Greeneville, Tenn., 1945), 36-42; William B. Sprague, *Annals of the American Pulpit* (9 vols.; New York, 1857-1869), III, 308-19; Albert C. Holt, *The Economic and Social Beginnings of Tennessee* (Nashville[?], 1923[?]), 138-42.

was renamed Maryville College, but its purpose remained the same.[15]

The establishment of schools in Kentucky by Presbyterians paralleled events in Tennessee. In 1780 Virginia set aside some public lands in Kentucky to be used for educational purposes. Caleb Wallace, a Presbyterian minister and Princeton graduate, took the lead in forming a board of trustees for a proposed Transylvania Seminary, which was incorporated in 1783. Two grants of land gave to the school some twelve thousand acres as endowment. In 1785 David Rice became chairman of the board and two years later the seminary was opened in his home in Danville. The income from the land was so small that the school faced financial difficulties and moved to Lexington where the prospects looked more promising than at the original location. Although the Presbyterians considered Transylvania largely their project, they lost control of the board in 1794 when Harry Toulmin, a Baptist preacher with Unitarian leanings, was appointed president.[16]

Within a short time Rice was instrumental in getting a charter for a new school to be called Kentucky Academy. In addition to a legislative grant of six thousand acres, he secured nearly ten thousand dollars, including gifts of one hundred dollars each from George Washington, John Adams, and Robert Morris. In 1797 the academy was opened at Pisgah, Kentucky, mainly because Pisgah had made the

[15] Sprague, *Annals*, III, 433-35; Stanley J. Folmsbee, "Blount College and East Tennessee College, 1794-1840," East Tennessee Historical Society, *Publications*, No. 17 (1945), 22-50; Samuel T. Wilson, *A Century of Maryville College, 1819-1919* (Maryville, Tenn., 1919); Samuel T. Wilson, *Isaac Anderson: Founder and First President of Maryville College* (Maryville, 1932).

[16] Walter W. Jennings, *Transylvania: Pioneer University of the West* (New York, 1955), Chaps. I, II; Robert Peter and Joanna Peter, *Transylvania University, Its Origin, Rise, Decline, and Fall* (Louisville, 1896), 18-20, et passim; Thomas D. Clark, *A History of Kentucky* (New York, 1937), 325-26.

largest offer of money and land. Apparently all did not go well, for in the following year Kentucky Academy and Transylvania Seminary united under the imposing title of Transylvania University, to be governed by a board of twenty-three, the majority of whom were to be Presbyterians. In 1799 a law and a medical department were added. After James Moore, an Episcopal rector, was removed from the presidency of Transylvania in 1804, a Presbyterian minister, James Blythe, became president and served for fourteen years. By criticizing the War of 1812 and politicians in Kentucky, Blythe became very unpopular with a liberal element which succeeded in driving him out of office in 1816 and replacing him two years later with Horace Holley, a graduate of Yale and a distinguished Unitarian minister. In less than a decade (1818-1827) Holley led Transylvania to the edge of greatness. The inevitable clash between Calvinism and liberalism brought Holley's resignation and the end of Transylvania's glory.[17]

In an effort to recoup the loss of Transylvania, the Synod of Kentucky secured in 1819 a charter for Centre College to be located in Danville. When the state had chartered the college and offered it to the Presbyterian Church, the church refused to accept an amendment to the charter which provided that "no religious doctrine peculiar to any one set of Christians shall be inculcated by any professor in said college." The college remained under state control until 1824 when the charter was amended to the complete satisfaction of the Synod of Kentucky. From that date Centre College has been in the continuous control of the Presbyterians. After the able John C. Young became president in 1830,

[17] "Subscription Lists for Kentucky Academy, 1794-1797," in Sweet, *The Presbyterians,* 583-89; MS Minutes of Kentucky Academy, March 11, 1797, Philadelphia; F. Garvin Davenport, *Ante-Bellum Kentucky* (Oxford, Ohio, 1943), 39-46; Sonne, *Liberal Kentucky,* passim; Davidson, *Presbyterian Church,* 298-318.

the college increased its endowment several times and expanded its student body to about 150.[18]

Leaders of the Cumberland Presbyterian Church, conscious of the need of an educated ministry, opened Cumberland College in March 1826 on a farm of five hundred acres at Princeton, Kentucky. Less than one-fourth of the twenty-eight thousand dollars pledged by the people of Princeton was ever paid, and from the opening days the school, established on the manual labor plan, was in deep financial trouble. Originally the church tried to finance the college through a pledge of fifty cents from each member. This and various other schemes of raising money failed, and in desperation in 1842 the college sold all but the ten-acre plot on which the buildings were located. The General Assembly immediately severed connections with the college, leaving the school to have an independent and tenuous existence until 1860.[19]

To the south in Alabama little was done for education by the Presbyterian Church for several years after the first preaching there. Despite various efforts nothing was accomplished until 1833 when the South Alabama Presbytery recommended the establishment of a manual labor institute in Perry or Dallas County. Under a most generous arrangement with the sellers, the trustees bought a plantation three miles west of Marion in Perry County as a site for the new school. Advantageous location and good management made the school a success, but, though this effort had "flattering prospects," the Presbyterians in Alabama tried no other. They were too few and too weak in the state, and they

[18] James H. Hewlett, "Centre College of Kentucky, 1819-1830," *Filson Club History Quarterly*, XVIII (1944), 173-91; MS (copy) Minutes of the Synod of Kentucky, 1822-1845, Oct. 15, 17, 1824, Oct. 18, 1841, Montreat. For the role of the Presbyterians in higher education see Thompson, *Presbyterians in the South*, Chap. XVII.

[19] Lindsley, "Sources and Sketches," *Theological Medium*, VII (1876), 132-71; McDonnold, *Cumberland Presbyterian Church*, Chap. XXII.

lacked the enthusiasm for education which had been so evident among Presbyterians in Tennessee and Kentucky.[20]

In 1829 within the states of Louisiana, Mississippi, and the territory of Arkansas, an area of 145,000 square miles, there was not a single Presbyterian college. In this year a committee meeting at Rodney, Mississippi, opened a subscription list which secured twelve thousand dollars in pledges for a projected Oakland College. The Mississippi Presbytery covering all the above region appointed a board of trustees for the school, chose a president, and selected a site, five miles east of the Mississippi River in Claiborne County. The singular position which this college enjoyed in the lower Southwest is shown in the spectacular growth of its physical plant. Within twenty years the institution had thirty cottages for students, two halls for literary societies, and a large main building containing class rooms and the library of four thousand books.[21]

The influence of the Presbyterian Church on higher education is clearly evident in the fact that of the forty permanent colleges and universities formed between 1789 and 1829, one-third were Presbyterian in origin. Of the forty, fourteen were in the West, and half of these were Presbyterian. By 1840 the Presbyterians had organized eleven colleges in the South. The highly educated minister had in many ways a tremendous advantage among an uneducated frontier folk. He possessed a driving determination to educate—especially Presbyterians—in order that they might the more fully participate in a religion that was established firmly on a rational basis of knowledge and thought.[22]

[20] MS Minutes, South Alabama Presbytery, 1833-1835, Oct. 30, Nov. 21, 1833, 1835-1840, Sept. 29, 1837, Montreat.

[21] John R. Hutchison, *Reminiscences, Sketches and Addresses* (Houston, 1874), 22-25; Sprague, *Annals,* IV, 590-95.

[22] Sweet, *The Presbyterians,* 75-76. Some students of American Christianity do not believe that the Presbyterians welcomed new ideas since the Westminster Confession of Faith contained "the entire body of truth."

Although Whitefield, the two Wesleys, and Coke of the Methodists were all college graduates, they set no educational pattern for preachers. Methodist preachers on the frontier for several generations put little premium on education, and in that respect differed from the Catholic, Presbyterian, and Episcopal ministers. Concerning this indifference, John Wesley succinctly asserted that "the Methodists are poor, but there is no need they should be ignorant."[23] Unfortunately the learned Dr. Coke was able to exert but little influence upon the education of Methodists in America. His one concrete effort was the abortive attempt to found Cokesbury College at Abingdon, Maryland.

Asbury was not college trained, but was a student of his own volition and deeply interested in education for people in general. As early as 1780 he tentatively planned to establish an academy somewhere in the colonies. Ten years later he was collecting subscriptions for a boarding school to be erected at Bethel in Jessamine County, Kentucky. When opened on a hundred acre farm on the Kentucky River in a remote section of the new state, the college declined rapidly, and its support was soon dropped by the church. Later educational efforts of Asbury were decided successes. By the year of his death (1816) he had established one or more schools in every Methodist conference in America.[24] For his great and continuing effort in behalf of education, one historian of Methodism has conferred upon Asbury the title of "Commissioner of Education in the United States."

The overt disinterest of the Methodists in the education of their ministry is explained in part by vast numbers of illiterate and poorly educated people to whom the Methodist preacher, like the Baptist, had an effective appeal. Many of the church leaders believed that the time and

---

[23] Charles C. Jarrell, *Methodism on the March* (Nashville, 1924), 36. Also see J. A. Faulkner, *The Methodists* (New York, 1903), 203-204.

[24] For his interest in Bethel see his *Journal*, II, 85, 148, 193, 260, 294, 473.

effort necessary to educate a ministry would be a sinful waste, and, considering their successes, they concluded that book learning might even be a hindrance to progress. Judging from the number of converts made by the Methodists and Baptists in comparison with that by the Presbyterians and Episcopalians, the observer has little doubt of the temporary advantage possessed on the early frontier by the unlettered preacher. However, as time passed the Methodist and Baptist attitude toward education changed for several identical reasons—contact with other sects, interdenominational discussions on theology, prosperity of church members, and growth of church printing presses.

Although the Methodist Discipline of 1784 had directed the preachers to study five hours a day and talk at intervals on the subject of education, thirty-two years elapsed before any further consideration would be given to this early outburst of interest. Then the General Conference admitted that a college education for the ministry was not essential, but insisted that a preacher should be able to understand and to illustrate the Holy Writ. In the General Conference of 1820 a committee was appointed "to inquire into the expediency of digesting and recommending the outline of a plan for the institution of schools." When a resolution concerning the establishing of literary institutions was approved four years later, the General Conference thereby committed the Methodist Church to an active educational program.[25]

In 1821 the Ohio Conference appointed a committee to meet with the Kentucky Conference for the purpose of building a college that would serve both. From this effort came an agreement to establish an institution of higher learning in Augusta, Kentucky, to be known as Augusta

---

[25] *Journals of the General Conference*, I, 149, 186, 208, 295. The "Report of the Committee on Education," to the conference of 1824 is in *Methodist Magazine*, VII (1824), 276-77.

College. A year later the college received a charter from the Kentucky legislature. At the time of its incorporation Augusta was the only Methodist institution in Kentucky possessing the right to grant degrees. In the same years it was further given body by the transfer from Bracken Academy in Augusta of money coming from the sale of six thousand acres of land received from the state in 1798. After a three-story brick building had been erected and agents appointed to solicit funds, the students arrived in good numbers and prosperity seemed inevitable. Events beyond the control of the college took their toll: the panic of 1837 strained the finances of the college to the breaking point, and agitation over the question of slavery contributed to its demise. The Ohio Conference became unwilling to support a college in a slave state, and Southerners refused to send their sons to a college so near abolitionists. In 1845, spurred by the prospect of getting control of Transylvania University, the Methodists abandoned Augusta College.[26]

Transylvania University had had an uncertain existence being successively under Presbyterian, Baptist, Episcopal, and Unitarian control before 1846, when it was tendered to and accepted by the General Conference of the Methodist Episcopal Church, South. Henry B. Bascom had been acting president of Transylvania since 1842, and he was appointed president when the Methodists officially assumed control. Under his administration Transylvania flourished briefly, but internal dissensions and denominational jealousies undermined the support of the Methodists and led to their abandonment in 1848 of the weak educational enterprise. Feebly surviving each change of ownership, Transylvania demonstrated great endurance. Whenever trouble arose, some similar college seemed ready to merge with Transylvania or another denomination was willing to assume

---

[26] Redford, *Methodism in Kentucky*, II, 98-100; W. E. Arnold, *A History of Methodism in Kentucky* (2 vols.; Louisville, 1935-1936) II passim.

both the control and the burden of supporting the wavering enterprise.[27]

As typical of the church colleges of the Old South, a history of LaGrange College affords a good view of the vicissitudes of such institutions. Lasting through a quarter of a century, the college experienced joys and sorrows and then passed into oblivion.[28]

Desiring to have a college, a few wealthy citizens of LaGrange, Alabama, offered ten thousand dollars as an inducement to locate a college there. In December 1828 their offer was accepted by the Tennessee and Mississippi conferences of the Methodist Episcopal Church whose preachers subscribed three thousand dollars to supplement the first pledge. The college was located in the village of LaGrange in Franklin County, ten miles south of Muscle Shoals, on a spur of the Cumberland Mountains four hundred feet above the surrounding country. Many visitors have left glowing accounts of the wealth of scenic beauty, of the good water, pure atmosphere, and a society offering "few temptations to vice, and no concealment for dissipation." Eight days after the college opened on January 19, 1830, the legislature granted to "a seminary of learning" for males, to be known as LaGrange College, a charter of incorporation which prohibited "the inculcation of the peculiar tenets or doctrines of any religious denomination whatsoever."

For its president the trustees selected the Reverend Robert Paine, just turned thirty years of age. A man of much courage and great strength of character, he was an admirable choice and held the post until he became a bishop in 1846. In addition to his administrative duties Paine served as professor of moral science and belles lettres. Two other

[27] Jennings, *Transylvania,* Chap. XI; M. M. Henkle, *The Life of Henry Bidleman Bascom* (Nashville, 1860), Chap. XIX passim.

[28] The pages devoted to LaGrange College are a condensation of my "LaGrange, Alabama's Earliest College," *Wesleyan Quarterly Review,* I (1964), 3-24. See it for references to quotations and to source material.

instructors completed the first faculty. Within two years the physical plant consisted of a main building and a dormitory. Besides classrooms, the two buildings contained forty-eight dormitory rooms—enough to accommodate 150 students.

LaGrange College began with 70 male students, increasing to 139 in 1845. During 1842 the enrollment of 106 students represented a good average—at which time the student body had 5 seniors, 12 juniors, 22 sophomores, 44 freshmen, and 23 preparatory students. In 1830 the tuition was ten dollars for a term of about twenty weeks and board cost forty dollars. By 1852 these figures had increased to twenty-five and fifty, respectively. Summer vacations were short so that the students might be on the hill during the "sickly" season. In the last fifteen years of the college's existence only one student died from the dreaded fever. An epidemic of small pox, however, forced the closing of the college for about a month in 1850.

Judged by the standards of the day, requirements for admission to the college were sufficiently high. The curriculum, heavily loaded with courses in Latin and Greek, would probably frighten a present-day student. In striking contrast to many of the colleges of its time LaGrange offered no courses in the Old or the New Testament, in keeping with the provisions of its charter. The college had two literary societies, the Dialectical and the LaFayette, each of which claimed a library of about two thousand volumes by 1842. Rivalry between the societies was extremely keen and "productive of useful and salutary consequences." At commencement time the two literary societies invited a speaker to address them jointly.

Careful supervision of student life was maintained day and night. Rooms were visited, delinquents and absentees reported, and the spending money of students limited. A great deal of wholesome fun enlivened the day and even the night, often at the expense of members of the faculty. Although the sale of liquor was prohibited on the campus, a student outbreak in 1837 was ascribed to the bad influence of a tavern keeper. And well it might have been, for certainly some spirit other than that of levity moved a student to point a pistol at the president!

LaGrange followed a system, then in general acceptance, of appointing a committee to hold oral examinations of all students at the close of the college year. Testing class by class from preparatory to senior, the examination usually consumed four to six days. In 1841 the committee reported that the examination "clearly evinced the unremitting application of the student; the peculiar talent and unwearied industry of the instructor; and the interest felt by the delighted spectators. . . ." The examinations were followed by the commencement exercises which differed little from those of today—except that each senior was required to deliver an address on some topic. A few of the ambitious titles indicate the confidence and self-assurance of the speakers at the conclusion of their college careers. As proof of their ability to face the world the declaimers spoke on subjects ranging from "Persia" and "Commerce" to "Spirit of Democracy" and "Westward the Spirit of Liberty Takes Its Flight."

LaGrange conferred its first A.B. degree in 1834. Between 1838 and 1854 the college conferred the degree on 144 candidates. As with the average church college the bestowal of honorary degrees scarcely knew any limitation. LaGrange gave the "regular" M.A. to forty-nine, while the "honorary" M.A. was given to fifteen people. The distinction in the types of degrees depended on the recipient, the "regular" going to alumni of the college. In 1843 LaGrange gave only four A.B. degrees, then reduced their value by granting three times as many "regular" and "honorary" M.A.'s. In 1847 the Alumni Society recognized the great generosity of the college by acknowledging the debt for "the high honorary degrees that she has conferred upon them."

Financial troubles threatened the daily life of LaGrange.

Opening with barely enough money to erect the necessary buildings and to purchase equipment, President Paine was sure that unless existing debts were paid the college would close. Few modern-day colleges have ever tried more different methods of raising money than LaGrange. Agents combed all possible avenues for pledges, gifts, and contributions of any type. The financial situation became so embarrassing in 1841 that the trustees pled for ten-dollar subscriptions which resulted in raising the small sum of nine hundred dollars. By 1844 the balance sheet was in poor state; the college indebtedness was some four thousand dollars, and its assets were chiefly unpaid pledges totalling fifty thousand dollars, much of which had been subscribed before the panic of 1837. Payment of the accumulated interest alone would have relieved the college of its most pressing debts. The trustees failed to reveal that President Paine had for several years returned to the college half of his salary of less than two thousand dollars.

Scarcely had the Reverend Richard H. Rivers entered upon his duties as president of the college in 1854 before a committee of citizens from Florence, Alabama, promising better buildings and larger endowment, proposed the removal of LaGrange to their town some ten miles distant. Although the supporters of the college seat at LaGrange claimed that only six of the twenty trustees had voted for removal, the college was moved in the winter session of 1855. The legislature granted a new charter under the name of Florence Wesleyan College. After the Civil War this property was given to the state of Alabama and today is the basis for Florence State College.

After the removal of faculty and students to Florence, those trustees who had voted to continue the college in LaGrange reorganized the school and elected a new faculty under the presidency of a Cumberland Presbyterian minister. In 1858 the college name was changed to LaGrange

College and Military Academy and two years later the title was slightly abbreviated to LaGrange Military Academy. In 1863 the school came to an end when federal cavalry burned the buildings. Long since the village of LaGrange has completely disappeared and today no person's memory reaches back that far.

During its quarter of a century of existence as a college under the control of the Methodist Church, LaGrange's roll of students included many who became prominent in the affairs of Alabama and the South. Through these formative years its influence was far-reaching and important. The culture and discipline which radiated from her academic circle softened the manner and broadened the mind of many young men.

The fierce antimissionary struggle among Baptist churches took a heavy toll in many ways and especially delayed the initiation of educational projects. In order to retain their members and avoid disturbances, the Regular Baptists found a decided advantage in poorly educated preachers whose intellectual pursuits rarely stirred existing conditions. When the Stone and Campbell schisms arose, the Baptists suddenly found themselves unequal in the task of debating with Alexander Campbell and many of his followers. The unlettered and ranting preacher had to give way to the new day. Baptists and Methodists alike would have to provide better educated ministers or lose their appeal to the prosperous people, especially in the towns and cities.

Influenced by the liberal intellectual atmosphere of Kentucky, some Baptists in the Salem Association became aroused over the appalling ignorance of the majority of their preachers. In 1815 the association urged its churches to send to the next meeting "a charitable mite" to be used for the education of young ministers. The leaven was at work. A gift of twenty thousand dollars, the income from which could be used for the education of Baptist preachers, hastened the formation in 1829 in Scott County of Georgetown College, the first Baptist institution claiming to be a college in the entire Mississippi Valley. For almost a decade, however, the new institution functioned merely as an elementary school that taught the three R's. Not until 1841 did it have as many as twenty-five students in the preparatory and college departments.[29]

In a long delayed effort to provide some semblance of ministerial education, the Western Baptist Association purchased land in Covington, Kentucky, and secured a charter for the Western Baptist Theological Institute, which opened in 1845 under good financial conditions. The president, Robert E. Pattison, a native of Vermont, became deeply involved in antislavery squabbles with Baptists in the South, but despite the lack of harmony the college prospered for several years. However, discord eventually led to controversy, and in 1855 the trustees of the once flourishing institution decided to close its operation and sell the property.[30]

Whether spurred by competition or more noble motives, the Baptists and Presbyterians attended to their educational responsibilities in Alabama about the same time. In 1832 the Alabama Baptist State Convention bought a farm of 355 acres near Greensboro to be used as a school site. Four years later a Manual Labor Institute, chiefly "for the education of indigent young men called to the ministry," was opened, but the bright prospects were quickly ruined by the hard times of 1837. Harassed by poor management and the dissatisfaction of the students with the manual labor plan, the trustees willingly closed the school in 1838. The property

---

[29] Leland W. Meyer, *Georgetown College* (Louisville, 1929), passim; Enoch Hutchinson, "Biographical Sketch of Rev. Howard Malcolm, D.D.," *Baptist Memorial*, X (1851), 317-22; Thomas M. Vaughan, *Memoirs of Rev. Wm. Vaughan* (Louisville, 1878), 231-39.

[30] "Western Baptist Theological Institute," *Baptist Memorial*, II (1843), 193-200; W. C. James, "A History of the Western Baptist Theological Institute," Kentucky Baptist Historical Society, *Publications* (Louisville, 1910), 29-100.

was sold to meet the debts, and the residue of two thousand dollars was put into a fund for the education of young ministers.[31]

In 1839 Judson Female Institute at Marion, Alabama, opened as a private school. When chartered by the legislature in 1841, the school was offered to and accepted by the state convention of Baptists. Providing instruction of college level, the school expanded both physically and numerically. In 1845 nearly two hundred young ladies were enrolled. The success of the college for girls encouraged a similar undertaking for men. In 1842 a school of "nine small boys" opened in a building previously occupied by Judson. Under excellent direction the school turned to a broader program, and took the name of Howard University which was later changed to Howard College. Within a year Howard had seventy students.[32]

A great change in the educational leadership of the Baptists is quite evident in the early life of the University of Alabama. Its first president was Alva Woods, a Baptist minister who served from 1831 to 1837. He was followed by the elder Basil Manly, who left the First Baptist Church in Charleston to serve the University as president from 1837 to 1855.

In Mississippi Baptist endeavors were distinguished by failures. Judson Institute was formed in 1836 on land purchased ten miles north of Jackson. When the location proved unhealthful, the school was moved to Spring Ridge and finally to Meddleton. Such relocations were expensive—too

[31] Carl B. Wilson, *The Baptist Manual Labor School Movement in the United States* (Waco, Texas, 1937), 127-28; Hosea Holcombe, *A History of the Rise and Progress of the Baptists in Alabama* (Philadelphia, 1840), 81-84; *Minutes of the Eleventh Anniversary of the Baptist State Convention* (Tuscaloosa, 1834), 5-7, 14.

[32] B. F. Riley, *A Memorial History of the Baptists of Alabama* (Philadelphia, 1923), 69-77, 84-86; Mitchell B. Garrett, "Sixty Years of Howard College, 1842-1902," *Howard College Bulletin* (Birmingham), LXXXV (1927), No. 4; *Alabama Baptist*, Oct. 14, Dec. 30, 1843.

expensive, in fact, for paper financing—and were excellent evidence of both haste and waste. Struggling against heavy odds, the school collapsed in 1845.[33]

In Tennessee the Primitive Baptists fought education with such vigor that no effort in behalf of higher education succeeded until about 1835. Under the leadership of Robert B. C. Howell a plan to build a Baptist college in each of the three natural divisions of the state resulted in the realization of only one—Union University in Murfreesboro which began operation in 1845. Six years later Union had 150 students in all departments.[34]

Although without the heritage of a liberally educated ministry like the Presbyterians or of college trained founders like the Methodists, the Baptist churches had done pretty well for education by 1860. When converted to the absolute necessity of theological training for preachers, the Baptists soon matched the efforts of their chief rivals the Methodists. Eventually both Baptist and Methodists excelled the Presbyterians in building and maintaining colleges and universities in the South.[35]

Bishop Stephen Elliott insisted, along with other bishops and leaders of the Protestant Episcopal Church, that their church should seek to combat ignorance especially since their services were liturgical and a deficiency in letters was almost a bar to participation. Once he said: "Every clergyman and layman should therefore strive to remove that ignorance, the fruitful parent of prejudice and· suspicion, and to enable every individual to feel that the prayer book does not stand as a dark mystery between him and the Church of Christ." Without a single exception all the

---

[33] Boyd, *Baptists in Mississippi*, 104, 296-97.

[34] Enoch Hutchinson, "Biographical Sketch of Rev. R. B. C. Howell, D.D.," *Baptist Memorial*, X (1851), 145-48; *Baptist Banner*, Oct. 29, 1840, Feb. 4, April 8, 1841.

[35] See Francis B. Simkins, *A History of the South* (New York, 1963), Chap. XXVI passim.

Episcopal bishops in the South before the Civil War were aggressive advocates of education and identified themselves with all school programs, ranging from elementary school to university. In 1840 Bishop Benjamin B. Smith of Kentucky was given the non-salaried position of Superintendent of Public Instruction. During his term he delivered lectures on education in seventy-six of the ninety counties in the state. As superintendent Bishop Smith's chief desire was the establishment of a system of common schools for all sections of the state. Francis L. Hawks, while rector of Christ Church in New Orleans, became the first president of the University of Louisiana, later named Tulane University.[36] Probably the great majority of the Episcopal ministry had, at one time, taught in some type of educational institution. Teaching provided a worthy and dignified means by which to supplement a meager income.

From various parishes, dioceses, towns, and cities of the South calls went forth for Episcopal ministers to open schools—often in places where there was no regularly established parish. A specific example from Mississippi indicates the activity of the church as an agent for education. In September 1838 an Episcopal minister in Woodville, Mississippi, informed a professor in the General Theological Seminary in New York City that the trustees of Jefferson College near "the rapidly rising city of Natchez" wished to place the college under Episcopal influence. He proposed that the college would pay a missionary bishop a salary of four thousand dollars a year in addition to free house rent. Seeing some difficulty in that offer, he suggested that it might be wise to appoint someone head of the college who might ultimately become bishop of the diocese. In 1839 the

[36] Pennington, "Stephen Elliott," *Historical Magazine*, VII, 222; W. Robert Insko, "Benjamin Bosworth Smith, First Bishop of Kentucky," *Historical Magazine of the Protestant Episcopal Church*, XXII (1953), 146-228; Carter and Carter, *Episcopal Church in Louisiana*, 74-80.

Reverend A. Stephens, an Episcopal rector, was installed as president of the college, but he failed to become a bishop.[37]

Soon after his marriage in 1821 the Reverend James H. Otey moved to Maury County, Tennessee, and opened a school for boys near Franklin. In 1835 he established the Columbia Female Institute, which for a few years was thought to be "the largest and most successful [Episcopal] church school in the United States." Yet this school functioned in a community in which the local parish had only seven or eight communicants. After the panic of 1837 the institute, struggling for existence, begged for books for its library. A blazer, dated August 1838, stated that, although the institute promised a full course of instruction by resident teachers, "the disasters of the last year have swept from the Churchmen of Tennessee all expectation of realizing their fondly cherished hopes of an Episcopal College. . . ."[38]

As the number of Episcopalians increased and simultaneously the demand for schools, here and there throughout the South appeared academies designed to meet the prevailing needs. Most of these efforts had the approval of some Episcopal minister, bishop, or diocese. In January 1849 at Tuscaloosa, Alabama, the Classical Institute and Mission School of the Diocese of Alabama was duly opened. It consisted of a theological and classical department, the one designed for training ministers and the other for educating boys. The classical department had a principal and two assistants with the title of ushers. It began with twenty-two students, six of whom paid no tuition. The theology department had one candidate for orders. On paper the framework of the school seemed solid enough, but fate soon tested the

[37] David C. Payne to William R. Whittingham, Sept. 12, 1833, in Whittingham papers, Duke. See William B. Hamilton, "Jefferson College and Education in Mississippi, 1798-1817," *Mississippi History*, III (1941), 259-76.

[38] Perry, *American Episcopal Church*, II, 203. The blazer of the "Female Institute, Columbia, Tennessee" is in the Duke University Library.

foundation and found nothing to support one man's dreams. When the principal died in July, the school closed. Numerous schools opened by or in the name of the Episcopal Church had equally short periods of existence.[39]

A parochial school organized in connection with the Episcopal church in Holly Springs, Mississippi, in 1842 became an institution for boys with as many as ninety students in 1855. It was closed during the Civil War, to be opened again in 1867 and permanently closed in 1898. Bishop William M. Green sought to establish for every parish in the state a school under Episcopal control or influence. His most ambitious effort was St. Andrews, a diocesan school and college opened at Jackson in 1852. Rose Gates College was begun in Okolona in the northeastern part of Mississippi in 1859. Neither survived the ravages of the Civil War.[40]

George W. Freeman, Missionary Bishop of Texas, in his address to the annual convention in 1850 urged the creation of a school. A committee of five was appointed to investigate the possibilities and was instructed to report in January 1851. After much haggling and dickering St. Paul's College and Diocesan School opened in 1852 at Anderson, Texas. Hardly had the institution started before a subscription had been raised in Austin to move the school there. After an adverse vote by the trustees on the question of removal to Austin, the college quickly failed. An attempt to revive it in Branham soon after the Civil War resulted only in reviving the preparatory school. Bishop Polk in a letter to other bishops in 1856 said that in the Southern dioceses the church did not have "a single seminary for the instruction of boys, under the distinct appointment or control of the Church, rising to the level of a first class grammar school." Further

[39] *Journal of the Eighteenth Annual Convention* (Tuscaloosa, 1849), 10-13.

[40] Nash K. Burger, "William Mercer Green, First Bishop of Mississippi, 1850-1887," *Historical Magazine of the Protestant Episcopal Church*, XIX (1950), 345-46.

he considered this situation incompatible with the duties of good citizens.[41]

A college education or its equivalent under the personal tutelage of an ordained clergyman was the general preparation for a candidate for the Episcopal ministry. At the beginning of the nineteenth century the only way for a candidate in America to obtain his theological training was through personal guidance. The shift to institutional training occurred almost simultaneously in several denominations. Despite the high standard of education which the Protestant Episcopal Church sought to maintain, the church did not have a single college under its control before the General Theological Seminary was established in New York City in 1817 and the Episcopal Theological Seminary at Alexandria, Virginia, in 1823. In the Lower South several plans reached a partial fruition; but the span of success was short, and schools established in Alabama, Texas, and Kentucky were feeble efforts.

Immediately after Benjamin B. Smith was made Bishop of Kentucky in 1832, he began an energetic campaign to form a theological seminary. Two years later his plan was far enough advanced to secure from the Kentucky legislature a charter which acknowledged a board of trustees already in existence. In the spring of 1834 the seminary bought the property of the old Eclectic Institute in Lexington, which would provide accommodations for forty students. The institution opened with only three students; in 1836 the enrollment increased to eighteen students, only one of whom was a native of Kentucky. Although the entrance requirements were quite low, the seminary failed to attract students. The affairs of the seminary became involved in the

[41] "A Brief History of the Rise and Progress of the Diocesan School in the State of Texas, and of St. Paul's College," in *Journal of the Seventh Annual Convention* (Anderson, Texas, 1856), 28-35; [Leonidas Polk], *A Letter to the Right Reverend Bishops . . . from the Bishop of Louisiana* (New Orleans, 1856), 9.

dissensions which prevailed in Kentucky, and the ecclesiastical trial of Bishop Smith was not beneficial to the educational activities of the Episcopalians. After abandoning the Lexington property, the diocese tried to operate a theological department in a diocesan seminary and this too failed.[42]

In 1835 Jackson Kemper was consecrated as the first Episcopal Missionary Bishop with jurisdiction over Missouri and Indiana. He became so discouraged over the inability of Eastern ministers to adapt themselves to the West that he sought to provide a college for the education of young men of the region. In the fall of 1836, with the support of a generous twenty-thousand dollar gift from a wealthy layman, he secured a charter for Kemper College to be located five miles southwest of St. Louis. For a while all went well, but, when Cicero S. Hawks became Bishop of Missouri in 1844, he found the college beset with a maze of financial problems and torn by faculty dissensions. The once promising endeavor closed a year later. Again the region west of the mountains had no Episcopal seminary for the education of sorely needed ministers.[43]

After years of preliminary discussions about a university for the Episcopalians of the South, Leonidas Polk, Bishop of Louisiana, made the first definite step by urging in 1856 that the bishops of the nine Southern dioceses take immediate action for a joint school to be erected in the high area of the southeastern corner of Tennessee. He, like Cobbs, had seen the need for training ministers in a school conveniently located in the South. Responding to his plea, the dioceses sent delegates the next year to Lookout Mountain

[42] Brewer, *Religious Education in the Episcopal Church*, 241; E. Clowes Chorley, *Men and Movements in the Episcopal Church* (New York, 1946), 45, 117; Caswall, *American Church*, 206-209; *Journal of the Twelfth Annual Convention* (Princeton, Ky., 1840), 11-13. The Whittingham papers contain a two-page printed prospectus of an Episcopal theological seminary proposed to be established in Lexington, Kentucky.

[43] Perry, *American Episcopal Church*, II, 259-60.

where final plans for a university were made. To the trustees was conveyed a land parcel of ten thousand acres on a mountain near Winchester, Tennessee, and a charter was granted by the state. In the fall of 1860 Bishop Polk laid the cornerstone for the first building of the University of the South. With the growing bitterness between the North and the South, the name caused comments and accusations of sectionalism. Bishop Otey in reply denied any aim to build a Southern university, but admitted that it was planned as "an institution of conservatism" which would "still the waters of agitation" and "bind the discordant elements" into a "Union stronger than steel."[44]

During the winter of 1860-1861 the families of Bishops Polk and Elliott lived at the small settlement designated for the future university. From there the two bishops addressed letters to the other Southern bishops proposing that a convention be held in Montgomery on July 3, 1861, to consider the status of the dioceses within the Confederacy. Before the next meeting of the trustees in the fall of 1861, Bishop Polk had entered the Confederate Army as a major general. In July 1863 Polk led a retreating army over the Cumberland Mountains, where the university buildings lay in burnt ruins. The greatest educational effort of the Episcopalians in the South had to wait for a more propitious day.

The poorly paid or wholly unpaid Disciples of Christ preacher had a tendency to criticize the salaried ministry. Some of the harshest articles found in the *Christian Baptist* were tirades against the "hireling clergy." Campbell and his preachers were really in revolt against the theological training of other churches. They felt oppressed and had little sympathy with seminaries under sectarian control. Since

[44] William M. Green, *Memoirs of Rt. Rev. James Hervey Otey* (New York, 1885), 65. Also see Arthur B. Chitty, *Reconstruction at Sewanee: The Founding of the University of the South and Its First Administration, 1857-1872* (Sewanee, Tenn., 1954), Chap. I; Joseph H. Parks, *General Leonidas Polk, C. S. A.* (Baton Rouge, 1962), 131-33, 144-52.

most of the early Disciples were proselytes from other churches, the first crop of preachers came already prepared for service. When this source of preachers dried up, the church had to recruit and train its own. In a short time the Disciples began to feel a great need for educated members and for a better educated ministry.

Within the ranks of the Disciples and Christian clergy no great number deliberately capitalized on their lack of education, as did some among the Baptists and Methodists of an earlier period. Some of these Disciples preachers earned their living by farming, but many of them taught schools or conducted schools of their own. Stone spent much of his life in a school room. He had taught in Georgia before moving to Lexington, Kentucky, where he was a teacher in a private school, after which he became principal of Rittenhouse Academy in Georgetown.

Thomas Campbell took a full three-year classical course at the University of Glasgow, followed by training in a theological seminary of the Presbyterian Church. Although he had decided on the ministry, he continued intermittently to teach school until he came to America. Between 1817 and 1819 the elder Campbell conducted an academy in Burlington, Kentucky, leaving there because of a Kentucky law that prohibited him from reading the Bible or preaching to Negroes except in the presence of one or more white witnesses. Thomas Campbell moved his family back to Pennsylvania not far from the Virginia line in order to aid his son Alexander in his newly organized Buffalo Seminary.[45]

Alexander Campbell had been well grounded by his father in Latin and Greek classics, French and English literature, and philosophy. At the age of nineteen he was an assistant in an academy in Ireland. While waiting to receive his father's call to come to America, Alexander studied for a year at the University of Glasgow. As a dele-

[45] Richardson, *Alexander Campbell*, I, 494-97.

gate to the Virginia Constitutional Convention of 1829-1830, he introduced a resolution providing for state recognition and supervision of public education. The failure of this resolution to pass may give evidence that Campbell was ahead of his time in his views on public schools. A short while after he returned home from the convention, he wrote in the *Millennial Harbinger* that he advocated levying taxes "sufficient to educate well every child born within the commonwealth" and to maintain as many schools as necessary for the convenience of all the children in every vicinity. Next to Campbell's influence as a churchman, his chief contribution was in the field of American education. He believed that, in his tireless advocacy of public education, he was giving the chief support to religion, morality, and representative government. In his several debates with Catholic priests Campbell indicated that he relied on universal education to combat the rising tide of Catholicism. He further believed that the training of students for the professions and for the ministry was the best method of spreading the religious movement to which he was devoting his life. To this end he turned to encourage the creation of colleges and established his own Bethany College.[46]

In 1836 the Disciples founded their first institution of higher learning in Kentucky, Bacon College in Georgetown, which already contained Georgetown College, a Baptist school. During Bacon's first four months of existence more than 130 students came from twelve states and the District of Columbia. The student body increased much faster than the financial support, which lagged despite the enthusiastic endorsement of Alexander Campbell. Because of promised aid, the trustees voted to move the college to Harrodsburg, where it began anew in September 1839. Bacon's financial situation became so desperate that a bill was passed in 1851

[46] *Millennial Harbinger*, 1830, 555. Also see Lunger, *Alexander Campbell*, Chaps. VI, XI.

by the Kentucky legislature granting to the college the privilege of a lottery. The Baptist church in Versailles was aroused by the "unchristian, sinful and unholy" effort and warned the college trustees that it would support no organization using a lottery. A "real friend" of Bacon College called for a disavowal of the act. Apparently the college did not take advantage of the lottery.[47] In 1858 Bacon merged with Kentucky University, which in turn joined Transylvania University in 1865. Into the hands of the youngest of the major church groups in Kentucky fell the permanent control of the oldest institution of learning.

For several years Alexander Campbell had considered plans for a college of his personal designing but had deliberately delayed action for fear of hurting the financial support of Bacon College. When this institution moved to Harrodsburg, Campbell decided that the opportune moment for his project had arrived. During the early part of 1840 a charter was granted by the Virginia legislature to Bethany College. In September the trustees held their second meeting at which time Campbell was elected president, a position he held until a few years before his death in 1866. On some of his land in Virginia, forty miles south of Pittsburgh and seven miles from Wellsburg on the Ohio River, Campbell proceeded to erect a large brick building. After having selected four professors, Campbell opened the college on the scheduled day of October 21, 1841.[48]

From its first day the college prospered under the presidency of a strict disciplinarian and a shrewd business man. In 1843, within three years after the first brick had been laid, the college had constructed buildings at a cost of twenty-five thousand dollars and enrolled 186 students from eleven states from New York to Louisiana. The entire expenses for

[47] "Bacon College," *Ecclesiastical Reformer*, March 1, 15, 1851. Also see John Rogers, *The Biography of Elder J. T. Johnson* (Cincinnati, 1861), 121-24, 145-47, 152-53.
[48] Richardson, *Alexander Campbell*, II, 468-70, 485, 491-92, et passim.

a session amounted to $150 and for this the college promised that "the inmates of this establishment will require and receive more attention, care, and management than is either necessary or expected at a College." The fact that twelve students were expelled during the year is convincing evidence that the care and attention were adequate. Bethany's charter provided "for the instruction of youth in the various branches of science and literature, the useful arts, agriculture, and the learned and foreign languages."[49] Although Campbell recognized a need for a trained and learned ministry, he forbade in Bethany's charter the establishment of a theological professorship. The Bible, however, was to be a textbook, like any other book. For this practice Bethany was charged with sacrilege and infidelity, but Campbell stood his ground and the storm of opposition soon subsided.

With Bethany successfully leading the way, other Disciples colleges arose in several states. "Soon the prairies were scattered with the bones of dead colleges whose very names have been forgotten. . . . It is not surprising that the Disciples of that period little realized what it took to make a college, in money, scholarship, and constituency." Finances were the rock upon which most of the colleges foundered and broke. Franklin College, established near Nashville in 1845 by Tolbert Fanning, an aggressive leader of the antisociety group of churches, attempted to function without an endowment. Campbell pointed out such folly by saying, "Not a College in the world has existed one century without endowment; nor can they. This fact is worth a thousand lectures. Can any one name a College that has seen one century without funds [other] than the fees of tuition?"[50] Had Campbell taken a quick look around at all the "bones

[49] *Millennial Harbinger*, 1840, 176, 1843, 277-79, 339. Also see Sterling W. Brown, *The Changing Function of Disciple Colleges* (Chicago, 1939), passim; *Millennial Harbinger*, 1846, 443-45.

[50] Garrison and DeGroot, *Disciples of Christ*, 251-53. Also see James E. Scobey (ed.), *Franklin College and Its Influences* (Nashville, 1954).

of dead colleges," he would have reduced his time element in his pronouncement of folly.

Campbell summarized succinctly his views on the value of an education: "All things else being equal, [an] educated mind will stand in all the ratios of its own superiority, in contrast with those equally gifted by nature and grace, but wanting in this particular." Having made this declaration in 1841, he repeated it whenever he made his extensive journeys through the South and West in behalf of his church and Bethany. He was a successful fund raiser, but not always to the degree which he experienced in 1857 as an overnight guest of the Gorees in Marion, Alabama.[51] Mrs. Goree's gift of five thousand dollars to Bethany refutes the accusation that all followers of Campbell were poor, ignorant, and uninterested in education.

In reaching the individual member, the religious press, next to the pulpit, was the most important educational influence in each of the respective denominations. In 1850 the editor of a Methodist paper, the *Western Christian Advocate* published in Cincinnati, said: "Thirty years ago there was scarcely a religious paper in existence. . . . Now, how changed is the scene. Each Church has its organs, through which religious intelligence is communicated, and its enterprises advocated, and its triumphs made known."[52]

Newspapers in the West gave very little space to religious or to church matters in general. An examination of the files of an early paper, such as the Knoxville *Gazette* for 1791-1796, reveals the almost complete absence of any reference to churches. In contrast much space was given to robberies, murders, runaway slaves, and even an occasional notice of a runaway wife. To counteract this neglect the churches had to supply their news by word of mouth or by church papers.

[51] *Millennial Harbinger*, 1843, 217, 1857, 504.
[52] Chester F. Dunham, *The Attitude of the Northern Clergy toward the South, 1860-1865* (Toledo, Ohio, 1942), 7.

The oldest religious paper established in the West was the *Kentucky Missionary and Theological Magazine,* begun in May 1812 in Frankfort by Stark Dupuy who was a young Baptist preacher. The magazine contained some sixty pages, appeared quarterly, and cost fifty cents a year. After one year Dupuy ceased the publication chiefly because of the effects of the War of 1812. Before the end of 1812 the Reverend Silas M. Noel began in the same town the *Gospel Herald* which lasted about a year and expired because of a lack of subscribers. The *Baptist Register* (soon changed to the *Baptist Recorder*), a weekly paper established in 1826 at Bloomfield, Kentucky, promised "to strip religion of everything like the traditions of men, and to present the truth in a plain and simple manner."[53] In contrast to earlier Baptist papers the *Recorder* was published for four years, then was changed to a monthly periodical bearing the name *Baptist Herald.* Through a long period the state was literally a breeding place for Baptist papers. Such fertility may be attributed to the presence of Campbellites, Parkerites, and Catholics—the chief targets against whom the Baptists directed their pens.

Several periodicals were published in the South under Baptist sponsorship. As early as 1821 the Baptists in Alabama began publishing the *Family Visitor* in Wetumpka. After twenty years the paper changed ownership and moved to Marion, where it was printed under the title of the *Alabama Baptist.* In 1835 Robert B. C. Howell began in Nashville, Tennessee, *The Baptist,* a well edited paper that had seventeen hundred subscribers in 1839. Since more than half of its subscribers were in arrears, the editor feared the paper could not long continue. *The Southwest Religious Luminary,* a monthly published in Natchez, Mississippi, came into being in 1836, but gaining no strength scarcely

53 Spencer, *Kentucky Baptists,* I, 218, 347, 567-68, 597.

lived out the year. A new paper, the *South-Western Monitor and Religious Luminary* survived for four years before consolidating with the *Baptist Banner and Pioneer* of Louisville, Kentucky. By 1880 of the forty-six Baptist papers printed primarily for the Southern and Southwestern states, thirty had died and only sixteen managed to survive.[54]

Methodist journalism gave to the church several organs for communication. *The Western Christian Monitor*, a short-lived paper established by William Beauchamp in 1816 at Chillicothe, Ohio, bears the honor of being Methodism's first Western periodical. In 1825 the *Wesleyan Journal* was established in Charleston, South Carolina, to be merged two years later with the *Christian Advocate* of New York City. By 1828 it had a circulation of twenty-eight thousand, surpassing that of the London *Times*. The wide circulation of the *Christian Advocate* in the mid-West and South probably accounts for the absence of a permanent paper until the appearance in Cincinnati in 1834 of the *Western Christian Advocate*, the first official Methodist paper west of the Appalachian Mountains. Six years later its fifteen thousand subscribers made it one of the largest circularized church papers in the entire country. In 1861 this Western paper had thirty-one thousand subscribers while the New York *Advocate* had only twenty-nine thousand. The General Conference of 1840 adopted a suggestion that a periodical for females be published, preferably in the West, to offset the activity of the Roman Catholics in this field. A year later the *Ladies Repository and Gatherings of the West* began publication in Cincinnati. During its earlier years the periodical, regarded by many as the leading magazine for women, contributed much to improving the general culture of the

[54] Charles A. Stakely, *History of the First Baptist Church of Montgomery, Alabama* (Montgomery, 1930), 152; *The Baptist*, V (1839), 28-29; Boyd, *Baptists in Mississippi*, 292; Victor I. Masters, *Baptist Missions in the South* (Atlanta, 1915), 126.

West and the South, both within and without Methodism. At one time the paper had a circulation of forty thousand.[55]

After the Methodist Episcopal Church, South was organized, each conference either sponsored a journal or adopted some journal as representative of its views and interests. When new journals were organized, conferences often transferred their support. Examples of important Southern Methodist papers established before the Civil War were the *Texas Christian Advocate* (1847); *St. Louis Christian Advocate* (1849); and the *New Orleans Christian Advocate* (1851). During the war all of these weeklies either ceased or suspended publication.

Conscious of the great need for a religious paper in the Lower Mississippi Valley, the Presbyterians in the Synod of Tennessee encouraged their churches to support the *Calvinistic Magazine*, which was published in Rogersville, Tennessee, beginning in January 1827. The editors, James Gallaher, Frederick A. Ross, and David Nelson, proposed "to defend the doctrines of the Bible as they are set forth in our Confession and Catechisms; also to discuss subjects in Church Government, to publish Sermons and Essays on Christian Duty, Missionary, Literary and Political Intelligence." During its five years of existence the well edited magazine contributed much to the welfare of the Presbyterian Church. The removal of Nelson to Danville, Kentucky, and of Gallaher to Cincinnati hastened the discontinuance of the paper in 1830. In 1846 Ross took the lead in the resumption of publication, this time at Abingdon, Virginia. After another five-year period the *Calvinistic Magazine* was merged with the *Weekly Presbyterian Register* of Knoxville, Tennessee. During the year 1830 Thomas T. Skillman published in Lexington, Kentucky, the *Presbyterian Advocate* which appeared monthly. He stated that the mission of the paper was,"to exhibit correct views of the doctrines and government of the Presbyterian church, to support their truth and scriptural authority and defend them against objections and misrepresentations." This declaration invited clashes with other denominations with differing points of view. After one year Skillman ceased this publication because the *Advocate* interfered with the circulation of the *Western Luminary*, an interdenominational journal which he also edited.[56]

In February 1830 the Cumberland Presbyterian Church sponsored the *Religious and Literary Intelligencer*, founded by Franceway R. Cossitt, president of Cumberland College, and printed in Princeton, Kentucky. Devoted to religion, literature, science, agriculture, and general information, this, the first Cumberland Presbyterian paper, lasted about two years. The paper was moved to Nashville in 1832 and its name was changed to *The Revivalist*. Two years later it was published as the *Cumberland Presbyterian*. Numerous church papers were published by individuals in the name of the church, but none was sponsored as an official church organ until 1874.[57]

The *Catholic Telegraph*, oldest surviving Catholic newspaper in the country, was founded in Cincinnati in 1831. At first it was a paper of eight pages, twelve by nine inches in format, without any advertisements. There is scarcely an early issue of the *Telegraph* that does not contain references to religious prejudices against the Catholic Church. The paper waged a relentless war on the Cincinnati *Journal*, a Presbyterian paper edited by a Reverend Mr. Blanchard, who referred to the *Telegraph* as "The Papal Newspaper."

The *Shepherd of the Valley* was first published in 1832 in St. Louis as a weekly paper. At first printed partly in

[56] Alexander, *Synod of Tennessee*, 62-63; Thomas H. Spence, "Southern Presbyterian Reviews," *Union Seminary Review* (Richmond), LVI (1945), 6.

[57] Lindsley, "Sources and Sketches," *Theological Medium*, VI (1875), 26, 386; McDonnold, *Cumberland Presbyterian Church*, 229-39, 460.

English and partly in French, the paper dedicated itself "to expand, defend and disseminate the real tenets of the Catholic Religion, and to counteract the unwearied efforts made in almost every portion of the United States, to check by calumny and misrepresentation the rapid increase of its members." From the first issue the paper lacked necessary patronage. In 1833 the Western Catholic Association was formed to save the paper, which managed to last another year. An examination of this weekly readily reveals a narrowness and intolerance not found in any other Catholic periodical in the West before the Civil War. No wonder the *Pittsburgh Catholic* felt constrained to write about the *Shepherd of the Valley*: "We regret the intemperate expressions of the writers alluded to, and we regret them the more if the common interpretation put on their words be correct."[58]

In 1836 the *Catholic Advocate* made its appearance in Bardstown, Kentucky. As an eight-page weekly costing $2.50 a year, the *Advocate* promised to contain a temperate defense of Catholic tenets and practices, articles on various subjects, statements against Catholics, foreign and domestic news, and miscellaneous items. At first the editorial control was vested in the faculty at St. Joseph's College, but in 1836 Bishop Flaget became the sole editor, a position he kept until the paper was moved to Louisville. Although there were twenty thousand Catholics in Kentucky in 1843, the *Advocate* had only 250 subscribers in nine states. In a long editorial on November 7, 1846, the editor complained of lack of support. Some aid came but not enough to prevent the paper from being combined with the *Catholic Telegraph* in 1850.

Bishop Blanc took the lead in establishing *Le Propagateur*

---

[58] Paul J. Foik, *Pioneer Catholic Journalism* (New York, 1930), 128-29, 141-48, 160-63. The most complete file of the *Shepherd of the Valley* is in the library of St. Louis University. See issue of Sept. 20, 1833. *Pittsburgh Catholic* is quoted in *Catholic Telegraph*, July 16, 1853.

Catholique, the first Catholic weekly in New Orleans. Its first issue edited by the paper's only editor, Abbé Napoleon Joseph Perche, appeared on November 13, 1842, and carried the caption "A family journal, published by a society of men of letters." Originally founded to support Bishop Blanc in his controversy with the trustees of St. Louis Cathedral and of other parishes in his diocese, the paper became the organ of the church in Louisiana. During most of its long life, the paper was printed in the French language. Abbé Perche's writings did much to convert many to orthodox thinking in church matters and to counteract the attacks of the nativists and the Know-Nothings. Once he so enraged the Know-Nothings that they attacked his printing plant and threatened to destroy his press. When the Civil War came, the priest, an ardent secessionist, was made a prisoner in his home and his paper was suspended in 1862.[59]

A list of Catholic weekly newspapers published in 1854 in the region south of the Ohio River and west of the mountains includes only *Le Propagateur Catholique, Shepherd of the Valley* (revived in 1851 as an anti-Know-Nothing organ), the *Catholic Messenger* in New Orleans, and *Der Herold des Glaubens* in St. Louis. The region had no monthly, quarterly, or annual periodical published by the Catholics.[60]

Alexander Campbell early saw the tremendous advantage of a literary vehicle by which he could propagate his own views and those of his associates. In 1823 he founded, edited, and printed the *Christian Baptist,* a monthly paper which stirred religious circles by its ceaseless fire on many fronts. Campbell was especially hard on the professional clergy, calling them "textuary divines" and "scrap doctors," charging them with ignorance, pride, and selfishness. Robert

[59] Baudier, *Catholic Church in Louisiana,* 331, 443; [Carroll], *Catholic History,* 273.

[60] See Joseph Belcher, *Religious Denominations in the United States* (Philadelphia, 1859), 766-67.

Semple, a leading Baptist minister in Virginia, said that the *Christian Baptist* was "more mischievous than any publication I have ever known and has succeeded in sowing seeds of discord among the brethren to an alarming degree." This situation arose largely as a result of Campbell's attack on three features of the existing church: clerical pretensions and titles; unauthorized associations such as missionary societies and Sunday schools; and creeds and confessions. Campbell's advocacy of a return to "the ancient order" and his clashing views on Calvinism soon led to an open break with Baptist churches and ministers.[61]

By 1830 Campbell's enormous activity had led him to change his position on church organization. Fears he once nursed and formed had abated to such a degree that he had begun to accept any organization that aided efficient church operation. This brought an end to the *Christian Baptist* and the beginning of the *Millennial Harbinger* which appeared monthly between 1830 and 1870. With Campbell as editor for thirty years and with adequate finances, the *Harbinger* had no equal among religious papers in the entire West and South. It was both heart and backbone of the periodical literature of the Disciples of Christ. Campbell's success in the publishing of the *Millennial Harbinger* served to encourage other Disciples members and ministers to publish periodicals. A list of seventeen papers appearing in the *Harbinger* in 1845 is highly impressive. Some of the papers did not circulate far and some did not last long, but their total contribution to the Disciples cause was significant. Campbell had converted his rapidly growing church to the value of a weekly or monthly paper.

By 1826 Barton Stone began his *Christian Messenger*, a twenty-four page monthly which continued with some intermissions until Stone died in 1844. Although never the equal in effectiveness of either of Campbell's papers, the *Messenger*

[61] Garrison and DeGroot, *Disciples of Christ*, 175-79.

was a journal of considerable importance among Stone's followers.[62]

Early Episcopal journals probably contributed little to winning converts. They were written largely for the clergy and the educated laity. "They bear ample testimony, however, to the fact that in those days readers were not easily bored." The *Gospel Messenger and Southern Christian Register*, a monthly published, with two changes in title, in Charleston, South Carolina, from 1824 to 1853 was the first Episcopal publication of any importance in the Southern states. Early in 1835 Dr. John E. Cooke, a prominent Episcopal layman, began publishing the *Church Advocate*, a fortnightly folio sheet in Lexington, Kentucky. This private venture became burdensome so that before the year closed Dr. Cooke decided not to continue the paper. In November 1835 the Reverend Henry Caswall, a professor in the theological seminary at Lexington, assumed the editorship but financial difficulties brought suspension of the *Advocate* by the end of 1836. In 1835 the prospectus of the *Southern Churchman* announced that, as a Southern paper, it would adapt itself to the "peculiar wants" of the Southern church and further that "its peculiar theology will be that of the Protestant Episcopal Church."[63] This periodical continued to be published in Richmond, Virginia, until 1957. No permanent church paper was published by Episcopalians in the Western area in the period covered by this study.

The average religious journal arose from the endeavors of a single person. He served as editor, business manager, and publisher. The opinions of the paper were usually his own personal views. Although he printed letters from correspondents, there is evidence that he used a highly selective method. The papers often copied articles from each other and thereby managed to fill the pages. Sub-

---

[62] Ware, *Stone*, 216.

[63] Addison, *Episcopal Church*, 120; Brewer, *Religious Education in the Episcopal Church*, 298-99; Chorley, *Men and Movements*, 130.

scribers were negligent in paying, and mounting arrears brought extinction to many journals. On the other hand, some of the papers were well managed; the *Millennial Harbinger* and the *Western Christian Advocate* were on sound financial bases. Despite the fluctuations of fortune of most journals, they reached places beyond the voice of the preacher, and so the influence of the religious presses cannot be measured in circulation or duration. Indeed, the need for them was best indicated by the numerous short-lived papers, which, as they fluttered out of existence, were succeeded by others. It was to the credit of the editors that they were not easily discouraged and that they allowed no other man's experience to dishearten them in their difficult ventures.

11

REFORM AND DISCIPLINE

THE EARLY SETTLER in the West and the South looked at the vast area before him and felt a sense of new independence and unaccustomed freedom from distant institutional and family restrictions. This situation challenged the churches to re-establish discipline as a barrier against the grave threats to a decent and respectable social order.

The one great evil that probably exceeded all others in the West was alcoholic intemperance. The drinking of large quantities of distilled liquors had become acceptable to all classes of society, and no small draught slaked a frontiersman's thirst. "Westward the Star of Empire takes its way" has been paraphrased "Westward the Jug of Empire takes its way." The spirit of corn became the van leader in the moving progress of American life. In 1787 Andrew Ellicott, leaving on a four-month surveying trip in the West, took for his party 256 gallons of rum, whisky, and brandy. Whisky and rum were among the staple items in every general store and dispensing them added to the social warmth of the place. A storekeeper in Georgia said that it was not uncommon for him to sell thirty pounds sterling of rum in a day and to see as many as fifty men drinking within a rod of his store. Ardent spirits were used for a great variety of practical reasons, especially as a preventive against such illnesses as agues and fevers. River boatmen who engaged in excessively strenuous labor demanded large quantities. And men whose emotions were aroused found solace in strong drink. Camp meetings, preaching services, funerals, weddings—all were likely occasions for serving or selling a quantity of liquor. The making or selling of whisky was not considered disreputable—even preachers engaged in both. They often carried a flask in their saddle bags and "did not scruple to invoke its inspiration when strength gave way under earnest labor."[1]

The increase in the per capita consumption rose rapidly from $2\frac{1}{2}$ gallons in 1792 to $4\frac{1}{2}$ in 1810 and $7\frac{1}{2}$ in 1823. Then occurred a decline in the consumption to 6 gallons in 1830 and $2\frac{1}{2}$ in 1840: the drastic lessening of the amount was largely attributed to a concerted campaign against an evil which the churches considered the greatest obstacle to social progress. Philip Lindsley, for twenty-six years president of the University of Nashville, declared in 1827 that nine-tenths of the criminals had been made by intemperance and that sixty thousand citizens died yearly either from the use of liquor or from disease caused by liquor. In 1834 John C. Young, the president of Centre College, stated that there was one death for every 1,866 gallons of whisky made and vended. He further declared that the country had 480,000 drunkards who constituted a greater menace to her safety than "the bayonets of four hundred and eighty thousand foreign foes."[2] Probably half of the dismissals of members by the Presbyterian and Baptist churches could be attributed to drunkenness.

The lack of transportation for corn largely explains the production of a great amount of liquor in the West and South. A horse could transport only four bushels of grain

[1] Edward Channing, A History of the United States (7 vols.; New York, 1907-1932), IV, 16-17; John A. Williams, Reminiscences (Cincinnati, 1898), 3.

[2] Othniel A. Pendleton, "Temperance and the Evangelical Churches," Journal of the Presbyterian Historical Society, XXV (1947), 15; Halsey, Lindsley, I, 129-30; John C. Young, An Address on Temperance (Lexington, 1834), 5. Also see Calvinistic Magazine (Rogersville, Tenn.), II (1828), 209-10.

but could carry the equivalent of twenty-four bushels when it was converted to a liquid form. Because of the small income from grain which would not bear transportation to a market, the people felt the absolute necessity of converting the grain to the more profitable whisky. Whisky became a convenient medium of exchange, and its use as such became a prevailing standard. Subscriptions to preachers' salaries were often paid in gallons of whisky, a payment adaptable to both personal and commercial uses. In 1798 John Shackleford, a Kentucky Baptist preacher, received three subscriptions of whisky amounting to thirty-six gallons. In 1807 the subscriptions for William L. Wilson, pastor of the First Presbyterian Church of Cincinnati, listed more than one hundred gallons. Little wonder that the region adopted a generous attitude toward both production and consumption of distilled liquors.[3]

The Methodist was the first denomination in America to oppose the wholesale use of ardent spirits. The ravages of liquor excited John Wesley and led to his ruling as early as 1743 that there should not be "drunkenness, buying or selling spirituous liquors, or drinking them, unless in cases of extreme necessity." This rule became the standard for American Methodists who at the Baltimore Conference of 1780 answered in the affirmative to the questions: "Do we disapprove of the practice of distilling grain into liquor? Shall we disown our friends who will not renounce the practice?" Three years later a stronger restriction was reached in a definite denial to the question: "Should our friends be permitted to make spirituous liquors, sell or drink them in drams?" By 1796 the retailing of liquor had become so offensive that the General Conference added a section to the Discipline which declared: "If any member of our Societies retail or give spirituous liquors, and anything disorderly be transacted under his roof on this account, the preacher who

<hr>

[3] Fortune, *Disciples in Kentucky*, 28; Sweet, *The Presbyterians*, 65.

has the oversight of the circuit shall proceed against him, as in the case of other immoralities. . . ."[4]

Although many Methodists flaunted the regulation of the church, many others obeyed largely because of preachers especially in the West who vigorously opposed the use of liquor. James B. Finley, Peter Cartwright, and James Axley were best known of the early Methodist preachers who took up the temperance work as a part of their pastoral duty. Finley frequently "would pledge whole congregations, standing upon their feet, to the temperance cause. . . ." Cartwright had no hesitancy in engaging in a fight, if necessary, to prove to drunken rowdies that they were not welcome to the camp meetings. Axley preached a famous sermon pointing especially to those who made and freely dispensed peach brandy in east Tennessee. If the frontier produced and consumed more than its share of whisky, it also produced a greater number of reformers than any other section. Bishop Asbury had numerous occasions to enforce regulations against intemperance which threatened the work of the church, finding it necessary to expel numerous preachers who failed to refrain from the use of liquor. The West supplied far more than its share of this group. Between 1817 and 1825 half of those expelled from ministerial ranks came from the new regions of the West.[5]

The expressions of several general conferences reflect a changing attitude toward the problem of liquor. In the conference of 1812 James Axley from Tennessee offered a motion that no stationed or local preacher should be permitted to retail spirituous or malt liquors. His proposal was vigorously voted down. Axley presented the same reso-

[4] Henry Wheeler, "Relations of the Methodist Episcopal Church to the Cause of Temperance," *Methodist Review* (New York), LVIII (1876), 629, 632; *Minutes of the Annual Conferences*, I, 12, 18.

[5] Finley, *Autobiography*, 251; Cartwright, *Autobiography*, 182-86, 212-14; Finley, *Sketches*, 238-40; Herbert Asbury, "The Father of Prohibition," *American Mercury*, IX (1926), 344-48; *Minutes of the Annual Conferences*, I, 287-470 passim.

lution at the next conference meeting in 1816, and by deleting the reference to malt liquors, he secured the passage of the motion "that no preacher shall distil or retail spirituous liquors without forfeiting his license." In 1828 the conference advised church members to cease the manufacture and sale of ardent spirits and to discontinue the practice of giving liquor to employees. Twenty years later the General Conference of the Methodist Episcopal Church adopted Wesley's original rule, but in their Pastoral Address two bishops felt under compulsion to urge moderation in its application.[6]

Daniel Dorchester in *Liquor Problem in All Ages* estimated that not one-third as much liquor was consumed in 1850 as had been in 1823. Beyond doubt the Methodist itinerant was instrumental in reducing the per capita consumption. The improved conditions reflect Methodism's war against "the two great potentates of this Western World— whisky [and] brandy" which Asbury once feared would be "the ruin of all that is excellent in morals and government."[7]

The Baptists also took an early stand in opposition to the prevailing use of liquor. The Philadelphia Association in 1788 adopted a resolution declaring that "this Association, taking into consideration the ruinous effects of the great abuse of distilled liquors throughout the country, take this opportunity of expressing our hearty concurrence with our brethren of several other religious societies, in discountenancing the use of them in the future; and earnestly entreat our brethren and friends to use all of their influence to that end . . . except when used as a medicine."[8]

Baptist oversight of individual members was far more constant and exacting than that of the Methodists. The

[6] *Journals of the General Conference,* I, 106, 107, 168, 239, 359, 384.

[7] Daniel Dorchester, *Liquor Problem in All Ages* (New York, 1884), 447; Asbury, *Journal,* II, 481, III, 391.

[8] John T. Christian, *A History of the Baptists of the United States* (Nashville, 1926), 165.

various jurisdictions passed innumerable resolutions against the use of the "tempting juice," and individual churches hesitated little in disciplining members for drunkenness or fighting. The first temperance society organized in Georgia had its initial meeting in 1827 at the call of Deacon Thomas Cooper and the Reverend Adiel Sherwood of the Eatonton church. A year later at the close of the Baptist State Convention, the State Temperance Society was organized. In Kentucky in the 1830s, largely through Baptist leadership, the Fayette County Temperance Society, first of its kind in the state, was organized with Alva Woods as its president. The formation of a temperance society in Kentucky, a locale of large production and consumption of liquor, was a bold and courageous move. One church member probably revealed the mixed sentiments by saying: "I saw Brother F. weeping freely under the sermon today, but when the preacher spoke of the evils of whisky drinking, he took his tears all back into his eyes again."[9]

In 1831 a correspondent to the *Baptist Chronicle*, presumably a Kentuckian, believed the practice of "treating" had changed a great deal especially in regard to ministers. Formerly when a minister called to visit the sick, or comfort the mourners, or for some other reason, it was the customary practice "to stimulate his gifts and graces with a little toddy." Now, the correspondent confided, it would be difficult to find a minister who would accept such an offer. In 1841 a temperance movement known as the Washingtonians had tremendous success in Kentucky, where thirty thousand signed total abstinence pledges. This occurred at the same time that the antimissionary group was being severed from the main body of Baptists. The antimissionaries opposed all organized societies even going to the point of dismissing any of their members who joined a temperance society or took the pledge.[10]

[9] F. L. Robinson, *History of the Georgia Baptist Association* (Union Point, Ga., 1928), 41-42; Spencer, *Kentucky Baptists*, I, 706-707.

In Alabama the Baptists seemed especially active against the evils of intemperance. The Alabama Association in 1836 "resolved, that . . . it is plainly the duty of all men . . . to abstain entirely in the trafficking in ardent spirits, as we believe the use of intoxicating liquors to be immoral . . . preparing them for eternal misery." A year later the Canaan Baptist Church ruled that no prospective member "in the habit of using those intoxicating liquors, as a beverage" would be admitted. By 1839 the Alabama Baptist State Convention was happy to report that the cause of temperance was advancing in the state and it hoped that "these sinks of pollution, grog-shops, from which distress and immorality proceed, will soon be hurled into oblivion." A few years later, in 1845, the convention was forced to report that "a mortifying and painful conviction exists" that much ground had been lost. In the following year, however, the Tuscaloosa County Baptist Association resolved that "henceforth we will not support any man for public office who is known to us to resort to treating with ardent spirits to secure his election." Evidently temperance had not succeeded satisfactorily enough, for in 1860 a report on temperance made before the Liberty (East) Baptist Association said that "so long as Baptists frequent drinking shops and drink with the drunken,—so long as Baptists holding prominent places in churches are engaged in buying and selling spirituous liquors,—we need not expect any great progress in the cause of temperance among our people."[11]

The temperance efforts elsewhere among the Baptists

[10] "Ministers & Jugs," *Baptist Chronicle and Georgetown Literary Register* (Georgetown, Ky.), Oct. 1831, 148; Spencer, *Kentucky Baptists*, I, 708-10.

[11] Holcombe, *Baptists in Alabama*, 113; MS Records of Canaan Baptist Church of Christ, July 22, 1837, in private possession; *Minutes of the Sixteenth Baptist State Convention* (Tuscaloosa, 1839), 9; *Proceedings of the Alabama State Convention* (Tuscaloosa, 1846), 17; Foster, *Tuscaloosa County Baptist Association*, 49; William C. Bledsoe, *History of the Liberty (East) Baptist Association of Alabama* (Atlanta, 1886), 99.

seemed to be far less successful than in Alabama. In 1836
The Baptist, published in Nashville, accused a sizable number of Tennessee preachers of owning and operating highly
profitable distilleries. "These ministers are upheld, and
defended in this practice, by the members of the Churches
to whom they preach, and who would turn out any one of
their members much more promptly for joining a Temperance Society, than they would for getting drunk." An old
minister in Georgia said that the Hardshells were accustomed to saying grace over their liquor before drinking it.
The Red River Association of Louisiana in 1854 adopted a
resolution prohibiting "the *sale* and *use* of intoxicating
liquors, except for Sacramental, Mechanical and Medical
purposes [which we regard] contrary to the genius of
Christianity, and injurious to the cause of Christ." The
position was too advanced and three years later was swept
away by a provision that no church should pass "stringent
prohibitory and condemnatory laws touching the question
of temperance. . . ."[12]

Baptist churches so diligently watched the behavior of
members that scarcely a page of some of the minute books
examined lacks a citation for drunkenness. Since there were
no laws against drinking, the church only sought to regulate
the conduct of its members in the matter of fighting or
disturbing the peace of the community or the church.
These books clearly show that the church disciplined erring
members.[13]

The evils of drinking had been a matter of general concern
in the Presbyterian Church for many years, but the Old
Synod of 1766 tackled a specific problem in the adoption
of a resolution which said: "The too great use of spirituous

---

[12] June 1836, 278; Henry A. Scomp, *King Alcohol in the Realm of King
Cotton* (n. p., 1888), 287; Christian, *Baptists of Louisiana*, 121-22.

[13] For strict Baptist discipline see Posey, "Baptist Watch-Care in Early
Kentucky," Kentucky State Historical Society, *Register*, XXXIV (1936),
311-17.

liquors at funerals in some parts of the country is risen to such a height as greatly to endanger the morals of many, and is the cause of much scandal. The Synod earnestly enjoins the several Sessions to take the most efficient methods to correct these mischiefs, and to discountenance, by example and influence, all approaches to such practices." In 1812 the General Assembly recommended to ministers "to preach as often as expedient on the sins and mischiefs of intemperate drinking, and to warn their hearers, both in public and private, of those habits and indulgences which may have a tendency to produce it." Despite such resolutions, the position of the church hardly seems as positive as that of the Methodist or Baptist churches.[14]

Until the second and third decades of the nineteenth century evidence is slight that the various Western judicatories adopted legislation that attempted to curb the sale and use of intoxicating liquor. Among many Presbyterians distilling and selling liquor was considered a respectable home industry conducted by laymen and often by clergymen. One has little reason to wonder about the absence of regulation when the activities of Gideon Blackburn are examined. Later to become one of the important figures in Presbyterian history of the South, Blackburn at one time sold whisky on a large scale, and he was able to collect from the federal government a claim for liquor destroyed by Indians. When M. W. Trimble, who had attended school with two of Blackburn's sons, heard Blackburn preach a temperance sermon in Mississippi in 1834, he remarked to several of his friends that "if any man ought to preach of temperance it ought to be Gideon Blackburn."[15]

[14] Hays, *Presbyterians*, 161; Gillett, *Presbyterian Church*, I, 451.
[15] "Personal Recollections of M. W. Trimble," (typed copy of articles printed in *The Witness*, Oct. 13–Nov. 17, 1866), 16-18, Philadelphia. John Sevier noted in his diary that some Creek Indians about 1807 had "seized upon & took away Parson Blackburn's whisky." John H. DeWitt (ed.), "Journal of John Sevier," *Tennessee Historical Magazine*, VI (1920-1921), 59.

Here and there through the West and South various judicatories of the Presbyterian Church took action against intemperance. In 1827 the Synod of West Tennessee passed a resolution against the use of liquor "except as a medicine in case of bodily infirmity." Two years later the Transylvania Presbytery of Kentucky warned her churches "to fly from this deadly plague." In 1832 a presbytery in Alabama refused, henceforth, to ordain any probationary for the ministry who continued to distill, sell, or drink the "inebriating fluid." The Synod of Mississippi and Alabama in 1833 regarded the traffic and manufacture of liquor "as a gross immorality and as utterly inconsistent with the high obligations of a Christian profession."[16]

The church became increasingly concerned over the widespread use of liquor and its consequences. An editorial in the *Calvinistic Magazine* in 1828 carried a charge that "intemperance is a vice which . . . is every year bearing its thousands to untimely graves, reducing thousands of virtuous and dependent families to poverty and disgrace. . . ." Three years later Robert J. Breckinridge, a Kentucky minister of much influence, delivered before a Kentucky temperance society an address in which he pointed out the tremendous cost of the liquor traffic and declared there was no solution save total abstinence.[17]

Probably the General Assembly of 1838 appraised the situation correctly when it declared: "The cause of temperance appears to be making but slow progress. In many places the friends of the Saviour appear to become discouraged, and to have relaxed their efforts." H. F. Taylor of the

[16] MS Minutes, Synod of West Tennessee, 1826-1849, Oct. 5, 1827, Montreat; "Minutes of the Transylvania Presbytery, 1786-1837," in Sweet, *The Presbyterians*, 262; MS Minutes, Elyton Presbytery (Cumberland Presbyterian), 1832-1869, April 13, 1832, in Alabama State Department of Archives and History—hereafter cited as Alabama. Also see *Synod of Mississippi and South Alabama*, 30.

[17] II, 209; *An Address Delivered before the Temperance Society* (Lexington, 1832), passim.

American Home Missionary Society reported on pastimes in east Tennessee in 1841: "Fishing, hunting, swimming, and strolling in bands from place to place" were so common they had become "*the order of the day*. Distilleries, doggeries (or perhaps more properly drunkeries), intemperance with its concomitants, card-playing, horse-racing, etc. are not wanting in different parts of the field." Fortunately he was able to form a temperance society that was enthusiastically aided by two lecturers from Blountsville, "the one a reformed drunkard, the other snatched from the very verge of the Maelstrom of intemperance."[18]

The position on temperance adopted by the Cumberland Presbyterian Church seems firmer than that of the parent church. The editors of the church papers consistently and vigorously opposed intemperance and the whisky traffic. In their formative years when the use of liquor was commonplace, the first three Cumberland presbyteries declared it an offense to make, sell, give away, or drink intoxicating liquors. Church courts continued for years to hold to this high standard. The General Assembly of 1851 passed a strong resolution against the use of liquor as being "not only unauthorized, but forbidden by the word of God." Two years later the assembly declared the use of ardent spirits "incompatible . . . with the Christian character of a Cumberland Presbyterian." Time after time men who sold liquor were declared unfit for membership in this church.[19]

In earlier years the Disciples of Christ heaped upon temperance societies the same condemnation and opposition that they had for all moral and religious societies. As the years advanced this opposition faded and the church leaders began to organize associations similar to those they had formerly condemned. This earlier opposition to societies,

---

[18] *Minutes of the General Assembly* (Philadelphia, 1838), 55; Taylor to AHMS, Sept. 10, 1841, CTS.

[19] McDonnold, *Cumberland Presbyterian Church*, 612-14.

however, did not prevent the Disciples of Christ from opposing the use, production, or sale of liquor. In 1837 Walter Scott, one of the foremost figures in the Disciples movement, approved the action of his own church at Carthage, near Cincinnati, when it passed a resolution against communing with anyone who sold liquor and wine. This sentiment was by no means universal in the church, for in the same decade an elder in another congregation in southern Ohio paid for the cost of the excavation and foundation of a new church building in return for the privilege of storing his liquor in its basement, just across the street from his general store.[20]

Alexander Campbell said surprisingly little about liquor, but what he did say carried great force among his people. He believed that "dram-drinkers, julip-sippers, chronic tipplers" should be examined and dealt with in the same manner as dealing with others who, although they may not violate any law, are in opposition "to the spirit and tendency of christianity." In 1842 Campbell wrote his ardent co-worker John T. Johnson that he had fought the distillation of ardent spirits for twenty years. Then he said, "And how a *Christian* man can stand behind the counter and dose out damnation to his neighbors, at the rate of four pence a dose, is a mystery to me. . . ." Earlier, in 1839, Campbell had railed against "the manufacture of the stiletto, dirk, Bowie knife, and other instruments of assassination." In the same category, he placed the man who earned his living by selling "ardent spirits," the use of which led to "poverty, distress, and ruin of his customers," and to "widowhood and orphanage of his neighbor's wife and family!" In one of his strongest utterances he declared: "We ought . . . [to] meet this monster, this insatiate murderer of our species, and break the arm, the puissant arm, that spreads poverty, moral

[20] Garrison and DeGroot, *Disciples of Christ*, 229, 422.

desolation and ruin through all ranks and conditions of men."[21]

Many of Campbell's colleagues—John T. Johnson, David Purviance, John Howard, and others—staunchly opposed the use and sale of liquor and devoted much of their efforts to the cause of temperance. There is little evidence that individual churches took action against the use of liquor, and apparently no agency representing the churches as a whole took a stand for many years. Probably this was not necessary, for Campbell had spoken and his words commanded attention.

The Episcopalians contributed their support in creating a congenial climate for the temperate use of liquors, but they did not support a legal form of control. The evangelicals among the Episcopalians usually favored temperance efforts as long as they stressed voluntary abstinence. Other Episcopalians looked with disfavor on efforts to secure moral reforms through societies or secular agencies, because such activity indicated a lack of confidence in Christian teachings. The individual churches passed no resolutions against the sale or use of liquor, and a preacher rarely prepared a sermon on temperance. One of the few exceptions was made by Bishop Cobbs, who about 1850 accepted an invitation to preach a sermon on temperance because the subject "has been too much given up by the church to other societies." Bishop John H. Hopkins, a High Churchman and an aristocrat, opposed any effort that would cause the church to lower its exalted position. He was pleased that the church did not endorse temperance societies, saying that "the church of Christ always was, and, with all its faults . . . is to this hour, the only sure school for temperance and for every other virtue." From the small effort made by Southern Episcopalians it seems that they endorsed Bishop Hopkins'

[21] Lunger, *Alexander Campbell*, 40-41; *Millennial Harbinger*, 1839, 316, 317, 1842, 171; Richardson, *Alexander Campbell*, II, 600.

pronouncement. The radical leaders disdainfully pointed out that Hopkins' views on temperance indicated that "fashionable, wealthy, wine-drinking congregations" had little sympathy for total abstinence. Although some church leaders had been charged with indifference, the *Southern Churchman* proudly pointed to Bishops Charles P. McIlvaine of Ohio and James H. Otey of Tennessee as supporters of the temperance cause.[22]

Little evidence exists that the temperance movement was accelerated by the Catholic churches and the priests throughout the West and South. Research reveals, here and there, an isolated case of temperance efforts. At Bardstown Flaget and David accepted no donation of liquor and totally abstained from its use. Their example was a "source of much edification to all the faithful of the diocese where, unfortunately, the use of strong drinks generally prevailed. . . ." In 1839 Father John Maguire visited a hundred or more Catholics who were working on the Western and Atlantic Railroad near Chattanooga. He found that the laborers had been without priestly care for a couple of years and that many, using the exertions of hard labor as an excuse, were heavy drinkers. The priest at once started some temperance work, organized a total abstinence society to which twenty-five pledged themselves, and secured a promise from a few others to sign the pledge later.[23]

A real crusader for the temperance movement arrived in New York in 1849 from Ireland. Father Theobald Mathew had had surprising success in his native land where he had enrolled thousands of Irishmen in a Temperance Society. Unfortunately for his work in America, Mathew had signed several years earlier a petition supporting abolitionism, and

[22] White, *Cobbs*, 128; John R. Bodo, *The Protestant Clergy and Public Issues, 1812-1848* (Princeton, 1954), 189; John A. Krout, *The Origins of Prohibition* (New York, 1925), 113, 166.

[23] Rosati, *De Andreis*, 140; O'Daniel, *Miles*, 367-69.

this taint was not likely to be forgotten by Southerners whom he met on his tour. After declaring that he had no intention of interfering in American institutions, Mathew was welcomed to Augusta, Georgia, in January 1850 with a torchlight parade. Despite the growing nativist opposition to Catholics, Mathew's trip through the South was considered quite successful. He encouraged the organization of additional Catholic Total Abstinence societies and administered the pledge to thousands. Meetings in Charleston, Richmond, Augusta, Columbus, Montgomery, and Mobile were satisfactory to him. The high point of his trip was reached in New Orleans where some twelve thousand people signed the pledge during the days that he preached in St. Louis Cathedral. When he left for Ireland in November 1851, about a half-million Catholics—one-third of all in the United States—had forsworn the use of liquors. Although Father Mathew condemned the distiller and the seller of liquors, he failed to urge the passage of legislation to prevent the trade in intoxicants. Many reformers believed that Mathew's reliance upon pledges was such a fragile symbol that it raised a question of grave doubt of the importance of his work.[24]

If the absence of pointed accounts of intemperance among Catholics is evidence of the absence of drinking, then the Catholics had fewer problems than churches like the Baptist, Methodist, and Presbyterian. It is also likely that the nature of the church's control over its individual members did not necessitate the type of supervision found in other churches. Despite the magnetism and apparent success of the enthusiastic reformer Father Mathew, there appears to have been in the West and South little Catholic interest in temperance or total abstinence societies or in the use of the press to prosecute a campaign in behalf of temperance.

[24] Krout, *Prohibition*, 219-22.

Another area of reform which interested some denominations was the use of tobacco. Probably the Methodist
Church took the lead in this area. James Axley, who fought
liquor harder than any other circuit rider, tackled tobacco
with equal force. He once delivered a biting sermon on
tobacco much to the discomfort of Judge Hugh Lawson
White who gave an interesting account of his embarrassment. "I was chewing and spitting my large quid with
uncommon rapidity, and looking up at the preacher to catch
every word and every gesture—when at last he pounced
upon the [topic of] tobacco, behold, there I had a *great
puddle* of tobacco spit! I quietly slipped the quid out of my
mouth, and dashed it as far as I could under the seats,
resolved never again to be found chewing tobacco in the
Methodist Church."[25]

Many Methodist preachers did not share Axley's aversion
and were constant users of tobacco. One circuit rider in
Indiana is said to have spat twice a minute during his
sermon until "the pulpit was as filthy as a stable" at the close
of the service. Bishop McKendree, a life-long opponent of
this "needless self-indulgence," wrote in his diary on September 30, 1790: "Some seemed a little moved [by my sermon],
but so soon as meeting was over and they were out of class,
one had a pipe, another was after a chew of tobacco, and the
women with their snuff-boxes, until my soul was grieved."[26]

Although ministers and preachers often delivered discourses against the use of tobacco, little official action
against it seems to have been taken by any church. This
inaction brought complaints from members of some Baptist
churches whose preachers were addicted to an excessive
use of tobacco. A correspondent to the *Baptist Banner* of

[25] Finley, *Sketches*, 245. For interesting pages on Axley see Redford,
Methodism in Kentucky, II, 420-58. Also see Posey, "The Public Manners
of Ante-Bellum Southerners," *Mississippi History*, XIX (1957), 219-33.

[26] Richardson Wright, *Hawkers and Walkers in Early America* (Philadelphia, 1927), 150; Paine, *M'Kendree*, I, 117.

Shelbyville, Kentucky, complained about preachers' spitting tobacco juice which is "disgusting, filthy, impolite, unkind, and generally unpleasing." He recounted a recent experience he had had at a meeting in which "the filthy minister" had spat so often during the sermon he was sickened by the sight and the smell. The editor of this paper did not see eye to eye with this writer. Previously the editor had stated that he had found nothing "reprehensible" in the chewing of tobacco by preachers, and he praised "a laudable zeal in encouraging the cultivation of the plant" which had been an important factor in the history of Virginia. The editor emphatically concluded that he had no intention of becoming "a member of an anti-using-tobacco society." Hosea Holcombe, early historian of his church in Alabama, bemoaned the fact that the money spent on tobacco by the Baptists in his state would supply all the churches with preachers twice a month, or pay every preacher in the state more than three hundred dollars a year.[27]

In the June 1830 issue of the *Millennial Harbinger* Alexander Campbell took a strong stand in opposition to the consumption of tobacco. Pointing out that a combination had already been formed against rum, brandy, and whisky, he called for a similar campaign against the use of tobacco in the three forms of chewing, smoking, and snuffing. Many lives would be saved and much disease prevented, he firmly believed, if people would eliminate the use of tobacco.

Presbyterian action against the use of tobacco was extremely mild. This position was indicated by an overture made to the Synod of West Tennessee in 1831. The question was asked of this group: "Is it the duty of ministers of the gospel and professing Christians to discourage by their example and influence the use of tobacco?" The matter was

[27] Issues of March 21, 1835, and Nov. 21, 1836, cited in Elias C. Miller, "Growth of American Baptists from 1845 to 1860" (M.A. thesis, University of Chicago, 1931), 80-81; Holcombe, *Baptists in Alabama*, 358.

considered by the synod and received an affirmative answer.[28]

While liquor and tobacco disturbed the Catholics very little, dancing and various amusements proved to be troublesome diversions in some of the early communities. In Kentucky Fathers Badin and Nerinckx were undeviating in their opposition to dancing and frowned on the Dominican priests who held more liberal views. Many people feared that Badin might be appointed bishop of Kentucky and from that position would bring effective control over those amusements which met his disapproval. Neighborhood dancing had been a favorite social activity among all classes and denominations in Kentucky before the Catholic priests arrived. Badin insisted that he had never declared dancing a sin, but that he was unalterably opposed to the custom of dancing far into the night or for the whole night. He had great distaste for public gatherings where "dances in this country are the repair of the most daring impudence, as the most profligate characters come thereto uninvited, and that they are infallible occasions of sin for most of the actors or Spectators. . . ." Badin liked to appear unexpectedly at a home while a dance was in progress, and, calming the flustered dancers who had not been able to escape by the back door, he would offer to hold a session of prayer and religious instruction.[29]

When Father Michael Fournier came to Kentucky in 1797, he believed that Badin was too severe on his parishioners, but later he became quite shocked by some of the rowdy practices and preached a few strong sermons against dancing. Nerinckx shared Badin's views on the excitement in dancing, but thought that horse racing was even more

[28] MS Minutes, Synod of West Tennessee, 1826-1849, Oct. 7, 1831, Montreat.

[29] Badin to Carroll, Sept. 7, 1804, in Records, American Catholic Historical Society, XXIII (1912), 154; Schauinger, Badin, 50-51; Schauinger, Cathedrals, 18-19.

stimulating than dancing. In error he said in 1807 that the Catholics in Kentucky had given up dances and balls. When new priests came to Kentucky, they, less strict than Badin and Nerinckx, permitted dancing, a favor which contributed to their popularity. To Bishop Carroll, Badin wrote numerous letters in which he questioned the faith of the new missionaries. They, in turn, accused Badin and Nerinckx of excessive harshness. Then Catholic laymen got involved in the accusing correspondence. Carroll quickly realized that personalities were contributing factors in the argument and that only a diocese and a bishop could put an end to the continual dispute over a matter no more important than dancing. Before the new Bishop Flaget reached the state, the wise and tactful Carroll had restored harmony and a spirit of friendship.[30]

A stern Presbyterian code of morals encouraged strict oversight of amusements in various forms. This regulation was especially rigid in respect to dancing. As early as 1799 David Rice in Kentucky wrote to James Blythe: "I believe promiscuous dancing, as commonly practised among us, is one of the works of the flesh, and irreconcilable with the self denying religion of Jesus. . . ." The General Assembly of 1818 condemned dancing as a "fascinating and infatuating practice" which "dissipates religious impressions, and hardens the heart." A year earlier the West Tennessee Presbytery had ruled that a dancer was guilty of "decidedly. criminal" conduct and should be denied the privileges of the church. The church in Murfreesboro, Tennessee, resolved to discipline parents who permitted their children to dance. In 1837 the Somerville, Alabama, church ordered a couple, guilty of holding dances in their home, to repent or leave the church. As late as 1841 a church in Courtland, Alabama, declared dancing "highly reprehensible" and "eminently deleterious to the true interests and real prosperity of our holy

[30] Mattingly, *Church on the Kentucky Frontier*, 135-36, 140-41.

religion." Many of the offenders against the Presbyterian
code of conduct accepted the reprimands and conformed
to the ruling; others rebelled and refused to alter their ways.
An offender in Tennessee presented Biblical support for his
defense of dancing.[31]

An inspection of Baptist congregation records reveals surprisingly few disciplinary instances for dancing. To conclude
from this evidence that the Baptists were not dancers may
not be entirely safe, but indications would point that way,
since their churches maintained such a strict watchcare over
their members. When the various types of Baptists are
taken into account, however, it should be pointed out that
in no other denomination did the individual churches have
such freedom in government or function with such differences. This accounts for the censoring of a person for a
certain offense in one section and the complete disregard of
the same offense elsewhere.

Other churches did not seem to be unduly concerned
about dancing. Here and there a preacher in a church like
the Methodist voiced his own personal opinion about dancing and the moral danger involved, but this opposition
expressed little reforming zeal compared to that expended
on liquor or on secret fraternities.

Most of the churches opposed secret fraternities in general
and the Masonic order in particular because they constituted
a rival religion for many of their members. The Catholic
Church was, over a long period of time, the most aggressive
opponent of the Masons. But some extreme Protestants even
saw similarities in the rituals of Catholics and Masons and

[31] Letter dated Dec. 11, 1799, Philadelphia; Baird, *Collection*, 802; MS
Minutes, West Tennessee Presbytery, 1810-1836, April 9, 1817, Montreat;
"Sessional Record of the First Presbyterian Church of Murfreesboro, Ten-
nessee, 1812-1829," June 23, 1829, in Sweet, *The Presbyterians*, 459; James
W. Marshall, MS The Presbyterian Church in Alabama, 1813-1898, 90,
Alabama; MS Minutes, North Alabama Presbytery, 1825-1844, April 8,
1841, Montreat; MS Session Record, Murfreesboro Church, 1812-1860,
Feb. 7, April 11, 27, 31, 1831, Montreat.

imagined grave implications in the secret ceremonies of the Masons. As a result some Protestants denounced both Popery and Freemasonry.[32] Since 1738 the Catholics have been forbidden, under penalty of excommunication, to join or to promote Masonic societies. Generally the papal decrees against Masonry have been the final directives for the various councils of the American bishops. It should be made clear, however, that there was a vast difference between Masonry in Europe and in America.

About 1793 Freemasonry was introduced to New Orleans, and two lodges were established outside the city walls. The organization grew with great rapidity—Spanish officers, Frenchmen, and influential Creoles joined. All the while, despite church decrees, these people considered themselves as members of the Catholic Church. During the administration in New Orleans of Luis Peñalver (1793-1801) the Masons were particularly obnoxious. In a pointed dispatch Peñalver attributed to the Masonic activities "a suspicious and criminal appearance." Particularly did they disturb the Indians by impressing upon them "their pernicious maxims, in harmony with their own restless and ambitious tempers. . . ." Freemasonry had its place among the many stories and rumors which hovered over the controversial Father Sedella in New Orleans. During his long and tempestuous residence, this influential priest did nothing to combat the Masons. In fact, his actions hinted that he approved the order, and some people asserted that they had knowledge that he belonged to the forbidden society. He was friendly with Masons, permitted Masonic paraphernalia on coffins in the church, and even buried Masons with the ceremonies of the church.[33]

In his correspondence with Propaganda in 1821 Bishop

[32] See Stokes, *Church and State*, I, 250-52.
[33] Lowenstein, *St. Louis Cathedral*, 35. Also see Baudier, *Catholic Church in Louisiana*, 219, 244, 275-76.

DuBourg discussed the problems created by the Masons in New Orleans. Under Sedella and his assistants the Masons had gotten such power that DuBourg had to proceed with "much prudence and forbearance" for fear "all hope for remedying things be nipped in the bud." Some twenty years later the situation seemed to be completely out of hand, for the Masons had managed to purchase ground in the Catholic cemetery, laid a cornerstone of a monument, and delivered an address within the consecrated ground. When the bishop investigated the matter, he found that the Grand Master of the lodge was also president of the board of trustees of the cathedral.[34] Although other Catholic priests and the hierarchy objected to the Masons, no other bishops in the Lower South were so bedeviled and disturbed as those in New Orleans.

Efforts were made to get Barton Stone to convert his paper the *Christian Messenger* into an anti-Masonic journal. In a sharp refusal he said: "I am afraid that anti-masonry is designed to be a political engine; it may be to effect what it ostensibly proposes to put down. We as Christians should preach and live the gospel, and not intermeddle with things we know not."[35] Apparently this ended Stone's relations with opponents of the order.

Alexander Campbell followed a very different course from Stone. Having a fear of all societies outside the church, Campbell declared that lodges came into existence because certain people felt the need of some type of organization which the church did not afford. Campbell objected to all types of secret societies, especially the Masons and Odd Fellows. He compared a Christian who became a Mason to a man who having five good fingers adds a sixth which is a wax finger for which he has no need. From observations

---

[34] "Documents from Our Archives," *St. Louis Catholic Historical Review*, III (1921), 110-12; "New Orleans Disturbances," *Catholic Advocate*, Sept. 23, 1843.

[35] Ware, *Stone*, 217.

he questioned if a man ever became more spiritually inclined after he turned "to the ribbon, the apron, or the mystic symbols of a secret conclave?"[36]

There were congregations of the Disciples of Christ who accepted aid from the Masons and praised them for their generosity. Often Masonic halls served temporarily in place of a church building. In some sections the Masons were so influential that their opinions were taken into account when preachers were appointed to church pulpits. In 1835 Philip S. Fall wrote Jacob Creath, Jr., that the Louisville church needed a minister and suggested that he consider the position. Fall concluded by saying that the Masons would have no objection to Creath. This same Creath made a difficult trip through Arkansas in 1860 and received so much assistance from the Masons that he gratefully said "God bless the Masons."[37]

As a whole the Baptists made no outcries against the Masonic order. Some Baptist churches excluded members for joining the Masons. In 1822 the Russell Valley (Alabama) Church excluded Thomas S. Pope, and seven years later restored him to fellowship "by recantation." The record does not state that he quit the Masons, but he later became a deacon. In 1822 two members of the White's Run (Kentucky) Church were excluded. A third was continued in fellowship because he merely attempted to join the lodge. It is safe to conclude that these and a few similar attacks were rare exceptions and by no means constituted a prevailing procedure among the Baptists.[38] The view of a moderate was expressed in a letter from W. F. Broaddus to the *Western Review* of Frankfort, Kentucky. He believed that

---

[36] *Millennial Harbinger*, 1845, 135. Also see 1845, 313-18, 1848, 685-93.

[37] *Christian Review* (Nashville), IV (1847), 4; P. Donan, *Life of Jacob Creath, Jr.* (Cincinnati, 1872), 69-70, 117.

[38] Josephus Shackleford, *History of the Muscle Shoals Baptist Association* (Trinity, Ala., 1891), 149; MS Minutes, Forks of Elkhorn Baptist Church, 1788-1831, Sept. 21, Oct. 16, 1822, Southern Baptist Theological Seminary, Louisville—hereafter cited as Baptist, Louisville.

membership in the Masonic order should not bar a man from the privileges of the church, provided his connections produced no bad effects on his character. Broaddus, however, did not encourage Baptists to join "an institution conceived in human wisdom," for the church had all kinds of charitable organizations for men to join. Furthermore, he deplored secrecy.[39]

Liquor, tobacco, dancing, and Masonry constituted the chief targets against which the churches directed their reforming zeal. Still other threats to church standards of conduct received varying degrees of attention. The Episcopal Church concerned itself over duels and lotteries; the Disciples of Christ over spiritualism; the Presbyterians over Sabbath mails; and on and on the catalog runs. Baptists and Presbyterians tried and dismissed their members for a variety of reasons—gambling, stealing, adultery, slander, horse racing, card playing, theatre going, worldly conversation, cursing, quarreling, and many other personal infractions of the moral code that the churches attempted to institute.

Years before the Methodist and Baptist churches divided, so much attention was given to the issue of slavery that a great deal of the reforming spirit of the churches relaxed or died. The division over slavery brought a positive lesson that any further dividing meant a dangerous lessening of the force of the church in great issues. Slaveowner and church member were usually the same person.

[39] Reprinted in *Catholic Advocate*, May 2, 1846.

12

THE SLAVERY PROBLEM
BEFORE THE 1840s

BEFORE THE EIGHTEENTH CENTURY had closed, Methodist,
Baptist, and Presbyterian churches were expressing by
various ways their concern with or opposition to the holding,
buying, and selling of Negro slaves. After the passage of
some forty or fifty years the slavery system had become
such a vital factor in the South's industrial, social, political,
and even religious life that toward it these same churches
became less aggressive and more indulgent. Along with
the conviction in the South that slavery was a necessary and
permanent institution, there arose in the North the demand
for its complete destruction. This chapter attempts to trace
the official attitude of the seven denominations toward
slavery prior to the division of the Methodists and the
Baptists.

The members of the Methodist societies made some strong
statements against the holding and buying of slaves, and
their sentiments were repeated and amplified by later members of the Methodist Episcopal Church. Just before sailing
for America in 1738, John Wesley was urged by an Oxford
associate, Dr. John Burton, to be aware of the great opportunity he would have in the conversion of Negro slaves.
Nothing had been done, said Burton, "but a door is opened
. . . the harvest truly is great." Eight years later Wesley
wrote into the General Rules of 1743 for the organization of
the English societies a regulation which forbade "buying or
selling the bodies and souls of men, women, or children,

with an intention to enslave them." For the next thirty years experience strengthened his initial attitude toward slavery, and Wesley regarded the slave trade as "that execrable sum of all villainies." Only four days before his death he urged William Wilberforce, the great British statesman and humanitarian, to continue his fight in behalf of the abolition of slavery "till even American slavery (the vilest that ever saw the sun) shall vanish away before it."[1]

Wesley's sentiment on the question of slavery was shared by many who felt his influence. Asbury's *Journal* contains reference after reference to slavery and many prayers that "its infernal spirit" might be banished. By 1798 Asbury seems to have become less sensitive to its existence in Virginia, where there was not "a sufficient sense of religion nor of liberty to destroy it." But three years later his dread of slavery had not lessened, and striking at the apologists he asked, "If the Gospel will tolerate slavery, what will it not authorize?" Freeborn Garrettson, an American-born preacher traveling in North Carolina and Virginia in 1777, wrote that his heart ached and his eyes wept as he thought of the slaves he had seen there. Of all the early preachers of significance only George Whitefield made no open declaration against slavery. On the contrary, he approved the action by which Georgia was changed from a free to a slave colony and sanctioned the purchase of Negroes to work at the orphanage which he founded near Savannah. As if justifying his decision to use slave labor, Whitefield said he thought the lives of the Negroes would be more comfortable than formerly and their posterity would grow up "in the nurture and admonition of the Lord."[2]

[1] Luke Tyerman, *Life and Times of the Rev. John Wesley* (3 vols.; New York, 1872), I, 109-10; Lucius C. Matlack, *The Antislavery Struggle and Triumph in the Methodist Episcopal Church* (New York, 1881), 54; John Wesley, *The Journal of the Rev. John Wesley* (4 vols.; New York, 1907), III, 461; John Emory (ed.), *The Works of the Reverend John Wesley* (7 vols.; New York, 1835), VII, 237.

Evidently considerable antislavery sentiment existed among both Methodist clergy and laity at the time of the writing of the Constitution of the United States. As the document took shape, John Marshall expressed his concern over the silent assent to slavery and feared that the support of the Methodists and the Quakers would be lost. Despite the fact that the annual conferences from 1776 to 1787 were held in slave states, the delegates were not always in complete agreement over the slave question. The conference of 1780 chose to express disapproval of slavery as "contrary to the laws of God, man, and nature." At the formation of the Methodist Episcopal Church in 1784 the organizers provided some rules of discipline for the member who traded in slaves and for the preacher who owned them. After a warning the member would be expelled from the church if he bought slaves with no design to hold them, and the preacher would be suspended if he held slaves in a state that permitted manumission. This ruling constituted the strongest position ever taken on slavery by the Methodist Church. Much evidence indicates that this action was pushed on an unwilling conference through the force exerted by Wesley, Coke, and Asbury. The legislation was too drastic for general compliance, and the rule was suspended within six months. In the quadrennial conferences of 1796, 1800, and 1804 concessions were made to slaveholders, and in 1808 all regulations that related to slaveholding among private members were removed and the governing right was given to the annual conferences. This change placed the control in the regional or state conferences, close to the people and sensitive to local opinion. Within the year the

---

[2] Asbury, *Journal*, I, 187, 374, II, 367, III, 10; William L. Grissom, *History of Methodism in North Carolina* (Nashville, 1905), 227; George Whitefield, *The Works of the Reverend George Whitefield* (2 vols.; London, 1771-1772), II, 405. Also see Stuart C. Henry, *George Whitefield: Wayfaring Witness* (Nashville, 1957), Chaps. III-V, et passim.

Western Conference, now having power to legislate, ruled
that any member or preacher who sold or bought a slave
"from speculative motives" should be expelled.[3]

Many of the first settlers who moved to eastern Tennessee
were firmly opposed to slavery. In his romantically written
history of the West, Theodore Roosevelt stressed the great
value which the people of Tennessee placed on the right of
the individual. Some farmers with small holdings both in
real estate and human property were accustomed to working
with their slaves and rarely considered themselves slaveholders like the people of the Atlantic seaboard. No other
adjective but illogical now seems appropriate to the Ten-
nessean who, owning a few slaves, was so moved at a Fourth
of July celebration that he joined in a toast to "the total
abolition of slavery." In the Knoxville *Gazette* of January 23,
1797, Thomas Embree called the citizens of Washington and
Greene counties to form abolition societies, but they were
not yet ready for such organizations. Antislavery sentiment
increased, however, and by 1815 it was sufficiently strong
to take the form of the Manumission Society of Tennessee.
This society was organized largely through the leadership
of a Quaker, Charles Osborn, with the assistance of a
Presbyterian minister, John Rankin. As late as 1827 east
Tennessee alone contained one-fifth of the antislavery societies in the United States and almost the same proportion of
members.[4]

In face of the successes of the antislavery organizations,
attitudes toward slavery began to change so rapidly that in
Tennessee the annual conference of the Methodist Church
in 1816, while admitting slavery to be a moral evil, stated

[3] Matlack, *Antislavery Struggle*, 57, 63; *Minutes of the Annual Confer-
ences*, I, 12, 20-21; *Journals of the General Conference*, I, 41, 63, 93;
"Journal of the Western Conference, 1800-1811," in William W. Sweet, *The
Rise of Methodism in the West* (Nashville, 1920), 148.

[4] Theodore Roosevelt, *The Winning of the West* (6 vols.; New York,
1905), VI, 10-12; Asa E. Martin, "The Anti-Slavery Societies in Tennessee,"
Tennessee Historical Magazine, I (1915), 261-81 passim.

that it could not adopt a rule compelling church members to free their slaves since the laws did not "admit of emancipation without a special act of the Legislature. . . ." In 1820 the General Conference resumed its control over slavery, and the right to regulate the traffic was withdrawn forever from the annual conferences. This transfer of authority was achieved by a minority party in the 1819 Tennessee Conference desiring to wrest the power from the hands of a group that occupied "the exact ground upon which the northern abolition party in the church" later stood. In the General Conference of 1828 a resolution which provided punitive measures against inhuman slaveholding was tabled with little opposition.[5] Three decades before the Civil War the antislavery spirit within the church had been trampled down by new forces.

The Methodist Church adopted a policy of compromise on the slavery question because of the threat of the separation of Southern churches and unashamedly because of various economic reasons. The New York *Christian Advocate* in 1834 urged preachers to oppose abolition societies recently created in New York, because they were "at variance with the vested interests and constitutional rights and obligations of the country." Critics of the *Advocate* said that the paper had assumed this point of view because it feared the loss of twelve thousand subscribers in the South from whom came annual receipts of twenty-five thousand dollars.[6] Bishops and conferences, regardless of geographical locations, unanimously condemned abolitionists.

Several factors rapidly transformed the Southern economy and Southern thought, the spread of the upland cotton plant in the South and Southwest being not the least. In 1801 the entire Western cotton production was about 1,000,000 pounds.

[5] McFerrin, *Methodism in Tennessee*, II, 401; *Journals of the General Conference*, I, 205, 337; Henkle, *Bascom*, 121.

[6] See Kenneth E. Barnhart, "The Evolution of the Social Consciousness in Methodism" (Ph.D. dissertation, University of Chicago, 1924), 81-85.

Thirty-three years later the four states of Alabama, Tennessee, Mississippi, and Louisiana produced 277,000,000 pounds, and the remainder of the country produced only 179,500,000 pounds.[7] The high productivity of the cotton belt of the South made it possible for poor farmers who had rushed there to become planters with Negro slaves, fertile fields, and good houses. Simultaneously this change in economic status slowed perceptibly the growth of democracy and brought about a great social change among people who once opposed bondage. As they changed from non-landholders to small farmers and later to planters, they changed their notions concerning slavery and privilege. Even in the Old Northwest where the Ordinance of 1787 had forbidden slavery, the Methodist preachers as well as those of other denominations were usually unwilling to censure the South. Some ministerial candidates who were known abolitionists were rejected by their conferences.

For many years prior to 1836 the church had maintained an almost unbroken silence on the slavery question. This had been assured by making numerous concessions to various elements and by adopting a generous system of toleration. But the abolitionists in the church, especially in New England, had long been busy before the General Conference met in 1836 in Cincinnati on the very boundary of the slaveholding area. By this time it was clearly evident that, despite accord maintained with great precaution, two separate and distinct parties had already formed in the Methodist Church. At this conference the Southern delegates placed in nomination for bishop William Capers, a slaveholder from South Carolina. When Capers failed of election, Southerners became incensed by what they termed "a proscription" and "an insult." Finally three non-slaveholders were elected to the episcopacy—one from the South and two from the North. Before the election, however, the delegates by a

---

[7] Channing, *History of the United States*, V, 409, 433.

wide margin had adopted a resolution declaring it "inexpedient to make any change in our Book of Discipline respecting slavery, and that we deem it improper to agitate the subject in the General Conference at present." Despite vigorous efforts by the extreme proslavery delegates, they could not get the Discipline changed to their view.[8]

At this General Conference of 1836 a majority of Southern delegates took the ground that slavery was not only right but a blessing to the slaves. In a private caucus William A. Smith of Virginia devised a plan for separation by the churches in the slaveholding section unless a revision of the Discipline would tolerate slavery and make it no bar to membership or office. Peter Cartwright, who was invited to attend, believed that some of the hotheads would follow Smith but that the moderates would not. The threat of secession was soon dropped, but the action of the caucus served as a warning of trouble just ahead. Smith told Cartwright that he would never be satisfied until the rule on slavery had been expunged from the Discipline. Smith's role in the General Conference of 1844 proved the strength of his determination.[9]

The increase of antislavery feeling and sentiment between 1836 and 1840 was evident in the sessions of numerous annual conferences. In New England the bishops, bent on keeping the peace, seem to have followed a policy of gagging some of the more outspoken antislavery advocates. During the session of the New England Conference of 1837 Bishop Beverly Waugh refused to accept an antislavery petition. The first Methodist abolition society had been formed in New York in 1833, quickly followed by the establishment of other societies in the New England and the New Hampshire annual conferences. Abolitionist ministers published

[8] David Cristy, *Pulpit Politics: or, Ecclesiastical Legislation on Slavery* (Cincinnati, 1863), 387-91; Matlack, *Antislavery Struggle,* 100-101.

[9] Swaney, *Methodism and Slavery,* 58-59; Cartwright, *Autobiography,* 361-64.

antislavery papers and held antislavery conventions.[10] By these and other procedures they rapidly increased agitation against slavery and against the soothing policy of the General Conference. In the South the situation was quite different. Slavery had been so generally received that it was considered fixed and permanent, and free debate concerning it was limited or not tolerated at all. The system that had been denounced by Wesley, Coke, and for a while by Asbury had become so vital to the South that the Methodist Church grew very indulgent toward slavery.

The total absence among the Baptist churches of any great ecclesiastical governing body or cooperating agency left members, preachers, and congregations free to adopt independent and varying attitudes toward the slavery question. The bond of sympathy in the church between slaveholders and antislavery people existed purely through voluntary action. The first recorded action in behalf of slaves occurred in 1778 when representatives from several Baptist associations met in Goochland County, Virginia, and discussed the framing of a petition to the next General Assembly of Virginia praying that slavery might be made more tolerable. After a lapse of eleven years a general committee in Richmond adopted a resolution condemning slavery as "a violent deprivation of the rights of nature," and urged that legal measures be used "to extirpate this horrid evil from the land."[11]

Gradually in early Kentucky and Tennessee, where the emphasis on cotton cultivation was not so great as in the Lower South, the Baptist preachers came to consider slavery as an evil. No concerted agreement, however, was ever adopted against this accepted condition of the Negro. A few early churches separately took uncompromising stands

[10] Matlack, *Antislavery Struggle*, 110; Stokes, *Church and State*, II, 158-59; Sweet, *Methodism in American History*, 238-39.

[11] Robert B. Semple, *A History of the Rise and Progress of the Baptists in Virginia* (Richmond, 1894), 103-105.

against slavery. In 1789 under the direction of Josiah Dodge the Rolling Fork (Kentucky) Baptist Church petitioned the Salem Association to take a stand. When the association decreed "it improper to enter into so important and critical matter, at present," Dodge led in the organization of New Hope Church, "the first emancipating church" in Kentucky. Action against slavery in the loosely organized associations with no dominating leader did not produce strong opposition. Although individual preachers and members of congregations in the Elkhorn (Kentucky) Association expressed their objections to slavery, the association rejected petitions and queries. In 1805 the association declared "it improper for ministers Churches or Associations to meddle with ema[n]cipation from Slavery" and advised them to have nothing to do with it. When David Barrow continued to be concerned over slavery, the association expelled him even though he was an able preacher. Barrow in 1807 formed a society of like minds who called themselves the Baptized Licking-Locust Association, Friends of Humanity. The organization made a bold expression of "abhorrence to unmerited, hereditary, perpetual, absolute, unconditional Slavery."[12] The sentiments for emancipation by Baptists in Kentucky increasingly weakened, so that Barrow's society soon began to decrease in membership.

In states south of Kentucky there were few examples of firm opposition to slavery. Churches in the cotton region acquiesced in the endeavor of their members to establish a mild but extremely profitable slave system. For reasons difficult to understand the Baptists made little effort to retard slavery in Tennessee in contrast to the Methodists who achieved their strongest opposition in that state. In the highly competitive Methodist versus Baptist struggle,

[12] Spencer, *Kentucky Baptists*, I, 184; John M. Brown, *The Political Beginnings of Kentucky* (Louisville, 1889), 224-26; *Minutes of the Baptized Licking-Locust Association, Friends of Humanity* (n. p., 1807), 2-3; Sweet, *The Baptists*, 82-88, 566-70.

one denomination tended to thwart the other on numerous occasions and in various places.

In 1814 the Baptists established the Triennial Convention, an organization of national scope which provided the first union of Baptists for missionary work. This organization evolved from the meeting in Philadelphia of thirty-three delegates from eleven states interested in a common missionary program. For twenty-one of its first thirty years of existence slaveholders served as presidents of the convention. In reality the convention was a missionary society with a board of managers who met annually. The headquarters was located in 1826 in Boston, where after 1841 an acting board functioned between the annual meetings. Under the constitution of the convention slaveholders and non-slaveholders were placed on terms of social and moral equality. This arrangement probably was a "fatal error," for it forced the convention "to sanction as Christian a slaveholding religion." At the death in 1815 of its first president, Richard Furman of South Carolina, his legal representatives advertised for sale his property which included twenty-seven Negroes, "some of them very prime."[13]

As slavery began to spread in Southern society, some Baptist preachers sought to oppose its further expansion; others began to advocate colonization, emancipation, and even abolition. In considerable numbers Baptist preachers and members left the South because they felt such strong revulsion to slavery. Some liberals who remained found themselves in trouble with their friends and neighbors. An overwhelming number of Baptists sought to maintain peace and harmony against all efforts to agitate the slavery subject. So successful was this effort that "a spirit of servility" became evident among the Baptists in the North. As early

13 Newman, *Baptist Churches*, 393-94; Mary B. Putnam, *The Baptists and Slavery, 1840-1845* (Ann Arbor, 1913), 19-20; William Goodell, *Slavery and Anti-Slavery* (New York, 1852), 186, 187.

as 1834 the *Baptist Magazine*, like magazines of other denominations, was closed to discussions on slavery.[14]

During the 1830s the first stage of the antislavery struggle gave way to a far more aggressive movement on the part of the abolitionists of the North. To the defense of slavery the Southern Baptists, having 115,000 slaves in their possession by 1837, quickly marshaled their forces. Quiet and peace, generosity and graciousness came to an abrupt end. The Richmond meeting in 1835 of the Triennial Convention was the "last harmonious meeting" of the most important Baptist body. The abolitionists accused Baptist papers in the South of printing intemperate statements about antislavery efforts. In its issue of September 1835 *The Baptist* of Nashville replied that Southerners would dispose of slavery matters as they saw fit. In Alabama, to a greater degree than in any other Southern state, the Baptists became angered by the interference of Northerners in their domestic affairs. To show contempt for their intervention, the Alabama State Convention in 1840 pledged the withholding of payments to the Board of Foreign Missions and to the Bible Society until they proved that they were not connected with the American Baptist Anti-Slavery Convention. In Alabama and elsewhere among Baptists in the South there was no turning back, for the ground had already been prepared for separation.[15]

The background and early history of the Presbyterian Church stands in marked contrast with that of the Methodist and Baptist churches, both largely products of America. A long period of existence and a Calvinistic theology gave to the Presbyterians a fixity of purpose and a surety of convic-

---

[14] Goodell, *Slavery and Anti-Slavery*, 493 ff.

[15] Putnam, *Baptists and Slavery*, 13; Jeremiah B. Jeter, *The Recollections of a Long Life* (Richmond, 1891), 187; *Minutes of the Twelfth Anniversary of the Alabama Baptist Convention* (Greensborough, Ala., 1835), 7; *Minutes of the Seventeenth Anniversary* (Tuscaloosa, 1840), 6. See also *Convention of the Baptist Denomination of Mississippi*, 17.

tion about numerous matters—especially about slavery. The Presbyterian Church made an early national stand against slavery. In its first official resolution on the matter the Synod of New York and Philadelphia in 1787 recommended that its members "use the most prudent measures, consistent with the interest and the state of civil society . . . to procure eventually the final abolition of slavery in America."[16]

Kentucky was the slave area in which the Presbyterian Church first took its strongest antislavery stand, although it had considerable success also in Tennessee. David Rice as a member of the Kentucky Constitutional Convention in May 1792 boldly spoke his views on slavery and urged the convention to put an end to involuntary servitude in the state. Although his proposal was not adopted by the convention, he wielded sufficient influence in the Transylvania Presbytery, which embraced all of Kentucky, to secure in 1794 a ruling which ordered all slaveholders in the church to teach children under fifteen years of age, so that they would be prepared "for the enjoyment of freedom." This legislation which was certainly looking toward emancipation frightened the General Assembly of 1795 to the extent that it warned against "differences of opinion" that "threaten divisions which may have the most ruinous tendency." Uninhibited by the rebuke, the Transylvania Presbytery in 1796 recommended that Presbyterians "emancipate such of their slaves as they may think fit subjects of liberty" and prepare others for eventual freedom. In the following year the slavery issue was declared "a moral evil," but the presbytery refused to consider all slaveowners guilty of the said evil.[17]

Death came in 1816 to David Rice, a valiant leader of

16 *Records of the Presbyterian Church*, 540.

17 David Rice, *Slavery, Inconsistent with Justice and Good Policy* (Philadelphia, 1792), 21; "Minutes of the Transylvania Presbytery, 1786-1837," Oct. 13, 1794, Oct. 5, 1797, in Sweet, *The Presbyterians*, 147, 169-70; *Minutes of the General Assembly, 1789-1820*, 104; Davidson, *Presbyterian Church*, 336.

antislavery forces in Kentucky. Toward the end of his life he lost some of the deep faith he had had in the power of the church to adopt "a rational plan for the gradual abolition of slavery." As he lay dying he charged a slaveholding society with depriving Negroes of their liberty. "Freedom," he said, "is a natural and unalienable right, belonging to them, as well as others, of which the proprietor of man has not authorized me to deprive them."[18]

The General Assembly in 1818 made a further "expression of views" in which slavery was declared to be "a gross violation of the most precious and sacred rights of human nature; as utterly inconsistent with the law of God . . . and . . . totally irreconcilable with the spirit and principles of the gospel of Christ. . . ." Unwilling to make a strong statement on the surrender of slavery, the assembly expressed some sympathy with that part of the church most affected and then exhorted Presbyterians to continue and increase their exertions to effect a total abolition of slavery. The force of the action was destroyed by a plea that the churches should take due regard for "the safety and happiness of the master and the slave." This policy proved to be only "temporizing and procrastinating."[19]

The great spread of cotton culture with its subsequent increase in the wealth of many farmers turned planters removed the odium from slave labor which cultivation of the crop required. Cotton and slavery had not only brought a halt to the spread of frontier democracy, but also contributed to the lack of religious zeal and enthusiasm. James Smylie, a well informed Presbyterian minister in Mississippi, claimed that three-fourths of all members of the Presbyterian Church owned slaves.

Six years after the establishment of the American Colonization Society, the Synod of Kentucky in 1823 appointed

[18] MS (copy) David Rice's Will, March 22, 1816, Philadelphia.
[19] Baird, *Collection*, 820-21; Goodell, *Slavery and Anti-Slavery*, 152.

some committees to promote the work of the society. From year to year the synod made recommendations urging participation in and contribution to the efforts of the organization. Records of various churches and presbyteries reveal considerable interest in the program and some financial contributions, but there is little evidence of actual colonization. The idea was good, but reality erected so many obstacles that actual plans moved slowly. An auxiliary society in Mississippi authorized the purchase of land on the African coast, but no colony was ever planted on it.[20]

The concept of the emancipation of slaves made little headway except in Kentucky and Tennessee where the plantation was less important than in the Lower South. Thomas T. Skillman was an early spokesman for the forces of emancipation. In the columns of the *Western Luminary* Skillman fought slavery so courageously that William Lloyd Garrison praised him in the *Liberator*. In 1832 and again in 1833 the antislavery members of the Synod of Kentucky introduced a resolution which declared slavery to be "a great moral evil" and recommended the favoring of "all proper measures for gradual voluntary emancipation." The tabling of the resolution for the second time led Robert J. Breckinridge, one of the antislavery leaders in the synod, to charge that any person who would not see that slavery was "founded on the principle of taking by force that which is another's has simply no moral sense. . . . Hereditary slavery is without pretense, except in avowed rapacity." The story was very much the same in Kentucky and in Tennessee. In 1833 in the Synod of West Tennessee the topic of slavery was introduced and then indefinitely postponed.[21]

The economic wealth of an average member of the Cum-

20 Davidson, *Presbyterian Church*, 337; New Orleans *Observer*, April 9, 1836.
21 Asa E. Martin, *The Anti-Slavery Movement in Kentucky prior to 1850* (Louisville, 1918), 64, 84; Bacon, *American Christianity*, 281-82; MS Minutes, Synod of West Tennessee, 1826-1849, Oct. 18, 1833, Montreat.

berland Presbyterian Church must have been considerably less than that of a member of the parent church, yet the slavery policies of the two churches differed very little. If there were a stronger antislavery disposition, it was in the Cumberland Presbyterian Church. *The Revivalist,* a semi-official church organ, kept up a strong editorial opposition to slavery. As late as the issue of March 19, 1834, the editor declared: "The negro will be freed; and we *must* liberate him, or God will do it at our expense." Finis Ewing declared that he had "determined *not to hold,* nor to *give,* nor to *sell,* nor to *buy any slave for life."* The author of an old and excellent history of the Cumberland Presbyterians says that he never knew "an extreme pro-slavery man" who was a member of the Cumberland Church. Living through the Civil War, the writer had good basis for his observations. It was his conviction that a majority of the members of the Cumberland Presbyterian Church would have rejoiced to have seen all the Negroes peacefully emancipated.[22] It seems safe to presume that the members of no other of the seven churches under consideration could have been in closer agreement.

While some clergymen were fleeing from the South, others aroused by the fanatical abolitionists had become apologists for slavery. Leonard Bacon believes that "Southern apostasy" from the generally accepted sentiments on slavery may be dated from about 1833. At this time James Smylie searched the Scriptures and said he was surprised to find that Negro slavery was justified under divine dispensation and that the duties of masters and slaves were clearly stated in the New Testament. At Port Gibson, Mississippi, Smylie greatly offended both the ministry and the members of the Presbyterian Church as he explained his discovery. Although covered with odium for a while, Smylie's interpretation soon

---

[22] Cossitt, *Ewing,* 273; McDonnold, *Cumberland Presbyterian Church,* 410.

became "not only prevalent, but violently and exclusively dominant" in most of the Lower South. Bacon is of the opinion that it would be difficult to find a similar example of "so sudden and sweeping a change of sentiment on a leading doctrine of moral theology. Dissent from the novel dogma was suppressed with more than inquisitorial rigor." The Synod of Mississippi in 1853, when preparing a notice of Smylie's death, acclaimed him "for giving the true exposition of the doctrines of the Bible in relation to slavery in the commencement of the abolition excitement."[23]

Southerners in the cotton sections of the country had become terrified by the force of abolitionism, and this fear led to the surrender of important principles held by most of the churches. From Tennessee to the Gulf of Mexico Presbyterian judicatories previously silent on the slavery issue united vigorously against the disturbers. By 1835 the Synod of Mississippi denied the right of a church to interfere in any of the political or civil relations of society. Two years later the South Alabama Presbytery agreed with the expressions of the Mississippi Synod and instructed its commissioners to the General Assembly to deny the right of the highest judicatory to interfere with slavery matters.[24]

By the mid-1830s unity within the Presbyterian Church was but a word. The mention of a few divisive factors will indicate the drift toward the schismatic action of 1838. In 1836 the New School or liberal wing composed the majority of the representatives to the General Assembly. In that year under the sponsorship of the New School group Union

[23] Bacon, American Christianity, 277-78; "Extract from the Minutes of the Synod of Mississippi," Journal of the Presbyterian Historical Society, XXI (1943), 200-205; John G. Jones, The Introduction of Protestantism into Mississippi and the Southwest (St. Louis, 1866), 240-42.

[24] As late as 1835 the Synod of Kentucky asserted that the New Testament condemned slaveholding "in the most explicit terms." Address of the Synod of Kentucky on Slavery in 1835 (Pittsburgh, 1862), 15. Also see New Orleans Observer, Dec. 12, 1835; MS Minutes, South Alabama Presbytery, 1835-1840, April 10, 1837, Montreat.

Theological Seminary was founded in New York, and Princeton Seminary remained the seat of learning for the Old School party. In a heated fight over slavery that threatened to disrupt the assembly, the matter was closed by the adoption of a resolution indefinitely postponing action. Within another year the composition of the assembly had changed so completely that the Old School or conservative wing had a safe majority for the changes it desired within the church. The Old School party, claiming that its traditional church had lost its identity in cooperating in the Plan of Union which had been made in 1801 between the Congregational and Presbyterian churches, abrogated the Plan of Union and created its own boards for education and missions. Seeking to curb the growing liberalism of the 1830s, the General Assembly in 1831 brought charges of heresy against Albert Barnes, pastor of the First Presbyterian Church in Philadelphia. After six years he was exonerated by the General Assembly. Lyman Beecher, president of Lane Theological Seminary in Cincinnati, and Edward Beecher, president of Illinois College, were also accused of heresy but were acquitted by their synods.[25]

When four synods, Western Reserve, Geneva, Utica, and Genessee, which had passed resolutions against slavery were exscinded by the general assembly in 1838, the church parties aligned themselves more firmly with regional attitudes. The New School presbyteries and synods were consistently antislavery in sentiment; the strength of the Old School party lay in the South and the group was sympathetic with regional problems. Thus it was that dissension crowded out unity, and the church fell into two well defined parts

---

[25] Sweet, *The Presbyterians,* Chap. V; Henry Woods, *The History of the Presbyterian Controversy* (Louisville, 1843), passim; Zebulon Crocker, *The Catastrophe of the Presbyterian Church in 1837* (New Haven, 1838), passim; C. Bruce Staiger, "Abolitionism and the Presbyterian Schism of 1837-1838," *Mississippi Valley Historical Review,* XXXVI (1949-1950), 391-414.

almost equal in size. After 1838 Presbyterian congregations distinguished themselves by the use of the initials O. S. or N. S., and for all practical purposes the schism of 1837-1838 was the first long step toward the complete and total division of 1861.

The problems of existence and growth facing a new church like the Cumberland Presbyterian or the Disciples of Christ enter of necessity into their attitudes and provisions regarding various issues. Only from this point of view is it possible to understand or explain the shifting position of Alexander Campbell as he led his church without schism or division through the intricacies and traps of the slavery question.

The issue of slavery among the Disciples of Christ revolved almost entirely around Alexander Campbell, with lesser roles played by his father Thomas Campbell and by his co-worker Barton Stone. Alexander Campbell so completely dominated the situation that individual congregations found little reason to be disturbed over issues concerning which Campbell made no pronouncements or gave no directives. Since there was no judicatory powerful enough to interfere with Campbell, he became the unchallenged spokesman of his followers. No person in the history of Southern churches ever so completely and so successfully directed the affairs of a denomination for so long a period as did Campbell. His attitude toward slavery, as was true of other immediate issues, "was tempered by considerations of long-range, political, national, and religious statesmanship."[26]

Fundamentally Campbell was antislavery in sentiment, but did not allow himself to be tinged with abolitionism. Although he remained a neutral throughout the Civil War, Campbell had earlier straddled the fence so well that Southerners thought he was pro-Southern in his sympathies and Northerners counted him among their own. The first issue

[26] Garrison and DeGroot, *Disciples of Christ*, 199-200, 468-69.

of the *Christian Baptist* contains an article, presumably by Campbell, in opposition to slavery. Desiring to assist in bringing an end to slavery in his state, Campbell successfully sought election to the Virginia Constitutional Convention of 1829. In the convention, however, Campbell raised no voice against slavery. He later attempted to explain his silence on the grounds that a clause in the constitution would be ineffectual so long as the legislature remained in the control of the slaveholders.[27]

Campbell effectively used his publications to broadcast his opinions and comments. Having his sympathies aroused by a violent slave insurrection in Southampton County, Virginia, in 1831, Campbell poured forth his hardest editorial blow against the "peculiar institution." Angered by circumstances that had caused the insurrection, he denounced slavery in no uncertain terms in the February 1832 issue of the *Millennial Harbinger* as "that largest and blackest blot upon our national escutcheon, that many-headed monster, that Pandora's box, that bitter root, that blighting and blasting curse, under which so fair and so large a portion of our beloved country groans—that deadly Upas, whose breath pollutes and poisons every thing within its influence." Shortly before events had so aroused his indignation, Campbell in writing about slavery in Virginia had described slavery as an evil from an economic point of view. He sustained his thesis on the grounds that the Negro had poorly used the lands which he cultivated and was responsible for the low value of farm land. Campbell was an advocate of a high tax on slaves, so high in fact that it would be a means to gradual emancipation.[28]

By the 1840s public opinion had been markedly influenced by the agitations of the abolitionists on the one hand and the Biblical defense of slavery on the other. Disunity was rife;

[27] Richardson, *Alexander Campbell*, II, 304-13; Lunger, *Alexander Campbell*, Chap. VI.
[28] Also see "Slavery in Virginia," *Millennial Harbinger*, 1832, 14-15.

already the Presbyterians had divided themselves, and the Methodists and Baptists were quickly moving toward a cleavage within their churches. Only ecclesiastical statesmanship could avert a similar fatality in the Disciples of Christ. The conflicting opinions of Alexander Campbell and Barton Stone had a tendency to divide their followers. This danger Campbell recognized and firmly met by preventing within the church the formation of parties with divergent views. Campbell had been an interested onlooker as the Presbyterian Church had been split largely over slavery issues, and he determined that such would not be the fate of the Disciples of Christ.

Thomas Campbell probably had firmer convictions about slavery than those held by his son, who carried the burden of a new sect on his shoulders. In 1819 the elder Campbell moved from Kentucky to Washington County, Pennsylvania, where he continued his work with the few Negroes in that area. Events and circumstances, however, influenced him to the point that he greatly modified his views on slavery. In 1845 he wrote in the *Millennial Harbinger* a revised defense of slavery, supporting his position with what he termed an examination of "the divine contents of the Good Book upon the subject of Bible slavery." He gave a surprising and baffling conclusion to his defense by saying that "Christians should have nothing to do with encouraging involuntary servitude."[29]

Standing firmer than either of the Campbells, Stone consistently opposed slavery for some fifty years. If he had ever been kindly disposed to human bondage, his mind was changed by the sight of slaves working in chains and wearing iron collars. While on a trip to South Carolina in 1797 Stone had come upon a group of half-naked Negroes driven at their work by the lash laid on by a merciless overseer. The sight so sickened Stone that for the rest of his life he was a

[29] *Millennial Harbinger*, 1845, 3, 6.

confirmed opponent of slavery. As a Presbyterian in 1800 he had written the antislavery resolution of the West Lexington Presbytery, a resolution originally coming from the churches at Cane Ridge and Concord. The resolution declared slavery to be "a subject likely to occasion much trouble and division in the churches" and defined it as "a moral evil, very heinous, and consequently sufficient to exclude such as will continue in the practice of it from the privileges of the church." In the *Christian Messenger* for 1829 Stone said that slavery was a political and moral wrong and that this nation had admitted its guilt by trying to stop the slave traffic. Although he was opposed to the indiscriminate emancipation of slaves, he felt that Providence had produced a means to freedom in the formation of the Colonization Society. Finding himself hampered in Kentucky, Stone moved in the fall of 1834 to Jacksonville, Illinois, where he could live without the daily reminders of slavery. He left his slaves in Kentucky, where "by common consent" they could be considered free.[30]

Alexander Campbell's strong inclination toward pacifism made him very conservative in his attitude toward abolitionism. Convinced that war was indefensible under any circumstance, Campbell continually talked of peace. Probably he stated his position the clearest when he said: "A Christian man can never, of right, be compelled to do that for the state, in defense of state rights, which he cannot do for himself in defense of his personal rights. Unless a Christian can go to war for himself, he cannot for the state." In his opposition to war Campbell remained consistent. His chief concern was "to preserve the unity of spirit among the Christians of the South and of the North. . . ." This was his "grand object."[31]

[30] Rogers, *Stone*, 27-28, 287-91; Ware, *Stone*, 217, 299-300; *Christian Messenger* (Georgetown, Ky. and Jacksonville, Ill.), March 1834, 94, Nov. 1835, 263. Also see West, *Stone*, Chap. XIV.
[31] Athearn, *Campbell*, 66-67; *Millennial Harbinger*, 1845, 194.

The Protestant Episcopal Church held itself aloof from involvement with slavery, refusing to express itself on any matter that could be classified as political in nature. Moral issues of a purely personal and private sort, such as the excessive use of liquor, gambling, dancing, and theater going, might be discussed in the church assemblies, but issues of a public nature, such as slavery, were the concern of the state. The church took the position that any interference in a social evil like slavery, which was neither primarily moral nor religious, would be contrary to the idea of the separation of church and state. Unfortunately for the Episcopal Church many opinionated people considered this position of the church as an implicit approval of slavery. But such was not the sentiment of the organization.[32]

In general the position taken by the Roman Catholics on slavery was strikingly similar to that of the Episcopalians. The Catholic Church neither condemned nor condoned slavery. It refused to approve abolitionism on the grounds that it offered many evils along with one good feature. The only large sections of the South where the Catholics came in contact with slavery were in portions of Maryland and Louisiana. In Florida, Kentucky, Tennessee, Alabama, and Mississippi there were not many Catholics either with or without slaves. But the attitude of the Catholic slaveowner was not different from that of his Protestant neighbor who owned slaves. The policy of the *Catholic Advocate,* published in Bardstown and later in Louisville, is very typical of that of other Catholic papers and presents the prevailing view of slavery as held by the church communicants throughout the country. The *Advocate* accepted advertisements for the sale of slaves, but at some time the editor must have questioned this policy. In 1837 the paper declared itself to be in a neutral position: "We are not advocates for slavery, yet

---

[32] See Addison, *Episcopal Church,* 192-93; William Manross, "The Episcopal Church and Reform," *Historical Magazine,* XII (1943), 339-66 passim.

we cannot persuade ourselves that it is, in its very nature, a *heinous* and *crying* sin; much less can we approve of the wild, fanatical, and barbarous schemes of the abolitionists."[33]

Within the ranks of the Catholic ministry a few priests challenged the slave system, a few participated in the fight for emancipation, and probably just as many priests supplied the proslavery group with a satisfying defense. The American hierarchy, predominantly European in birth, had little sympathy with reform movements, a reminder of changes from which they had fled in Europe. Concerning the American officials, an able student of the Catholic attitude toward slavery had made some telling observations: "During the years of the slavery discussions members of the hierarchy by taking refuge in a conservative church tradition, entirely remote from the contemporary issue, contributed to the general impression that their church was proslavery. They helped also to retard the development of a constructive Catholic approach to the slavery issue and encouraged the persistence among their followers of racial and nationalist antipathies which had no place upon the American scene."[34]

The majority of Catholics belonged to the Democratic Party and of these the majority were Irishmen who had little sympathy with the sad plight of the Negro. The Irish, bound by poverty and the lack of skills, were concerned first with their own economic insecurity and had little time for the hard luck of others. The unfair accusation of being proslavery added fuel to the charges and tirades of the Know-Nothings. When this movement was at its height, Alexander H. Stephens rushed to the defense of the Catholics by declaring that "they have never warred against us or our peculiar institutions. No man can say as much of New England Baptists, Presbyterians or Methodists; the long roll of abolition petitions, with [which] Congress has been so

[33] Gillard, *Colored Catholics*, 42-43; Rice, *Catholic Opinion*, 75, 76.
[34] Rice, *Catholic Opinion*, 156-57.

much agitated for past years, come not from the Catholics; their pulpits at the North are not desecrated every Sabbath with anathemas against slavery."[35]

In the presidential campaign of 1840 Secretary of State John Forsyth of Georgia attempted to influence the voters of Georgia against General William H. Harrison by interpreting Pope Gregory XVI's famous Apostolic Letter on the slave trade as a condemnation of American domestic slavery. Since this letter antagonized Southerners, Bishop John England of series of letters printed in the *United States Catholic Miscellany* during the winter of 1840-1841 set forth his explanation that the Pope spoke not of domestic slavery but of the African slave trade. Bishop England stated that the Apostolic Letter did not condemn American slavery but regarded it as not "incompatible with the natural law." Since England's explanation went unchallenged, it appears evident that the American Catholic bishops did not oppose domestic slavery. The attitude of the church, however, was so neutral it could easily have been interpreted as either proslavery or antislavery in position. Bishop England disliked abolitionism so much that he was accused of favoring slavery. In a letter to the *Miscellany* of February 25, 1841, he represented the opinion of many Catholics in the North and in the South when he said that he was not friendly to "the existence or continuation of slavery," but he saw no possibility of abolishing it.[36]

The three largest denominations in the South—Methodist, Baptist, and Presbyterian—receded from an earlier position of attacking slavery and compromised with it. As cotton

[35] Maynard, *American Catholicism*, 345; William G. Bean, "An Aspect of Know-Nothingism—the Immigrant and Slavery," *South Atlantic Quarterly*, XXIII (1924), 333.

[36] See Stokes, *Church and State*, II, 186-87; Stephen Theobald, "Catholic Missionary Work among the Colored People of the United States," *Records, American Catholic Historical Society*, XXXV (1924), 334-39.

and slavery took a firm hold on Southern society and economy, the churches took their stand with an expanding slavocracy. Expediency produced compromise; compromise gave countenance to an institution, which, without the direct and indirect support of the churches in the South and Southwest, might have been shortlived. As with similar issues in Southern history, the general outline is familiar, a retelling of the old theme—cotton and slavery, expediency and compromise. Eventually the day of reckoning would come. Some churches would divide; others would remain intact.

13

CRISES AND DIVISIONS

FOR FORTY YEARS after its organization in America, the Methodist Episcopal Church by means of various rules and regulations sought to rid itself of the moral responsibility for slavery. But from 1824 until the division of the church in 1844 the generous rules on slaveholding remained unaltered. The Southern clergy ceased its denunciations of slavery and became slaveholding itself, basing its position on the idea that a successful program in the church depended on a common understanding and mutual interest between preacher and congregation. The slavery interest had gained strength by supporting legislative acts, which were aided and abetted by ministerial advocacy in virtually all the denominations of the South. In order to hold the churches in the South, Bishop Asbury had been forced to compromise on slavery and to accept a position which permitted Southern members and clergy to dominate the Methodist Church until about 1840.

Prior to the General Conference of 1840 the annual conferences had been requested to pass judgment on "the buying or selling, or holding men, women, or children as slaves, or giving them away, except on purpose to free them." When the conference met, the delegates acknowledged slavery as an evil, for the destruction of which the Discipline of the church did not provide. This General Conference declined to express an opinion on the question of whether "slavery was a moral evil, or only a social and political evil."

Here was a matter on which the annual conferences had already given "uncertain and conflicting testimony." The struggle went on despite rebuffs; abolitionists continued a policy of boring from within. Many Southern delegates began to believe that the end to tolerance had been reached in relations with the Northern conferences, which under the whip of abolitionists continued to pass resolutions calling slavery a great moral evil.[1]

A resolution which had been passed by the Georgia Conference of 1837 contributed to the mounting tension. By a unanimous vote the conference had resolved "that it is the sense of the Georgia Annual Conference that slavery, as it exists in the United States, is not a moral evil . . . and we view slavery as a civil and domestic institution. . . ." The Reverend S. K. Hodges, a delegate from Georgia to the General Conference of 1840, first attempted to explain the conditions under which the resolution had been written, then proceeded to defend the resolution. Bishop Elijah Hedding, seeking harmony on the convention floor, explained how much less disturbing the resolution would have been if it had stated that slavery as it existed in the Methodist Church rather than in the United States was not a moral evil. The suggestion of the bishop eased the tension, but a great hurt to a continuing peace had been given.[2]

Through the years the smoldering fire of controversy, smothered by compromise and by arbitrary rulings, broke out in several places, especially in New England. In the midwestern states antislavery sentiment had increased in the early 1840s to the point that many members withdrew from the Methodist Church and joined other denominations. The fear of losing the church in New England led Methodist bishops in that section to relax their rule over annual conferences, thereby permitting the conferences to adopt vigor-

[1] Matlack, *Antislavery Struggle*, 106, 133.
[2] Matlack, *Antislavery Struggle*, 104; David W. Clark, *Life and Times of Rev. Elijah Hedding* (New York, 1856), 552-55.

ous proposals.[3] Abolitionist successes tended to cease, but the suspicion of the South sharply increased.

When the General Conference met in New York City on May 1, 1844, the antislavery element possessed the balance of power. Among the 180 delegates were men of great stature and ability, who constituted the real leadership of American Methodism. The South was ably represented by Henry Bascom of Kentucky, William Capers of South Carolina, William Winans of Mississippi, Lovick and George F. Pierce, father and son from Georgia, and a host of others of genuine importance. Peter Cartwright, who had moved to Illinois in order to make his residence in a free state, was there. Directly or indirectly the slavery issue dominated the long convention that lasted from May 1 to June 11.[4]

On May 7 the celebrated Harding case came up and the discussion lasted for five days. Francis A. Harding, a minister, had been suspended by the Baltimore Conference for refusing to free some slaves that had come into his possession by marriage. Appealing his case to the General Conference, Harding had sought protection under a rule in the Discipline that exempted slaveholders from the obligation of emancipation when they lived in states which had declared emancipation of slaves illegal. The decision of the Baltimore Conference was upheld by a decisive vote of 117 to 56. This was the first devastating blow suffered by the South in the slavery quarrels. Murmurs of discontent were rampant. Capers believed that the church had become lenient on the radicals in order to keep them loyal. One delegate quickly expressed his opinion of the situation by saying: "the great question of unity is settled, division is inevitable."[5]

[3] Robert D. Clark, *The Life of Matthew Simpson* (New York, 1956), 117; Holland N. McTyeire, *A History of Methodism* (Nashville, 1884), 611-12; Sweet, *Methodism in American History*, 241-42.

[4] See Swaney, *Methodism and Slavery*, Chap. X.

[5] John N. Norwood, *The Schism in the Methodist Episcopal Church, 1844* (New York, 1923), 61-63.

Despondency prevailed among the Southern delegates and was intensified when the conference heard the report on May 21 of the Committee on Episcopacy in the James O. Andrew case. After Andrew had been elected in 1832 to the office of bishop, he by no actual choice of his own came into the ownership of some slaves. To Bishop Andrew had been given a girl, whom with her consent he was to send to Liberia. When the Negress refused to go, she legally remained the property of Andrew. From his wife Andrew inherited a boy whom he could not free under Georgia laws. In his second marriage he was further endowed by a widow who had inherited slaves from her deceased husband's estate. Although Andrew's status as a slaveowning bishop had been ignored for years, in 1844 it became the subject of much controversy. Before Bishop Andrew arrived at the General Conference, he had heard that his ownership of slaves was causing great excitement. His first impulse in reaction to the criticism was to resign the office, and to his daughter the modest bishop wrote: "I would most joyfully resign, if I did not dread the influence on the Southern church." Knowing how explosive the situation was, he feared that if he relinquished his office or left the assembly floor all the delegates from churches in the South would walk out.[6]

A full investigation of Bishop Andrew's connections with slavery by the Committee on Episcopacy resulted in a resolution asking the bishop to resign. On the following day James B. Finley offered a second resolution, milder in tone, which requested Bishop Andrew to "desist from the exercise of his office so long as this impediment remains." When Andrew realized that the substance of the resolutions intimated that he had broken faith with the church and that he must resign or be deposed, he was no longer receptive

[6] George G. Smith, *The Life and Letters of James Osgood Andrew* (Nashville, 1883), 336-37, 355.

to the idea of resignation with which he had earlier toyed. The Southern delegates almost to a man supported his position.[7]

An impasse had been reached; the delegates from neither the Northern nor the Southern churches could afford to yield the position they held. If the North had surrendered its tenet that the episcopacy should remain free from slavery, this equivocating would have been wholly unacceptable to the free states and considered as a sacrifice of a great principle. On the other hand, for the Southern churches to accept the deposition of a bishop, merely because he had involuntarily come into possession of slaves, would have been equally disastrous to the church in that region. The General Conference had arrived at its hour of crisis and of decision, but for the nonce the majority of the delegates failed to sense the decisive moment. The bishops presented a peace measure requesting that action be postponed until the next general conference, but the delegates were in no mood to temporize and asked for a vote on the Finley resolution.[8]

In eleven days numerous speeches were made on both sides of the important resolution. Few were longer remembered than that of the impassioned young George F. Pierce of Georgia. In accusing the New England churches of being the intermeddlers, Pierce said he was willing that all New England should secede from the Methodist Church rather than pass the Finley amendment. "I say," he cried, "*let New England go, with all my heart*; she has been for twenty years a thorn in the flesh, a messenger of Satan to buffet us; let her go, and joy go with her, for peace will stay behind." If the resolution should pass, Pierce predicted that in ten years there would not be left any of the distinctive features

[7] Smith, *Andrew*, 342-45; Matlack, *Antislavery Struggle*, 171-72. Also see Albert H. Redford, *History of the Organization of the Methodist Episcopal Church, South* (Nashville, 1871), Chap. III.
[8] Clark, *Hedding*, 589-92.

of Methodism, the people would desert the divided church and preachers would stand idle because they had not been hired. Although this oratorical burst of feeling had a profound effect on Southern delegates, it did not alter the direction of the vote. Finley's substitute resolution passed by a vote of 111 to 69. Only one of the 111 votes came from a delegate in a slaveholding conference.[9]

Tempers flared, and the issue broadened with Bishop Andrew at its center. The Southern delegates were angered over their colleagues from the North attempting to depose Andrew without trial although admitting that, except for this one defect, he was "pure and spotless" and "in every way qualified for the Christian ministry." Sentiment throughout the South condemned the action of this conference. Peter Cartwright, although he had spent a great deal of his life in the South, was no friend of the slavery cause. He insisted that the conference should have arraigned Bishop Andrew for improper conduct, as the Discipline provided, and then suspended him from all official acts of the church. If it had proceeded in the suggested cautious manner, the conference would not have been liable for hasty actions. Then if the South chose to secede, let her secede. The Southern delegation in answer to this type of attack contended that Bishop Andrew had violated no rule of the church, and that the conference had no constitutional right to suspend a bishop. The delegates from the North, on the other hand, insisted that an officer of the church was amenable to the General Conference and that this was not a matter of constitutional law but one of expediency. Abel Stevens, distinguished historian of Methodism, believes that Andrew held the key to peace and unity of the church. Gross Alexander, a highly sympathetic critic of Bishop Andrew, insists that if Andrew did not know the explosive effect of

[9] George G. Smith, *The History of Methodism in Georgia and Florida* (Macon, Ga.), 374-75, 381.

the slavery situation and could not foresee the results of his own holding of slaves, "his ignorance, for a man in his position, was inexcusable." John N. Norwood's scholarly study is inclined to agree with both Stevens and Alexander.[10]

The Southern delegation in the General Conference of 1844 had become convinced of the futility of any further effort to maintain the unity of the church. On June 3 William Capers offered a group of resolutions providing for a separation from the Methodist Episcopal Church. Four days later a committee of nine, with Robert Paine of Alabama as chairman, made a report which became known as the Plan of Separation. In the event of separation the main provisions in this plan were: the General Conference would proceed with kindness and equity; all societies, stations, and conferences in the Southern church should remain unmolested; and ministers of the Methodist Episcopal Church in the North would not organize in the limits of the Methodist Episcopal Church in the South. The plan was adopted by a vote of 136 to 15. Northern bishops sanctioned the action which was taken and offered no objections.[11] There being no further business, the General Conference of the Methodist Episcopal Church adjourned on the night of June 10, 1844, after an unprecedented session of forty days.

While the Plan of Separation was still in the hands of the committee, the details had been discussed with John C. Calhoun. Just before the General Conference had closed, Calhoun had sent a letter to William Capers inviting him to stop in Washington on his way home in order to discuss with him the probable direction to be taken by the church

---

[10] Clark, *Simpson*, 124-27; Cartwright, *Autobiography*, 416; Norwood, *The Schism*, 70, 71; Gross Alexander, "A History of the Methodist Church, South," in *American Church History*, XI (New York, 1900), 20. Also see *History of the Organization of the Methodist Episcopal Church, South* (Nashville, 1845), Chap. II passim.

[11] Swaney, *Methodism and Slavery*, Chap. XI. For a bitter Southern account see Edward H. Myers, *The Disruption of the Methodist Episcopal Church, 1844-1846* (Nashville, 1875), passim.

in the South. Capers wisely declined the invitation for fear, as was later true, that the charge would arise of an alliance of politicians and preachers.[12] But this invitation of Calhoun's was indicative of the seriousness of the rift in the church.

On the morning after the adjournment of the conference the Southern delegates who had been in attendance agreed to call a convention in Louisville on May 1, 1845. Fifty-one delegates from thirteen annual conferences signed a letter calling attention "to the proscription and disability under which the Southern portion of the Church must of necessity labour, . . . unless some measures are adopted to free the minority of the South from the oppressive jurisdiction of the majority in the North."[13]

At Louisville in May 1845 in a movement peacefully and unanimously executed, the Southern delegates voted 94 to 3 to separate from the Methodist Episcopal Church, and, then and there, to organize a new church to be known as the Methodist Episcopal Church, South. Bishop Andrew and Bishop Soule gladly accepted the invitation to become bishops in the Southern church. With some justifiable warrant the Southern delegates laid a variety of charges at the feet of the church in the North, but they were very careful to please Kentucky and not to lose the border conferences.[14]

The Southern Methodists refused to change the Discipline on slavery until the year 1858, and the Northern Methodists made no alteration until 1860. In their General Conference of 1858 the Southern Methodists voted by 140 to 8 to rescind the rule on slavery on the basis that it was "ambiguous in phraseology, and liable to be construed as antagonistic to the institution of slavery in regard to which the Church has no right to meddle, except in enjoining the duties of

[12] Wightman, *William Capers*, 514.
[13] William W. Sweet, *The Methodist Episcopal Church and the Civil War* (Cincinnati, ca. 1912), 26.
[14] *Organization of the Methodist Episcopal Church, South,* passim.

masters and servants as set forth in the Holy Scriptures."
Two years later the Methodist Church in the North adopted
a new rule on slavery which declared that "we believe that
the buying, selling, or holding of human beings, to be used
as chattels, is contrary to the laws of God and nature. . . .
We, therefore, affectionately admonish all our preachers and
people to keep themselves pure from this great evil, and
to seek its extirpation by all lawful and Christian means."[15]

When the delegates to the General Conference of 1844
had returned to their homes in the North, a storm of protest
broke out against the actions of the conference. Questions
from congregations and annual conferences arose over the
authority of the delegates to the General Conference to do
whatever they pleased. The majority of the delegates to the
1848 conference went instructed to repudiate the Plan of
Separation. This business was speedily attended to when
the conference convened in Pittsburgh. Numerous motives
were assigned for this reversal of opinion, but the chief
reasons were opposition to dividing the church and the fear
of the withdrawal of several New England conferences
which were dominated by abolition sentiment.

In the Plan of Separation which had been adopted in 1844,
provisions had been made for the transfer to the church in
the South of all Book Concern property located in the area
and all accounts owned by ministers and citizens of the
South. Furthermore, the agreement provided for a division
of Book Concern property and general funds. This, of
course, was part of the Plan of Separation which was
reversed in 1848. When no proposal for settlement came
from the agents of the Book Concern, the Methodist Episcopal Church, South decided to bring legal suit. Accordingly
a suit was instituted in the United States Circuit Court for

[15] Charles Elliott, *South-Western Methodism* (Cincinnati, 1868), 110;
Journals of the General Conference . . . 1860 (New York, ca. 1860), 260.
Also see J. M. Buckley, *A History of Methodists in the United States* (New
York, 1896), 501-502.

the Southern District of New York for a division of the property of the New York Book Concern. A second suit for the division of the property of the Western Book Concern was brought in the United States Circuit Court for the District of Ohio.[16]

With a great array of fine legal talent each side shuddered at the prospect of a scandal arising over a squabble for money. Arbitration was refused by the North, for that would involve recognition of the validity of the claim of Southerners to the property. The Southern church stood squarely on the binding features of the Plan. The New York suit was decided in favor of the Southern plaintiffs, and the Ohio suit in favor of the Northern defendants. The latter case was then appealed to the United States Supreme Court which reversed the decision and upheld the Plan of Separation as a valid arrangement. These settlements brought an end to the long and unfortunate quarrel over church property. Some people in the North insisted that slavery influences in the courts had affected the decisions, but it should here be pointed out that the Supreme Court decision was unanimous.[17]

Before the separation was generally accepted, clashes along the border between the churches North and South became frequent, disturbing, and even destructive. It is true, however, that most of the episodes were on the local level in areas where the Northern and Southern sympathizers were rather evenly divided. It was not rare for services conducted by one side of the controversy to be broken up by the other. Despite the enormous amount of writing on this topic a few accounts of the border clashes must suffice. At Parkersburg, Virginia (later West Virginia), well within

---

[16] See R. Sutton (reporter), *The Methodist Church Property Case* (Louisville, 1851); W. P. Harrison, *Methodist Union, Threatened in 1844, Was Dissolved in 1848* (Nashville, 1892).

[17] Harrison, *Methodist Union*, Chap. XI; Redford, *Organization of the Methodist Episcopal Church, South*, 561-84, 644-60.

the bounds of the Ohio Conference and according to Northern opinion not a border section, some Southern sympathizers in 1845 ran the Methodist preacher out of town and
seized the church property. In June 1855 in Andrew County,
Missouri, a preacher of the Methodist Church in the North
attempted to conduct a protracted meeting despite threats
against him. When he reached the church, he was met by
a mob of about one hundred who tarred and feathered him
and then ordered him to leave town at once. Probably the
best known and most publicized case of clashing involved
Anthony Bewley who moved from Tennessee to Missouri.
Having been admitted to the Missouri Conference in 1843,
Bewley decided to remain with the Northern church. From
this period until his death he was the victim of continuing
persecution. In 1860 he and a companion were charged with
poisoning wells and burning towns in Texas. Fearing the
rising opposition to him, he decided to return to Missouri.
On the way he was apprehended by a mob and hanged
near Fort Worth. Perhaps, as one author claims, Northern
Methodists had not been hanged by Southern Methodists,
but the harm had been done and continued to be done.
Right was not always on the side of the church in the North,
but the bulk of printed material indicates that the Southern
sympathizers had been more aggressive in the campaign to
control the border regions. The reaction in the North
mounted to a boiling point.[18]

Anger and bitterness now ruled in a divided church.
Bishops on both sides of the border were uttering statements
that later seem to have been wholly unjustified. Radical
Methodists in the North contributed to the hatred and antag-
onisms of Methodists in the South. One New England minister urged that no missionary be sent to the South unless he
adopted the most radical proslavery views. William Hosmer,

[18] Norwood, *The Schism*, 136; Sweet, *Methodist Church and the Civil
War*, 30-31; W. M. Leftwich, *Martyrdom in Missouri* (2 vols.; St. Louis,
1870), I, 109-16, 150 ff.

editor of the *Northern Christian Advocate,* appealed to slaves to rise against their masters. Any slave who had been converted and refused to fight for freedom, he insisted, should not be considered a Christian. George F. Pierce, who had pleaded Andrew's cause so effectively, was chosen bishop by the Church South in 1854, and became the spokesman for the radical opposition to Northern ministers in the South. In 1860 he declared that they came into the South only as enemies of the people and institutions of the slave states, interested in aiding runaway slaves and sympathetic "with blood, and murder, insurrection, and carnage." Designating these ministers as abolitionists, he spoke with no moderation: "Rank, rotten with the foul virus of an incurable disease, foes of God and man, spies and traitors of their country and their kind, let them stay where they belong!"[19] Intensive investigation has revealed no countercharge able to match this tirade by Bishop Pierce.

Many people believed that there was a direct relation between the division of the Methodist Church and the origin of the Civil War. John C. Calhoun, a spokesman for this group, in the great debate with Clay in 1850 said that the cords that had bound the nation together were unable to resist the force of slavery. "The numerous ties which held it [Methodist Church] together are all broken and its unity gone. They now form separate churches, and instead of that feeling of attachment and devotion to the interests of the whole church which was formerly felt, they are now arrayed into two hostile bodies, engaged in litigation about what was formerly their common property."[20]

The Baptist denomination in sharp contrast to the Methodist was characterized by the independence of each congregation, although congregations united in numerous voluntary organizations ranging from the Triennial Convention

---

[19] Swaney, *Methodism and Slavery,* 251-52.
[20] Sweet, *Methodism in American History,* 276.

at the top to some regional associations or even local efforts. Despite the absence of a central organization various churches, associations, and conventions expressed their opinions on the issues of the day. In the South these expressions generally favored slavery and condemned abolitionism and antislavery agitation.[21] Rapidly the day approached when the slaveholder no longer merely excused slavery but justified it with the support of the Holy Writ. As the slavery and antislavery lines grew tighter and threats against the institution daily increased, the moderate Baptist leaders, North and South, strove valiantly to keep peace between the radicals in both sections. Harmony prevailed at the Triennial Convention which met in Richmond in 1835, but the next three meetings were disturbed by the slavery controversy, and the last one culminated in the formation of the Southern Baptist Convention.

During the winter of 1839-1840 the Board of Missions asserted in a resolution the positive neutrality of itself in regard to the slavery question. The real controversy broke forth in April 1840 with the organization in New York City of the American Baptist Anti-Slavery Convention which issued immediately "An Address to Southern Baptists." The address caused great resentment. A few months later the members of the Fellowship Baptist Church in Wilcox County, Alabama, adopted resolutions expressing "utter detestations of the principles, accusations and threats" in the address, "believing them to be unkind, untrue, unchristian, and unscriptural." They urged their Southern brethren "to speak out their sentiments fully on this subject, and let the Northern Baptists know, distinctly, that we cannot cooperate with those who thus stigmatize and excommunicate us." Typical reaction to the address was apparent in the Alabama Baptist Association in its resolution of October

21 By 1837 Baptist members owned about 115,000 slaves, exceeded only by the Methodists who held about 220,000. Putnam, *Baptists and Slavery*, 13.

1840 "to resist all interference of Northerners in our domestic relations," for those engaged in abolition are "in an unholy cause—in one which is condemned by the Bible, and wholly unauthorized by the blessed Savior."[22]

By November the Board of Managers of the Triennial Convention issued an address pointing "with painful interest" to the withdrawal of brethren from the missionary work. The utterances of various abolition and antislavery groups declaring the sinfulness of slavery and the urgency for immediate emancipation frightened Southern Baptists. Basil Manly, Sr., president of the University of Alabama, had warned William C. Crane, a Mississippi preacher, that Northern Baptists disagreed so thoroughly with the Southern Baptists that the latter would be *"tried to the core"* if they attended the Triennial Convention in 1841. Manly urged Crane in the event he should go to "determine beforehand that you will be as *impassable* as a stone, that *nothing* shall move you, that the inglorious malevolence, the taunting insolence, the vaporing black guardism of any of them 'Jack O'Lantern' fellows can devise" will not faze you.[23]

At the 1841 convention the Southerners with the aid of Northern moderates managed to get Elon Galusha, an active abolitionist, removed from the office of vice president of the Board of Foreign Missions and to fill the vacancy with Richard C. Fuller of South Carolina. The messengers reached an agreement that slavery should not be discussed by the convention. Before leaving the meeting the Southern messengers addressed a letter to the Board of Managers stating their conviction that abolitionism would fail if a spirit of mildness prevailed.[24] Unfortunately, abolitionism did not

[22] Newman, *Baptist Churches*, 443-44; *Baptist Banner*, Aug. 20, 1840, March 11, 1841.

[23] Putnam, *Baptists and Slavery*, 21-23. The Manly letter is quoted in Henry F. Snapp, "The Mississippi Career of William Cary Crane" (M.A. thesis, Baylor University, 1958), 31-32.

[24] Goodell, *Slavery and Anti-Slavery*, 498-99; Sweet, *Religions in America*, 428-29.

subside among the Baptists, and antislavery sentiments
increased. The compromise only served as an agent to
bring the inevitable division.

In 1844 "A Southern Baptist" published a significant
twelve-page pamphlet with the title *A Calm Appeal to
Southern Baptists, in Advocacy of Separation from the North
in All the Works of Christian Benevolence.*[25] In the first
half of the booklet the author denied any hostility or
grievance against boards or societies, but admitted that he
sought to show that consistency required a separation of
the Southern from the Northern societies. Despite his denial
of grievance, the writer insisted that the boards were dominated by Northerners and that representatives from the
South were mere "spectators." The second half of the publication declared that expediency required immediate separation while it could be done with good feelings. Separation
would tend to guarantee or contribute to the maintenance
of peace, spiritual welfare, the work of various societies,
intelligence of people, and welfare of the political union of
the country.

When the Triennial Convention met in Philadelphia in
the spring of 1844, only 85 of the 456 messengers represented associations or churches in slaveholding states. So
completely were the moderates in control, they introduced
a resolution declaring that "in cooperating together as
members of this Convention in the work of Foreign Missions,
we disclaim all sanction either expressed or implied, whether
of slavery or of antislavery, but as individuals, we are
perfectly free both to express and to promote our own views
on these subjects in a Christian manner and spirit." Received
with much satisfaction, the resolution was passed by a
unanimous vote, which for the time seemed to have freed
the church of the vexing issue.[26]

25 A copy of this rare pamphlet is in the library of Crozer Theological
Seminary, Chester, Pa.

26 Newman, *Baptist Churches*, 444-45.

During the meeting of the Triennial Convention the Georgia Baptist Convention recommended to the Board of the Home Mission Society the appointment of James E. Reeves, a slaveholding preacher, as a missionary. This was definitely intended to be a test case, for the application declared: "We wish his appointment so much the more as it will stop the mouths of gainsayers. . . . There are good brethren among us, who notwithstanding the transactions of your society at Philadelphia, are hard to believe that you will appoint a slave-holder a missionary, even when the funds are supplied by those who wish his appointment." Finally, after five sessions of three hours each, a decision was reached by a vote of 7 to 5 against appointing Reeves. The corresponding secretary reported that the application introduced the subject of slavery which violated the letter and the purpose of the constitution of the society, hence the board could not receive the application for appointment. This action led to the withdrawal of Southern associations from the Board of Home Missions, and a subsequent formation of a Board of Domestic Missions to be supported by Southern Baptists.[27]

After the adjournment of the Triennial Convention of 1844 some Southern Baptists claimed that the General Board of Baptist Foreign Missions had forced from its service Jesse Bushyhead, a successful and respected Cherokee preacher who owned a plantation and several slaves. The Southerners seemed to have assumed that the board would no longer countenance slaveholding by its representatives. In the same year the dismissal of Bushyhead was brought to the attention of the Alabama Baptist State Convention through a query from the Tuscaloosa Church, probably inspired and even written by Basil Manly, Sr. The question asked: "Is it proper for us at the South, to send any more money to our brethren at the North, for missionary and other benevolent

[27] Putnam, *Baptists and Slavery*, 49-50; Sweet, *Religions in America*, 430-31.

purposes, before the subject of slavery be rightly understood by both parties?" On November 25, 1844, resolutions addressed to the Acting Board demanded "the distinct explicit avowal that slaveholders are eligible, and entitled equally with non-slaveholders to all the privileges and immunities of their several unions, and especially to receive any agency, mission or other appointment which may run within [the scope] of their operation or duties." On December 17 the board replied in a kind but unequivocal statement that "we can never be a party to any arrangement which would imply approbation of slavery." "If our brethren in Alabama . . . can co-operate with us, we shall be happy to receive their aid. If they can not, painful to us as will be their withdrawal, yet we shall submit to it. . . . [Our] sentiments avowed in this communication . . . are . . . dearer to us than any pecuniary aid whatever."[28]

This action by the agents of the convention was a flagrant violation of an accepted compromise. "There is no adequate defense of their conduct," says a competent Baptist historian, "in thus disobeying the plain mandate they had received from the Convention only a few months before." The outcome had been clearly foreseen, and a separation of Southern churches was deemed inevitable. The Virginia Baptist Foreign Missionary Society took the lead in separation by urging a called meeting for the purpose of organizing a purely Southern convention.[29]

On May 8, 1845, amidst great enthusiasm 377 messengers from Maryland, Virginia, North Carolina, South Carolina, Georgia, Alabama, Louisiana, Kentucky, and the District of Columbia met in Augusta, Georgia, to organize the Southern Baptist Convention. After the election of officers the assem-

---

[28] Riley, *Memorial History*, 82; Putnam, *Baptists and Slavery*, 53-56. Also see Harold Wilson, "Basil Manly, Apologist for Slavocracy," *Alabama Review*, XV (1962), 38-53.

[29] Henry C. Vedder, *A Short History of the Baptists* (Philadelphia, 1897), 235, 236.

blage unanimously resolved "that for peace and harmony, and in order to accomplish the greatest amount of good, and for the maintenance of . . . Scriptural principles . . . it is proper that this Convention at once proceed to organize [a society] for the propagation of the Gospel." Two boards were formed—the Foreign Mission Board with headquarters at Richmond and the Home Mission Board with offices at Marion, Alabama. In harmony with the old convention, a provision was made for triennial meetings. An address sent forth by the convention insisted that the rupture involved only the foreign and domestic missions of the denomination, and pointed out that the constitution adopted was that of the original union making no break with the foundation principles. But it did say clearly that "for years the pressure of men's hands has been upon us far too heavily. Our brethren have pressed upon every inch of our privileges and our sacred rights. . . ." In parting with their brethren, the framers of the address declared that "we could weep, and have wept, for ourselves and for them; but the season, as well of weeping as of vain jangling, is . . . just now past."[30]

Richard Fuller, a leader of the Southern moderates, contended that the formation of a new convention "did not divide the Baptist Church: that could not be separated, it was independent and republican, having no general head, and only associated for a general purpose." Yet the Charleston *Mercury* in commenting on the division of the Methodists and Baptists said: "The two greatest religious sects in the United States sever a union that was thought to be secured by indissoluble ties. . . . In this contest of religion we have an entire and remediless severance of the Union— a division that henceforth creates in the two most numerous denominations of the country a Northern and a Southern religion . . . [despite] efforts that yielded only to a settled

30 Newman, *Baptist Churches*, 449-50, 452-53.

conviction that reconciliation was impossible."[31] The practical significance of the new Baptist organization meant that another of the great spiritual and ecclesiastical ties that bound the Union was severed and simultaneously another great bulwark of slavery had taken concrete form.

All Baptists seemed relieved that the separation had been completed; each side, dreading the removal of an infected portion, felt the better when the task was finished. It cannot be said that the rescinding of harmony was accomplished without bitterness, but the degree was milder than the Methodists had experienced. The ease of separation was due to the absence of any central governing agency. The autonomy of the Baptist congregations gave strength to disunity. Energy and effort that previously were aimed at abolitionists and antislavery advocates could now be directed to better purpose. There were among the Baptists few financial problems and these were arranged readily and without rancor. Even the American Baptist Publication Society, organized in 1824 for the publishing and circulating of Baptist literature, was not divided. Perhaps the Baptists had demonstrated that ties could be amicably broken. Separation may have eased the political tensions and delayed national disunion.

David Benedict was present at the first anniversary of the Southern Baptist Convention which met in Richmond in June 1846. He was deeply impressed by the fact that among 150 messengers no reference was made to the difficulties that had led to its formation. He regretted the necessity for the new institution, but thought well of the organization for several reasons. He believed that Southern Baptists would give more support to an organization under their own

---

[31] Sweet, *Religions in America*, 433; Putnam, *Baptists and Slavery*, 88. In his famous speech on slavery, March 4, 1850, John C. Calhoun pointed out that "the Episcopal Church is the only one of the four great denominations which remains unbroken and entire," Richard K. Crallé (ed.), *The Works of John C. Calhoun* (6 vols.; New York, 1855-1874), IV, 557-58.

management and control; that a great saving in money and labor would result from holding conventions in the South; that future collisions between Northern and Southern Baptists might be avoided; and that harmony would prevail among delegates representing a single geographical area.[32]

Most of the future which Benedict foresaw actually came to pass. The great increase in contributions to missions was significant. In the first thirteen years of the existence of the Southern Convention, the Baptists in the South contributed seven times as much money as they had given during the preceding thirteen years. As a result of assembling boards and conventions in the South, an intense denominational loyalty developed. The old and destructive antimissionary spirit that had long pervaded many Southern Baptist churches gave way to an aggressive missionary spirit.[33] By the time of the Civil War there was much evidence that certain gains had resulted from the early split in the churches and in the organization of a Southern convention.

If one were able to separate Baptist churches from the broad aspects of Southern society, it would be easy to conclude that slavery should not have been permitted to disrupt the Baptist denomination. Each individual church was virtually a law unto itself and bound only in the loosest manner by boards and societies. But Baptists had taken a role in Southern society similar to that of the Methodists, and this activity led to an involvement from which even Baptists could not escape. An extensive study of the social emphases of Southern Baptist journals before 1861 finds that most of the editors were ardent supporters of slavery. A few had misgivings about certain evils attached to the system, but they continued to believe that, until the Lord revealed a better way, an acceptable relation between labor and capital lay in a slaveholding society. In the border

[32] Benedict, *Fifty Years*, 217-19.
[33] Newman, *Baptist Churches*, 455.

states the support of emancipation schemes by several editors is evidence of a lack of support for slavery. But a majority was on the side of Southern slavery, and this encouraged the church leaders to withdraw from the various boards.[34]

Long before any serious divisions had occurred in the Presbyterian Church, the sentiment of American Presbyterians generally had been "decidedly anti-slavery, and the utterances of the Assembly from year to year showed that it fully responded to that sentiment." In several sections of the country the effect of the division into the Old School and the New School bodies in 1837-1838 proved to be disastrous, particularly in respect to the missionary enterprises. Continual agitation of the slavery question tended to misrepresent the actual position of the church in the North and in the South. Although some of the small and strict bodies of Presbyterians excluded slaveholders, neither the Old School nor the New School group was yet ready to adopt a positive and unrelenting position. From the General Assembly of 1818 Presbyterians as a whole had inherited "an authoritative denunciation of slavery," which demanded that steps should be taken leading to emancipation. This declaration, however, long remained unenforced—in fact, it had been defied.[35]

After 1838 two bodies of Presbyterians, almost equal in size, continued for a quarter of a century a course that deviated little from the drift or the direction of prevailing opinion in the particular section of the country. Possessing the same name and the same standards, each stood in sharp antagonism to the other. Presbyterian historians, especially Southerners, have been wont to contend that slavery was not

[34] See Roger H. Crook, "The Ethical Emphases of the Editors of Baptist Journals Published in the Southeastern Region in the United States up to 1865" (Th.D. dissertation, Southern Baptist Theological Seminary, 1947).

[35] Gillett, *Presbyterian Church*, II, 555; Thompson, *Presbyterian Churches*, 133.

the central issue which divided the two branches. Later evidence and research seem conclusive that slavery was "a determining factor" and far more important than these historians have acknowledged.[36]

Entanglement in the fabric of the expanding slave institution, desire to retain the advantages of a slavocracy, fear of the effects of emancipation, dangers from abolitionism, acceptance of the changing ecclesiastical and political philosophy of slavery—all contributed to the continuation of slavery by the Southern Presbyterian laity, which was essentially more proslavery than the ministry. Opposition to the leadership of the liberal members of the clergy can be illustrated readily by pointing out some activities which occurred during the 1840s and 1850s in the border state of Kentucky. When an advocate of emancipation heard that the Synod of Kentucky had proposed measures for the immediate emancipation of slaves or preparation for their freedom, he wrote an acquaintance that he believed the plan was doomed because many slaveholders would more readily "part with their church privileges rather than with their slaves." The slave system had gotten such a stranglehold on the people around Frankfort that they had become "Godless & Christless." Such was the opinion of the Reverend B. Mills, presumably a Presbyterian living in that vicinity. He thought that the people respected him only because he was a minister and listened to him only "as a pleasant means of killing time on a dull day." Depressed by the failure of emancipation and colonization efforts, Mills had hopes that the introduction of white labor into central Kentucky would lessen the demand for slave labor and turn it into a burden rather than a profit.[37] Other sections offered other examples,

[36] Staiger, "Abolitionism and the Presbyterian Schism," *Mississippi Valley Historical Review*, XXXVI, 391, 413-14.

[37] Robert G. Wilson to Joseph I. Irwin, Jan. 10, 1845, Philadelphia; B. Mills to AHMS, June 1, Aug. 1, 1854, Chicago.

but a pattern of similarity prevailed in the area of the Cotton Kingdom.

For several years the Old School Assembly denied demands of antislavery commissioners and laid memorials on the table. In 1845, however, the number of petitions was so large that a committee was appointed to consider them. When the report was heard and the committee's recommendations were adopted, the assembly denied all antislavery demands and, in a sense, accepted slavery as a Christian way of life. In this manner the church sought to push aside the whole issue and remain aloof from the agitation. It recognized no responsibility to remove the evils of slaveholding except to preach the duty of masters to slaves. Commissioners from several Northern presbyteries walked out of the 1845 assembly as an expression of their position. In the 1849 assembly a commissioner from an Ohio presbytery asked that slavery be declared a sin and that its presence should not be tolerated. The assembly replied that it was "inexpedient and improper for it to attempt or propose" emancipation measures. In this way the Old School managed to preserve its unity until 1861.[38]

The General Assembly of the New School sidestepped a decision concerning slaveholding about as adroitly as did the other branch of the Presbyterian Church. In 1846 the assembly in answer to numerous petitions and memorials adopted a resolution declaring slavery a wrong and urging churches to eradicate the evil, but set no machinery in movement to further this position. Three years later the assembly declared that the church had the duty "to efface this blot on our holy religion," yet the effacing did not become a matter of discipline until 1850. And then a protective hedge was added that special circumstances would be grounds for excuse. Defying the official position of the church, the Presbytery of Lexington, Kentucky, in 1853 reported to the

[38] Thompson, *Presbyterian Churches*, 135-36.

assembly that some of its ministers and members held slaves since they believed that the Bible sanctioned slavery. The assembly "disapproved and earnestly condemned" the position taken by the Lexington Presbytery and called upon it to review and alter its position, for "such doctrines and practice" could not be permanently tolerated. Five years later a group of Southern churches withdrew from the New School and formed the United Synod of the Presbyterian Church, made up of six synods, twenty-one presbyteries, and about fifteen thousand communicants. For years this slaveholding element had hindered the efforts of the New School Presbyterians. Now shortly before the Civil War peace and harmony prevailed in both Old and New School divisions.[39]

Prior to 1860 the clergy in all Southern churches had played an insignificant role in the official discussion of political questions on state and national levels. The South had produced no ecclesiastical figures similar to Lyman Beecher, William E. Channing, or Theodore Parker. As the Civil War drew near, many Southern clergymen emerged from the closet and began to express themselves on various aspects of the slavery issue. Earliest of the truly great ecclesiastical defenders of slavery was James H. Thornwell, Presbyterian theologian and educator from South Carolina. In 1850 Thornwell declared that "slavery is a part of the curse which sin has introduced into the world and stands in the same general relations to Christianity as poverty, sickness, disease, or death." Ten years later, by teaching that Christianity taught sympathy for slaves, he defended the slaveholder against the charge that slavery was immoral. Probably the best known of all pulpit statements on slavery came from the Thanksgiving Day sermon preached in 1860 by Benjamin M. Palmer, pastor of the First Presbyterian

[39] Sweet, *Religions in America*, 440-41; Gillett, *Presbyterian Church*, II, 557-58.

Church in New Orleans. There he asserted the great duty of Southerners was to serve as *the constituted guardians of the slaves themselves.*" In order to save the slave "from a doom worse than death," Palmer declared that the relationship with the slave had to be preserved, for "it is a duty which we owe, further, to *the civilized world.*" One who had heard the sermon wrote of the profound effect it had on the audience. "After the benediction, in solemn silence, no man speaking to his neighbor, the great congregation of serious and thoughtful men and women dispersed; but afterwards the drums beat and the bugles sounded, for New Orleans was shouting for secession." The effectiveness of this sermon moved a Confederate general to say that Palmer's "services were worth more to the cause than a soldiery of ten thousand men."[40]

Although the Old School General Assembly of 1860 was a harmonious body, the editor of the *Princeton Review*, generally considered a firm friend of the South, stated in the issue of January 1861 that Southern complaints were either unfounded or without cause for secession. On March 16, 1861, the *Southern Presbyterian* carried an editorial declaring that a new church in the South would be "desirable and proper." By the time the General Assembly convened in Philadelphia on May 16, nine of the Southern states had left the Union, and war had been under way for a month. Thirty-three of the sixty-four presbyteries in the South sent no commissioner to the assembly. Not a single representative was present from South Carolina, North Carolina, Georgia, Alabama, and Arkansas. Other than commissioners from border states, only sixteen people represented thirteen Southern presbyteries. Thornwell, the acknowledged leader of Southern Presbyterians, sent a message to the assembly

[40] William S. Jenkins, *Pro-Slavery Thought in the Old South* (Chapel Hill, 1935), 214-15, 240; Thomas C. Johnson, *The Life and Letters of Benjamin Morgan Palmer* (Richmond, 1906), 210-11, 220; Thompson, *Presbyterian Churches*, 156.

expressing his hope that God would restore harmony between the sections.[41]

When the General Assembly of the Old School Presbyterians began its meeting, the leaders had reason to believe that a division could be averted by preventing the body from expressing an opinion on the slavery question. But the leaders lost control of the floor action, and a majority of the commissioners forced the political issue. A sense of duty to the Union exerted pressure that paved the way for the introduction of the resolution made by Dr. Gardiner Spring, pastor of the Brick Presbyterian Church of New York City. The assembly was asked "in the spirit of that Christian patriotism" to acknowledge its obligation "to promote and perpetuate, so far as in us lies, the integrity of these United States, and to strengthen, uphold, and encourage the Federal government in the exercise of all its functions. . . ." After several days of debate the resolution was adopted by a large majority. Many of the Southern leaders considered the offensive proposal "simply a writ of ejectment of all that portion of the Church within the bounds of eleven states, which had already withdrawn from the Federal Union, and established a government of their own." John N. Waddell, a Tennessee minister and educator, addressed an open letter to Dr. Spring in which he deplored the introduction of "a set of resolutions of the most incendiary nature" in an hour which demanded "the exercise of forbearance" and the omission of "expression of any opinion, or the utterance of any voice, in one way or another, in regard to the state of the country. . . ."[42] The Spring resolution probably was not the immediate cause of the division of the church, but the resolution had the effect of forcing out Southern delegates

[41] T. Watson Street, *The Story of Southern Presbyterians* (Richmond, 1961), 55-56.

[42] Bacon, *American Christianity*, 353-54; Benjamin M. Palmer, *The Life and Letters of James Henry Thornwell* (Richmond, 1875), 501; Street, *Southern Presbyterians*, 57.

on a political issue and convincing them and other leaders that the political question had been settled for all Presbyterians by those who had seized control in the assembly. Interest in the formation of a Southern Presbyterian Church was easily aroused, and especially so, since more than three-fourths of the Southern Presbyterians belonged to the Old School.

A call was issued for delegates to attend a convention to meet in Augusta, Georgia. On December 4, 1861, the convention opened with fifty ministers and thirty-eight elders from forty-seven presbyteries representing eleven hundred churches and seventy-five thousand members. Benjamin M. Palmer was chosen moderator of the new body which adopted the name of the Presbyterian Church in the Confederate States, a name which was changed after the war to the Presbyterian Church in the United States. Under Thornwell's leadership a committee prepared "An Address to All the Churches of Jesus Christ." This paper set forth the causes which impelled the separation. It emphatically stated that "true religion will be more effectually subserved by two independent Churches, under the circumstances in which two countries are placed, than by one united body."[43] Many of the delegates believed that separation was demanded for the sake of peace and for the protection of their liberties. When the convention adjourned, another link had been broken in the religious chain that had helped to hold the country together during the trying slavery period.

Although the Cumberland Presbyterian Church originated in a slave state and had its greatest strength in the South, it did not divide when war came. Of the three ministers who had founded the first presbytery of the church only Ewing owned slaves and later he emancipated them. McAdow had opposed slavery, and so strong were his convictions that he

---

[43] Palmer, *Thornwell*, 502-509. The Spring Resolutions and the "Address to All the Churches" are found in Thompson, *Presbyterian Churches*, 379-80, 388-406.

moved from Tennessee to Illinois to be freed from the burden of seeing it daily. Undoubtedly a majority of the Cumberland Presbyterians believed slavery to be an evil and approved of emancipation.

In 1847 the Synod of Pennsylvania adopted a resolution declaring "that the system of slavery in the United States is contrary to the principles of the gospel, hinders the progress thereof, and ought to be abolished." The General Assembly, meeting in Memphis the following year, expressed regret at this resolution or "any attempt of judicatures of the church to agitate the exciting subject of slavery," since it "would gender strife, produce distraction in the church, and thereby hinder the progress of the gospel." In 1851 the General Assembly at Pittsburgh received six memorials on the subject of slavery. The committee to which these memorials were referred took a stand in line with the Old School of Presbyterians when it declared that "the church of God is a spiritual body, whose jurisdiction extends only to matters of faith and morals. She has no power to legislate upon subjects on which Christ and his apostles did not legislate, nor to establish terms of union, where they have given no express warrant." The committee expressed its belief that any legislation in regard to slavery belonged to civil authority rather than to ecclesiastical. When the General Assembly of the Cumberland Church convened in St. Louis in 1861, sixty-one of the ninety-seven presbyteries had no representatives in attendance. There were only twenty-nine delegates from Southern presbyteries and twenty-one from Northern. Here as in earlier conventions a spirit of compromise prevailed among the members from the North and the South.[44] Division did not threaten this conservative, democratic church.

Apparently only three Episcopal clergymen in the North, E. M. P. Wells, Evan M. Johnson, and John McNamara, took an active part in the struggle against slavery. Whatever

[44] McDonnold, *Cumberland Presbyterian Church,* 380, 410-11, 417.

they accomplished must undoubtedly have been offset by those men of greater influence on the opposite side of the issue. The pronouncements of two leaders will indicate the position of many churchmen who lived outside the rich farmlands of the South. During the Civil War, John H. Hopkins, Bishop of Vermont, declared that slavery was not in opposition to God's will and that slavery as it was found in the South was far more desirable than the system of the employer and the hired worker. Samuel Seabury, a Protestant Episcopal clergyman of New York, expressed his acceptance of the point of view of Southern slaveholders in a book *American Slavery . . . Justified,* which he published just before the war. He like others reasoned that slavery was acceptable because it was not forbidden by the New Testament and had been established by Divine Providence. The same sentiment had been expressed as early as 1834 by Bishop Levi S. Ives of North Carolina in a sermon which was later printed: "No man or set of men are entitled to pronounce slavery wrong; and . . . as it exists in the present day it is agreeable to the order of Divine Providence." These attitudes, he said, sprang from the sincere conviction that what is is right and that it is not the duty or privilege of man to depreciate or criticize the powers ordained of God. The action taken in 1843 by the Diocese of Louisiana seems now most typical in interpreting the attitude of the church toward slavery. The Episcopal churches, it declared, are "not political crusaders, but simple and guileless teachers" of the Gospel, and they should not "dogmatize on the civil relations or rights of individuals" but rather should be "chiefly concerned with the hearts and consciences of those to whom we go."[45]

[45] Posey, "Protestant Episcopal Church," *Journal of Southern History,* XXV (1959), 27-28. In 1856 the Pastoral Letter to the bishops at the General Convention advised that the ministry, "the constituted rulers of the Church," should have no dealings with party politics and sectional disputes. Addison, *Episcopal Church,* 192.

Bishop Samuel Wilberforce of the Anglican Church criticized the aloof unity which distinguished the American Episcopalians in the heat of controversy over the "clinging curse" of slavery. In 1844 in *A History of the Protestant Episcopal Church in America* he denounced in no uncertain terms its weak position toward slavery. The church, he said, "raises no voice against the predominant evil; she palliates it in theory; and in practice she shares in it." The cruelty of slavery should lead the church "to reprove the sins of others, not to adopt them into her own practice; to set, and not to take the tone." It was to the "greater shame" of the Episcopal Church that some small sects maintained "the witness she has failed to bear."[46]

As sectional differences became more marked by vested interests and as controversies over slavery reached white heat, the Protestant Episcopal Church by virtue of its class solidarity was in a unique position on the eve of the Civil War. The church had neither stretched itself over a large area nor gathered into its folds people of widely different taste, culture, and background. Although a church of national scope, it had great sectional strength—three-fourths of the Episcopalians in America were residents of free states in 1850. Denominations whose members were evenly distributed in slave states and free states were split by slavery; sectional churches were able to avoid division. Had the Episcopal Church permitted itself to be involved in the political storm prior to the Civil War, any attempt to adopt in the General Convention a resolution condemning slavery would have been resisted solidly by Southern bishops, other clergy, and laity and would have precipitated a division in the church. A split in the church body was too dear a price to pay for the enforcement of a different social pattern on its Southern members. When political secession was first

[46] [Samuel Wilberforce], *A History of the Protestant Episcopal Church in America* (New York, 1844), 303-305.

proposed, Bishop Otey wrote to Bishop Polk: "It is God alone that can still the madness of the people. . . . To what quarter shall we look, when such men as you and Elliott deliberately favor secession? What can we expect, other than mob-law and violence among the masses, when . . . the Ministers . . . are found on the side of those who openly avow their determination to destroy the work which our fathers established. . . ?"[47] Polk had hoped for peaceable secession; Cobbs with clearer vision saw that it was impossible, for there was no natural boundary between the peoples of divergent sentiments. The combination of conservative Southern slaveholding church members and High Churchmen in the North had won in the struggle to keep the church united.

When secession of the states became a reality, Southern leaders in the Episcopal Church, following the precedents and principles of 1789, maintained that political separation necessitated the formation of a new church. On July 3, 1861, delegates met in Montgomery to draft a constitution for the Protestant Episcopal Church in the Confederate States. Not until September 19, 1862, three days before Lincoln issued the Emancipation Proclamation, was the official announcement made of the acceptance of the constitution by the requisite number of dioceses.

Holding to "the ancient order of things," Alexander Campbell recognized the relation of master and slave as not immoral, since it had Biblical status. In company with some other church leaders Campbell insisted that the relations of slave and master were not condemned in the New Testament; therefore slaveholding should not be made a test of Christian membership. He argued "that no Christian community, governed by the Bible, Old Testament and New, can constitutionally and rightfully make the simple relation of master and slave a term of Christian fellowship or a

---

[47] Green, *Otey,* 91.

subject of discipline. . . ." His extreme reliance on Biblicism permitted him to justify slavery; his shrewd outlook encouraged him to choose a middle course and maintain the unity of his church.[48] In the absence of any pyramidal form of church government, no pronouncements, edicts, rulings, or resolutions disturbed the congregations of Disciples of Christ. There was no rule of the majority to strengthen or alter the opinion of the individual. The Methodist, Baptist, and Presbyterian churches, having been torn by schisms and permanent divisions, looked enviously at the isolated security which each Disciples congregation enjoyed. The Disciples, like the Episcopalians, relied on the basic element of Christian unity to keep them removed from sectional and temporal disruptions. If any group was justified in questioning Campbell's attitudes toward the slavery issue, it was his own followers, for Campbell had given evidence of shifting positions when he looked the institution of slavery squarely in the face.

Alexander Campbell was a highly successful businessman and a large property holder, whose sympathies were probably closer to the slaveholder than to the slave. In order to explain his position, Campbell wrote a series of eight articles in 1845 on "Our Position to American Slavery," which he published in the *Millennial Harbinger*. He defended himself very well with such statements as: "As a political economist, and as a philanthropist, I have many reasons for preferring the prospects and conditions of the Free to the Slave States; but especially as a Christian, I sympathize much more with the owners of slaves, their heirs, and successors, than with the slaves which they possess and bequeath." He insisted that he was "neither the advocate nor the apologist of American or any other kind of slavery." In answer to a letter asking his position on slavery, Campbell replied in 1851 that he deeply regretted

[48] Richardson, *Alexander Campbell*, II, 531-32.

the existence of slavery since he thought it was disastrous to all it touched. He doubted that the abolitionists were motivated by more humane or benevolent sentiments than those of other people. Then he revealed his personal leaning by saying: "There is as much humanity, benevolence and magnanimity, at the South as at the North, in proportion to the Anglo Saxon population in either."[49]

The Disciples of Christ constituted the largest Protestant body that did not divide as a result of the slavery issue or of the Civil War. The best history of the Disciples gives four major reasons for the prevalence of harmony: ethics a matter of faith not opinion; pacifistic leaders; loose ecclesiastical organization; and appeal for unity. To these must be added the heavy hand of Alexander Campbell. He had owned slaves and had freed them, but he did not condemn slaveholding. In 1860 the Disciples had 829 churches in the South and 1,241 in the North.[50] The membership of no other church was so heavily concentrated on the border where trouble was more likely to occur. Yet the Disciples, far more interested in evangelizing individuals than in reforming the social and political system, rode out the storm and profited from the wisdom of both leaders and members.

Despite the hierarchical organization of the Catholic Church, the people, according to an eminent Catholic historian, were given "complete freedom of political action." Sectional differences did not disturb church councils. The slavery question was at its height when the First Plenary Council of the Roman Catholic Church in the United States met at Baltimore in 1852. Slavery or abolition was not mentioned in the decrees or in the Pastoral Letter. In 1856

[49] *Millennial Harbinger*, 1845, 108-109, 234, 356, 1851, 529.

[50] Garrison and DeGroot, *Disciples of Christ*, 330. According to a report of the American and Foreign Anti-Slavery Society, Disciples owned 101,000 slaves in 1851. If this is correct, on a per capita basis the Disciples were the leading slaveholders in the country. Garrison and DeGroot, *Disciples of Christ*, 468.

the *Miscellany* of Charleston smugly observed: "Catholics as such are the only religious body exempt from fanaticism on the slavery question and bound by their creed to the support of the Constitution." In the Ninth Provincial Council, meeting in Baltimore in 1858, the bishops took note of slavery but said that lay Catholics "should be free on all questions of polity and social order, within the limits of the doctrine and law of Christ." In 1861 at a meeting of the Provincial Council in Cincinnati, the bishops stated that they did "not think it their province to enter into a political arena." This statement has significance, for it was made two weeks after the shots had been fired at Fort Sumter. Although the Catholic clergy had taken little part in the slavery struggle, many of the priests had openly asserted their support of the Union. But a considerably greater number had remained discreetly silent on social and moral issues. The nature of the Catholic Church and the traditional unwillingness of its hierarchy to disturb the *status quo* had assured the complete absence of any effort to create a division in the church. This apparently negative position gave the Protestants a pretext to charge the Catholic Church and its clergy with disloyalty to the Union. As was true of Episcopalians the Catholics could also be described as located midway "between a glacier of pacifism and a cauldron of patriotism."[51]

Slavery had brought division to four of the seven important denominations in the Old South. Hard feelings between individuals and difficult settlements over property encrusted the lines of schism, so that, when the immediate war situation closed, the edges of demarcation were as sharp as ever. It is significant that the two denominations, Methodist and Episcopal, which have effected a reunion are both distinguished for strong central control remote from the local

[51] Ellis, *American Catholicism*, 92; Stokes, *Church and State*, II, 188; Dunham, *Attitude of the Northern Clergy*, 15, 18.

scenes. The General Convention of the Episcopal Church
so tactfully ignored the existence of ecclesiastical secession
that it was possible for the seceding dioceses to return
agreeably to their former status at the end of the war. The
devotion of Episcopal churchmen to the catholic aspects of
their religion had outweighed whatever concern there may
have been for social and political issues. The branches of
the Methodist Episcopal Church were slow in resolving
their differences, but time eased the hurts, and, after almost
a century, the Methodist Episcopal Church and the Methodist Episcopal Church, South fused in 1939 into a peaceful
and prosperous union. The Northern and Southern branches
of the Baptist and Presbyterian churches have chosen to go
their separate ways even after their geographical nomen-
clatures have lost their importance.

14

ON THE EVE OF
THE CIVIL WAR

ANY DREAMS that ecclesiastical leaders may have had of an ideal religious community in the great area beyond the Appalachians had vanished by the 1840s, for the shadow of slavery lay on many parts of the country. As early as 1843 it had been estimated that in the Methodist Church two hundred traveling ministers and one thousand local preachers held nearly twelve thousand slaves. The small farmer, landless newcomer, and preacher who had once opposed slavery changed their views, as they eventually shared in the profits from tobacco and cotton. Clergymen, both Protestant and Catholic, generally became apologists for slavery and "formulated a strong Biblical and patriarchial defense of the South."[1] Slavery was no longer regarded by the majority of Southerners as an evil institution, but was considered with favor as able ministers built scriptural foundations for its existence.

By the 1830s most Protestant societies—missionary, Bible, tract, and other—had shifted positions on issues, reorganized, or collapsed. With these agencies stabilized, the several denominations turned their attention to matters of more immediate concern, and the result was a strengthening of denominational lines. Each denomination in the South and Southwest busily engaged in trying to sustain itself. All lacked sufficient properly trained ministers, suffered from niggardly giving, supported only a minimum of schools and seminaries, and expanded here and there as the opportunity arose. Yet these same churches enjoyed many outward evidences of success—especially in the addition of members, the erection of buildings, and in increased social and political power in the face of threatening conditions.[2]

The newly organized Methodist Episcopal Church, South, rapidly expanded throughout the southern part of the United States. In 1846 the church had 455,217 members and in 1860 the membership had risen to 749,068—about one-third being Negroes. Beyond question the Methodists had enrolled more Negroes than any other church. Numerical growth, establishment of churches and missions, and material prosperity were found from Georgia to Texas. In the latter state the Methodists established missions among the German people, published the *Texas Christian Advocate,* and formed schools in several communities. Among the Germans in New Orleans a church was dedicated costing about fifteen thousand dollars. Proudly the congregation boasted of a chandelier lighted by gas and of seats with spring cushions. Farther to the west the Indian Mission Conference, which had been organized in 1844, adhered to the Southern church and in 1846 reported thirty-two missionaries and 3,404 members. The discovery of gold in California in 1848 followed by the quick populating of the state challenged the church to establish a mission there. In February 1850 the Reverend Isaac Boring of Georgia went to California accompanied by two assistants. His work laid the foundation for the Pacific Conference, organized in 1852.[3]

[1] Buckley, *Methodists in the United States,* 406; William E. Dodd, *Expansion and Conflict* (New York, 1915), 144. Also see William E. Dodd, *The Cototn Kingdom* (New Haven, 1919), 103-109; Jenkins, *Pro-Slavery Thought,* Chap. V.

[2] For a general survey of the period see Bacon, *American Christianity,* Chaps. XVII-XIX.

[3] McTyeire, *History of Methodism,* 651, 653, 670. Lewis G. Vander Velde (*The Presbyterian Churches and the Federal Union, 1861-1869,* Cambridge, 1932, 104) reprints an estimate of slaves in the several denominations in 1861. Also see William L. Duren, *The Trail of the Circuit Rider* (New Orleans, 1936), 156-57.

Until the General Conference of 1854 only four bishops, James O. Andrew, Joshua Soule, William Capers, and Robert Paine, administered the church. In 1854 much strength was added by the election to the office of bishop of John Early of Virginia, Hubbard H. Kavanaugh of Kentucky, and George F. Pierce of Georgia. At the 1854 conference, meeting in Columbus, Georgia, plans were made for the establishment of a publishing house in Nashville, head-quarters for the Board of Missions. A report on the schools under the jurisdiction of the Methodists in the South re-vealed a total of eighty-one institutions, twenty-five of which were called colleges, although nineteen of them had no endowment. Survival of half of these colleges indicates good management and foresight despite financial straits. Al-though the endowment of the colleges totaled only $182,000, there was other evidence that the financial and social level of the church membership had risen perceptibly. William H. Milburn lived from 1848 to 1853 in the South, a region which favorably impressed him with its affluence and the social level of his church members.[4]

Methodist leaders worried, however, about uneasy de-velopments among their brethren in the border states. Both sides of the division were continually threatened with the loss of conferences and churches. Disputes over property ranged from the division of the Book Concern to the posses-sion of some small church buildings. Tensions were daily reflected in Methodist papers, North and South. All of the periodicals in the North held slavery to be a great evil and sought its destruction. The papers in the South screamed back rebuking their brethren above the border.[5]

Some of the Methodist leaders in the South began to see what was forthcoming while others failed to appraise the

[4] Duren, *Circuit Rider*, 287-88; William H. Milburn, *Ten Years of Preacher-Life* (New York, 1859), Chaps. XIX-XXI passim.
[5] Sweet, *Methodist Church and the Civil War*, 35-36; Clark, *Simpson*, 211.

situation correctly. Bishop Andrew, a peace-loving Whig of
the Webster school, believed that the Southerners did not
desire secession or that the Northerners would not force
abolition on the country. Even after the war had started,
he refused to face the facts and, writing to his son in April
1861, prayed that "God have mercy on us, and save us from
bloodshed." Bishop Paine also sought to ignore the crisis.
Among his papers no direct reference to war was recorded
between 1861 and 1865. The imperturbable attitude of
Andrew and Paine hardly satisfied the Northern Methodists
who listened to such outspoken people as Peter Cartwright.
He had charged that Southern delegates, on leaving the
conference of 1844, sounded "the tocsin of war," denounced
the Methodist Episcopal Church as "an abolition Church,"
and then uttered "a cry of self-defense." Tauntingly Cartwright warned that the Methodist abolitionists would steal
all the Negroes belonging to Southern Methodists.[6]

William G. Brownlow, "the fighting parson," who, although a strong Unionist, had ardently championed slavery
on scriptural grounds, came to believe that the Methodist
preachers as a whole had had a larger hand in secession than
any other group of people. "I bring the charge," he wrote,
"of political preaching and praying against the great body
of clergymen in the South, irrespective of sects; and I have
no hesitancy in saying, as I now do, that the worst class of
men who make tracks upon Southern soil are Methodist,
Presbyterian, Baptist, and Episcopal clergymen, and at the
head of these for mischief are the Southern Methodists.
I mean to say that there are honorable exceptions in all
these churches; but the moral mania of Secession has been
almost universally prevalent among the members of the
sacred profession." Brownlow supported his charge by citing
the example of the Reverend William A. Harrison, pastor of

6 Smith, *Andrew*, 437; R. H. Rivers, *The Life of Robert Paine* (Nashville, 1916), 146; Cartwright, *Autobiography*, 452.

the First Presbyterian Church in Knoxville, "who boasted in his pulpit that Jesus Christ was a *Southerner*, born on Southern soil, and so were His apostles, except Judas, whom he denominated a *Northern* man!" Harrison declared that "he would sooner have a Bible printed and bound in hell, than one printed and bound north of Mason & Dixon's line!"[7]

The period between the division of the church and the clash of arms witnessed little healing of the wound or lessening of the tension. In January 1860 the editor of the Richmond *Christian Advocate* predicted that the dissolution of the Union was inevitable. Alfred Brunson charged that "no well-informed person doubts that if those Southern Methodist preachers had not fomented the rebellion, it would not have occurred. The statesmen who led it could not have carried the mass of people with them, if those preachers had been against them, nor if they had been neutral."[8] Beyond question this Northern Methodist revivalist ventured too far in placing the full burden of starting the Civil War on the Southern Methodist ministers. By no stretch of imagination did they have that much influence or power.

Shortly after the Southern Baptist Convention was organized in 1845, some leaders of Baptist churches in the South took a realistic view of the field for their endeavors. Too much time had been spent in sectional bickerings. Vast areas had been neglected while the churches had been involved with the slavery issues. A revealing article in the *South-Western Baptist Chronicle*, published in New Orleans, on July 3, 1847, reflected the barren condition of the church in the South and Southwest. Describing the paucity of preachers and the untouched areas, the writer covered the

[7] William G. Brownlow, *Sketches of the Rise, Progress, and Decline of Secession* (Philadelphia, 1862), 143, 189-90.

[8] Swaney, *Methodism and Slavery*, 291-92; Brunson, *Western Pioneer*, I, 395. See Clement Eaton, *The Mind of the Old South* (Baton Rouge, 1964), Chap. VIII.

whole gloomy scene. In Alabama a colporteur had found
mature people who had never heard a sermon. In Mississippi a missionary had gone into a region 150 miles square
where he found one Baptist preacher. In Arkansas there
was not more than one intelligent minister for each sixty
square miles, and nine-tenths of the people rarely saw a
preacher. From Texas reports told of the labors of one
Baptist preacher ministering to the people between the
Brazos and Colorado rivers—a region 150 miles long and 40
miles wide.

When the newly organized Southern Baptist Convention
began to function smoothly, the Baptist picture gradually
changed for the better. In 1849 James M. Russell, a minister
from Alabama, reported the highly improved religious situation in his state. Previously while proclaiming the promise
of salvation to small congregations, he had been inter-
rupted by "the sportsman's horn, and hounds, and sharp
report of his rifle." It was his opinion that before the change
the congregation had been "more pleased with these sounds
than the sound of the gospel." In 1850 the editors of the
Tennessee Baptist, in a letter to James Whitaker of North
Carolina, boasted that "the baptists are now triumphing
most gloriously in most of the counties in the state." The
writer waxed so enthusiastic about Baptist prospects that he
prophesied "the baptists are soon destined to make a clean
sweep of the state. Whole platoons are coming over from
the sects & joining the church of Jesus Christ." In 1858 the
Reverend Thomas C. Teasdale estimated that the members
of the Baptist church in Columbus, Mississippi, possessed
wealth amounting to about two million dollars. Readily he
accepted from this church a call which promised a generous
salary of three thousand dollars, a "commodious parsonage,"
and everything "to render the situation pleasant and promising in the highest degree."[9]

[9] *Southern Baptist Missionary Journal* (Richmond), Oct. 1849, 139;

Such flourishing conditions did not prevail in Louisiana. In 1854 the Baptists in New Orleans were without a house of worship and gladly used as a meetingplace the hall of a railroad station. This situation was a matter of great embarrassment and concern to Baptist leaders. A Reverend Dawson, a Baptist preacher from Georgia, had gone to New Orleans in the winter of 1853 to assist in the raising of funds for a church building. Discouraged by the miserable failure of the Baptists to gain a foothold in a city of several churches and large congregations, he wrote his wife that the Baptists "are either going to other churches, or relapsing into a worse feeling. . . . The old church is not in a very good condition, and having no house of worship, must grow worse until defunct." A correspondent from New Orleans to the *Western Recorder,* published in Louisville on May 21, 1856, pointed out the great disparity between the Baptists and others. He enumerated the success of other denominations: the Presbyterians were erecting a building on Lafayette Square that eventually would cost a hundred thousand dollars; the Episcopalians had a good house; the Methodists had a meetinghouse on Carondelet Street that would seat one thousand and two other churches with a seating capacity of six or seven hundred each. He was aware that the Baptist cause languished in the entire state of Louisiana. After a survey made in 1860 Baptist fortune seemed no better, and a plea was issued for help from Baptists everywhere. "They must send the well armed missionary, over our pine hills, broad prairies, up and down our rich bayous, rivers, lakes, seacoasts, and in our villages and cities, with the light of the glorious gospel of Jesus Christ."[10]

Probably the greatest need was an adequate supply of

---

editors to Whitaker, July 17, 1850, Duke; Thomas C. Teasdale, *Reminiscences and Incidents of a Long Life* (St. Louis, 1887), 181.

[10] *Western Recorder* (Louisville), April 26, 1854; Mrs. A. P. Hill, *The Life and Services of Rev. John E. Dawson* (Atlanta, 1872), 80; Christian, *Baptists of Louisiana,* 113.

educated ministers. The old method of relying on expedients and makeshifts had failed. In July 1855 in "A Plea for Theological Education" a correspondent from Talladega, Alabama, to the *Christian Repository* stated that he had utmost confidence in the tenets of the Baptist churches, but he was "not willing to stake the maintenance of success of them upon an unlettered ministry." Similar sentiments were expressed by Robert J. Breckinridge, professor of Exegetic, Didactic and Polemic Theology in the Presbyterian seminary at Danville, Kentucky, who complained that Baptist ministers were illiterate and unfriendly to education. Bristling under such criticism, one who held an opposite view replied that in thirty-three years these "illiterate Baptists" had founded twenty-four colleges, ten theological seminaries, and employed as many educated ministers, regularly graduated, as any Protestant denomination in America.[11]

Although Baptist efforts did not thrive in some areas, the Southern Baptist Convention enjoyed a remarkably rapid rise in the membership of its churches. In its first year there were 350,000 Southern Baptists of whom 125,000 were Negroes. The convention had increased by 1860 to 640,000 of whom 225,000 were Negroes—an increase much greater in percentage than that of the population in the same period. Among the predominantly rural people of the South the Baptists were more numerous than any other denomination. Formerly attracting a large percentage from the low economic bracket of society, the church now drew heavily from the middle class and had a sizable sprinkling of planters. Another indication of newly found strength arising from the reorganization was the increased interest in missions. By 1861 the Home Mission Board was able to send out 750 missionaries, to build 200 churches, and to spend nearly $300,000. Missionaries had been sent to China and Japan,

11 *Christian Repository*, VI (1857), 67.

and preliminary plans had been made to establish missions in Central and South America.[12]

Unfortunately many of the efforts of the Baptists were dissipated in sectional strife and a rush to war. "In the whirlwind of the rage, people were ready to sacrifice their fortunes, their sons, and themselves, and submit to anything that might be demanded, if only the enemy could be destroyed." Here and there in the South a few Baptist preachers refused to follow the Southern banner. The case of James M. Pendleton is worthy of notice. Born in Virginia in 1811, he was moved to Kentucky at the age of one. Considerably better educated than the average Baptist minister, he accepted the call to the Bowling Green, Kentucky, church, which he served for twenty years. During this period he strongly supported Henry Clay's emancipation ideas, especially through the medium of numerous articles for newspapers. In 1857 he became professor of Theology in Union University in Murfreesboro, Tennessee. Convinced of the sinfulness of slavery and imbued with a deep and abiding faith in the Union, Pendleton was unsympathetic with the Confederacy and heartily wished to see its destruction. Despite grave danger and fear of personal violence, he managed to remain in Murfreesboro until August 1862.[13]

Probably the position taken by the Alabama Baptist State Convention represented the prevailing attitude of most of the conventions of the South. In its 1860 meeting this assembly declared that "the union of the states in this Confederacy has failed in important particulars to answer for the purpose for which it was created." With "no particular mode of relief" the body felt constrained to declare itself "subject to the call of proper authority in defense of the sovereignty

[12] Masters, *Baptist Missions*, 134; Newman, *Baptist Churches*, 455; T. B. Ray and others, *Southern Baptist Foreign Missions* (Nashville, 1910), passim.

[13] Riley, *Memorial History*, 146; J. M. Pendleton, *Reminiscences of a Long Life* (Louisville, 1891), passim, esp. 121-31.

and independence of the state of Alabama, and of her sacred right as a sovereignty to withdraw from this union. . . ."[14] Some people believed that this particular pronouncement, more than any other event, led Alabama into secession. Elsewhere in the South this position was repeated in other conventions. There is no denying the importance of the Baptists in sustaining the movement for secession or of supporting the Confederacy once the war had begun.

With the possible exception of the time spent on doctrinal quarrels, the Presbyterian Church seems to have functioned with few problems and little disturbance. This resulted in part from the nature of the Presbyterian organization and in part from the earlier division among the Presbyterians into the Old and New School groups. Furthermore, the Presbyterians were not aggressive about increasing their membership and therefore became a conservative church body whose problems were not numerous and generally not acute. The Old School, the dominant Presbyterian group in the South, had studiously avoided meddling with the slavery subject until the years immediately before the war.

Throughout the denomination for several years there had been a satisfactory increase of members, church buildings, financial contributions, and interest in education. The Southern Presbyterian ministers usually received the very best training supplied by any Protestant denomination with the possible exception of the Episcopal. Between 1820 and 1860 one-third to one-half of all the students at Princeton College were from the South.[15] Many of these eventually became Presbyterian ministers in their native sections.

But all was not well everywhere. For example, troubles arose in Kentucky from the failure to get the right minister for a specific congregation. The American Board missionaries, usually Presbyterian or Congregational clergymen,

[14] Riley, *Baptists of Alabama*, 279-80.
[15] Bodo, *Protestant Clergy*, 15.

were often antislavery in sentiment, and the Kentucky people generally considered them unacceptable. In various sections of the South, as in Tennessee in 1847, strong prejudices arose against Presbyterian doctrine and thwarted numerous attempts to organize Presbyterian churches.[16] To win the section, the doctrine would have to be subordinated, and untrained or partially educated ministers would have to be used. Conservative Calvinistic Presbyterians were not ready to accept those innovations or to make those concessions. The Cumberland Presbyterian schism had proved the parent church was far more willing to permit a segment to separate than to yield on basic beliefs.

Beyond question the Presbyterians furnished the South with great religious leaders out of all proportion to the membership of larger denominations. In New Orleans Benjamin M. Palmer became the intellectual spokesman of those who believed slavery was a product of "the imperfect state of human society" in which "it pleases God to allow evils which check evils that are greater." Probably Palmer's biographer was partially justified in the great praise that he lavished when he wrote that Palmer was "endowed with a force and splendor and enthusiasm like Homer's, a fiery and convincing logic, like Paul's . . . [and] an eloquence like Edmund Burke's. Habitually an honest and comprehensive student . . . on great occasions he was in possession of the resources and the mettle to respond to the unusual pressure."[17] Palmer, Thornwell, James Smylie of Mississippi, Stuart Robinson of Kentucky, and similar Presbyterian ecclesiastics more than held their ground against many of the charges of abolitionists and opponents of slavery.

[16] Antislavery sentiment is evident in numerous letters in the files of the AHMS, Chicago. A typical letter was written at Cynthiana, Kentucky, April 8, 1850, by Benjamin Mills who promised to use "the influence of the gospel and the tactics of politicians" against slavery. For opposition to doctrine see letter of George H. Blair, Spring Hill, Tenn., March 1, 1847, to AHMS.

[17] Jenkins, Pro-Slavery Thought, 216; Johnson, Palmer, 247.

Characterized by its position on slavery, the Southern branch of the Presbyterian Church took positive form. In a resounding declaration in regard to the war the convention at Augusta, which organized the new church, urged its constituents to "put your treasures in the lap of your Country; throw your stout arms about her . . . if need be let your blood flow like water. . . ." On December 7 the assembly spent half an hour in prayer for the cause of the Confederate States, and then adjourned convinced that God was on the Southern side. Four years later, in the spring of 1865 when the South was faced with immediate defeat, Harmony Presbytery was still "fondly anticipating and expecting the day when God will put down our haughty and wicked foes."[18]

The Cumberland Presbyterian Church had no minister who approximated Thornwell or Palmer. But J. A. Cornwall, one of its clergy, had led a colony to Oregon in 1846, and five years later was active in the formation of the Oregon Presbytery. In 1853 this frontier body organized a short-lived college in Eugene City. John E. Braly, another Cumberland minister, went from Oregon to California, and, on July 4, 1849, preached what may have been the first Protestant sermon in the future state. The young church had experienced phenomenal growth by 1861 when it had ninety-seven presbyteries, sixty-nine of which were in slave states. Efforts were made to induce them to return to the parent church, but steering a neutral course, they wisely declined any connection.[19]

The churches of the Disciples of Christ had the most successful church organization developed on American soil. Without anything that resembled a national organization

---

[18] Street, *Southern Presbyterians*, 59, 67. In "The State of the Country," a defense of the secession of the Southern states, printed in the *Southern Presbyterian Review*, Jan. 1861, Thornwell declared that "the Constitution, in its relation to slavery, has been virtually repealed. . . ." Palmer, *Thornwell*, 595.

[19] See McDonnold, *Cumberland Presbyterian Church*, Chap. XXXIII.

until 1849, the Disciples made great strides before 1860. Quickly they became unified in purpose and organized into state and national conventions. During Campbell's long leadership hardly any important voice was raised against his dictation and his direction. Opposition by leaders and spokesmen of other churches was, however, often hostile, bitter, and even cruel. Campbell was the worthy adversary of any of these foes. If he ever suffered a signal defeat, neither he nor his colleagues admitted the loss. In these controversial years he wrote and spoke against a paid clergy, Bible and missionary societies, and theological schools. Time softened the intensity of his distaste and even found him taking the lead in promoting some of the very projects that he had once opposed. As these years progressed, he became one of the best known ecclesiastical figures in America. While on numerous trips through the South and West, Campbell was showered with commendation and congratulations instead of denunciation from churches that once opposed him and his sect. He was even praised as a logician and as a profound thinker. When he came to Nashville in 1854, he was invited to speak in the leading Methodist church, where among his auditors was the well known Methodist Bishop Soule. One who heard Campbell's address that same evening commented that his discourse showed "clearly the genius and talents of the speaker."[20]

In the midst of the overall expansion and success of the Disciples, Campbell was vexed with problems as were the leaders of other churches. For example, he was deeply disturbed by the activity and defection of James Ferguson, a "courteous, eloquent, fascinating" Disciples minister at Nashville. Fired by Ferguson's leadership, the Disciples had erected in 1847 a spacious church costing thirty thousand dollars. The building had not been conceived with austerity.

[20] *Millennial Harbinger*, 1855, 44, 1856, 536-37; Archibald McLean, *Alexander Campbell as a Preacher* (New York, 1908), 10-11, 20-25; O. P. Fitzgerald, *John B. McFerrin* (Nashville, 1888), 250-51.

The spire towered 150 feet, and the interior was ornamented by a brass chandelier burning gas which lighted the splendid auditorium with its white walnut pews and crimson cushions. A deeply spiritual person, Ferguson developed a mystical disposition which led him into spiritualism and, according to some of his opponents, into universalism. When twenty-five members of the church withdrew from Ferguson to form a new congregation, the parent church appeared for a time on the verge of expiring, but it was saved by recalling a former pastor. A church composed largely of accessions from other churches always stood in danger of defections for one cause or another.[21]

Campbell in the mellow years became a leader very different from what he once had been as the young editor of the *Christian Baptist* and the belligerent champion of the combined Disciples-Christian movement of the 1830s. More than any other significant ecclesiastical figure in the entire Mississippi Valley he had exhibited a firm and undeviating opposition to war with all its horrors. In 1861 Campbell uttered some of his strongest objections: "Of all the monstrosities on which our sun has ever shown, that of professedly *Christian* nations, glutting their wrath and vengeance on one another, with all the instruments of murder and slaughter, caps the climax of human folly and gratuitous wickedness." Extremely conservative in many areas, "in the matter of war he adhered to the characteristic radical sect position even to the end."[22] Although some of his colleagues had misgivings about the wisdom of Campbell's position, his beloved church weathered the storm and did

[21] *Millennial Harbinger,* 1855, 96-97, 104; James A. Cox, "Incidents in the Life of Philip Slater Fall" (B.D. thesis, College of the Bible, Lexington, 1951), 93 ff. Fall succeeded Ferguson. When Nashville was captured by the Union armies, Fall was the only minister in the city permitted to continue his duties.

[22] *Millennial Harbinger,* 1861, 348; Lunger, *Alexander Campbell,* 262. Not only was the editorial policy of the *Millennial Harbinger* pacifistic but so were most of the correspondents.

not divide. Geography had helped a great deal, for the Disciples were strongest in the border states where enthusiasm for war was generally at the lowest point.

A story is often cited in Disciples literature that a sermon supposedly prevented Kentucky's secession from the Union. At Frankfort a week before the legislature voted on secession, W. T. Moore preached a sermon filled with a plea for loyalty to the Union. Four of the five undecided members of the legislature belonged to Moore's church, and their votes were cast in opposition to Kentucky's secession. Evidence clearly indicates that the position on slavery taken by Campbell and other church leaders like Benjamin Franklin, at that time editor of the *American Christian Review*, led the Disciples of Christ to contribute more pacifists, proportionate to membership, than any other Southern denomination. But when the war came, soldiers from this new church of some 200,000 members were found in the ranks of both armies.

By the middle of the nineteenth century the Protestant Episcopal Church, when compared with other Protestant denominations had made little progress. Less than 5 percent of the total membership of the Protestant Episcopal Church in the United States lived in the Tidewater section and a smaller percentage in the backcountry of the Southern states. Yet nationally it ranked third in the value of church property —positive evidence of the social and economic status of its members.[23] Appealing to the upper middle class, the church had financial resources and social prestige considerably beyond that which its membership would indicate. When judged by education, devotion, sincerity, refinement, and courage, the bishops who served the church in the Lower Mississippi Valley had no superiors among the ecclesiastical leaders in other churches.

In many areas the 1850s were considered to be a church-

[23] Addison, *Episcopal Church*, 138-39.

building era among the Episcopalians. Small, neat chapels were new sights in Alabama where the liturgical church was growing. Although the Diocese of Mississippi had been formed in 1826, its growth was exceedingly slow. When William M. Green became its bishop in 1850, the diocese had less than five hundred communicants in ten regularly organized parishes with suitable houses for worship. In 1851 William T. Leacock began a half century of consecrated service to Christ Church in New Orleans. Ten years later the state of Louisiana had thirty-two Episcopal clergymen in forty parishes, presided over by Bishop Polk who as a lieutenant general would die on a battle field of the Civil War. Bishop Otey in Tennessee was impressed by the progress in his state. By 1852 he was able to report sixteen parishes, twenty clergymen, and several mission stations. On the other hand, Bishop Smith seemed depressed over the state of the church in Kentucky. In 1858 he looked at the statistics and sighed over the fact that only two young men had entered the Episcopal ministry in Kentucky in a quarter of a century. No wonder he felt that "hope has well nigh expired." He described the situation by asking a question: "What have we to offer, but harder work, more discouraging prospects and poorer pay than elsewhere?" Expansion was slow in Texas in the twenty-year period between the first Episcopal efforts made there and the arrival of Bishop Alexander Gregg in 1859. At a convention held in 1860 a report stated that in Texas there were fourteen clergymen and 456 communicants. A token of mission work touched Missouri, but it thrived only in St. Louis, where Christ Church was the first Episcopal church organized west of the Mississippi River. This congregation had begun a building that was scheduled to cost $175,000. By 1860 St. Louis had seven Episcopal churches and more than a thousand communicants.[24]

[24] Whitaker, *Church in Alabama*, 70-79; Burger, "William Mercer Green,"

Since so many disappointments beset Southern bishops, it is difficult to understand their staying power. Salaries were very low and were difficult to raise. Prior to 1853 Bishop Polk had had a private income that permitted him to serve the church without salary for thirteen years. When he lost his plantation, he found it necessary to accept a New Orleans pastorate in addition to his bishopric. Bishop Cobbs in Alabama complained about the narrow and somewhat uninteresting life that he led. "It is to be observed," he wrote, "that for obvious reasons the entire literary product of southern churchmen . . . was homiletic and apologetic, that is, purely practical. There existed no incentive to theological reflection, no opportunity for profound historical and critical research." The Oxford Movement had made little impression on Episcopalians in the United States until the 1840s, when it began to pour a stream of Anglo-Catholicism into the churches. Many of the converts to the Episcopal Church had come from narrow Protestant backgrounds. When these people came under the influence of the Oxford Movement, they were swept away by the totalitarian concepts of Roman Catholicism. Between 1825 and 1855 about thirty clergymen withdrew from the Episcopal connection and joined the Roman Catholic Church. In comparison with the remainder of the country the Episcopalians in the South furnished more than their share of defecting ministers. Some of the Southern bishops like Cobbs were angered by the use of Romanish symbols which threatened to lead to trouble in the church.[25]

For a time the reaction to the slavery issue came in the

Historical Magazine, XIX, 344; Carter and Carter, Episcopal Church in Louisiana, Chaps. VIII, IX; Green, Otey, 56; Journal of the Thirtieth Annual Convention (Frankfort, 1858), 35; Arthur H. Noll, Alexander Gregg, First Bishop of Texas (Sewanee, 1912), 64-66; Journal of the Twentieth Annual Convention (St. Louis, 1860), 17.

[25] Whitaker, Church in Alabama, 84-104; Parks, Polk, Chap. VI; William M. Polk, Leonidas Polk, Bishop and General (2 vols.; New York, 1913), I, 209; White, Cobbs, 120, 131-34; Addison, Episcopal Church, 161.

form of a firm stand against disunion. In the immediate prewar years Bishops Cobbs, Meade, and Otey were concerned about the fate of the country and had no desire to see it divided. William L. Yancey, "the Fire-Eater" from Alabama, swore at the "Union-loving fogies" of which Cobbs was one of the strongest among the Episcopal hierarchy. Cobbs died on January 11, 1861, a few minutes before the announcement of the ordinance of secession of Alabama. Bishops Polk, Elliott, Freeman, and Thomas S. Davis of South Carolina had supported the South in the early threats against its social concepts.[26]

True to its traditional policy of non-interference in church and state relations, the Episcopal Church contributed few elements to encourage division or to hinder reunion of itself. Its General Convention so tactfully ignored the existence of ecclesiastical secession that it was possible for the seceding dioceses to return agreeably to their former status at the end of the war. The devotion of Episcopal churchmen to the catholic aspects of their religion had outweighed whatever concern they may have had for social and political issues which had disturbed and divided other churches.

In numerical strength in the United States the Catholics had passed the Congregationalists in 1850 and ranked behind the Methodists, Baptists, and Presbyterians. Between 1850 and 1860 the gain in membership was more rapid in the Catholic Church than in any other religious body except the Disciples of Christ. Catholic membership in the South was approximately 100,000, with Louisiana accounting for three-fifths of the total. This growth, mainly arising from immigration, had created a church of foreigners whose "membership was so largely illiterate and so new to the country that prior to the Civil War its chief function was to serve as an occasional scapegoat for Protestant discontent.

[26] See George W. Freeman, *The Rights and Duties of Slave-Holders* (Charleston, 1837), passim; White, *Cobbs*, 139, 173.

. . ." As late as the Plenary Council of 1852 only nine of the thirty-two bishops present were native Americans. Nine years later of the eleven bishops serving the South none had been born in the region.[27] As pointed out earlier, the area of Catholic activity in the United States was limited to relatively few sections.

The 1850s were unfortunately disturbed by the Know-Nothing movement, especially directed against foreigners and Catholics and resulting in such deplorable events as a disturbance of religious services at Nashville, the bloody election in Louisville, an attack on a medical school in St. Louis, and assaults on convents in Galveston and Charleston. Prejudices against Catholics were part of the long past and did not temporarily abate except in unusual periods such as the Civil War.[28]

Catholics failed definitely in the role of producing leaders. According to John Tracy Ellis, "the weakest aspect of the Church in this country lies in its failure to produce national leaders and to exercise commanding influence in intellectual circles. . . ." Written for the more recent period, this criticism would be equally true of the pre-Civil War times. Still another vital defect lay in the failure of the church to contribute to the formation of the general culture. According to a Protestant student of the religious background of America, Roman Catholic art, literature, and music have not "until quite recently been even very distinctly recognizable as the important contribution they might have been to the enrichment of the early life of the United States."[29]

The Catholic Church in the North had stood firm and had

[27] Bates, American Faith, 321; Ellis, American Catholicism, 89; Olmstead, Religion in the United States, 328; Benjamin J. Blied, Catholics and the Civil War (Milwaukee, 1945), 53.

[28] See Ray A. Billington, The Protestant Crusade, 1800-1860 (New York, 1938); Agnes Geraldine McGann, Nativism in Kentucky to 1860 (Washington, 1944); Gohmann, Nativism in Tennessee; W. Darrell Overdyke, The Know-Nothing Party in the South (Baton Rouge, 1950).

[29] Putz, Catholic Church, U.S.A., 317-18; Hall, Religious Background, 257.

never lent any strength to the excitement over the slavery issue. An article "The Union and Catholicity," in the *Catholic Telegraph,* published in Cincinnati, on December 1, 1860, insisted that the church, "so far from being a source of danger to our republican government, is one of its strongest safe-guards." The writer of the article accused all Southern churches, except the Episcopal, of refusing to check the dissension, a policy which tended "to broaden its sphere, and heighten its intensity." When the war came, the Catholic leaders, laity and clergy, adopted the same general policy of the Protestants. Practically all of the Catholic religious papers of the South supported the Confederacy while a small majority in the North supported the Union. Had he been alive in 1861 Bishop England of Charleston undoubtedly would have upheld the Southern cause. His successor, Bishop Patrick Lynch, sympathized with the South although neither he nor England upheld slavery. It must be restated that the Catholic Church had never condemned slavery nor approved abolitionism. Father Napoleon Perche, editor of *Le Propagateur Catholique* in New Orleans, was such an ardent secessionist and so assertive that after the federal occupation of New Orleans his paper was forced to suspend publication and he was placed under arrest. The one notable exception to Southern loyalty was James Whelan, Bishop of Nashville, who expressed sympathy for the Union, fraternized with Northern military officers, resigned his office, and entered a Dominican priory in Ohio.[30]

The war had a very salutary effect on Protestant-Catholic relations. The necessities of war assumed precedence over interdenominational squabbles. Old animosities and hatreds gave ground to a concerted effort to halt a more pressing enemy on the borders of the Southern Confederacy.

[30] Maynard, *American Catholicism,* 343; Ellis, *American Catholicism,* 93-95.

15

THE BALANCE SHEET

WHEN PRIESTS LANDED with the De Soto expedition in Florida in 1539, Catholicism entered the South. More than a half-century later Protestantism made its entry with the arrival of an Anglican minister at Jamestown. In the long stretch of time from these two important events to the opening of the Civil War, seven denominations dominated the religious life in the expanse of land from the Appalachian Mountains to Missouri, Arkansas, and Texas and from the Ohio River to the Gulf of Mexico.

Most of the migrants who came from Europe to the Atlantic coastal colonies and from there to the interior of North America were people in search of an improved way of life for themselves and their families. In the course of this transplanting men rarely relied on religious philosophy in their search for fertile land, good water, and freedom from restriction or oppression. All their energies were directed toward a material betterment. Time was the important element, and it seemed all too brief for the strong and the determined.

The American Revolution brought patriots together in a common unity against the tyranny of the mother country. Being bound together in the colonial cause, Protestants and Catholics ceased bickering, merged their energies, and enjoyed agreeable relationships, the like of which would not be duplicated for another century. By the close of the Revolution all the major denominations then planted in the colonies had achieved distinctive organizations which the years would alter but little.

A significant feature of the post-colonial period in the history of the United States was the rapid movement of people beyond the colonial boundaries and across the mountains. Here and there a preacher accompanied a group, or he joined them after a settlement had been made. After the arrival of the preacher, a church was raised without much delay and some semblance of religious activity was begun. Europe, especially the Catholic portion, regarded America as a mission field and aided it materially with men and money. Eventually the eastern portion of the United States considered the West in the same light and sent a sprinkling of missionaries and a modicum of money. After a brief lapse of time the frontiersman took stock of the situation and saw valid reasons for welcoming the preacher and the church. Life was hard, monotony threatened sanity, danger lurked at every turn, and death took an early toll. Men had need for more than material gains.

Great distances, a widely scattered population, and poor transportation created problems for the preachers as they planned for some religious activity. A solution lay in a system of worship that could gather a large number of people at a selected place. Picking up an earlier development in Virginia, the preachers introduced the camp meeting to the Western regions near the end of the eighteenth century and there used it successfully for many years. Although the Presbyterians had first used the camp meeting, it easily became the special agency of the Methodists for converting, temporarily or permanently, thousands of frontier folk. To a degree the Baptists refrained from participation in a joint meeting, but, on seeing its potentialities, they adopted a quite similar system. The Episcopalians had no association with the revivalists, and the Catholics, scandalized by the emotional excesses that were generated, made no use of the method. The excesses that some preachers permitted or tolerated as religious experiences gave foundation to the rumors that some camp meetings had descended to the level of religious orgies. Whatever the final appraisal of the camp meeting may be, one fact is generally accepted —religious enthusiasm which emphasizes the heart instead of the head creates anti-intellectualism.

All the denominations eventually came to see the need for a clergy that was educated, to some degree at least. The Episcopal, Catholic, and Presbyterian churches, having a long history of an educated ministry, resisted the demands for a lowering of standards. The Methodists, forgetting the college groups in which the Methodist societies had originated, considered an untrained clergy adequate for frontier needs. The Baptists, as if in defiance of the Anglicans in Virginia, chose to use uneducated preachers. Both Methodists and Baptists changed their attitude toward education when sectarian competition put their self-made preachers in poor positions. Public demand for improved education exerted strong pressure on the emerging Cumberland Presbyterians and Disciples so that they were able to avoid some of the early errors of the Methodists and Baptists.

Before public education became the responsibility of federal or state government, the churches provided some type of primary or elementary school for the children of the congregation and of the community. The extensions of these efforts into the field of secondary schools were frequent failures. All churches used in some form the manual labor type of school and profited not at all by the mistakes of early ventures. Most of the so-called colleges were little more than academies. Their existence depended on the personality of a single individual whose removal, resignation, or death brought an end to his particular school. None was administered on a long range program. Usually conceived in a spurt of inspiration and planned in haste, these schools struggled for financial stability, and the administrators or trustees willingly moved them if a more attractive site and monetary inducements were offered. The frequency with which schools were moved and names were changed indicates no awareness of the efficiency lag and the loss of identity. When in the hands of educated ministers like the Presbyterians and Catholics, some schools offered fair educational opportunities. The Sunday school, in terms of effort and cost, was perhaps the most successful educational endeavor attempted by the several churches.

All denominations took some interest in Christianizing the American Indians, but the actual missionary efforts were slight and were ineffectual largely because they sought to mold the Indians after the fashion of white men. Specific attempts to aid the Indians were counteracted by deeds of some whites whose insatiable greed for land knew no bounds. Against a concerted effort to drive the Indians out of the fertile territory, the churches offered little resistance. Perhaps they should have directed their efforts toward bringing religion to the rapacious whites instead of the Indians, who had found no reason to ravish the land.

In missionary efforts to the Indians language was an important barrier to communication, but, even if communication had been better, the problem of introducing a new religion to the Indians would never have been easy. To the Indians their own rites were very satisfactory; a meaningful pantheism provided them with spiritual direction. A small scale effort by the Moravians in North Georgia probably had a more rewarding result than that of any other denomination. Although some missionaries followed the Indians in the forced move across the Mississippi River, their financial support rarely came from people in the region from which the Indians had been driven. A great deal of the money for the mission work came from the interdenominational American Board of Commissioners for Foreign Missions and from the federal government.

While yet saturated with the spirit of liberty, men expressed some sentiment against human bondage. The condition of the Negro in slavery was distressing. People with strong antislavery attitudes spoke out sufficiently to cause the churches to take an official position against slavery. Some regulations against the buying and selling of slaves were intermittently made by church organizations, but these usually lacked any means of enforcement. When the extension of cotton culture and the demand for cheap labor fastened the institution of slavery firmly on the economic life of the South, the churches made compromises with previous legislation and increased their efforts to evangelize the Negro. By offering the slave a religion with a covenant of a better life in the future, the churches sought to make his condition bearable. The eradication of slavery was not considered by churchmen as their responsibility. Since the Baptists and Methodists allowed emotionalism to be lavishly displayed at their services, they captured the bulk of the Negro membership. Many planters, not genuinely concerned with the experiences of a religious life, quickly perceived the disciplinary force that the churches could exert on their Negro members.

Mountains, streams, and plains invited the Western man to stretch himself beyond old confines. The churches were frequently plagued by the inquisitive members who, turning against the old, were eager to try the new. There was always a group willing to follow a new leader in a new direction. As a result, splinters from denominations could easily and quickly be formed into new sects—two of which became the Cumberland Presbyterian Church and the Disciples of Christ. Of all the new sects that arose in the area only these two achieved permanency. In the main these groups were led by defectors whose background was Presbyterian or Baptist. There were few lasting dissensions in the autocratically governed Catholic, Methodist, and Episcopal churches. Power in the hands of a few wise administrators often proved highly effective. One group of Baptists, for example, turned completely away from its missionary origin. This change probably resulted from too much democracy in the Baptist system of government.

After the 1830s there was no significant defecting group in Protestant ranks. The Disciples of Christ had been accepted by other churches, and this sect was in the process of becoming a denomination. Harangues among Protestant churches had largely ceased in exchange for a concerted campaign against the Catholics. Hordes of Irish immigrants had come to the United States, and their pressure on the country's economy aggravated Catholic-Protestant relations. The presence of a large group of Irish priests also cast an unpleasant light on Catholics in America. Protestant opposition flourished on historic and economic sources rather than on personal differences. Church members seldom assumed the leading role in the skirmishes. This was left to the clergy who enjoyed the mental exercise of debating. In fact, the people often ignored their differences since necessity demanded that they support the various community agencies. Frequently the Catholics had the only school, and to this the Protestants gratefully sent their children. There were some Protestants, however, who were fearful of the influence of Catholic teachers. And there were Catholics who under similar circumstances would have had an equal uneasiness of Protestant schools.

Each of the several churches had definite advantages and disadvantages in presenting its doctrine and its form of government to prospective members. As a rule, the early Westerner did not like the looks of much that was Episcopal or Catholic. Since his own dress was plain or even shabby, he preferred a preacher dressed "not too fancy" so the saying went. He likewise wanted a preacher who used the same idioms as his own, that is a man "not too educated." Many people preferred the freedom in backsliding which the

Methodists allowed rather than the relentless Calvinism of the Presbyterians. Since most early settlers lived in cramped, crude cabins, they had little desire to contribute hard earned and scarce money for expensive church buildings. Naturally a religion that cost the membership nothing or very little had an attraction. As economic conditions improved, the brush arbor and the log church were replaced by a better sanctuary. The uneducated preacher, relying on his quick wit and sharp tongue, no longer satisfied a people who were building schools and educating children. When the new day arrived, a church like the Catholic, which always had had an educated ministry and often an adequate chapel, found itself in a favorable position. The educated clergy of the Presbyterian and Episcopal churches gave to them a leadership out of all proportion to their numerically small membership. In fact, the Presbyterian Church, when judged by many standards, was the most influential church in the area.

All churches exerted a potent influence in checking lawlessness and in bringing stability to the area. They opposed the same infractions of the moral code, such as dishonesty, licentiousness, and drunkenness. Some churches, like the Methodist, attempted to control the use of intoxicating liquors, and others, like the Episcopal and Catholic, exerted their efforts to reform in less personal ways. Temperance societies flourished in many churches, but their existence was not so much an evidence that the membership wanted to curb an excess, as that it had a penchant for joining something. When economic gain was involved, as in distilling liquor and raising tobacco, the opposition of churches in some areas was appreciably tested. The communities most willing and eager to fight the use of liquor and tobacco were those in which the issues did not hurt the local economy. A genuine evidence of material sacrifice is difficult to find. Church legislation seldom varied from the sentiment of the community. It is true, however, that the ministers often took a position considerably in advance of the church members.

As the rough edges of frontier life wore smooth, the patterns of an old society grew visible and on heritage and custom a premium was placed. Vague, but positive, influences provided some cultural enrichments for which people had nostalgically yearned. Shifting settlers had become a stable population. Among the contributing factors to this change the church would rank high.

Living among the people as a representative of a religious body was the preacher—a personification of the church. It was the preacher whose simple theology convinced his neighbors that religion should be basic in the foundation of Western society. He stood for moderation—in law and order, and in all emotions that moved men to action. He was the same as other men with whom he lived—full of error and corruption. But the vision of his task kept him to the purpose of his calling. Until someone better came along, he could serve right well. He was a weak agent of an imperfect agency. His imperfections perhaps enhanced his worth in a community. With feet of clay, he never lost touch with people around him nor soared in heights too great to see the needs of mundane living.

As the years progressed the state of religion was directed and altered by the political and economic conditions of the country. The church at last had to turn full face to the issue of slavery. Condemnation of slavery grew in the North directly from the peculiar economic development of the country. Defense of the institution came from the importance of cotton in the South and an agricultural society based thereon. The Southerner, long accustomed to the use of slave labor, was faced with a reversal of his ideology. His manner of living was now touched with guilt, sin, and judgment. His loyalty to the federal government was questioned. These accusations poured over him to a disrupting degree. And the Northerner was not free of liability in the disruption of the unity of the nation. These Northern and Southern men made up the church. It was not an institution nor an organization, but it was men, frail, weak, and ambitious—willing to sacrifice but unwilling to be sacrificed. As groups of church members with sectional allegiances, none had the intent nor the power to prevent the holocaust of a civil war.

The endeavors of the church were a blend of success and failure. To separate the two is difficult. Perhaps the failures are more evident than successful achievements, for the obstacles which encompassed them loom large. There was too little money for the support of priests and ministers; too little communication between isolated churches and a supporting society; too much emphasis on numerical strength of church rolls; too much attention to the pettiness of individual infractions of church discipline; and too little regard for total service to a community. When such obstacles are enumerated, the significance of the successes increases, and gratitude multiplies for men who dared to assume tasks of such magnitude.

Musing about the scope of the church, John Calvin sought an answer to this question: "How could the church be made not simply an institution for the worship of God, but an agency for the making of men fit to worship Him?" It is beyond the power of any man to judge with a degree of accuracy the contribution made to individual men by an institution like a church. But certain claims seem evident and valid. As agents for the churches, missionaries, ministers, and laymen of the several denominations zealously had entered the new territory. Unwittingly they assumed a task too large for human accomplishment, but knowingly they labored to the best of their ability and to the utmost extent of their energy. The scope of their challenge was too great: the territory was too vast to cover; the needs were too demanding to meet; the problems were too manifold to solve; and the material lure too strong for frail men to resist. Many who came late into the West and South became much occupied with practical tasks, but there were many who never lost sight of the initial ideals and aspirations that had brought them there. Although hindered by circumstances and lacking necessities, these men executed in a very acceptable way the same charge which Isaiah had given to other forerunners: "Prepare ye the way of the Lord, make straight in the desert a highway for our God. Every valley shall be exalted and every mountain and hill shall be made low: and the crooked shall be made straight, and the rough places plain."

APPENDIX

THE MEMBERSHIP FIGURES on the following charts are estimates derived from United States census data on church seating accommodations for 1860. They represent the application of the ratio between seating accommodations and church membership in 1890 (the first year membership data was included in the census) to the figures on seating accommodations given in 1860. Figures on the graphs are percentages. State population (P) and church membership (CM) are given in thousands.

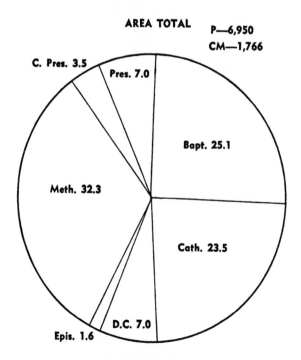

AREA TOTAL   P—6,950   CM—1,766

C. Pres. 3.5
Pres. 7.0
Bapt. 25.1
Meth. 32.3
Cath. 23.5
D.C. 7.0
Epis. 1.6

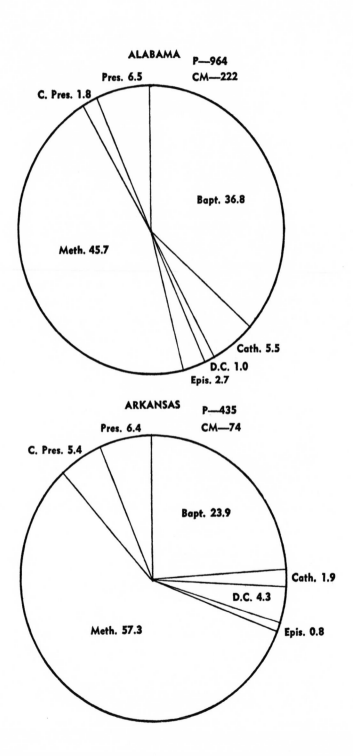

ALABAMA   P—964
           CM—222

Pres. 6.5
C. Pres. 1.8
Bapt. 36.8
Meth. 45.7
Cath. 5.5
D.C. 1.0
Epis. 2.7

ARKANSAS   P—435
            CM—74

Pres. 6.4
C. Pres. 5.4
Bapt. 23.9
Cath. 1.9
D.C. 4.3
Meth. 57.3
Epis. 0.8

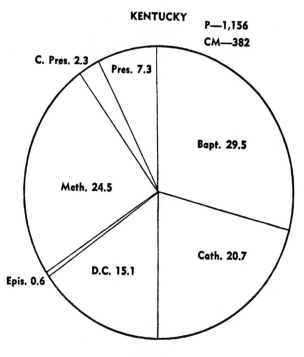

KENTUCKY

P—1,156
CM—382

C. Pres. 2.3   Pres. 7.3

Bapt. 29.5

Meth. 24.5

Cath. 20.7

Epis. 0.6   D.C. 15.1

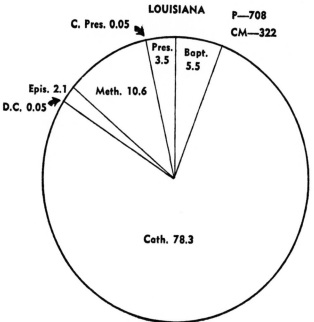

LOUISIANA

P—708
CM—322

C. Pres. 0.05

Pres. 3.5   Bapt. 5.5

Epis. 2.1   Meth. 10.6
D.C. 0.05

Cath. 78.3

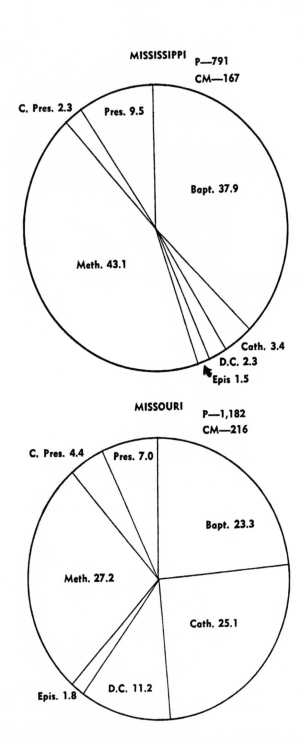

MISSISSIPPI P—791
CM—167

C. Pres. 2.3 Pres. 9.5

Bapt. 37.9

Meth. 43.1

Cath. 3.4
D.C. 2.3
Epis 1.5

MISSOURI P—1,182
CM—216

C. Pres. 4.4 Pres. 7.0

Bapt. 23.3

Meth. 27.2

Cath. 25.1

Epis. 1.8 D.C. 11.2

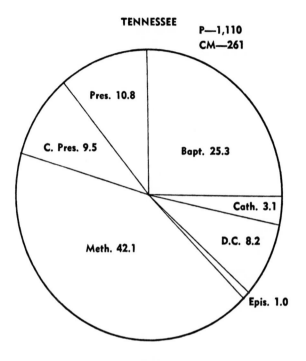

TENNESSEE

P—1,110
CM—261

Pres. 10.8

C. Pres. 9.5

Bapt. 25.3

Cath. 3.1

D.C. 8.2

Meth. 42.1

Epis. 1.0

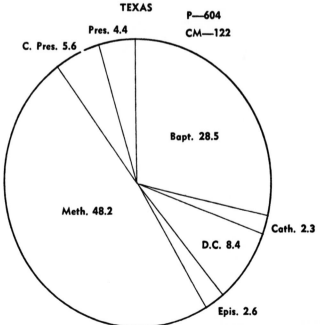

TEXAS

P—604
CM—122

Pres. 4.4

C. Pres. 5.6

Bapt. 28.5

Cath. 2.3

D.C. 8.4

Meth. 48.2

Epis. 2.6

INDEX